SHAKESPEARE STUDIES

EDITORIAL BOARD

SHAKESPEARE STUDIES VOLUME XXII

EDITED BY
Leeds Barroll

BOOK-REVIEW EDITOR

Susan Zimmerman

Rutherford • Madison • Teaneck
Fairleigh Dickinson University Press
London and Toronto: Associated University Presses

Associated University Presses
440 Forsgate Drive
Cranbury, NJ 08512

Associated University Presses
25 Sicilian Avenue
London WC1A 2QH, England

Associated University Presses
P.O. Box 338, Port Credit
Mississauga, Ontario
Canada L5G 4L8

The paper used in this publication meets the requirements of the American National Standard for Permanence of Paper for Printed Library Materials Z39.48-1984.

All editorial correspondence concerning Shakespeare Studies should be addressed to the Editorial Office, Shakespeare Studies, Department of English, University of Maryland (Baltimore County), Catonsville, Maryland 21228. Send two copies of submitted articles and return postage. Correspondence concerning orders and subscriptions should be addressed to: Associated University Presses, 440 Forsgate Drive, Cranbury, New Jersey 08512.

International Standard Book Number 0-8386-3580-6 (vol. xxii)
International Standard Serial Number 0582-9399

Contents

6   *Contents*

Reviews

List of Contributors

CAROLYN E. BROWN is Assistant Professor of English Literature at the University of San Francisco and has written articles on Shakespeare for journals such as *American Imago, Literature and Psychology*, and *English Literary Renaissance*. She is currently exploring the Shrew and Griselda traditions in relation to Shakespeare's *The Taming of the Shrew*, and is also serving as the associate editor of an anthology of women's literature for McGraw-Hill.

S. P. CERASANO is Associate Professor of English at Colgate University and a member of the Editorial Board of *Shakespeare Studies*. She has published extensively on the English Renaissance stage and is completing a biography of Edward Alleyn.

MAURICE CHARNEY is Distinguished Professor of English at Rutgers University.

WILLIAM M. HAMLIN is Assistant Professor of English at Idaho State University. His current research interests include the influence of Montaigne on English Renaissance thought, relations between early modern ethnographic writings and literary texts, and skepticism in Jacobean tragedy.

LORI SCHROEDER HASLEM is Assistant Professor of English at Le Moyne College in Syracuse, New York, and regularly teaches courses in Shakespeare and Elizabethan/Jacobean drama. Her scholarly interests lie especially in culturally informed representations of women in the early drama. Her essay on portrayals of the maternal body in plays by Jonson and Webster is forthcoming in *Modern Philology*.

THOMAS B. HORTON is Assistant Professor in the Department of Computer Science and Engineering at Florida Atlantic University.

JOHN S. HUNT is Assistant Professor of English at the University of Montana in Missoula. He has published articles on Sidney, Shakespeare, and Joyce and has reviewed books in Renaissance and twentieth-century literature. He is currently writing a book on embodiment, transcendence, and ego in Shakespeare's plays.

WILLIAM INGRAM is Professor of English at the University of Michigan.

ARTHUR F. KINNEY is Professor of English at the University of Massachusetts and Editor of *English Literary Renaissance*.

ROSLYN L. KNUTSON is Professor of English at the University of Arkansas, Little Rock.

NINA S. LEVINE is Assistant Professor of English at the University of South Carolina. She is currently completing a book on representations of women in power in Shakespeare's history plays and in Elizabethan culture.

JOYCE GREEN MACDONALD is Assistant Professor of English at the University of Kentucky. She has published on Shakespeare in the Restoration, on modern women's productions of Shakespeare, and on race in Shakespeare and Jonson. She is currently editing a collection of essays on racial representations in Renaissance drama.

BARBARA A. MOWAT is Director of Academic Programs at the Folger Shakespeare Library and Editor of *Shakespeare Quarterly*. She has published extensively on Shakespeare and on the English Renaissance and is the coeditor (with Paul Werstine) of the New Folger Library Shakespeare.

MARGA MUNKELT is in the Department of English at the University of Münster.

MARGARET LOFTUS RANALD is Professor of English at Queens College, City University of New York.

PEGGY MUÑOZ SIMONDS is an Independent Scholar specializing in the iconographic approach to Shakespeare's works. Her recent study *Myth, Emblem, and Music in Shakespeare's "Cymbeline"* (1992) won the University of Delaware Press Shakespeare Award.

Her *Critical Guide to Iconographic Research in English Renaissance Literature* will be published in 1994, and she is currently studying Shakespeare's use of wild and green man figures.

Lynne M. Simpson is completing her doctoral studies at the University of Massachusetts and has served as Associate for the Humanities and Fine Arts at the university's Office of Development. Her dissertation, *Shakespearean Loss: Mourning Interminable,* explores the depiction of grief in Shakespeare throughout his development as well as the idea of mourning from Freud to contemporary psychological theorists.

Marta Straznicky is Assistant Professor of English at Queen's University, Kingston, Ontario, where she teaches Renaissance literature. She is currently finishing a book on women writers and closet drama in the English Renaissance.

Paul Werstine is Professor of English at King's College, the University of Western Ontario.

Robert F. Willson, Jr., is Professor of English at the University of Missouri, Kansas City.

SHAKESPEARE
STUDIES

ARTICLES

Men of Inde: Renaissance Ethnography and *The Tempest*

WILLIAM M. HAMLIN

I

AUDIENCES AND SCHOLARS have long recognized that the plays of Shakespeare allude in various places and various ways to the New World. Many of these allusions are wholly conventional, signalling nothing more than a repetition of standard Renaissance stereotypes about America; among these may be counted lighthearted references to the mineral wealth of the New World in *The Comedy of Errors*, *The Merchant of Venice*, *Henry the Fourth, Part One*, *As You Like It*, *The Merry Wives of Windsor*, and *Twelfth Night*, and metaphors in which love is likened to Amerindian sun worship in *Love's Labour's Lost* and *All's Well That Ends Well*.[1] Others, such as the mention of the "strange Indian with the great tool" in *Henry VIII* (5.3.34), are perhaps equally stereotypical but at the same time more suggestive of familiarity with individual New World natives; long ago Sidney Lee speculated that Shakespeare "doubtless caught a glimpse" of most of the natives of Virginia, Guiana, and New England who were brought to London in the late sixteenth and early seventeenth centuries.[2] Still others constitute examples of linguistic borrowing, such as "hurricanoes" in *King Lear* (3.2.2), "potato" in *Troilus and Cressida* (5.2.56), and, more indirectly, "Setebos" in *The Tempest* (1.2.373, 5.1.261).[3] Finally, there are dramatic allusions, dependent not so much upon explicit references to the "Indies," "Mexico," or "Bermoothes" as upon situations resonant with contemporary New World associations. A particular abundance of these may be found in *The Tempest*—at least according to an ever-growing number of critics—and as a result, readings of *The Tempest* in which the European consciousness of

America serves as a contextual ground have become increasingly
common in recent years. As Alden T. Vaughan has pointed out,
"The 'Americanist' reading" of *The Tempest*, while "only one of
many that have flourished in the past three and a half centuries,
. . . has dominated twentieth-century interpretations."[4] Prospero's
assumption of rulership, Gonzalo's imagined "plantation," and Caliban's slavery and rebellion are just a few of the facets of this drama
that make it, in Leo Marx's words, Shakespeare's "American
fable."[5]

Discussion of Shakespeare's sources for *The Tempest* and for his
New World allusions in other plays has taken interesting directions
of late, resulting, among other things, in a critical revaluation of
conventional source study of the past. No one, of course, denies
that a reference such as that in *Twelfth Night* to "the new map, with
the augmentation of the Indies" (3.2.79–80) provides persuasive
evidence that Shakespeare had glanced through the second edition
of Hakluyt's *Principal Navigations* (1598–1600), or that certain passages in *The Tempest* bear strong witness to Shakespeare's acquain-
tance with Florio's 1603 translation of Montaigne and with the
Bermuda narratives of Strachey and Jourdain.[6] But source study
relying on parallel passages and grounded on the principle of a
writer's acutal familiarity with source texts quickly loses its air of
objectivity and shades into varying degrees of speculativeness, as
the articles and books of Margaret T. Hodgen and Robert Ralston
Cawley clearly reveal.[7] Thus it should come as no surprise that we
find more recent commentators abandoning all pretense of demonstrating that Shakespeare "knew" a given text; instead, we discover
an increasing interest in models and in informing discursive contexts. Charles Frey, for example, while noting curious parallels between incidents in *The Tempest* and in narratives of early
circumnavigations such as those of Magellan, Drake, and Caven-
dish, nonetheless points out that

> Whether or not Shakespeare had read Eden's narrative of Magellan's
> voyage, such accounts can inform or illuminate *The Tempest* because
> they provide models of Renaissance experience in the New World . . .
> We need to read the voyage literature, therefore, not necessarily to find
> out what Shakespeare read, but what Shakespeare and his audience
> together would have been likely to know—what they would have gath-
> ered from a variety of sources.[8]

Similarly, Francis Barker and Peter Hulme, drawing on Julia Kristeva's articulation of intertextuality, argue that what they term "con-

textualization" "differs most importantly from source criticism when it establishes the necessity of reading *The Tempest* alongside congruent texts, irrespective of Shakespeare's putative knowledge of them, and when it holds that such congruency will become apparent from the constitution of discursive networks to be traced independently of authorial 'intentionality'."[9] In defense of traditional source criticism, I think it only fair to note that even such conventional practitioners as Cawley and Hodgen occasionally advance beyond the stage of unproblematic attribution; Cawley suggests that certain texts which post-date *The Tempest* are also valuable inasmuch as they "illustrate the general spirit of the times"; Hodgen argues convincingly that if Shakespeare had never read Montaigne's "Des Cannibales," Gonzalo's "plantation" speech might well have been written anyway, perhaps very much as it now exists.[10] Similarly, Maynard Mack cautions us, in discussing the sources of *King Lear*, against "ignoring larger, admittedly vaguer, but equally cogent influences, which freqently determine the way in which the specific source is used."[11] In short, an awareness of textual "congruencies" is by no means unique to post-structuralist critics. In contrast to their predecessors, however, these critics have much more satisfactorily articulated the theoretical grounds for such an awareness, principally on the basis of discursive networks and practices; and, in addition, they have contended that all texts, whether construed as "poetry," "history," "travel writing," or otherwise, are equally permeable by ideology and by cultural norms and presuppositions.

The discourse most frequently brought forth as an informing context for *The Tempest* is English colonialism in the late sixteenth and early seventeenth centuries. Such contextualization, of course, has been more or less implicit in many earlier readings and productions of the play; witness, for instance, the procolonial production mounted in 1904 by Herbert Beerbohm Tree, the anticolonial production by Jonathan Miller in 1970, and the suggestive remarks of such writers as A. L. Rowse, Roberto Fernández Retamar, and Leslie Fiedler.[12] But only in the past dozen or fifteen years has there been a concerted effort to locate the play explicitly within the complicated network of ideas, preconceptions, goals, schemes, rhetoric, and propaganda that constitutes colonial discourse. Barker and Hulme, for example, see *The Tempest* as "imbricated within the discourse of colonialism" and Paul Brown writes that the play "serves as a limit text in which the characteristic operations of colonialist discourse may be discerned—as an instrument of exploitation, a

register of beleaguerment and a site of radical ambivalence."[13] One
of the interesting consequences of this explicit contextualization is
that recent critics have found a means whereby to demonstrate the
extent to which earlier commentators either occluded or missed
altogether the text's "anxieties" about colonialism due to their sympathy—conscious or unconscious—with colonialist ambitions and
ideology.[14] In contrast, and without (thankfully) pursuing at length
this sort of *ad hominem* criticism, such writers as Barker, Hulme,
and Brown have drawn attention to the ways in which *The Tempest*
illuminates common tropes of colonialist discourse and offers resistance both to procolonial and antihistorical readings. Brown argues, for instance, that Prospero "produces" Caliban as a dangerous
and threatening other, and that the containment of Caliban, Stephano, and Trinculo unifies Prospero and Alonso's party in their
colonial and aristocratic hegemony.[15] Hulme makes the useful
point that "Prospero is [a] colonial historian, and such a convincing and ample historian that other histories have to fight their way
into the crevices of his official monument."[16] All three writers demonstrate an acute awareness that "truths" about Caliban, Ariel, and
the beginnings of Prospero's rule on the island have too often been
conflated with Prospero's own allegations. As Hulme puts it, critics
have time and again shown an "uncritical willingness to identify
Prospero's voice as direct and reliable authorial statement, and
therefore to ignore the lengths to which the play goes to dramatize
its problems with the proper beginnings of its own story."[17] In a
strange way, then, it would appear that emphatic historical contextualization has allowed recent readers of *The Tempest* to make
valuable contributions to what in the past has emphatically *not*
been considered an activity deeply dependent upon this sort of
historical knowledge: reading the play as a *play*, a dramatic construct that continually comments upon its own existence and assertions through its inherently dialogic nature.

A sampling of the interchanges and dramatic incidents in *The
Tempest* which tend to receive greater attention in colonialist considerations might begin with the following pair of speeches: Stephano's remark to Trinculo that "the King and all our company else
being drown'd, we will inherit here" (2.2.174–75), and Prospero's
reminiscence to Alonso and others that "most strangely / Upon this
shore ... was [I] landed, / To be the lord on't" (5.1.159–62). The
first of these pronouncements is uttered in the presence of Caliban—clearly a more rightful "inheritor" than Stephano, if only on
the grounds of prior inhabitation—and both reveal a complete

obliviousness to the idea that indigenous non-Europeans might have a legitimate claim to lands upon which Europeans have stumbled. Yet the idea was not foreign to European jurists of the period—Francisco de Vitoria offers one of its classic statements in his *De Indiis prior* (1539)[18]—and even Francis Drake delayed claiming Nova Albion (northern California) for England until after a ceremony in which the native king "made several orations, or rather supplications, that hee [Drake] would take their province and kingdome into his hand, and become their King, . . . which thing our Generall thought not meete to reject, because he knew not what honour and profit it might be to our Countrey."[19] Stephano's further remark to Caliban, "Trinculo and thyself shall be viceroys" (3.2.108), reminds us that viceregal government was a standard form of colonial rule in Spanish America; and Prospero's command, "Let them be hunted soundly" (4.1.262), follows directly upon the stage direction "Enter divers Spirits in shape of dogs and hounds, hunting them about; Prospero and Ariel setting them on," thereby reinforcing the sense in which the punishment of Caliban and the Neopolitan drunkards recapitulates the many early modern accounts of New World natives being terrorized by dogs.[20]

Other incidents highlighted by situating *The Tempest* within colonialist discourse might include the initial reciprocity of the relationship between Prospero and Caliban (1.2.332–38); the disagreement among Gonzalo, Adrian, Antonio, and Sebastian as to the nature of the island (1.2.35–58); Trinculo and Stephano's talk of transporting Caliban to Europe in a get-rich-quick scheme (2.2.27-33, 2.2.76–78); Stephano's use of liquor to inspire Caliban's devotion (2.2.82–188); Ariel's exclamation "Thou liest" as a veiled suggestion that *he*, in fact, is the rightful ruler of the island (3.2.45); Gonzalo's articulation of entrenched European ignorance regarding the wondrousness and variety of the things of this world (3.3.42–49)[21]; Prospero's excessive discomposure upon suddenly remembering Caliban's feeble plot against his life (4.1.139–42); Sebastian and Antonio's comments on buying and marketing Caliban (5.1.265–66); and, above all, the various ways in which Caliban is demonized and his status as a human being mystified or otherwise rendered uncertain. Because this last aspect of the play constitutes my principal subject in the latter half of this essay, I will say no more about it here. I will add, however, that inasmuch as Caliban's attempted rape of Miranda is adduced as justification for his enslavement and proof of his unregeneracy (1.2.344–62), Prospero's "colonial rule" may be said to rely in part upon a rhetorical process of selective forgetting: many men in Prospero's home of Milan might also have attempted to violate the honor of his child, but such behavior would not necessarily have stigmatized them as incapable of civility or wholly irredeemable. Prospero, however, occupies an ideal position from which to "forget" this fact, since Caliban has no cognizance of it and thus no compelling reason to contradict Prospero's characterization of him as one upon "whose nature / Nurture can never stick" (4.1.188–89).

Perhaps the major problem with recent colonialist readings of *The Tempest* is that they tend to condemn too categorically other readings as ahistorical while remaining dogmatic in their own insistence that, as Barker and Hulme put it, "The ensemble of fictional and lived practices, which for convenience we will simply refer to here as 'English colonialism', provides *The Tempest*'s dominant discursive con-texts" [sic].[22] Rather than positing colonialism as a useful and illuminating discursive frame for the play, critics in this vein imply that *The Tempest* remains in many important respects unintelligible without the particular historical imbrication which they bring to it. Brown claims, for instance, that Prospero's rule is "after all a colonialist regime on the island," yet in saying so he ignores several crucial facts: there is never any indication that the island is perceived as the permanent property of Milan, there was no initial intent to "plant" or colonize it, and Prospero obviously does not wish to remain there. Brown also asserts that "Stephano the 'drunken butler' and the 'jester' Trinculo obviously represent . . . 'masterless men', whose alliance with the savage Caliban provides an antitype of order, issuing in a revolt requiring chastisement and ridicule."[23] But while this claim is valuable insofar as it extends the political discourse of colonialism so as to include the class discourse of masterlessness, its schematic dogmatism is highly limiting.[24] Even Terence Hawkes, a critic generally more nuanced than Brown in his speculations upon Prospero and Caliban, argues that the "roots" of their relationship "find their true nourishment in the ancient home-grown European relationships of master and servant, landlord and tenant"—which of course is simply a way of abandoning colonialism for another and perhaps less controversial historical contextualization.[25] In short, colonialist readings tend to fail through narrowness of focus just as they succeed through acuity. And while their grounding in historical process and detail prompts fascinating interpretive speculations, moral and sociopolitical agendas often predetermine their conclusions. Hawkes, in the above-quoted passage, remains historicist in method but eschews colonial contextualization in favor of a class discourse undoubtedly more familiar to Shakespeare and equally amenable to contemporary Marxist/materialist interpretation. What I would like to suggest is that one may retain the New World context and the historicist approach without necessarily committing oneself to the near-dogmatism that seems endemic to colonialist readings. Such a strategy has been used recently by Jeffrey Knapp, who, in a book remarkable for its complex presentation of relations between English colonialism and English literature, claims that Shakespeare "wants to recommend American colonies as essential to England's well-being, and essential precisely because of the dangerous treasure those colonies may secure," but adds that in so doing Shakespeare "must 'remove' such motives and even America itself from direct consideration in order to promote the temperate homebodiedness without which, he believes, a colony cannot last."[26] I propose that the strategy also becomes possible by shifting the contextual ground from the highly politicized discourse of colonialism to the more taxonomic, speculative, polyvalent, and autonomous discourse of ethnography. This is by no means to imply that ethnographic contextualization is apolitical; clearly it is not. But just as clearly, ethnography is connected by no necessary ties to the familiar and seemingly unalterable dynamic of exploration, domination, plantation, surveillance, and containment which—at least according to many recent accounts—constitutes a core structure of the colonialist project.

Obviously, the incidental or inchoate ethnography of the early modern period may be construed as merely one more facet of the vast network of thoughts, words, and deeds that we call "colonialism." David B. Quinn hints at this when he writes that "The earliest stages of contact between Englishmen and non-English cultures were likely to be governed by the desire to define and limit their inferiority (or non-Englishness) and to find ways of forcing them into a new English pattern, reforming them or obliterating them." But Quinn acknowledges that there also existed "the tendency to observe alien cultures for their own sake," and, at least in the case of England and Ireland, "The making of notes, the taking of an interest—scornful or superior, earnest or objective—led from casual observation to some measure of systematic study of Irish life and Irish society, to an elementary ethnology, if not precisely to a social anthropology."[27] The same holds true more generally, I maintain, in the case of Europe and the New World; the accounts of such writers as Ramon Pané, Bartolomé de Las Casas, Toribio Montolinía, Alvar Núñez Cabeza de Vaca, Jacques Cartier, Diego Durán, Bernardino de Sahagún, Jean de Léry, Arthur Barlowe, Thomas Harriot, and John Smith—to name just a few—exhibit in varying degrees and varying ways the kinds of interest in and description of alien cultures that may be considered legitimately ethnographic.[28] And while Quinn's supposition that this interest can be "objective" is rendered false by the inevitable subjective assimilationism that accompanies the interpretation of any alterological encounter, his larger point remains valid: cultural description separable from overt colonial aims and emanating primarily from curiosity and the desire to record and contemplate the unfamiliar may be found in the Renaissance.[29] The significance of this is that one may utilize early ethnography as a distinct contextual ground within which to locate *The Tempest* or any other relevant text: colonial discourse, in and of itself, has no intrinsic superiority as a historical frame, but is simply one of many "force-fields" we can "bring to the play to disclose its meanings."[30] I believe an ethnographic contextualization is likely to prove valuable precisely because of its lack of strict connection to political ends. This is not to say that it is wholly dissociated from ideology; we should never forget, for example, that Friar Ramon Pané assembled his ethnographic notes because Columbus *commanded* him to do so, or that Las Casas, Motolinía, Durán, and Sahagún were zealous Christian missionaries, or that Barlowe and Harriot were employees of Ralegh in one of his grand colonial schemes.[31] At the same time, though, I think we must acknowledge that the documents of these writers—and numerous other texts such as the glossaries of Léry, Smith, and Richard Eden—emblematize a genuine European curiosity about alien cultures that would almost certainly have manifested itself under any historical circumstances.[32] Inasmuch as Renaissance ethnography is primarily a descriptive rather than a manipulative or hegemonic discourse—fully capable of registering curiosity, ambivalence, confusion, and even self-condemnation in representing and attempting to understand the cultural other—using it as a discursive context promises to yield readings less dogmatic or programmatic than those typically brought forth by colonialist critics. In what follows, therefore, I propose to situate *The Tempest* within the context of this inchoate Renaissance ethnography, and in particular to examine the extent to which Caliban may be perceived as a product of conflicting accounts regarding the savagery or civility of New World natives.

II

Throughout *The Tempest* an air of ambiguity surrounds Caliban. His name—almost certainly an anagram of "cannibal"—appears in the First Folio's cast list among the play's human characters (as opposed to its spirits) and above those of Trinculo and Stephano, but he is described there as "a salvage and deformed slave."[33] And when Prospero first mentions him to Ariel in act 1, it is difficult to decide whether the bestial or the human plays a greater role in his constitution:

> Then was this island
> (Save for the son that [she] did litter here,
> A freckled whelp, hag-born), not honor'd with
> A human shape.
>
> (1.2.281–84)

Although Peter Hulme cites these lines as proof of Prospero's "grudging admittance of Caliban's humanity" and rails against those who seize upon the last six words as "'evidence' of Caliban's lack of human shape,"[34] I think rather that a sense of uncertainty is exquisitely balanced here, that "litter," "whelp," "hag-born" and the parenthetical exception play off against "son" and the main clause in such a way as to reveal Prospero's own deep confusion about Caliban's status. I will argue later that *The Tempest* moves gradually—almost inexorably—toward affirming Caliban as a man, but I believe that in the play's earlier scenes his status is deliberately mystified. However, unlike many colonialist readers, who interpret this mystification as Prospero's ruse to justify usurpation, I think its presence is due primarily to the genuine uncertainty regarding the human status of cultural aliens that emerges as a pervasive motif in the early modern period. Again and again in the travel literature, ethnographic description reveals a deep-seated ambivalence toward ethnic otherness and perceived savagery, and while this ambivalence is undoubtedly exploited at times by conquerors and colonists, its initial presence does not appear to be a necessary function of the European will to power.

Take, for example, Richard Johnson's 1609 description of the natives of Virginia near the colony at Jamestown:

> [The region] is inhabited with wild and savage people that live and lie up and downe in troupes like heards of Deere in a Forrest: they have no law but nature, their apparell skinnes of beasts, but most goe naked, . . . they are generally very loving and gentle, and do entertaine and relieve our people with great kindnesse; they are easy to be brought to good, and would fayne embrace a better condition.[35]

Here we see a people likened to "heards of Deere" and alleged to have "no law but nature," yet we also hear that they are capable of "great kindnesse" and—like Caliban when he claims that he will "be wise hereafter, / And seek for grace" (5.1.295–96)—desire to "embrace a better condition." Similarly, in the writings of Captain John Smith we encounter such seemingly contradictory portrayals of the Chesapeake Algonquians as that, on the one hand, they are "sterne Barbarians," "fiends," "inconstant Salvages," and "naked Divels," and that, on the other, they "have amongst them such government, as that their Magistrates for good commanding, and their people for due subjection, and obeying, excell many places that would be counted very civill."[36] It is as if the authors of these passages can relinquish neither their wonder at the seemingly "natural" or "bestial" condition of American natives nor their ever-recurring recognition—or suspicion, at any rate—that these people, like Europeans, possess genuine forms of "civility." And while such a comment as Johnson's that the Virginians "would fayne embrace a better condition" may certainly be read within the frame of colonial discourse as a projection of the colonists' desire for defensible hegemony, it also may reflect a more concrete kind of observation—perhaps of the sort we see in Thomas Harriot when he tells us that despite the coastal Algonquians' clear exhibition of spiritual culture, "they were not so sure grounded, nor gave such credite to their traditions and stories, but through conversing with us they were brought into great doubts of their owne, and no small admiration of ours."[37]

Critics who have touched, however perfunctorily, upon the presentation of Caliban as in some way indebted to New World ethnography have tended either to trace a speculative genealogy through specific travel accounts or to allude somewhat unassuredly to the sort of ambivalence reflected in the above quotations. The former inclination has been present at least since the time of Edmund Malone—who claimed in 1821 that Caliban was Shakespeare's version of a Patagonian—and perhaps reached its apogee in Leslie Fiedler's pronouncement that "Caliban seems to have been created, on his historical side, by a fusion in Shakespeare's imagination of Columbus's first New World savages with Montaigne's Brazilians, Somers's native Bermudans, and those Patagonian 'giants' encountered by Pigafetta during his trip around the world with Magellan, strange creatures whose chief god was called, like Caliban's mother's, 'Setebos'."[38] The latter tendency, however, while relatively common, has provoked few interesting observations beyond the rather obvious generality that Caliban's portrayal relies upon a conflation of contradictory descriptions and evaluations of cultural otherness—particularly American otherness. Geoffrey Bullough, for example, writes that "the ambiguity of travelers' opinions about the American natives affects Shakespeare's handling of Caliban," and Peter Hulme goes so far as to say that "Caliban, as a compromise formation, can exist only within discourse: he is fundamentally and essentially beyond the bounds of representation."[39] But few critics have, to my knowledge, explored the ambiguity or the "compromise formation" of Caliban at any length. Many seem inclined, after acknowledging ambivalence, to settle upon rather reductive conclusions; a representative example is the claim that "By every account in the play, Caliban is something less than a man .... He is an American savage, clearly humanoid though not fully human."[40]

Two commentators, however, have come close to focusing on the sort of ambivalence to which I want to draw attention. In stressing the distinction between the European views that, on the one hand, "Indian language was deficient or non-existent" and that, on the other, "there was no serious language barrier," Stephen Greenblatt anticipates Tzvetan Todorov's useful schematization of European perceptions of native Americans as either acknowledging *difference* and concluding *inferiority*, or acknowledging *equality* and concluding *identity*.[41] Greenblatt writes, for instance, that the tensions of this dichotomy "either push the Indians toward utter difference—and thus silence—or toward utter likeness—and thus the collapse of their own, unique identity."[42] And in a slightly different vein, Richard Marienstras has observed that Caliban possesses a "dubious ontological status"; he "can be seen as a complete and irreducible contradiction or, alternatively, as having two positive but separate natures, each stemming from a different scale of values."[43] What Greenblatt and Marienstras do not do, however, is point toward a middle range of perception that either acknowledges *difference* without immediately concluding *inferiority* or acknowledges *equality* without positing *identity*. Yet we see views within this range expressed implicitly, for example, by various early writers in their recognition and description of distinctly different tribes and social groups among native American peoples:

> Alvar Núñez Cabeza de Vaca (1542): The inhabitants of all this region [Malhado] go naked. The women alone have any part of their persons covered, and it is with a wool that grows on trees. The damsels dress themselves in deerskin. The people are generous to each other of what they possess. They have no chief. All that are of a lineage keep together. They speak two languages; those of one are called Capoques, those of the other, Han. They have a custom when they meet, or from time to time when they visit, of remaining half an hour before they speak, weeping; and, this over, he that is visited first rises and gives the other all he has, which is received, and after a little while he carries it away, and often goes without saying a word. They have other strange customs; but I have told the principal of them, and the most remarkable, that I may pass on and further relate what befel us.

> Jean de Léry (1578): Although like other Brazilians [the Ouetaca] go entirely naked, nonetheless, contrary to the most ordinary custom of the men of that country (who, as I have already said and will later expand upon, shave the front of their head and clip their locks in the back), these wear their hair long, hanging down to the buttocks .... The Margaia, Cara-ia, or Tupinamba (which are the names of the three neighboring nations), or one of the other savages of that country, without trusting or approaching the Ouetaca, shows him from afar what he has—a pruning-hook, a knife, a comb, a mirror, or some other kind of wares brought over for trade—and indicates by a sign if he wants to exchange it for something else.

> José de Acosta (1589): It is a popular error to treat the affairs of the Indies as if they were those of some farm or mean village and to think that, because the Indies are all called by a single name, they are therefore of one nature and kind .... The nations of Indians are innumerable, and each of them has its own distinct rites and customs and needs to be taught in a different way. I am not properly qualified to handle the problem, since a great many peoples are unknown to me, while even if I knew them well it would be an immense task to discuss them all one by one. I have therefore thought it proper to speak primarily of the Peruvians in this work.

> William Strachey (1612): [T]hus it may appear how they are a people who have their several divisions, provinces, and princes, to live in and to command over, and do differ likewise (as amongst Christians) both in stature, language, and condition; some being great people, as the

Susquehannas, some very little, as the Wicocomocos; some speaking likewise more articulate and plain, and some more inward and hollow, as is before remembered; some courteous and more civil, others cruel and bloody; Powhatan having large territories and many petty kings under him, as some have fewer.

John Smith (1624): Upon the head of the Powhatans are the Monacans, whose chiefe habitation is at Rasauweak, unto whom the Mowhemenchughes, the Massinnacacks, the Monahassanughs, the Monasickapanoughs, and other nations pay tributes. Upon the head of the river of Toppahanock is a people called Mannahoacks. To these are contributers the Tauxanias, the Shackaconias, the Ontponeas, the Tegninateos, the Whomkenteaes, the Stegarakes, the Hassinnungaes, and divers others, all confederates with the Monacans, though many different in language, and be very barbarous, living for the most part of wild beasts and fruits. Beyond the mountaines from whence is the head of the river Patawomeke, the Salvages report inhabit their most motall enemies, the Massawomekes, upon a great salt water, which by all likelihood is either some part of Canada, some great lake, or some inlet of some sea that falleth into the South sea.[44]

To the extent that these descriptions register plurality and allow a varied yet specific cultural inheritance to the native groups introduced they represent anti–*tabula rasa* views and thus stand in opposition to such bald and overarching characterizations as Samuel Purchas's that American natives are "bad people, having little of Humanitie but shape, ignorant of Civilitie, of Arts, of Religion; more brutish then the beasts they hunt, more wild and unmanly then that unmanned wild countrey, which they range rather then inhabite."[45] Yet to the extent that they point explicitly to differences among these natives—and implicitly to differences between them and Europeans—they resist both the easy conclusion of inferiority and the more insidious one of identity. In short, they fall outside the polarizing rubric suggested by Greenblatt and Todorov. Rather than countering claims that native Americans are subhuman *tabulas rasas* by wholly assimilating them into Europeanness, these descriptions—and others like them—allow the natives their difference and in fact stress their cultural diversity. Thus they provide a more subtle contrast than that proposed by Greenblatt, a contrast more relevant, I think, to *The Tempest*. If we can admit that early modern ethnography allows for an ambivalence not solely between the binary opposites of subhumanity and virtual identity, but also among the range that includes subhumanity, identity, and cultural—but fully human—difference, we can sharpen our account of the way this ambivalence sheds light on the characterization of Caliban.

An interesting way of producing this account lies in situating Caliban within an ethnographic context and then contrasting him with another curiously ambiguous character from English Renaissance drama: the "wild man" Bremo in the anonymous and highly popular play *Mucedorus*.[46] Caliban has been connected to Bremo before, notably by Frank Kermode in his eclectic genealogy of Caliban's character; but while Kermode points to Bremo's conventionality as a wodewose or salvage man, he does not dwell on the association with Caliban.[47] Yet there is much of interest to focus on, particularly given an ethnographic contextualization.

Like the Wild Man in Book Four of *The Faerie Queene*, Bremo lives in a cave in the woods (7.7, 17.94), carries a club (7.5,21,29), and is lustful and cannibalistic (11.16–19, 11.21, 11.25–30, 15.59–60); but unlike Spenser's Wild Man (or, for that matter, the Salvage Man of Book Six), Bremo possesses language and demonstrates an ability to relent and to recognize changes within himself (11.38–54, 15.105). Moreover, he is represented as having the capacity to fall in love (11.37–55, 15.1–55), though exactly what this love means to him remains unclear.[48] Finally, like Caliban, he is poetic, particularly in the description of his immediate surroundings (15.23–55): he knows the forest's oaks, quail, partridges, blackbirds, larks, thrushes, nightingales, springs, violets, cowslips, marigolds, and deer, and if his catalogue strikes us as more conventional and symbolic than realistic, it nonetheless suggests a genuine love of place. Bremo seems, therefore, a rather more attractive character than the standard wodewose or *homo ferus*, and certainly less violent and lecherous than the type described as common in the late sixteenth century by R. H. Goldsmith.[49] Yet Bremo is duped and then brutally killed onstage by Mucedorus late in the play (17.35–67), and nothing in the response of Amadine or Mucedorus to the murder invites us to regard it as anything more consequential than the slaughter of an offending beast. Bremo is dismissed as a "tyrant" and "wicked wight" (17.68,74); that he has grown progressively more sympathetic and dies in the act of providing instruction to Mucedorus (17.51–67) is utterly forgotten. The play seems to tell us that a wild man, regrdless of his apparent capacity for improvement or potential for civility, is subhuman and may be killed without remorse or consequence.

Contrast this with Caliban's portrayal in *The Tempest*. Like Bremo, who is called a "cruel cutthroat" and a "bloody butcher"

(17.6,27), Caliban serves as the target of many dubious allegations: Prospero terms him a "demi-devil" (5.1.272) and a "poisonous slave, got by the devil himself / Upon thy wicked dam" (1.2.319–20); Miranda reviles him as an "Abhorred slave, / Which any print of goodness wilt not take, / Being capable of all ill!" (1.2.351–53). Yet much more than *Mucedorus, The Tempest* offers forms of resistance to these allegations, both in the speeches of Caliban and in the words and actions of other characters. For every suggestion that Caliban is not fully human, a counter-suggestion emerges that he *is;* Miranda's dual attitude (1.2.445–46; 3.1.50–52) becomes emblematic of this tendency. Moreover, in opposition to the view that Caliban is devoid of goodness, we have the uncontested claim of Caliban himself that his initial relationship with Prospero was thoroughly reciprocal:

> When thou cam'st first,
> Thou strok'st me and made much of me, wouldst give me
> Water with berries in't, and teach me how
> To name the bigger light, and how the less,
> That burn by day and night; and then I lov'd thee
> And show'd thee all the qualities o' th' isle,
> The fresh springs, brine pits, barren place and fertile.
> Curs'd be I that did so!
>
> (1.2.332–39)[50]

Caliban goes on to point out that he is now Prospero's subject, when earlier he was "mine own king" (1.2.342), and of course Prospero responds to this implied charge of usurpation by making the counter-accusation that Caliban attempted to rape Miranda and thus deserves his subjugation. But if, as Stephen Orgel has suggested, Caliban's unrepentant attitude toward this attempted rape may be partly explained by the fact that "free love in the New World is regularly treated [in Renaissance travel narratives] not as an instance of the lust of savages, but of their edenic innocence,"[51] Prospero's allegation that Caliban is a "slave / Whom stripes may move, not kindness!" (1.2.344–45) loses much of its persuasiveness. Indeed, the problems of subordination and rebellion highlighted by the Prospero/Caliban relationship may be usefully contrasted with the relative absence of such problems in the Prospero/Ariel interdependence; Ariel's nearly perfect modelling of subservience and service ultimately rewarded may be possible precisely because Ariel, quite explicitly, is *not* human. Such behavior, and such social relations, are far more problematic for Caliban.

Many Renaissance descriptions of New World natives have been adduced as sources or models of the subhuman or near-human element of Caliban's characterization, among them Peter Martyr's depiction of "certeyne wyld men" in Española who "neuer . . . wyll by any meanes becoome tame . . . . [and] are withowte any certaine language" and Robert Fabian's portrayal of three Eskimos who "spake such speach that no man could understand them, and in their demeanour like to bruite beastes."[52] But far fewer descriptions have been produced in support of another side of this characterization: Caliban as fully human, though radically different. Giovanni Verrazzano's observation that the native peoples of Florida "did not desire cloth of silke or of golde, much lesse of any other sort, neither cared they for things made of steele and yron" is perhaps typical of these descriptions in that it serves as an analogue of a specific incident in *The Tempest*: Caliban's rejection of the "glistering apparel" so attractive to Stephano and Trinculo (4.1.222–54).[53] But there are other anti–*tabula rasa* ethnographic views available in the Renaissance, views less likely to be seen as pertinent to *The Tempest* because broader in scope and not as easily associated with particular passages in the play. And I refer not only to the comparatively well-known writings of Las Casas and Montaigne. Jean de Léry, for instance, emphasizes the social harmony of the Tupinamba even as he exposes the conceptual limitations attendant upon his own religious bias: "As for the civil order of our savages, it is an incredible thing—a thing that cannot be said without shame to those who have both divine and human laws—how a people guided solely by their nature, even corrupted as it is, can live and deal with each other in such peace and tranquility."[54] José de Acosta describes the Incas' indigenous form of literacy: "Unbelievable as it may seem, the Peruvians made up for their lack of letters with so much ingenuity that they were able to record stories, lives, laws, and even the passage of time and numerical calculations by means of certain signs and aids to the memory which they had devised and which they call *quipos*. Our people with their letters are commonly unable to match the skill of the Peruvians with these devices. I am not at all certain that our written numerals make counting or dividing more accurate than their signs do."[55] Alexander Whitaker writes that the inhabitants of Virginia are "lustie, strong, and very nimble: they are a very understanding generation, quicke of apprehension, suddaine in their dispatches, subtile in their dealings, exquisite in their inventions, and industrious in their labour . . . . there is a civill government amongst them which they strictly observe"; William Strachey characterizes the elaborate dressing and ornamentation of a Virginian queen as "ceremonies which I did little look for, carrying so much presentment of civility"; and Thomas Harriot, in a passage to which I will return, avers of the Algonquians, "Some religion they have alreadie, which although it be farre from the trueth, yet being as it is, there is hope it may be the sooner and easier reformed. They beleeve that there are many Gods."[56] It is true that Léry's and Whitaker's remarks, like those of Las Casas, emanate from a Christian essentialist perspective; this emerges explicitly in Whitaker's opinion that "One God created us, they have reasonable soules and intellectuall faculties as well as wee; we all have *Adam* for our common parent: yea, by nature the condition of us both is all one, the servants of sinne and slaves of the divell."[57] It is true as well that Acosta's "Unbelievable as it may seem" and Harriot's "farre from the trueth" disclose the strongly ethnocentric tendencies of these early ethnographic accounts. But some degree of subjective assimilationism is inevitable in any description of a cultural other; the above quotations— and others like them—are remarkable in the degree to which they avoid the easy conclusion of *identity* and insist upon a measure of *difference.* And if, as I believe, such views as these played a role in the evolution of Caliban's character, it is not hard to understand why Caliban seems far less "unaccommodated" than *Mucedorus's* Bremo. Even Bremo's portrayal reveals certain suggestions of contemporary ethnographic influence, but by and large his conventionality as a wodewose preempts the possibility of any lasting ambivalence in his character: like Doctor Chanca's New World natives, whose "bestiality is greater than that of any beast upon the face of the earth," Bremo is essentially less than fully human; like them, easy to kill without remorse.[58] But Caliban, whose depiction relies heavily on Renaissance ethnography—and particularly on the ambivalences I have stressed between the other as subhuman, identical, and human but different—is thereby rendered far less easy to dismiss. If he is a "salvage" man, his savagery is nonetheless treated by Shakespeare with more tolerance and more respect for its potential or concealed civility than is Bremo's by his anonymous creator.

A final word about *Mucedorus.* The play's *Dramatis Personae* not only lists the characters but provides instructions for the doubling (and tripling) of parts; thus, for example, Bremo is to be played by the same actor who plays Tremelio and Envy.[59] I find this intriguing for several reasons. Tremelio is a would-be assassin, a captain persuaded by the jealous Segasto to kill Mucedorus (6.62–82); in fact, precisely the opposite occurs, Mucedorus killing *him* in self-defense, calling him a "Vile coward" (6.81). And Envy, a figure who appears only in the induction and epilogue, is constantly reviled by his allegorical counterpart, Comedy, as, among other things, a "monster" (Ind. 16), an "ugly fiend" (Ind. 75), a "hellhound" (Epi. 24), a "Nefarious hag" (Epi. 26), and a "bloody cur, nursed up with tiger's sap" (Ind. 35). In short, the trio of Bremo, Tremelio, and Envy—all playable by the same actor—represents something like a principle of monstrosity or unnaturalness, and these characters' purpose in the play is perhaps indirectly suggested by Comedy's urgent wish that Envy "mix not death 'mongst pleasing comedies" (Ind. 50). In fact, death *is* present in *Mucedorus*, and the play becomes more a tragicomedy than a simple comedy treating "naught else but pleasure and delight" (Ind. 51). In spite of the play's happy ending, Envy insists to Comedy, "yet canst thou not conquer me" (Epi. 12) and threatens that in the future he will overthow her by the following strategem:

> From my study will I hoist a wretch,
> A lean and hungry neger cannibal,
> Whose jaws swell to his eyes with chawing malice;
> And him I'll make a poet.
>
> (Epi. 34–37)

This implies that if an outcast or "native monster" (Epi. 20) of the sort Envy describes had the linguistic command of a poet, he would represent a true threat to Comedy's complacence; he would have the power of subversion. And while Comedy dismisses this threat as nonsense and easily manages to subdue Envy by the epilogue's end, the description of a poetic "neger cannibal" nonetheless has a strangely prophetic ring for readers familiar with *The Tempest*. In spite of Caliban's alleged aphasia at the initial contact with Prospero, he learns language—learns it astonishingly well—and this acquisition, perhaps more than any other trait, marks his humanity and signals his potential dangerousness to the intruding Europeans. Envy's threat, with its suggestion that characters like Bremo and the "neger cannibal" are necessary to the workings of comedy even as they endanger its survival and structural integrity, prefigures in a peculiar way Prospero's elusive remark about Caliban: "this thing of darkness I / Acknowledge mine" (5.1.275–76). Comedy cannot thrive without the dangerous potency of Envy: *Muced-*

orus needs Bremo and Tremelio just as *The Tempest* needs Alonso, Antonio, and Sebastian—and just as Prospero needs Caliban.

One of *The Tempest's* most explicit mystifications of Caliban's status lies in Stephano's reference to him as "My man-monster" (3.2.12). Clearly, such a phrase would be less appropriate with respect either to Bremo, notwithstanding his command of language, or to *The Faerie Queene's* Salvage Man, in spite of his aphasia; but for Caliban—especially at this point in the play—it seems a perfect designation, emblematic of the pervasive ambivalence regarding his condition which the play has created. Stephano utters it early in the second of four scenes in which he and Trinculo appear with Caliban. In the first of these scenes, Trinculo makes the thoroughly ambiguous remark—after coming upon Caliban wrapped in a gaberdine—that in England "would this monster make a man; any strange beast there makes a man" (2.2.30–31); Stephano seconds this ambiguity by alluding to "salvages and men of Inde" (2.2.58) and marvelling that the composite Caliban/Trinculo is "some monster of the isle with four legs, . . . Where the devil should he learn our language?" (2.2.65–67). Interestingly, however, this uncertainty regarding Caliban is mirrored by Caliban's own uncertainty regarding the Neapolitans—especially Stephano. And it is in this pair of corresponding and reinforcing ambivalences that we begin to see perhaps the greatest value of locating *The Tempest* within an ethnographic context.

Prompted by his drinking of Stephano's sack—itself an action resonant with contemporary New World associations—Caliban exclaims to himself, "These be fine things, and if they be not sprites. / That's a brave god, and bears celestial liquor. / I will kneel to him" (2.2.116–18). This is followed by such exclamations as "Hast thou not dropp'd from heaven? . . . I do adore thee . . . . I prithee, be my god . . . . Thou wondrous man" (2.2.137–64). Like *The Faerie Queene's* Artegall when he meets Britomart—or the satyrs in their encounter with Una—Caliban "makes religion" of his wonder.[60] It is true that he swears allegiance to Stephano, and true also that this willing subordination is often interpreted as proof of his natural slavishness[61]; but Shakespeare makes it clear that Caliban takes Stephano for a "brave god" (2.2.117) *before* he promises to be his "true subject" (2.2.125). Thus, notwithstanding the comic mode of the scene or its status as subplot in the play's larger design, Caliban does not necessarily reveal an abject propensity to be a slave. Stephen Greenblatt has written, in a discussion of the *Diario,* that Columbus occasionally demonstrates a recognition of "reverse wonderment" among the native Americans he encounters in the Caribbean[62]; I would argue that Caliban's behavior here suggests a literary transformation of that wonderment. His subservience, initially, is not that of man-monster to man, but of man-monster to man-god; and while it is in some respects comic, it merits far more than ridicule.[63] We must not forget, for example, that Caliban possesses a concept of divinity of godhead: his references to his "dam's" god, Setebos, make this clear (1.2.373, 5.1.261). And since it is virtually beyond dispute that Shakespeare takes "Setebos" from Antonio Pigafetta's account of Magellan's voyage, it bears noting that in an adjacent passage Pigafetta describes the reaction of a Patagonian native confronted by Europeans: "When he sawe the capitayne with certeyne of his coompany abowte hym, he was greatly amased and made signes holdynge vppe his hande to heauen, signifyinge therby that owre men came from thense."[64] Indeed, the motif of native Americans regarding Europeans as gods appears frequently in the voyagers' accounts.[65] And while this representation, due to its utter one-sidedness, is clearly unreliable as a descriptive characterization, its implicit reliance upon the idea that idolatry can evolve into "true" religion suggests that at its core lies the accurate perception, among European observers, that the native inhabitants of America practiced forms of devotion that could only be categorized as "religious." Thomas Harriot, in a passage quoted earlier, expresses this best:

> Some religion they have alreadie, which although it be farre from the trueth, yet being as it is, there is hope it may be the easier and sooner reformed.[66]

The Europeans' very theory of evangelization—or, at any rate, their most successful theory—relied in part upon the premise that what they deemed idolatry was in fact a conclusive indication of humanity and a positive step toward Christian conversion. The ability to confuse men for gods, as Caliban does, is thus a confirmation of the views expressed in the anti–*tabula rasa* descriptions quoted above. When American natives are represented as overestimating the status of Europeans, they are simultaneously—if indirectly— represented as fully human in status and as possessing cultural forms of their own. They are not blank pages, not unaccommodated.

The emphasis which Shakespeare gives to the ambivalences I have discussed both highlights the play's debt to voyagers' accounts and propels it toward its romantic conclusion. Stephano cannot decide whether Caliban is monster or man; Caliban, equally, cannot decide whether Stephano is man or god. And, as if in sympathy with these uncertainties, Miranda wonders whether Ferdinand is human or divine (1.2.410–20), and neither Ferdinand nor Alonso can initially decide whether Miranda is a maid or a goddess (1.2.422–29, 5.1.185–88).[67] Gradually, however, the uncertainties are resolved, the multiple possibilities collapsed. Prospero assures Miranda that Ferdinand "eats, and sleeps, and hath such senses / As we have" (1.2.413–14); Miranda describes herself to Ferdinand as "No wonder, sir, / But certainly a maid" (1.2.427–28); Ferdinand tells his father that Miranda "is mortal" (5.1.188); and Caliban curses himself for his error: "What a thrice-double ass / Was I to take this drunkard for a god, / And worship this dull fool!" (5.1.296–98). And while no explicit recognition surfaces in Stephano or Trinculo that Caliban is human, there remains the far more significant remark by Prospero that "this thing of darkness I / Acknowledge mine" (5.1.275–76). As Stephen Greenblatt has pointed out, Prospero "may intend these words only as a declaration of ownership, but it is difficult not to hear in them some deeper recognition of affinity, some half-conscious acknowledgment of guilt."[68] Affinity and guilt indeed; many years ago, assuming the persona of Caliban and addressing a composite Prospero/Shakespeare, W. H. Auden characterized this recognition as follows:

> Striding up to Him in fury, you glare into His unblinking eyes and stop dead, transfixed with horror at seeing reflected there, not what you had always expected to see, a conquerer smiling at a conquerer, both promising mountains and marvels, but a gibbering fist-clenched creature with which you are all too unfamiliar, for this is the first time indeed that you have met the only subject that you have, who is not a dream amenable to magic but the all too solid flesh you must acknowledge as your own; at last you have come face to face with me, and are appalled to learn how far I am from being, in any sense, your dish; how completely lacking in that poise and calm and all-forgiving because all-understanding good nature which to the critical eye is so wonderfully and domestically present on every page of your published inventions.[69]

Prospero's acknowledgment may imply that Caliban is what he—Prospero—can become, or what he has *in futurum videre* within himself, or what his nurture may, in the end, amount to; in any of these cases, his remark hints at the same interpenetration of the conventionally savage and the civil suggested by the portrayal of *The Faerie Queene*'s Salvage Man. Perhaps Prospero is also implicitly admitting that Caliban possesses a perceptive subjectivity and thus stands in a dialogic relationship with him. At all events, this acknowledgment—coming as it does from the character who, more than anyone else, has been responsible for the mystification of Caliban's status—goes far toward finally drawing Caliban within the bounds of humanity.

Throughout *The Tempest* we look at Caliban much in the way that Renaissance explorers must have looked at New World natives. In some ways he seems bestial; but in others—among them his intimate knowledge of the isle, his initial nurturing of Prospero and Miranda, his later resentment of Prospero's rule, his capacity for forming warm attachments, his vulnerability, and his dreamy, reflective poetry—he seems entirely human. Above all, there is his decision, late in the play, to "be wise hereafter, / And seek for grace" (5.1.295–96).[70] Perhaps this means that he will seek Christian prevenient grace—the divine favor of God—or perhaps the pardon or indulgence of Prospero.[71] But in this particular instance, the word "grace" need not necessarily refer either to divine dispensation or human forgiveness; it *could* be being used in the alternative sense of "virtue," as it is twice elsewhere in the play (3.1.45, 5.1.70) and in such other instances as Donne's famous lines about "man, this world's vice-emperor, in whom / All faculties, all graces are at home" or the moment in *Macbeth* when Malcolm speaks of "The King-becoming graces" and mentions, among other traits, "justice," "temp'rance," "lowliness," "Devotion," and "patience" (4.3.91–94).[72] Caliban, in vowing to "seek for grace," may very well be vowing not submission (and thus containment by the dominant culture) but rather an independent project of self-betterment; the virtue he may be seeking is that of proper judgement, so that in the future he will not again make his past mistake of confusing humans and gods. In any case, though Shakespeare never explicitly resolves the matter of Caliban's status, he suggests—to the extent that he gradually allows the play's other uncertainties about character identity to dissolve into thin air—that Caliban, like Ferdinand, Miranda, and Stephano, is a fully human being. And this suggestion is reinforced by *The Tempest's* thorough contradiction of Prospero's allegation that Caliban is ineducable, "a born devil, on whose nature / Nurture can never stick" (4.1.188–89); the same could be said, after all, of Antonio and Sebastian, neither of whom—unlike Caliban—show any sign of repentance for their conspiracy, though both have had the advantage of more refined and extended nurture. One might even argue that Caliban, in his initial and fully reciprocal relationship with Prospero, exhibits a nurture that, far from failing to "stick" to his nature, lies at is very essence.

Placing *The Tempest* within an ethnographic context goes far toward explaining why Caliban cannot be discarded in the way that Bremo is, for example, in *Mucedorus*. Caliban is not merely a "wild man," a sinister, shadowy figure derived from European folklore and medieval tradition; he remains far more complex and distinct, and though his portrayal certainly reveals bestial elements, it is also vivified by an acknowledgment of the existence of culturally alien humans across the ocean. Like the ambivalences of New World ethnography, the ambivalences of *The Tempest* gradually move toward human inclusiveness. And this levelling tendency, which shows the failings of aristocrats as well as the virtues of an alleged "demi-devil," bears a resemblance both to movements in other late plays of Shakespeare and to the ideals of what might be referred to as "Montaignesque pastoral"—a more radical pastoral than that typical of Spenser, more informed by the speculative and critical spirit that characterizes the *Essais*. As the whoreson and the Bedlam beggar must be acknowledged in *King Lear* (1.1.24, 3.4.28–180) and the strange Tupinamba in Montaigne's "Des Canni-bales," so, too, must Caliban.

Notes

I wish to express my gratitude to Joanne Altieri, David Bevington, and Charles Frey for reading and carefully responding to earlier drafts of this essay. I have learned much from their acuity and generosity.

1. See *Err.* 3.2.132–37, *MV* 1.3.19–20, *1H4* 3.1.166–67, *AYL* 3.2.88–89, *Wiv.* 1.3.69–72, *TN* 2.5.13–14, *LLL* 4.3.218–21, and *AWW* 1.3.204–7. All quotations from the plays and poems of Shakespeare are drawn from *The Riverside Shake-speare*, ed. G. Blakemore Evans, et al. (Boston: Houghton Mifflin, 1974). I have retained the brackets indicating editorial choices among variant readings.

2. Sidney Lee, "The American Indian in Elizabethan England," *Elizabethan and Other Essays*, ed. F. S. Boas (London: Oxford University Press, 1929), 285. Lee claims that Shakespeare's "strange Indian" was in fact the New Englander known as "Epenow" who was exhibited about London—for money—in 1611 (284).

3. For "hurricano," see also *Tro.* 5.2.172; for "potatoes," *Wiv.* 5.5.19. "Hurri-cane" is derived, through Spanish, from the Arawakan word "hurakan," according to Peter Hulme in *Colonial Encounters* (London: Methuen, 1986), 95; see also Hulme's "Hurricanes in the Caribbees: The Constitution of the Discourse of En-glish Colonialism," in *1642: Literature and Power in the Seventeenth Century*, ed. Francis Barker, et al. (Colchester: University of Essex Press, 1981), 77, 9n. "Potato," according to the *OED*, is derived from the Haitian (i.e., Taino) "batata"; Richard Eden (1555) and John Hawkins (1565) are cited as having used variant forms. "Setebos," as *Tempest* commentators have long known, comes from Antonio Piga-

fetta's account of Magellan's circumnavigation in 1519–22; two Patagonians who were deceived and captured by Magellan's men "cryed vppon theyr greate deuyll *Setebos* to helpe them" (Richard Eden, *The Decades of the newe worlde or west India* [London, 1555; Ann Arbor: University Microfilms, 1966], 220).

4. "Shakespeare's Indian: The Americanization of Caliban," *Shakespeare Quarterly* 39.2 (Summer 1988): 137. See also Alden T. Vaughan and Virginia Mason Vaughan, *Shakespeare's Caliban: A Cultural History* (Cambridge: Cambridge University Press, 1991); chapters 2, 5, and 6 provide excellent overviews of various "Americanist" readings of *The Tempest*.

5. "Shakespeare's American Fable" is the title of chapter 2 of Marx's *The Machine in the Garden* (London: Oxford University Press, 1964).

6. The first volume of the second (and enlarged) edition of Richard Hakluyt's *Principal Navigations* was accompanied by a world map based on the Mercator projection. Further evidence that Shakespeare knew this collection of travel narratives is suggested by a speech of one of *Macbeth*'s Witches: "Her husband's to Aleppo gone, master o' th' Tiger" (1.3.7); we read in "The voyage of M. Ralph Fitch . . . in the yeere of our Lord 1583" of "a ship of London called the Tyger, wherein we went for Tripolis in Syria: & from thence we tooke the way for Aleppo" (*The Principal Navigations, Voyages, Traffiques and Discoveries of the English Nation* [London, 1598–1600; New York: AMS Press, 1965], 5: 465). William Strachey's account of the 1609 Bermuda shipwreck of the *Sea Venture*, bound for the new English colony at Jamestown, is titled *A True Repertory of the Wrack and Redemption of Sir Thomas Gates*; it was first published in Purchas's *Hakluytus Posthumous* (London, 1625), but circulated in manuscript around London in 1610. Silvester Jourdain's account of the same voyage, *A Discovery of the Barmudas, Otherwise Called the Isle of Devils*, was published in London in 1610.

7. See Hodgen, "Montaigne and Shakespeare Again," *Huntington Library Quarterly* 16 (1952): 23–42, and Cawley, "Shakspere's Use of the Voyagers in *The Tempest*," *PMLA* 41 (1926): 688–726. Cawley greatly extends and further catalogues his study of source material in *The Voyagers and Elizabethan Drama* (Boston: MLA, 1938) and *Unpathed Waters* (Princeton: Princeton University Press, 1940).

8. "*The Tempest* and the New World," *Shakespeare Quarterly* 30.4 (Winter 1979): 34.

9. "Nymphs and reapers heavily vanish: the discursive con-texts of *The Tempest*," *Alternative Shakespeares*, ed. John Drakakis (London: Methuen, 1985), 196. Barker and Hulme cite Kristeva's *Le Texte du roman* (The Hague, 1970) as their source for the concept of intertextuality. In a separate work, Hulme quotes Charles Frey approvingly as a critic who "rejects the idea of an autotelic text" in favor of careful study of *The Tempest*'s "discursive milieux" (*Colonial Encounters*, 93).

10. Cawley, "Shakspere's Use of the Voyagers," 688n; Hodgen, "Montaigne and Shakespeare Again," 40.

11. *King Lear in Our Time* (Berkeley: University of California Press, 1965), 49.

12. On the Beerbohm Tree and Miller productions, see Virginia Mason Vaughan, "'Something Rich and Strange': Caliban's Theatrical Metamorphoses," *Shakespeare Quarterly* 36.4 (1985): 390–405, Trevor R. Griffiths, "'This Island's mine': Caliban and Colonialism," *Yearbook of English Studies 13*, ed. G. K. Hunter and C. J. Rawson (London: Modern Humanities Research Association, 1983), 159–80, and Anthony B. Dawson, *Watching Shakespeare* (New York: St. Martin's, 1988), 231–41. See also, for a discussion of earlier productions, Michael Dobson, "'Remember / First to Possess his Books': The Appropriation of *The Tempest*, 1700–1800," *Shakespeare Survey* (1991): 99–108. Rowse writes that "perhaps in

the subconscious corridors of the mind we think of what happened to the red-skins" (*The Elizabethans and America* [New York: Harper, 1959], 197–98); Reta-mar argues, in the tradition of José Martí and Frantz Fanon, that *The Tempest* aids us in articulating a Marxist critique of European and Yankee imperialism in Latin America: Ariel is a Gramscian intellectual and Caliban a symbol of the oppressed proletariat ("Caliban: Notes Toward a Discussion of Culture in Our America" [1971], in *Caliban and Other Essays* [Minneapolis: University of Minnesota Press, 1989], esp. 39–45); Fiedler claims that by the end of *The Tempest*, "the whole history of imperialist America has been prophetically revealed to us in brief parable: from the initial act of expropriation through the Indian wars to the setting up of reservations, and from the beginnings of black slavery to the first revolts and evasions" (*The Stranger in Shakespeare* [New York: Stein Day, 1972], 238). See also Dominique Octave Mannoni, *Prospero and Caliban: The Psychology of Colonization* (New York: Praeger, 1956); Philip Mason, *Prospero's Magic* (London: Oxford University Press, 1962); D. G. James, *The Dream of Prospero* (Oxford: Oxford University Press, 1967); Harry Berger, Jr., "Miraculous Harp: A Reading of Shakespeare's *Tempest*," *Shakespeare Studies* 5 (1969): 353–83; John Gillies, "Shakespeare's Virginian Masque," *English Literary History* 53 (1986): 673–707; and, most recently, Jeffrey Knapp, "Distraction in *The Tempest*," in *An Empire Nowhere: England, America, and Literature from Utopia to* The Tempest (Berkeley: University of California Press, 1992), 220–42.

    13. Barker and Hulme, "Nymphs and reapers," 204; Paul Brown, "'This thing of darkness I acknowledge mine': *The Tempest* and the discourse of colonialism," *Political Shakespeare*, ed. Jonathan Dollimore and Alan Sinfield (Ithaca: Cornell University Press, 1985), 68.

    14. "Anxiety" in this sense is drawn from Barker and Hulme, 198. Barker and Hulme offer a critique of Frank Kermode's introduction to the Arden *Tempest* (London: Methuen, 1954), 195–96. See also Terence Hawkes's remarks on the English critic Sir Walter Raleigh in *That Shakespeherian Rag* (London: Methuen, 1986), 51–72, and Meredith Anne Skura's brief mention of G. Wilson Knight in "Discourse and the Individual: The Case of Colonialism in *The Tempest*," *Shakespeare Quarterly* 40.1 (Spring 1989): 46.

    15. Brown, "'This thing of darkness'," 53.

    16. Hulme, *Colonial Encounters*, 125.

    17. Hulme, *Colonial Encounters*, 124. Richard Marienstras makes a similar point when he argues that because Prospero knows more than any other character, spectators "see and judge events from his point of view"; he adds, however, that "it is not possible, in the conflict between [Prospero] and Caliban, entirely to eliminate or discredit the reasoning of the latter" (*New Perspectives on the Shakespearean World* [Cambridge: Cambridge University Press, 1985], 171).

    18. Vitoria writes that the title to possession of a given territory, when based upon the discovery of that territory, is legitimate in certain cases (prior lack of inhabitation, for instance); but such a title is *not* legitimate in most parts of America: "the barbarians were true owners, both from the public and from the private standpoint. Now the rule of the law of nations is that what belongs to nobody is granted to the first occupant, . . . (quoted in Stephen Greenblatt, *Marvelous Possessions* [Chicago: University of Chicago Press, 1991], 61).

    19. "The famous voyage of Sir Francis Drake into the South sea," *Principal Navigations*, 11: 121–22. Apropos of this, Louis B. Wright has accurately observed that "the doctrine that particular regions [of the New World] had been set aside until such time as Englishmen might need to emigrate . . . helped to create an English version of the belief in Manifest Destiny which profoundly influenced

colonial enterprise in the seventeenth century" (*Religion and Empire* [Chapel Hill: University of North Carolina Press, 1943], 85–86).

20. See, for example, Las Casas's *The Spanish Colonie* (London, 1583; Ann Arbor, University Microfilms, 1966) sig. A4, and Montaigne's "Of the Caniballes" (*The Essayes of Michael, Lord of Montaigne*, trans. John Florio [London: 1603; New York: Modern Library, 1933], 166–67). Sister Corona Sharp argues in her article "Caliban: The Primitive Man's Evolution" that "Shakespeare could hardly have missed hearing about [Las Casas'] *The Spanish Colonie*, and the numerous passages in this work that are analogous to portions of *The Tempest* are worth noting" (*Shakespeare Studies* 14 [1981]: 279). See also Skura's "Discourse and the Individual," 51.

21. On this, compare Montaigne in "Of Coaches": "Our world hath of late discovered another (and who can warrant us whether it be the last of his brethren, since both the *Damons*, the *Sibylles*, and all we have hitherto been ignorant of this?) no lesse-large, fully-peopled, all-things-yielding, and mighty in strength, than ours" (*Essayes*, 821).

22. Barker and Hulme, "Nymphs and reapers," 198. Skura points to this limitation in colonialist readings when she writes that "the exploitative and self-justifying rhetoric [of colonialism] is only one element in complex New World discourse" ("Discourse and the Individual," 54).

23. Brown, "'This thing of darkness',", 60, 52–53.

24. For a useful and balanced critique of Brown's article and the view that Shakepeare endorsed the colonial project, see Deborah Willis, "Shakespeare's *Tempest* and the Discourse of Colonialism," *Studies in English Literature* 29 (1989): 277–89. See also Russ McDonald, "Reading *The Tempest*," *Shakespeare Survey* 43 (1991): 15–28, esp. 15–17.

25. Hawkes, *That Shakespeherian Rag*, 3.

26. Knapp, *An Empire Nowhere*, 235.

27. *The Elizabethans and the Irish* (Ithaca: Cornell University Press, 1966), 20.

28. Jack Beeching observes in his introduction to Hakluyt's *Voyages and Discoveries* (Harmondsworth: Penguin, 1972) that "Shipmen breaking in upon more primitive, hitherto untouched societies for the purpose of trade had a faculty of observing and recording curious customs with the lack of prejudice which distinguishes the anthropologist, who is their historical legatee" (12); while the claim that these accounts reveal a "lack of prejudice" is certainly naive, Beeching's point is still pertinent.

29. On Renaissance ethnography see, among other studies, Margaret T. Hodgen, *Early Anthropology in the Sixteenth and Seventeenth Centuries* (Philadelphia: University of Pennsylvania Press, 1964); two articles by John Hawland Rowe: "Ethnography and Ethnology in the Sixteenth Century" (*Kroeber Anthropological Society Papers* 30 [1964]: 1–19) and "The Renaissance Foundations of Anthropology" (*American Anthropologist* 67 [February 1965]: 1–20); Michael T. Ryan, "Assimilating New Worlds in the Sixteenth and Seventeenth Centuries," *Comparative Studies in Society and History* 23.4 (October 1981): 519–38; Caroline B. Brettell, "Introduction: Travel Literature, Ethnography, and Ethnohistory," *Ethnohistory* 33.2 [1986]: 127; and Mary B. Campbell, "The Illustrated Travel Book and the Birth of Ethnography: Part I of De Bry's *America*," in *The Work of Dissimilitude*, ed. David G. Allen and Robert A. White (Newark: University of Delaware Press, 1992), 177–95.

30. Charles Frey contrasts the idea of "sources" with that of "linguistic and narrative force-field[s]" in "*The Tempest* and the New World," 33. Alden T. Vaughan cites Frey's article, along with Stephen Greenblatt's "Learning to Curse:

Aspects of Linguistic Colonialism in the Sixteenth Century" (in *First Images of America*, ed. Fredi Chiappelli, 2 vols. [Berkeley: University of California Press, 1976], 2: 561–80), as a forerunner in "the new interest in historical contexts" ("Shakespeare's Indian: The Americanization of Caliban," 151n).

31. Indeed, Stephen Greenblatt has brilliantly argued that what appears in Harriot's *Briefe and true report* to be "a conversation among equals, as if all meanings were provisional, as if the signification of events stood apart from power" is in fact "part of the process whereby Indian culture is constituted as a culture and thus brought into the light for study, discipline, correction, and transformation" ("Invisible Bullets," in *Shakespearean Negotiations: The Circulation of Social Energy in Renaissance England* [Berkeley: University of California Press, 1988], 36–37). I am, I suppose, more sanguine than Greenblatt in my conviction that Renaissance ethnography, by and large, is only haphazardly tied to colonial aims; one encounters, I believe, abundant instances of relatively disinterested description.

32. Eden, "The Indian language," in *Decades*; Léry, *History of a Voyage to the Land of Brazil*, trans. Janet Whatley (Berkeley: University of California Press, 1990) chap. 20; Smith, *A Map of Virginia* (London, 1612), in *The Complete Works of Captain John Smith*, ed. Philip L. Barbour (Chapel Hill: University of North Carolina Press, 1986) 1: 136–39. See also Jacques Cartier, "The language that is spoken in the Land newly disouered, called new Fraunce" and "The names of the chiefest partes of man, and other wordes necessarie to be knowen," in *A Shorte and briefe narration of the two Nauigations and Discoueries to the Northweast partes called Newe Fravnce*, trans. John Florio (London, 1580; Ann Arbor: University Microfilms, 1966), 27, 79–80. Stephen Greenblatt contends that "In Cartier, as in almost all early Eurpean accounts, the language of the Indians is noted not in order to register cultural specificity but in order to facilitate barter, movement, and assimilation through conversion" (*Marvelous Possessions*, 104); while there is certainly a good measure of truth to this, I think that such documents as Cartier's and Léry's glossaries inevitably *do* register cultural specificity and difference, thereby both demonstrating European interest in the other and providing a discourse in which that interest may perpetuate itself.

33. As Skura points out, these words appear in the Folio's "Names of the Actors"; Shakespeare may or may not have written them ("Discourse and the Individual," 48).

34. Hulme, *Colonial Encounters*, 114.

35. *Nova Brittania* (London: 1609), in *Tracts and Other Papers, Relating Principally to the Origin, Settlement, and Progress of the Colonies in North America*, ed. Peter Force, 4 vols. (New York: Peter Smith, 1947), 1 (6): 11.

36. *The Generall Historie of Virginia* (London, 1624), in *The Complete Works of Captain John Smith*, ed. Philip L. Barbour (Chapel Hill: University of North Carolina Press, 1986) 2: 152, 183, 189, 198, 125–26.

37. *A briefe and true report of the new found land of Virginia* (London, 1588), in *Virginia Voyages from Hakluyt*, ed. David B. Quinn and Alison M. Quinn (London: Oxford University Press, 1973), 70.

38. Edmund Malone, *The Plays and Poems of William Shakespeare*, 21 vols. (London, 1821) 15: 11–14; Leslie Fiedler, *The Stranger in Shakespeare*, 233. Sidney Lee also points to the varied ethnographic roots of Caliban, including the Guianans described by Ralegh, but he curbs his enthusiasm enough to recollect—unlike Fiedler—that there were no "native Bermudans" ("The American Indian in Elizabethan England," in *Elizabethan and Other Essays*, ed. F. S. Boas [London: Oxford University Press, 1929], 263–301).

39. Bullough, *Narrative and Dramatic Sources of Shakespeare* (London: Routledge & Kegan Paul, 1975) 8: 257; Hulme, *Colonial Encounters*, 108. See also Robert Ralston Cawley, who argues that Caliban is not a mélange of types but a representation of the changing attitudes toward native Americans held by the colonists ("Shakspere's Use of the Voyagers in *The Tempest*," *PMLA* 41 [1926]: 719n); Sister Corona Sharp, who writes that Caliban's character "took shape under the influence of conflicting opinions held on the American Indians during Shakespeare's lifetime" ("Caliban: The Primitive Man's Evolution," 267); and Karen Flagstad, who adds that "the savage Caliban conflates contradictory stereotypes" ("'Making this Place Paradise': Prospero and the Problem of Caliban in *The Tempest*," *Shakespeare Studies* 18 [1986]: 221).

40. Bernard W. Sheehan, *Savagism and Civility: Indians and Englishmen in Colonial Virginia* (Cambridge: Cambridge University Press, 1980), 85, 87.

41. Greenblatt, "Learning to Curse: Aspects of Linguistic Colonialism in the Sixteenth Century," 574; Todorov, *The Conquest of America* (New York: Harper & Row, 1984), 42–43.

42. Greenblatt, "Learning to Curse," 575.

43. *New Perspectives on the Shakespearean World* (Cambridge: Cambridge University Press, 1985), 169–70. I disagree with Marienstras, however, when he asserts that Caliban's uncertain status "gives the reader a feeling of instability that remains with him through to the end of the play" (170).

44. Cabeza de Vaca, *Relation of Nuñez Cabeza de Vaca*, trans. Buckingham Smith (New York, 1871; Ann Arbor: University Microfilms, 1966), 82; Léry, *History of a Voyage to the Land of Brazil*, 29; Acosta, *How to procure the salvation of the Indians*, excerpted in John Howland Rowe, "Ethnography and Ethnology in the Sixteenth Century," 16; Strachey, *Historie of Travell into Virginia Britannia*, excerpted in *The Elizabethans' America: A Collection of Early Reports by Englishmen on the New World*, ed. Louis B. Wright [Cambridge, Mass: Harvard University Press, 1965], 215; Smith, *Generall Historie*, in *The Complete Works of Captain John Smith* 2: 119.

45. "Virginias Verger," in *Hakluytus Posthumous, or Purchas His Pilgrimes* (London: 1625), 20 vols (Glasgow: J. MacLehose & Sons, 1905–7) 19: 231.

46. All quotations from *Mucedorus* (London, 1598) are drawn from *Drama of the English Renaissance*, ed. Russell A. Fraser and Norman Rabkin, 2 vols. (New York: Macmillan, 1976), 1: 463–80. *Mucedorus* was published in seventeen separate editions between 1598 and 1658. It was performed by the King's Men in 1610 "before the King's majesty at Whitehall on Shrove-Sunday night" (Fraser and Rabkin, 463); thus Shakespeare probably knew the play, and may have acted in it.

47. Introduction to the Arden *Tempest* (London: Methuen, 1954), xxxviii–ix. Norman Rabkin writes that "Bremo the wild man is something of a forerunner of Caliban, suggesting the interest of an age of exploration in the phenomenon of natural man while ensuring that the play remains fairy tale" (Introduction to *Mucedorus*, 463).

48. Bremo's encounter with Amadine in scene 11 reveals obvious similarities to the conventional motif of the wild man's transformation to civility in the presence of a beautiful and virtuous woman. But this particular encounter is presented, I think, as a more sentimental and less thoroughly transforming experience.

49. Goldsmith, "The Wild Man on the English Stage," *Modern Language Review* 53 (1958): 481–91.

50. This speech, with its indication of Caliban's intelligence and appreciation of Prospero's gifts, echoes numerous accounts of New World natives, among them

James Rosier's 1605 description of Indians along the New England coast: "They seemed all very civil and merry, showing tokens of much thankfulness for those things we gave them. We found them then (as after) a people of exceeding good invention, quick understanding, and ready capacity" (A True Relation of the Most Properous Voyage Made This Present Year 1605 by Captain George Weymouth, excerpted in The Elizabethans' America, 149). On Weymouth's voyage, see Sidney Lee, "The American Indian in Elizabethan England," 282.

51. Orgel, introduction to the Oxford Tempest (Oxford: Oxford University Press, 1987), 34. Sister Corona Sharp takes this view even further in calling the attempted rape "Caliban's failure in European sexual ethics" ("Caliban: The Primitive Man's Evolution," 273). And Paul Brown asserts that Caliban's "inability to discern a concept of private, bounded property concerning his own dominions is reinterpreted as a desire to violate the chaste virgin, who epitomizes courtly property" ("'This thing of darkness I acknowledge mine': The Tempest and the discourse of colonialism" 62). See also Orgel's "Shakespeare and the Cannibals," in Cannibals, Witches, and Divorce, ed. Marjorie Garber (Baltimore: Johns Hopkins University Press, 1987), 55.

52. Martyr, Decades, decade 3, bk. 8, p. 134; Fabian, in Hakluyt, Principal Navigations 7: 155. The three Eskimos Fabian describes were brought by Sebastian Cabot to England from the North American Arctic in 1502 and presented to Henry VII. See Sidney Lee, "The American Indian in Elizabethan England," 270.

53. "The relation of John de Verrazzano a Florentine, of the land by him discovered in the name of his Majestie. Written in Diepe the eight of July 1524," in Hakluyt, Principal Navigations 8: 433.

54. Léry, History of a Voyage, 158.

55. Acosta, How to procure the salvation of the Indians, 17.

56. Whitaker, Good Newes from Virginia (London: 1613; New York: Scholars' Facsimiles and Reprints, 1936), 26–27; Strachey, Historie of Travel into Virginia Britannia (London: 1612), excerpted in The Elizabethans' America, 212; Harriot, A briefe and true report (London: 1588), in Virginia Voyages, 68.

57. Whitaker, Good Newes from Virginia, 24.

58. Diego Alvarez Chanca, a Spanish surgeon, accompanied Columbus on his second voyage to the West Indies (1493–96) and wrote about the natives in his "Letter addressed to the Chapter of Seville" (Four Voyages to the New World: Letters and Selected Documents, trans. and ed. R. H. Major [Gloucester, Mass.: Peter Smith, 1978], 66).

59. Alan C. Dessen discusses this role-doubling as "a means to call attention to structural or thematic analogies" in "Conceptual Casting in the Age of Shakespeare: Evidence from Mucedorus," Shakespeare Quarterly 43 no. 1(Spring 1992): 67–70.

60. The Faerie Queene, ed. Thomas P. Roche, Jr. (New Haven: Yale University Press, 1981), 4.6.22 and 1.6.7–19.

61. Marienstras, for example, writes that Caliban "rushes into servitude even when striving for freedom" (New Perspectives, 175).

62. Greenblatt, Marvelous Possessions, 77.

63. For a fascinating and sustained example of native Americans confronting Europeans whom they cannot, at first, satisfactorily categorize, see Diego Durán, The Aztecs: The Indies of New Spain (New York: Orion, 1964), esp. chap. 69–74. Durán claims, for instance, that Moteczoma and his ministers plotted various strategies of resistance to Cortés and the other conquistadors even while alluding to them as immortal beings: "'I do not know' [said Moteczoma] 'what measures to take to prevent these gods from reaching the city or seeing my face. Perhaps

the best solution will be the following: let there be gathered enchanters, sorcerers, sleep-makers and those who know how to command snakes, scorpions and spiders, and let them be sent to enchant the Spaniards. Let them be put to sleep, let them be shown visions, let the little beasts bite them so that they die.' . . . 'O powerful lord' [responded Tlillancalqui] 'your decision seems good to me, but if they are gods who will be able to harm them? However, nothing will be lost in the attempt'" (276).

64. Martyr, *Decades*, 219.

65. Drake's men found that the Miwok natives of California "supposed us to be gods, and would not be perswaded to the contrary" (Richard Hakluyt, "The famous voyage of Sir Francis Drake into the South sea," *Principal Navigations* 11: 119). And Thomas Harriot writes of the Indians near the Roanoke Colony, "some people could not tel whether to thinke us gods or men" (*A briefe and true report*, 73). See also Cawley, *The Voyagers and Elizabethan Drama*, 385–88. In one of the classic English fictions dealing with the encounter of European and native American, Daniel Defoe exploits this motif in portraying the relationship between Crusoe and the "savage" Friday: "I believe, if I would have let him, he would have worshipped me and my gun" (*The Life and Adventures of Robinson Crusoe*, ed. Angus Ross [Harmondsworth: Penguin, 1965], 214).

66. Harriot, *A briefe and true report*, 68.

67. On connections between Miranda and the American native Pocahontas, see Morton Luce's Arden edition of *The Tempest* (London: 1902) 169–70; Geoffrey Bullough's *Narrative and Dramatic Sources* 8: 241; and Jeffrey Knapp, *An Empire Nowhere*, 240–41.

68. Greenblatt, *Shakespearean Negotiations*, 157. See also Skura, "Discourse," 66; Knapp, *An Empire Nowhere*, 239; and Lynda E. Boose, "The Father and the Bride in Shakespeare," *PMLA* 97.3 (1982): 341. When Ferdinand speaks to Prospero of "our worser genius" as a force that can potentially "melt . . . honor into lust" (4.1.27–28), he perhaps anticipates Prospero's "thing of darkness" speech inasmuch as he suggests that a principle of wildness or savagery lies within all humans.

69. "The Sea and the Mirror," in *The Collected Poetry of W. H. Auden* (New York: Random House, 1945), 387–88.

70. In claiming that he will "be wise hereafter, / And seek for grace" (5.1.295–96), Caliban is almost certainly not speaking ironically; the tone of self-annoyance in which he castigates himself for taking the drunkard Stephano for a god and worshipping the "dull fool" Trinculo (5.1.297–98) seems strongly to preclude this.

71. On prevenient grace, see article 10 of the Church of England's thirty-nine articles (1571): "The condition of man after the fall of Adam is such, that he cannot turn and prepare himself, by his own natural strength and good works, to faith and calling upon God: Wherefore we have no power to do good works pleasant and acceptable to God, without the grace of God preventing us, that we may have a good will, and working with us, when we have that good will" (from Thomas Rogers, *The Faith, Doctrine, and Religion, Professed and Protected in the Realm of England . . . Expressed in 39 Articles* [Cambridge, 1607; rpt. New York: Johnson Reprint Corporation, 1968], 103). If Caliban is capable of seeking prevenient grace, the presumption is strong that he is fully human.

72. Donne, "An Anatomy of the World: The First Anniversary" (ll. 161–62) in *John Donne: The Complete English Poems*, ed. A. J. Smith (Harmondsworth: Penguin, 1973), 274. See also *As You Like It*, 3.2.11 and 3.2.17, and *Hamlet*, 4.7.21. The *OED* defines this meaning of "grace" as "In persons: Virtue; an individual virtue; sense of duty or propriety" (2.13b).

"Borrowed Robes," Costume Prices, and the Drawing of *Titus Andronicus*

S. P. Cerasano

Even after the witches warn Macbeth that he will soon acquire a greater rank and title, he expresses some surprise when their prophecy is realized. In 1.3, Ross bears the king's tidings along with his reward for Macbeth's courage and loyalty: "He bade me, from him, call thee Thane of Cawdor" (l. 105)[1] to which Macbeth replies: "The Thane of Cawdor lives; why do you dress me / In borrow'd robes?" (11.108–9). Of all the things that are borrowed and lent in Shakespeare's plays, life is most often lent, and title borrowed. At the opening of *King John*, for instance, the French ambassador delivers a message to the "borrow'd majesty" of England (1.1.4–5)[2]; and in *I Henry IV*, Douglas suggests to Hotspur, "A borrow'd title hast thou bought too dear" (5.3.23).[3] Around such rhetoric the issues of right rulership are fought. Yet in Macbeth's "borrow'd robes" another suggestion is embedded, one less involved with the philosophical and political debates on statecraft and one more tied, instead, to the practicalities of theatrical production. The robes that the actor playing Macbeth wore onstage were not his own, workaday dress, but were literally "borrowed" from the stock that belonged to the company with which he performed. Consequently, by drawing attention to them Macbeth might also have been drawing attention to his "actorly," deceptive nature, the condition of seeming to be Duncan's host while actually being his murderer. Focusing on Macbeth's "borrow'd robes" and other costuming customs reminds us of the conventions of production that might well add a new dimension to the way in which we envisage play productions in the 1590s and finally come to interpret the drawing of *Titus Andronicus*.

The drawing of *Titus Andronicus*, preserved among the papers

Fig. 1. The drawing of *Titus Andronicus* from the Harley Papers, vol. 1, fol. 159ᵛ. (Reproduced by permission of the Marquess of Bath, Longleat House, Wiltshire, Great Britain.)

of the Marquess of Bath at Longleat House, Wiltshire, is well known, and it has been the object of scholarly discussion since 1925 when E. K. Chambers pronounced it "The First Illustration to Shakespeare" (see fig. 1).[4] At the top of the page are seven figures interacting, as if to represent a specific scene from the play. In the lower left-hand margin (in a different hand) is a signature ("Henry Peacham") and a date (possibly 1595). Either of these could, or could not relate to the text and/or to the drawing. Written sideways near the right-hand margin (in yet another hand), on a flap of paper that was folded over in an endorsement is: "Henrye Peachams Hande/ 1595." One central scholarly puzzle concerns the relationship of the visual evidence to the verbal components of the manuscript and how these perhaps fit together. However, for the purposes of this essay I wish to concentrate on the drawing that heads the page, rather than on other issues. I do not, by this emphasis, mean to argue that the drawing can be disengaged completely from the complexity of questions raised by the rest of the manuscript page, but that the drawing deserves greater attention, especially as it relates to issues of actual staging.

Interestingly, the artist seems to have produced a single drawing by conflating several distinct moments in 1.1. of Shakespeare's play. On the far left are two characters (identified by various scholars as soldiers or Titus' sons), each holding a halberd and each wearing different costumes. The one on the far left is dressed in baggy breeches (called Venetians or slops) which taper at the knees. On the top he wears a traditional doublet. His hat, likewise, has a tall, conventional crown and is decorated with a feather. A long sash (baldrick) tied at the right shoulder dresses up the costume. (Perhaps it serves as an elaborate shoulder belt for the sword.) He carries a curved sword on his left side. Overall, the patterned breeches, baldrick, and sword suggest the flavor of an eastern-type costume, while the other components of the costume represent common contemporary dress. The helmet, breastplate armor, and straight sword complement this effect, and all appear to be strictly in period. Both men wear what appear to be conventional shoes.

In front of these men stands a character (seemingly Titus) in a tunic, toga, and sandals, with a laurel crown on his head. In his left hand he holds a large ceremonial staff. Tamora kneels in front of him wearing a voluminous gown with richly embroidered sleeves. There also is a long train down the back of the dress. Although she is the queen of the Goths, it is unclear whether the gown is distinctive in style. In its outline and details it could well resemble any English woman's ornate gown; and in its overall effect it quite resembles the style of gowns in portraits of the queen during the 1590s.

Just behind Tamora are two young men kneeling. Both wear tunics and one has a baldrick tied across his right shoulder. The one closest to the viewer has a beard and is wearing sandals. Both men appear to be prisoners, not only because they are suppliant, but because neither carries arms. Closer to the viewer is another figure on the far right, a black-skinned man in a tunic with sandals. He wears a head band and carries a long sword, which he points menacingly in front of him. He seems to be speaking straight ahead (perhaps to Titus) while, with his right hand, he points at the two kneeling men further upstage to his right.

Although J. Dover Wilson argued that the artist depicts "without doubt, what he actually saw at a performance of the play," R. A. Foakes has demonstrated quite convincingly that the drawing lacks certain elements that would anchor it absolutely to the tableau at 1.1.130 when Tamora pleads for Alarbus. Most notably, Foakes points out, the coffin draped in black (which is supposed to con-

tain the bodies of Titus's dead sons slain by Alarbus) is missing.
Foakes writes:

> There is, in fact, no reason to suppose this drawing was made at a
> staging of the play; it is more likely that it was drawn from recollection
> afterwards, possibly bringing together into a group separate sketches
> of individual actors made when watching a performance.[5]

If this is the case, it would easily explain why the drawing does
not identify any specific moment in the text, and also why the
forty-two lines of text (Tamora pleading for her sons) beneath the
drawing were excerpted from a point somewhat earlier in the
scene than those moments with which the drawing can be
vaguely identified.

About costuming Foakes concluded that "this medley of costumes suggests a casual attitude towards both historical accuracy
and consistency."[6] The Goths appear as Romans, and Titus "as an
ancient Roman, but his two sons or followers in variations of contemporary costume of the Tudor period."[7] Yet Dover Wilson sought
a more concrete, thematic approach to explain the distinct styles
of costuming: the lower classes wear contemporary dress while the
upper classes, he explained, adopt "the attire worn by patricians."[8]
In plays written during Shakespeare's lifetime references to contemporary dress were common. Casca refers to Caesar's "doublet"
in *Julius Caesar* (which conflicts with Dover Wilson's thesis concerning patrician and proletariat dress) and Hamlet wore his "inky
cloak" and his hat indoors thus observing the conventions of dress
for the time. Foakes questioned Dover Wilson's thesis by suggesting
that "the two soldiers on the left may be Titus' sons and 'patricians'."[9] But in addition to this consideration I would like to present another complementary possibility: that the mixed costuming
of the *Titus Andronicus* drawing reflects standard performance
practice, and that the costs of costuming were an important factor
in creating the mixture of costumes.

The costs of everyday dress can be found in a variety of sources.
Records from Newcastle upon Tyne keep fairly careful account of
the city's expenses for clothing fools, and these figure prominently
in the city's charitable expenses. Almost twenty different articles
of clothing are named including shirts, waistcoats, doublets,
breeches, jerkins, hats, gloves, and shoes. Fabrics were usually
basic, coarse types such as broadcloth, cotton, linen, and silk russet.
One man, John Watson, is mentioned frequently throughout the

accounts of the 1560s, during which time the city provided him with four shirts, four pairs of hose, a pair of gloves, two coats, one cap, and five pairs of shoes (totalling £3 11s. 10d.) for the 1562–63 fiscal year.[10] These expenses, although they define the most basic articles of clothing and the least expensive fabrics, are still modest, particularly when compared with what the average citizen or gentleman would have paid for clothing in a year. Edward Alleyn noted clothing expenses in his diary many years later, in the period from 1618 to 1622, when he spent almost £11 per year for apparel, and in some years he laid our a far greater sum, £78 18s. 8½d. in 1622, for instance.[11] Comparatively speaking, the expenses laid out for John Watson were also modest by comparison with similar articles of clothing purchased for a play performed by the Fullers and Dyers of Newcastle in 1561. Whereas the combined companies paid 3s. for a pair of gloves and 3s. 2d. ob. "for Gods coot," Watson received a pair of gloves and a dozen points for 4d. During the same year "fools" (plural, of which Watson was probably one) receive coats at Easter time, the costs of which totalled £2 1s. 6d.[12] Therefore the city of Newcastle allocated more financial support for costuming plays than for clothing the mentally impaired.

Whether the clothing worn in dramatic productions was generally of a better quality than the average street dress is still open to question. However, it is the assumption of most theater historians that it was, a hypothesis supported by many records, including those in Coventry, to cite only one case. There dress for civic ceremonies was traditionally of a better quality and a more elaborate design, the range of fabrics extending from taffeta (a thin silk) and linen to satin, velvet, and cloth of gold.[13] Descriptions also include such items as lace and ribbons, decorative materials that are notably absent from everyday dress.[14] Theatrical costumes shared the same distinctive qualities as ceremonial dress. Although the fabrics are not always specified, the sense that theatrical costumes were dress produced for special occasions pervades the records. Most commonly, coats, crowns, gloves, gowns, and hats were specially ordered, and they are often described as being in lively colors— gold, silver, scarlet, green—to match their wearers (King Arthur, Pilate, God, demons, giants, witches). In addition, items such as beards, helmets, and armor were specially ordered. Because these were not a part of ordinary dress they tended to make dramatic productions expensive.

In light of the expense of outfitting a man for a year, it appears that even a well-to-do citizen would think himself comfortably suited if he owned four pairs of hose and six shirts, two doublets and three cloaks, four coats and three cassocks, one sleeveless coat, four gowns, and one "workaday gown." This is the inventory of Edmund Brownell's wardrobe written in 1573 upon his death.[15] Brownell was a wealthy Coventry draper who died leaving fourteen houses, in addition to the one in which he lived, and the inventory of his possessions is fairly typical when compared with others of the same period. But wealth was not the sole factor in determining a man's wardrobe. Brownell presumably abided by the sumptuary laws dictated by both the national and local governments, laws which legislated what items of dress could be worn by various ranks of people. Yet these restrictions notwithstanding, Brownell's wardrobe is less extravagant than what we might expect.

The expense of clothing makes it easy to understand the regularity with which ordinary people bequeathed clothing to others in their wills. Amongst many testators who made provisions for their clothing, Shakespeare bequeathed £20 and all his apparel to his sister Joan Hart; and William Byrd, a player in the Palsgrave's Men, left his son his "Ash color suit and cloak trimmed with green silk and silver lace."[16] And some players provided costumes for the acting companies through bequests. When Christopher Beeston died he stipulated that his wife (also his executrix) should use two of his shares in the Cockpit to "provide and find for the said Company a sufficient and good stock of apparel fitting their use."[17]

The expense of clothing also serves to explain why John Alleyn (Edward's brother) purchased second-hand clothing for use as theatrical costumes: a long black velvet cloak from a London yeoman in 1589 (for £5) and a velvet cloak, a cape embroidered with gold and pearls, and a robe made of gold cloth from a gentleman of Clifford's Inn in 1590 (for £16).[18] All were priced much more cheaply used than new, as were the articles of theatrical clothing included in Richard Jones's "share"—a collection of playbooks, musical instruments, and apparel—which Jones sold to the Alleyn brothers and Robert Brown for £37 10s.[19] Also, as Henslowe's *Diary* shows, clothes were often pawned in times of economic crisis. In 1597 Henslowe lent a player's widow £5 10s. to recover several items from a pawnbroker.[20] In his own pawnbroking business, for which the documentation is especially good, Henslow's annotations are full of doublets, cloaks, and other articles of clothing. And in November 1598, Henslowe sold the Admiral's Men one of his own cloaks for £4.[21]

What can be learned about costuming from traditional scholarly sources is that apparel constituted a substantial investment for a playing company. Henslowe sold the stock of Lady Elizabeth's Men (without their playbooks) for £400 in 1615; and E. K. Chambers calculates "if the sums of £50 to £80 received by retiring sharers early in the seventeenth century may be taken as representing their interests in the stocks, the total value of the contents of a tiring-house might be anything from £500 to £1,000."[22] In context, then, the contents of the tiring house at the Rose Playhouse, for instance, seem to have been worth as much, or slightly more than the cost of the playhouse itself.[23] Moreover, although the value of the contents of the tiring house is difficult to assess—because stock grew over time and a certain amount of it depreciated, as Henslowe's "coat eaten by rats"—it also is clear that the players kept costs to a manageable level by buying second-hand garments and purchasing new costumes for only the major actors (or the unusual characters, such as giants and demons) for each production. An inventory list in Edward Alleyn's hand (dated 1598 or 1602 by various scholars) lists a collection of costumes that could only be judged as slight if indeed the list is meant to represent the entire contents of the tiring house: 14 cloaks, 18 gowns, 15 "antique suits," 17 jerkins and doublets, 11 pairs of hose, and 8 "venetians." Several of the articles specifically described as being "for a boye" suggest that not all of the items in this modest stock list could have been worn by adult actors.[24]

Of all the available evidence, that provided by Henslowe's *Diary* bears the fullest implications for our understanding of costuming procedures. Over a six-year period (1597–1603), Chambers concluded that Henslowe laid out £561 for apparel and properties, the greatest portion of which was apparel. However, Chambers did not note other significant trends in Henslowe's accounts; and many of the additional facts recorded in the *Diary* increase our understanding of the economics of costuming players. In the period from 1597 through 1603, the Lord Admiral's Men purchased one hundred and fifty pieces of apparel. Additionally, Henslowe's more general category labeled "diverse things" might well have included smaller items of apparel such as gloves and hats which aren't mentioned in other descriptions. However, while all of this information is extremely useful, costume lists sometimes provide ambiguous evidence. Of all the purchases of costumes, only twenty are clearly articles of women's apparel, and it is difficult to determine how many "gowns" were purchased for women (as opposed to the "gowns" purchased for men).

In general, Henslowe's annotations and the costs quoted in the *Diary* are marked by consistency throughout the six years of expenses he recorded, in terms of both the quantity and the quality of the costumes purchased. When Henslowe noted specific fabrics, he mentioned satin and velvet, and he regularly described the style of hose as "ornate."[25] The average cost of a doublet was £3. Most women's gowns ranged from £4 to £7 (with the odd £2 spent for a gown), and the average set of skirts cost £2. When accessories (gloves, hose, hats) were noted, they frequently cost as much or more than the rest of the costume; but the players' willingness to bear this expense makes sense when we consider that accessories served an important purpose. In a situation in which the number of costumes was limited, accessories could be used to provide variety and to lend visual interest to aging or basic costumes. Moreover, the costs recorded in Henslowe's *Diary* seem to provide realistic estimates and to represent actual costs to the company. Henslowe was fastidious in noting the unusual case in which fabric and tailoring were paid for separately. Consequently, it is probably safe to assume that his figures usually represent the price of the finished clothing.

Finally, it is useful to note that the costs for costumes seem to have been in accord with the expenses laid out for everyday clothing to clothe the members of Henslowe's extended family. In 1593 Philip lent his brother Edmund £2 10s. to buy "A new gowne for his wiffe."[26] He lent his nephew John (Edmund's son) 17s. to buy himself a cloak, and 5s. 6d. to purchase two shirts, both in 1596.[27] A year later Henslowe lent Edward Alleyn (by then his son-in-law) £2 to buy a gown for his wife.[28] Of course, expenses depended entirely upon the material chosen and the complexity of the tailor's work; however, the pawn accounts kept by Henslowe indicate that the average doublet could be pawned for 10s. to 20s., probably only a third or a quarter of its original cost.

Whether the stock in the tiring house at the Rose or the Fortune playhouses was supplemented by Henslowe's pawn business is a question that remains to be answered; but it would seem that Henslowe kept the theatrical business separate from the pawn business. On the occasions when the company purchased second-hand clothing it seems to have come from an outside source (not from one of Henslowe's pawn clients), and Henslowe nearly always specified the source of the purchase.[29] When substantial purchases were made for a given production, Henslowe was careful to note the name of the character for whom the costume was being prepared.

For instance, there was a purchase of a gray gown for Grissel (in *Patient Grissel*); of a suit for the boy in *Cupid and Psyche*; of a robe for Thomas Downton to wear when he played Hercules.[30] It also appears that some productions were fitted out much more elaborately than others and that the expenses of these special productions were simply accommodated by the normal costume budget of the company without relying upon outside sources, such as the pawn broking business. One example in which expenses were managed in this way is the costumes for *The Life of Cardinal Wolsey* (1601) which took better than two weeks to prepare, beginning with "tawny coats" (7 August), and moving on to "coats" (11 August), and a "doctor's gown" in velvet (20–21 August).[31] The inventory taken by Henslowe in March 1598, suggests that the company anticipated the expenses of unusual costumes: that Henry V wore both a doublet and a velvet gown for example; that Longshanks's costume was specially made; that unique costumes were made up for the lead actors in *Thomas More* and *Dido*. In addition, it is clear that clowns, fools, friars, and the boy players received special attention and that frequently their costumes were more expensive than the average costume.[32]

But primarily, the financial evidence preserved by Henslowe suggests that only two or three new costumes were purchased for most productions, that these were tailored for lead actors or for unusual characters (clowns, devils, and such), and that the other actors were attired from the stock in the tiring house. Obviously the leading actors, like Edward Alleyn, were privileged in this; some apparently had their own private stock, as it were, of costumes made for them (and, in some cases, even owned by them as the example of Richard Jones and others attests).[33] Paying attention to the economic dimension implies, furthermore, that a high rate of turnover in the number of productions would have made costuming costs prohibitive. A spectacle such as *Tamburlaine the Great, Part I*, requiring at least eighteen major roles, could have cost almost £60 if every actor was apparelled at the average minimal cost of £3 per costume.

This is not to say that all playing companies invested equally in apparel. There is too little evidence to support such a conclusion, and each company was limited by the shareholders' investments, which differed from company to company. Yet interestingly, the known expenses for costume investments from several companies seem to fall within a similar range. The £400 which Henslowe received from the sale of the stock from Lady Elizabeth's Men is not far off from the £561 that he invested in costumes for the Admiral's Men. Nor are either of these estimates far afield from the £500 to £600 in shares that the Admiral's Men contributed originally for investment in costumes, playbooks, and other necessities.[34] The available evidence indicates that apparel was the costliest portion of a company's outlay; and that, in terms of the Lord Admiral's Men, which paid dramatists a set £6 for playbooks, the costumes often seem to have cost as much or more than the playbooks. Still, the disparity between productions could be great. Aside from the standard £6 to purchase the playbook and the £3 paid the Master of the Revels for licensing the play, *Patient Grissell* only cost £3 in costumes; however, the company ended up spending £48 on costumes for both parts of *Cardinal Wolsey* in addition to their usual costs. It was probably for this reason that John Suckling purchased the costumes for the performance of his *Aglaura* himself and donated them to the company.[35]

In returning to the drawing of *Titus Andronicus*, if we accept the premise that the sketch captures some reflection of a live performance, it seems useful to reconsider Dover Wilson's assumption that a two-tiered social hierarchy was visibly in operation, one that divided the characters shown in the drawing into upper-class characters ("patricians" in special costume) and lower-class characters (in contemporary Elizabethan dress). Because we have no other sketches of *Titus Andronicus* or any other play, and because the major characters in *Titus* are by their very social standing "patrician," Wilson's theory can easily stand or fall depending upon whether we choose to identify the two characters on the left side of the sketch as Titus's sons (and therefore as "patricians") or as minor characters. In Foakes's estimation this point of ambiguity is the factor that makes Wilson's thesis untenable. In my estimation, Wilson's thesis is also untenable, but for slightly different reasons. I suggest that his thesis can stand only in the strictest sense: the "patrician" characters in the *Titus* drawing are so costumed because they are, after all, socially defined as patricians, and not because they are the lead actors in the company. Further, I depart from the broader social implications of Wilson's thesis by noting that the lead actors are specially costumed because of the economic constraints and costuming conventions within which the acting companies were operating. I argue that it was simply conventional to purchase special costumes for the actors who played prominent parts, while the supporting actors were outfitted from the tiring house stock. (Or, supporting actors might even have worn their own clothing on stage.) Some historians might argue that the hierarchy of the acting compnay was reflected in the "social hierarchy" of the costuming, that lead actors were treated as "patrician" while the supporting actors were not. This issue is certainly open to debate. However, I would like to suggest that hierarchy was not the only factor in determining costuming habits, that the "medley of costumes" was also financially determined. This factor has not been discussed for the full force of its effect by historians of Elizabethan theater companies.

In addition to this, there is a bit of irony offered by historical hindsight. The incidences of the gentry selling their clothes to the players, their social inferiors, were common enough knowledge that both John Donne and Ben Jonson made light of this practice. Donne, whose daughter married a player (Edward Alleyn), commented on suitors at court:

> As fresh, and sweet their apparels be, as be
> The fields they sold to buy them; "For a king
> Those hose are," cry the flatterers; and bring
> Them next week to the theatre to sell.
>
> (*Satire IV*, 180–84)

Jonson spoke of the patricians who change their clothes three times a day in order to teach each suit the way to walk to the theater "where at last / His dear and borrowed bravery he must cast."[36] Accounts of the Elizabethan theater are replete with references to the sumptuary laws and the frequent complaints against players who "jett in their silks" thus aping their social betters.[37] Finally the playing companies were capable of purchasing clothing that individual actors were legally prohibitied from wearing, except on the stage where they impersonated those who had sold them the clothes, thus "borrowing" both robe and title. If, in the future, historians decide to draw attention to the sketch of *Titus Andronicus*, they might also explain the complex and practical reasons why the costumes were mixed, noting both the financial and practical reasons behind costuming habits in the Elizabethan theater.

Notes

1. *Macbeth*, in The Arden Edition, ed. Kenneth Muir (London: Methuen, 1965).
2. *King John*, in The Arden Edition, ed. E. A. J. Honigman (London: Methuen, 1959).

3. *I Henry IV*, in The Arden Edition, ed. A. R. Humphreys (London: Methuen, 1960).

4. The manuscript is identified as MS. Harley Papers, vol. 1, fol. 159^v in the library of the Marquess of Bath. E. K. Chambers's well-known discussion of the *Titus* drawing is "The First Illustration to Shakepeare," *The Library*, 4th ser., 5 (1925), 326–30. Other discussions of the manuscript include John Munro, "Titus Andronicus," *TLS*, 10 June 1949, p. 385, and the reply by J. Dover Wilson, *TLS*, 24 June 1949, p. 413. Also, Eugene Waith has written a very thoughtful reconsideration of Henry Peacham's potential involvement in the manuscript in his edition of *Titus Andronicus* (Oxford: Oxford University Press, 1984), 20–27. There is also a woodcut illustration preserved in the Folger Library copy of a broadside ballad (printed between 1655 and 1665) entitled "The Lamentable and Tragicall History of Titus Andronicus, with the fall of his five and twenty sons, etc." which seems to be a composite presentation of several of the principle incidents from the play and the story of Titus; however, it does not bear upon the drawing under discussion here.

5. J. Dover Wilson, "Titus Andronicus on the Stage in 1595," *SS*, 1 (1948): 17–22. This quotation is from p. 20. R. A. Foakes's comments are contained in *Illustrations of the English Stage, 1580–1642* (London: Scolar Press, 1985), 48–51; this quotation is from p. 50. For useful information of Elizabethan costume see C. Willett Cunnington and Phillis Cunnington, *Handbook of English Costume in the Sixteenth Century* (London: Faber & Faber, 1970), and, by the same authors, *Handbood of English Costume in the Seventeenth Century* (London: Faber & Faber, 1972). Also useful is Stella Mary Newton, *Renaissance Theatre Costume and the Sense of the Historic Past* (London: Rapp & Whiting, 1975).

6. Foakes, *Illustrations*, 51. Newton comments, "The leading characters wear historical costume but the attendants Jacobean dress." (p. 284, n.5)

7. Ibid., 50–51.

8. Wilson, "Titus Andronicus," 21.

9. Foakes, *Illustrations*, 51, and Wilson, "Titus Andronicus," 21.

10. *Newcastle upon Tyne* (Records of Early English Drama), ed. J. J. Anderson (Toronto: University of Toronto Press, 1982), xvii-xix, and passim.

11. George F. Warner, *A Catalogue of Manuscripts and Muniments of Alleyn's College of God's Gift at Dulwich* (London: Longmans, 1881), 175, 182, 194.

12. *Newcastle upon Tyne*, 29–31.

13. *Coventry* (Records of Early English Drama), ed. R. W. Ingram (Toronto: University of Toronto Press, 1981), 401, 404, 487–89, 492.

14. Ibid., 423, 488–89, 492.

15. Ibid., 488–89.

16. Shakespeare's will is PRO, Prob 1/4; William Byrd's is PRO, Prob 11/143.

17. For a bequest that includes apparel, see Simon Jewell's will, proved 23 August 1592 (PRO, PCC 63 Harrington). Christopher Beeston's will is transcribed in G. E. Bentley, *The Jacobean and Caroline Stage* (Oxford: Clarendon Press, 1941), 2:632.

18. Warner, *Catalogue*, 3.

19. Ibid.

20. R. A. Foakes and R. T. Rickert, eds., *Henslowe's Diary* (Cambridge: Cambridge University Press, 1968), 242; hereafter, *HD*.

21. Ibid., 102, 253–61.

22. E. K. Chambers, *The Elizabethan Stage* (Oxford: Clarendon Press, 1923), 1:372; hereafter, *ES*.

23. Ibid., 2:406.

24. *HD*, 184; the inventory is transcribed in *HD*, 291–94.

25. *HD*; see, for example, 74–75, 99, 216, and 219 among many examples.

26. *HD*, 226.

27. *HD*, 230.

28. *HD*, 238.

29. *HD*, p. 99, for example: "Bowght of mʳ Jewbey the 28 of september 1598 / A blacke vellvet gercken & a payer of har coler clothe of sylver hoose."

30. *HD*, 93, 130, 135.

31. *HD*, 179–80.

32. *HD*, 317–23.

33. Richard Jones's sale to Edward Alleyn of all his "share, parte and porcion of playinge apparelles, playe Bookes, Instrumentes and other commodities" (3 January 1588/89) is cited in Warner, *Catalogue*, 2–3.

34. *HD*, xxxvi–xl, and 8, 50, 84, 87, 136, 198.

35. John Aubrey remarked of Suckling's play: "When his *Aglaura* was acted he bought all the clothes himself, which were very rich; no tinsel, all the lace pure gold and silver, which cost him . . . I have now forgot" (spelling modernized, as quoted from *Brief Lives*, 2:244, ed. Andrew Clark, 2 vols. (Oxford, 1898) cited by Bentley, *The Jacobean and Caroline Stage*, 1:58.

36. John Donne, *Satire IV* ("Well; I may now receive"), ll. 180–84, from *John Donne* (The Oxford Authors), ed. John Carey (Oxford: Oxford University Press, 1990), 36–42 and 427, from the 1631 edition of Donne's poems, conjecturally dated 1597 by Carey. Ben Jonson, *No. 15* ("An Epistle to a Friend, to Persuade Him to the Wars"), in *The Underwood*, as quoted in Ben Jonson, *Poems*, ed. Ian Donaldson (London: Oxford University Press, 1974), 155–61, ll. 109–10 from the 1640 edition of Jonson's poems.

37. *ES*, 4:304.

Rogues, Shepherds, and the Counterfeit Distressed: Texts and Infracontexts of *The Winter's Tale* 4.3

Barbara A. Mowat

As I look at a particular intertextual moment in *The Winter's Tale* (the scene in which we meet Autolycus), I begin by assuming that the first printing of the play in the 1623 Shakespeare First Folio is a "text"—that is, dialogue initially crafted as a script for performance but nevertheless preserved for us as printed symbols, inked pages. I also assume that this moment of Autolycus's appearance came into existence within a field of printed texts to which it was contextually related. By describing and thus delimiting the moment's context as "printed," I do not deny it other contexts; rather, I argue that among the many contexts—social, cultural, variously semiotic—implicated in Shakespeare's text, one of the more significant is that massive field of discourse that issued from printing houses.

Not that the boundary between printed discourse and surrounding discourses is fixed or impermeable. Indeed, as we trace the interweavings of printed texts within Shakespeare's *Winter's Tale*, we trace at the same time the social and moral worlds represented in those texts, and we hear the debates in which the texts engaged. There is merit, though, in focussing attention as unwaveringly as possible on printed discursive systems. Such careful focussing forces us to acknowledge the constructedness of even supposed eye-witness accounts and heightens our awareness of the ideological freight carried by both the most fanciful of mythological tales and the most laconic of statutes and chronicles.

The word *text* in my title, then, refers primarily to the Folio words that preserve and transmit *The Winter's Tale* 4.3 and secondarily to printed discourse in general. The word *infracontext* I borrow from Claes Schaar, whose work in intertextual theory I find particularly helpful vis-à-vis Shakespeare.[1] Schaar suggests that the works of certain poets can best be described as vertical context systems; in these works, within and beneath, as it were, the surface context are embedded infracontexts that "constitute a matrix, a bed or mould which serves as the base for the surface context" and which, when recognized, expand and stratify meaning. The surface context functions as signal, sometimes in an overt or covert allusion, sometimes as a mere reminiscence or faint echo. Once the reader or listener recognizes the infracontexts and "recognition turns to understanding, the signal . . . and [the] infracontexts coalesce"; in some cases, the surface context is, in effect, annotated by the infracontext; in other cases, the meaning of the surface context is expanded through a vaguer merging as the infracontexts "rub off" on the surface context. Schaar's construct is a variant of familiar intertextual models from Bakhtin through Kristeva to Riffaterre.[2] It differs from other intertextual models in that it bases itself "on distinctive, mostly verbal similarities between surface and infracontexts" and in that it focusses on a given intertextual moment as "a closely connected semantic whole, a functional entity" whose meaning is expanded and enriched by its infracontexts.

In these pages I argue that *The Winter's Tale* 4.3 is a dramatic moment in which the surface context and its infracontexts create a wonderfully complex contextual universe, one that, like so much of Shakespeare's work, constitutes a special variant of Schaar's vertical context system. Beneath the moment's surface context are distinct sets of infracontexts, some of which supplement and intensify each other, while others set up sharply contrasting associations and patterns. These conflicting infracontexts generate intensely complex meanings as, to quote Schaar, "irreconcilable worlds and value systems are pitted against each other."[3]

The Winter's Tale as a whole is, of course, an interesting intertextual transformation of Robert Greene's *Pandosto*. Woven into and transforming Greene's story of jealousy, attempted incest, and suicide are Ovidian, Apuleian, and Euripidean incidents and motifs that lift the play out of Greene's sordid and prosaic pages and into an almost mythic world of metamorphoses: of shepherdesses into princesses, of raging tyrants into repentant fathers, of statues into living women. Act 4, scene 3, has no parallel in *Pandosto*. It opens with the entrance of a new character who introduces himself to the audience as a thief and explains how he got the name Autolycus. A second character, the son of the Old Shepherd, enters, trying to calculate the money that this year's shearing will bring in; unable to do it "without counters," he abandons the effort and instead begins to read aloud his shopping list for the coming sheepshearing festival: sugar, currants, rice, saffron, mace, nutmegs, ginger, "four pound of prunes, and as many of raisins o' the sun."[4] Autolycus, to lure this "prize" into his trap, lies down and cries out for help, claiming that he has been robbed and beaten. As the shepherd charitably lifts him up, offering him money and offering to take him to shelter, Autolycus cleans out the shepherd's purse. They part, the shepherd going, he thinks, to buy spices for the feast, and Autolycus making plans to attend the festival himself, where, he says, he will turn the shearers into sheep for his own fleecing.

The signals in this scene that have alerted previous scholars to two of the scene's infracontexts are Autolycus's name and the general configuration of the trick he plays on his victim. "My father named me Autolycus," he tells us, "who, being, as I am, littered under Mercury, was likewise a snapper-up of unconsidered trifles." This single sentence compresses several Greek-mythological pieces of text (most of them reprised in Ovid's *Metamorphoses*) that tell the story of the master thief Autolycus, son of the god Mercury. While Shakespeare's Autolycus is "littered under Mercury" in the sense, one presumes, that he was born when the planet Mercury was in the ascendant, his namesake was actually sired by the god Mercury, inheriting from his father the magic power to transform stolen booty into new, unrecognizable forms. As Ovid writes (in Golding's 1567 translation), the maiden Chyone

> . . . bare by *Mercurye*
> A sonne that hight *Awtolychus*, who provde a wyly pye
> And such a fellow as in theft and filching had no peere.
> He was his fathers owne sonne right; he could mennes eyes so bleere
> As for to make the black things whyght, and whyght thinges black appeere.[5]

Shakespeare's Autolycus does his namesake proud. He, too, is "a wyly pye" who "in theft and filching" has no peer. His link to Mercury—the trickster god, god of thieves, lord of roads, known primarily for his "subtle cunning"[6]—gives Shakespeare's Autolycus a quasi-mythological status, casting a kind of glamor on his thieving. One finds a parallel glamorizing of the thief in the second infracontext that has been cited by scholars, a story in Robert

Greene's *Second Part of Conny-Catching*, one of five such books written by Greene in 1591–92 that describe con men (or, as he calls them, conny-catchers); Greene's announced purpose is to display the evil doings of conny-catchers and alert honest citizens to their tricks. Among Greene's tales of clever crooks versus innocent gulls is that of a wary farmer unknowingly stalked by conny-catchers. As he walks the inner regions of St. Paul's, the farmer refuses to take his hand off his "well lined purse." The hero/villain of this tale is a master deceiver—"one of the crue," writes Greene, "that for his skill might haue bene Doctorat in his misterie."[7] Having tried a series of ploys to get the wealthy farmer to remove his hand from his purse, the thief disguises himself as a gentleman and falls down as if ill at the farmer's feet, begging the farmer to help him; as the farmer "stept to him, helde him in his armes, rubd him & chaft him," the farmer's purse is neatly removed. This tale, "A kinde conceit of a Foist performed in Paules," is generally accepted as underlying the Autolycus gulling-incident.[8]

The tale of the wary farmer and the clever pickpocket is a London story, set in the middle aisle of St. Paul's. *The Winter's Tale* sets its parallel incident in the country and has its con man fall down beside what, within the fiction of the play, is a country road. This seemingly minor shift in the story's location begins the process of bringing into play sharply conflicting infracontexts. As I have already suggested, the mythological context and the conny-catching context, though they take us into radically different discourses, do not themselves markedly differ in the stance taken toward Autolycus the thief. Both contexts convey a more-than-sneaking admiration for the trickster. It is not such a long step from Ovidian commentary on the subtle cunning of Mercury, god of thieves, and on his son Autolycus as a "wyly pye," to Greene's statement that his pickpocket "for his skill might haue bene Doctorat in his misterie." However, when Greene's young gentleman is taken from London and put in rags and made to cry out for help from beside a roadway, a signal is given that opens another, immensely complicating set of infracontexts in which Autolycus is far from glamorized. When, in his seeming distress, the ragged Autolycus is succored by a stranger passing along the road, what is replayed is the familiar story of the Good Samaritan[9]—except that in Shakespeare's version of the story, the part of the man set upon by thieves, stripped, beaten and left by the side of the road, is enacted by Autolycus, the thief, and the charitable Samaritan is presented as a gullible fool taken in by outward signs of victimization and suffering.

This complicated dramatic moment represents with remarkable economy the essence of a century-long struggle among and within texts as to how individuals and states should respond to those in distress. In the biblical text, Jesus tells the story of the Good Samaritan to illustrate what is meant by "loving one's neighbor." Loving one's neighbor means aiding anyone in distress.[10] But, beginning in texts in the late fifteenth century, one finds the question posed again and again: how can one know whether apparent distress is genuine? In Brandt's *Ship of Fools*, in "Cocke Lorelles Bote," and in the *Liber Vagatorum*—all published around 1500 and all drawing, to a greater or lesser extent, on an advisory issued by the Senate of Basel around 1475[11]—we read about healthy "beggars who sit at the church doors . . . with sore and broken legs . . . [tying] a leg up or besmear[ing] an arm with salves . . . and all the while as little ails him as other men"; we read about beggars who pretend to suffer from epilepsy, falling down "with a piece of soap in their mouths, whereby the foam rises as big as a fist"; we read about beggars who apply corrosives to their skin or who leave their clothes at the hostelry

> and sit down against the churches naked, and shiver terribly before the people that they may think they are suffering from great cold. They prick themselves with nettle-seed and other things, whereby they are made to shake. Some say they have been robbed by wicked men; some that they have lain ill and for this reason were compelled to sell their clothes. Some say they have been stolen from them; but all this is only that people should give them more clothes, [which] they sell . . . and spend a whoring and gambling.[12]

When the *Liber Vagatorum*—from which the above quotations are taken—went into its nineteenth printing in 1528, it included a preface by Martin Luther, who wrote that "the . . . true meaning of the book . . . is . . . that princes, lords, counsellors of state, and everybody should be prudent, and cautious in dealing with beggars, and learn that, whereas people [who] will not give and help honest paupers and needy neighbors, as ordained by God, . . . give . . . ten times as much to Vagabonds. . . . I have myself of late years been cheated and befooled by such tramps and liars more than I wish to confess."[13]

The theme of the evil perpetrated by what I call "the counterfeit distressed" continues throughout the century. In Robert Copland's *Hye way to the Spyttell house*, written in the 1530s, the truly poor and infirm are shown as left to die in the cold while those merely pretending to be poor and sick receive charity:

> Some beggarly churls . . .
> . . . walk to each market and fair
> And to all places where folk do repair,
> By day on stilts or stooping on crutches
> And so dissimule as false loitering flowches,
> With bloody clouts all about their leg,
> And plasters on their skin when they go beg.
> Some counterfeit lepry, and other some
> Put soap in their mouth to make it scum,
> And fall down as Saint Cornelys' evil.
> These deceits they use worse than any devil;
> And when they be in their own company,
> They be as whole as either you or I.[14]

The tricks purportedly used by healthy beggars to prey upon the pity of charitable individuals appear in text after text as warnings to gullible Christians: from the *Liber Vagatorum* and the *Ship of Fools* to Copland, from Copland to Awdeley (in 1561) and thence to Harman (in 1567), and from Harman verbatim into Dekker's 1608 *Bellman of London*.[15] Nor does it stop there: Robert Burton, who, in his copy of the *Bellman of London*, traces Dekker's liftings from Harman, includes in his 1621 *Anatomy of Melancholy* a discussion of beggars who "counterfeit severall diseases, . . . dismember, make themselves blind, lame, to haue a more plausible cause to beg, and lose their limmes to recover their present wants."[16]

But it was not only individuals who were represented as concerned about how to be charitable but not gullible. English statutes, annals, and chronicles beginning in the second half of the sixteenth century represent the state as aware of the need to distinguish the distressed from the counterfeit distressed so that those who genuinely need help can be relieved. Earlier in the century, English statutes and royal proclamations attack vagabonds and sturdy beggars (i.e., beggars who are healthy enough to work) not on the grounds that they fraudulently receive aid that rightfully belongs to the legitimately distressed but rather because, as a statute passed in 1547 put it, "Idelness and vagabundry is the mother and roote of all theftes Robberyes and all evill actes and other mischiefe."[17] Although the 1547 statute does not address the question of how the state should take care of the truly distressed when the realm is purportedly filled with "a multitude of people given to" idleness and begging, chronicles represent the state as becoming aware of this issue by mid-century.

For example, in Grafton's 1569 *Chronicle* (from which it was picked up by later chroniclers) we read that in 1553, the last year of Edward VI's reign, Bishop Ridley preached a sermon on poverty and the urgent need for charity that so moved the king that he had Ridley set up a council to find a solution to the problem of how to relieve the needy. The council began its work by classifying the poor into three major categories and recommended that two of the three (those legitimately in need) should receive charity, and that those in the third category, "the thriftless poor" (i.e., "the riotous that consumeth all," "the vagabond that will abide in no place," and "the idle person, as the strumpet and other"), should be sent to workhouses.[18]

A statute passed in the fifth year of Elizabeth's reign suggests that Edward's plan did not solve the state's problem. "To thintent," it begins, "that idell and loytering persons and valiant [i.e., healthy] Beggers may be avoyded, and thimpotent, feble, and lame, which are the Poore in very dede, should bee hereafter relieved and well provided for: Bee it enacted . . ."—and the statute goes on to order that the truly distressed should be taken care of by local governments while the healthy unemployed poor should be publicly whipped and put to work.[19] Statutes from the fourteenth and thirty-ninth years of Elizabeth's reign and from the first and seventh years of James I's reign make clear that the state's response to the truly distressed and to the counterfeit distressed were represented as a problem throughout the period, up to the very year in which *The Winter's Tale* was probably written.[20]

When Autolycus pretends to be in need of aid, then, and when he caps that pretense by robbing the man who ministers to him, he incarnates a figure presented in a host of texts as an evil disrupter of the commonwealth. Autolycus himself calls attention to this ominous infracontext of pamphlets, statutes, and chronicles when, in his dialogue with the shepherd, he labels his current knavish profession as that of "rogue." Pretending to describe the thief who robbed him, Autolycus says: "I knew [Autolycus] once a servant of the Prince. . . . He hath been since an ape-bearer, then a process-server . . . , and, having flown over many knavish professions, he settled only in rogue." "A rogue," of course, is what Autolycus is called in the Folio dramatis personae list. Shakespeare had used this word in earlier plays in some of its looser senses, but in *The*

Winter's Tale 4.3 it seems technical, as if it were the name of a "knavish profession."

The word did, in fact, have such a specific, legal meaning. The word *rogue* entered the English language—in print, at least—in 1561, with John Awdeley's *Fraternity of Vagabonds*.[21] There, *rogue* is the name given a particular kind of vagabond, a beggar who uses as his excuse for being on the road the tale that he is seeking a kinsman. Thomas Harman, who, in 1567, expanded Awdeley's small book into the more substantial *A caueat or warening for common cursetors vulgarely called Vagabones*, gives a much fuller character sketch:

> A Roge is neither so stoute or hardy as the vpright man. Many of them will go fayntly and look piteously when they see [or] meete any person, hauing a kercher, as white as my shooes, tyed about their head, with a short staffe in their hand, haltinge, although they nede not, requiring almes of such as they meete, or to what house they shal com. But you may easely perceiue by their colour that thei cary both health and hipocrisie about them, wherby they get gaine, when others want that cannot fayne and dissemble. Others therebee that walke sturdely about the countrey, and faineth to seke a brother or kinsman of his, dwelling within som part of the shire. . . . These also wyll pick and steale. . . .[22]

Harman's *Caueat* puts the rogue primarily among the counterfeit distressed, one of the twenty-three kinds of vagabonds and beggars Harman claims to have himself met.

The word *rogue* spread quickly after Harman's very popular book was published in 1567.[23] As the word spread and was taken up into legal terminology, it lost much of the meaning that Awdeley and Harman had given it and became a more general term used to name the healthy unemployed poor. Most significantly, in the statute against vagabonds passed and published in 1572 (14 Eliz. c.5), a rogue is legally defined as a healthy person who has neither land, nor master, nor a legitimate trade or source of income. In that same statute, the phrase "Beggars, Vagabonds, and Idle Persons"—a phrase that had appeared with slight variations in comparable statutes back to the time of Richard II[24]—now becomes, for the first time, "Rogues, Vagabonds, and sturdy Beggars," and thus it appears in every statute for punishment of the unemployed poor throughout the reign of Elizabeth and into the reign of King James. From the 1572 statute the word *rogue* passed immediately into Stow's 1573 *Summarye of the Chronicles* and from there directly into Holinshed's 1577 *Chronicles*—and even into the *Chronicles'* index.[25]

We learn from the statutes and the chronicles that, for the crime of having neither land nor master nor legitimate source of income, the rogue received various punishments: from 1572 to 1597, he or she was stripped to the waist, whipped until bloody, and had a hole burned through the gristle of the right ear; from 1597 to 1604, he or she was merely whipped until bloody, then sent back to his or her place of birth and put to work. In 1604, in James's first parliament, the 1597 statute was declared ineffective

> for that the said Rogues hauinge no marke upon them . . . may . . . retire themselves into some other parts of this Realme where they are not knowne, and soe escape the due punishmente . . .: For remedie whereof be it ordained and enacted, That such Rogues . . . shall . . . be branded in the lefte Shoulder with an hot burning Iron . . ., with a greate Romane R upon the Iron, . . . [so] that the letter R be seene and remaine for a perpetuall marke upon such Rogue during his or her life.[26]

The fierceness of attack—both physical and rhetorical—on the unemployed destitute is usually linked in the chronicles, statutes, and pamphlets to the biblical injunction against idleness. God had ordered man to labor; anyone who did not labor did not deserve to live. As Sir John Cheke wrote in 1549, people think of drones, caterpillars, and vermin as noisome beasts in the commonwealth. But what, he asks, is an idle person?

> A sucker of honie, a spoyler of corne, a destroyer of fruite, Naye a waster of money, a spoyler of vittaile, a sucker of bloud, a breker of orders, a seeker of brekes, a queller of life, a basiliske of the commune wealthe, whiche by companie and syght doth poyson the whole contrey and staineth honeste mindes with the infection of his venime, and so draweth the commune wealthe to deathe and destruction.[27]

According to Cheke (and to many others writing throughout the century), unemployed persons simply hated work,

> leauing labour, which they like not, and following idlenes, which they should not. For euery man is easely and naturally brought, from labor to ease, . . . from diligence to slouthfulnesse. . . . [V]aliaunte beggers play in tounes, and yet complaine of neede, whose [beggar's] staffe if it be once hoat in their hande, or sluggishnes bred in their bosome, thei wil neuer be allured to labour againe, contenting them selues better with idle beggary, then with honest and profitable labour.[28]

William Harrison's "Description of England," printed as an introduction to Holinished's 1577 and 1587 *Chronicles*, includes a section entitled "Of Provision Made for the Poor."[29] Echoing the commonplace that many are idle because they hate to work—they "straie and wander about, as creatures abhorring all labour and euerie honest exercise," he writes—Harrison lashes out at the unemployed poor with a vigor comparable to Cheke's:

> [the idle] are all theeues and caterpillers in the commonwealth and by the word of God not permitted to eat, sith they do but licke the sweat from the true laborers browes & bereue the godlie poore of that which is due unto them . . ., consuming the charitie of well disposed people . . . after a most wicked & detestable maner.[30]

But Harrison, in describing the numbers of rogues and beggars in the commonwealth, asks a question of the situation that places Autolycus and his shepherd victim in a different light. Noting that "[i]dle beggers are such either through other mens occasion, or through their owne default," he writes that,

> By other mens occasion (as one waie for example) when some couetous man . . . espieng a further commoditie in their commons, holds, and tenures, doth find such meanes as thereby to wipe manie out of their occupiengs and turne the same unto his priuate gaines.

In the margin of Harrison's text appears this statement: "A thing often seene." The text then continues: "Hereupon it followeth, that . . . the greater part [of those so dispossessed] commonlie hauing nothinge to staie vpon . . . do either prooue idle beggers, or else continue starke theeues till the gallows do eat them vp." The marginal comment on this sentence reads: "At whose hands shall the bloud of these men be required?"[31]

This small questioning of who is to blame for the numbers of unemployed poor who haunt the English streets and countryside summons up a host of texts that present the story of the vagrant from quite a different perspective than that shown in the statutes against vagabonds or in the moralizings by Harman and Cheke and all the others who attack the idle poor. The other side of the story, as Harrison so briefly suggests, is that many are unemployed because their lands or jobs have been taken away from them, a point that is made in statutes "for the maintenance of husbandrie and tillage" throughout the century and in numerous pamphlets and tracts that plead to various English monarchs on behalf of the dispossessed.[32] Nowhere is this side of the story told more poignantly than in More's *Utopia*. There the point is made that England is overrun by thieves, not because thieves enjoy stealing (as one of the characters in *Utopia* claims) but because people have lost their livings: serving men out of work, returned soldiers, evicted farm laborers thrown out of work when farms are sold—these are the men and women frantic for food and driven to begging and stealing: "they that be thus destytute of seruice, other [i.e., either] starue for honger, or manfullye playe the theaues. For what wolde yow haue them to do?" Hythloday asks.[33] "I pray you," he goes on to ask, "what other thing do you [Englishmen do, but] . . . make [people into] theues and then punish them?" That which sets England apart from other nations, Hythloday says, is the way English sheep are responsible for such problems. These supposedly peaceful animals "consume, destroy, and deuoure hole fieldes, howses, and cities." Noblemen, gentlemen, and abbots, he explains, "leaue no grounde for tyllage, [but] enclose all in pastures: they throw downe houses; they plucke downe townes, and leaue nothing stondynge." One greedy sheep owner may

> inclose many thousand acres of grounde together . . . [while] the hus-
> bandmen be . . . compelled to sell all; by one meanes . . . or by other,
> . . . by howke or crooke they must nedes departe awaye, pore, sylie [i.e.,
> simple], wretched soules, men, women, husbandes, wyves, fatherles
> chyldren, widdowes, woful mothers, with their yonge babes. . . . Awaye
> they trudge . . . out of their . . . howses, fyndying no places to rest in.
> . . . And when they haue wanderynge about sone spent [all that they
> have], what can they then els do but steale, . . . or else go about beggyng?
> And yet then also they be caste in prison as vagaboundes, because they
> go aboute and worke not: whom no man will set a worke, though they
> neuer so willingly offer them selfes thereto.[34]

This yet darker side of vagrant life in England, with its textually familiar picture of wealthy, covetous men who buy up land for pasturage and in the process dispossess thousands of people, shadows the scene in *The Winter's Tale* at which we are looking, a meeting between a rogue and a wealthy owner of sheep. Their vocations can hardly be seen as coincidental: it is not alone in More's *Utopia* that the sheep owner is blamed for the plight of vagrants and thieves.[35] Nor can it be a coincidence that the shepherd enters calculating the amount of money that will come in from this year's shearing—more than £140, a goodly sum at that time—and that he then lists the expensive delicacies that he is off to buy. In the previous scene, we were told that this shepherd and his father had "beyond the imagination of [their] neighbors . . . grown into an unspeakable estate" (4.2.39–40). We know that the money that purchased that estate was the money found with the baby Perdita sixteen years before (3.3.116–20), but the shepherd's calculation of the money coming in this year merely from the wool of fifteen hundred of their sheep tells us that, as More and others make clear—and as is wonderfully exemplified by the fortunes of the sheep-raising family of Spencers (by 1610 having achieved a baronetcy and the reputation of having the most money of any family in England[36])—the wealth from their sheep-herding estate will bring in annually more and more wealth. In contrast, Autolycus's downward descent from serving man of the prince to the profession of rogue echoes the progress catalogued by More and many others describing the background of England's thieves. Autolycus is thus reminiscent of one of More's wretched souls who steal because "what would you have them do?"

But here the struggle between infracontexts becomes intense. Autolycus may incarnate the unemployed vagrant, a figure represented as either scandalously evil or truly pitiable. But Autolycus is given songs and dialogue that signal contexts in which he is neither evil nor pitiable. Like the vagabond poets of the twelfth and thirteenth centuries, he claims to love his life of wandering: he enters singing songs that echo both the well-known medieval "Confessions of a Vagabond," in which the wandering life is celebrated, as well as goliardic rejoicings in spring and in casual sexual encounters.[37] This lyric infracontext immensely complicates the emotive and ideological stance of the scene. Further, Autolycus's catalog of the history of his progress from one knavish profession to another signals yet another complicating infracontext, that of sixteenth-century picaresque tales that recount the adventures of the antihero who moves from profession to profession, celebrating himself and being celebrated by others for his quick wit and ability to survive.[38]

The vagabond songs and the dialogue's picaresque tonality supplement and intensify the infracontexts mentioned at the outset—the mythological texts that make Autolycus a trickster in the likeness of Mercury and the conny-catching tales that point up his cleverness vis-à-vis the foolish gull. One set of infracontexts, then, makes of the dramatic moment a variously nuanced celebration of the cunning of the trickster. Another set makes the moment instead an enactment of frightening social conflicts. When Claes Schaar briefly discusses this kind of complicated variant of his vertical context system, he notes that, in texts like this, "complex significance is very clearly to the fore" and "meaning is movable, shifting radically as different infracontexts are brought into focus." "The semantic result," he writes, is "quite different as we 'tilt' the text one way or the other."[39] In *The Winter's Tale* 4.3, if we tilt the text toward Autolycus the trickster, the moment becomes resonant with the mythology of the trickster archetype, and Autolycus can be seen as a stand-in for the artist himself, endowed with Mercury's gifts of eloquence and illusion-making, a kind of earlier-day Felix Krull.[40] If we tilt the text toward Autolycus the rogue, mentally branding his left shoulder with a great Roman R, the moment speaks more of social and economic struggle, of counterfeiting, of acting, if you will, as Autolycus first licks the sweat off the true laborer's brow and then exits to change his costume for his next actorly role.

Over the centuries, *The Winter's Tale* 4.3 has been read primarily as tilted toward the trickster infracontexts, and Autolycus has been seen as a great comic creation, a figure in which to delight. In 1611, the tilt—at least for Simon Forman—was instead toward Autolycus the rogue. As Forman wrote, after having seen the play at the Globe:

> Remember also the Rog that cam in all tottered like coll pixci. and howe he feyned him sicke & to haue bin Robbed of all that he had and howe he cosoned the por man of all his money. . . . beware of trustinge feined beggars or fawninge fellouss.[41]

Forman's use of the terms "rog," "feyned him sicke" and "feined beggars" foregrounds the moment's economic and social infracontexts; his reference to the play's wealthy shepherd as "the por man" and his warning to "beware of trustinge . . . fawninge fellouss" place Forman himself on the side of those who, like Martin Luther, felt threatened by such impostors. Forman's description of Autolycus as coming in "all tottered [i.e., tattered] like coll pixci" suggests that Forman had picked up (from the costuming, it would seem) an infracontext with links to the mythological (a coll-pixie was a mischievous supernatural being that lured people astray, into pixie paths and bogs),[42] but, for Forman, even the mythological infracontext tilts the meaning of Autolycus toward the ominous.

Today, the word *rogue* has lost its darker pejorative resonance, shepherds are no longer viewed as a primary enemy of the downtrodden, and one suspects that few readers or auditors pick up the allusion to Autolycus's namesake. For today's audience, these contexts, then, are mostly "absent structures," to borrow Umberto Eco's phrase, infracontexts that "remain inaudible like . . . voice[s] out of earshot."[43] As with so many moments in Shakespeare, though, once the voices are heard, the moment becomes tantalizing in its complexity. Thus, although Shakespeare turned printed texts not directly into other printed texts but into air, into scripts for the ephemeral breath of the stage, I would add his name to those of such poets as Dante, Milton, and Eliot, artists whose poetic effects are "powerful and dynamic [in part because they are] based . . . on . . . complex meanings emerging along vertical axes."[44] To read Shakespeare intertextually, as I've tried to show, is to recover those complex meanings, to recognize "powerful and dynamic" poetic *and* dramatic effects, and to exchange the amusing surface context of *The Winter's Tale* 4.3 for a supercharged contextual world.

Notes

An earlier version of this paper was presented at the annual meeting of the Shakespeare Association of America in Vancouver, March 1991. I am grateful to the Newberry and the Huntington Libraries for research support.

1. Claes Schaar, *The Full Voic'd Quire Below: Vertical Context Systems in Paradise Lost.* Lund Studies in English 60 (Lund: CWK Gleerup, 1982), 11–33.

2. See, e.g., Mikhail Bakhtin, *The Dialogic Imagination*, trans. C. Emerson and M. Holquist (Austin: University of Texas Press, 1981); Julia Kristeva, "Word, Dialogue, and Novel," trans. Alice Jardine, Thomas Gora and Léon S. Roudiez, in *The Kristeva Reader*, ed. Toril Moi (New York: Columbia University Press, 1986), 34–61, and *Revolution in Poetic Language*, trans. Margaret Waller (New York: Columbia University Press, 1984), 13–17, 57–61; and Michael Riffaterre, "Syllepsis," *Critical Inquiry*, 6 (1980). For helpful discussions of intertextuality, see John Frow, "Intertextuality," *Marxism and Literary History* (Cambridge, Mass: Harvard University Press, 1986), 125–69, and Louise Schleiner, "Latinized Greek Drama in Shakespeare's Writing of *Hamlet*," *Shakespeare Quarterly* 41 (1990): 29–48, esp. 45–48.

3. Schaar, *The Full Voic'd Quire Below*, 24.

4. All quotations from *The Winter's Tale* are from *The Complete Works of Shakespeare*, ed. David Bevington (New York: Harpercollins, 1992).

5. *The xv. Bookes of P. Ouidius Naso, entytuled Metamorphosis, translated oute of Latin into English meeter by Arthur Golding* (London: Willyam Seres, 1567), bk. 11, ll. 359–63. Lewis Theobald, in his edition of *The Winter's Tale*, writes that "The Allusion is, unquestionably, to this Passage in Ovid. . . . The true *Autolycus* was the Son of Mercury; our fictitious one, born under his Planet; the first a Copy of his Father; the other, suppos'd to derive his Qualities from natal Predominance." *The Works of Shakespeare*, 1733, 3:116, n. 23.

6. Walter F. Otto, "Hermes," in *The Homeric Gods*, trans. Moses Hadas (London: Thomas and Hudson, 1979; orig. pub. 1954), 104–24, esp. 104. Otto notes that Hermes (i.e., Mercury) "distinguished his son Autolycus among all men in the accomplishments of thieving and perjury," citing *Iliad* 10.267 and *Odyssey* 19.395 (p. 104; see also p. 108). See also Robert Graves, *The Greek Myths*, 2 vols. (Pelican Books), 1:65, 216–19, and passim.

7. Robert Greene, *The Second Part of Conny-Catching*, 1592, in The Bodley Head Quartos, ed. G. B. Harrison (London: John Lane, The Bodley Head, 1923), 40–42, esp. 41.

8. Sir Arthur Quiller-Couch, in his introduction to the New Cambridge *Winter's Tale*, 1931, seems to have been the first scholar to note the parallel: "let anyone turn to Greene's *Second Part of Conny-catching* (1592), he will find the trick played by Autolycus on the Clown so exactly described as to leave no doubt that poor Greene was again drawn upon." Kenneth Muir, in *The Sources of Shakespeare's Plays* (1977), writes that "Autolycus . . . might have stepped out of one of the pamphlets of Harman, Greene, or Dekker, exposing the iniquities of the criminal underworld. Several of his tricks do in fact come from Greene's coney-catching pamphlets," one of which "describes . . . Autolycus' . . . robbing of the shepherd's son" (275–76).

9. The parable is found in The Gospel of Saint Luke 10.25–37. This parable, according to the 1539 *Book of Common Prayer*, was to be read in church each thirteenth Sunday after Trinity.

10. Jesus tells "a certain expounder of the law" (Geneva translation) that, in order to inherit eternal life, he must "love thy Lord God with all thine heart . . ., & thy neighbour as thy self." When the lawyer "said unto Iesus, Who is then my neighbour? . . . Iesus answered, and said, A certeine man went down from Ierusalem to Ierico, and fell among theues, and they robbed him of his rayment, and wounded him, & departed, leauyng him halfe dead." "A certeine Priest" and then "a Leuite" pass by the wounded man while "a certeine Samaritan . . . had compassion on him and went to him, & bounde vp his woundes, and powred in oyle and wine, and put him on his owne beast, and brought him to an ynne, and made prouision for him. And on the morowe when he departed, he toke out two pence [marginal note: which was about 9 pence of sterling money], and gaue them to the hoste, and said unto him, Take care of him, and whatsoeuer thou spendest more, when I come againe, I wil recompense thee." Jesus then asks the lawyer, "Which now of these thre, thinkest thou, was neighbour vnto him that fell among the theues?" "And he said, He that shewed mercy on him. Then said Iesus unto him: Go, and do thou lykewyse." In the Geneva Bible (from which this is quoted) the marginal gloss on Jesus's final sentence reads: "Helpe him that hath nede of thee although thou knowe him not."

11. Sebastian Brandt, *Narrenschiff*, 1494 (trans. Alexander Barclay as *Shyp of folys* [London: Pynson, 1509]); "Cocke Lorelles Bote" (London: Wynkyn de Worde, 1510? [reprinted in *Ancient Poetical Tracts of the Sixteenth Century*, ed. E. F. Rimbault [London: for the Percy Society, 1843]); *Liber Vagatorum der betler orden* (Augsburg: Joh. Froschauer, ca. 1509; reprinted eighteen times before being issued in 1528 under the title *Von der falschen Betler Bueberey*. It is this 1528 edition that is translated as *The Book of Vagabonds and Beggars with a Vocabulary of Their Language and a Preface by Martin Luther*, ed. D. B. Thomas [London: Penguin Press, 1932]).

The relationship among these books is not clear, in part because it has been impossible to determine when "Cocke Lorelles Bote" and *Liber Vagatorum* were first printed. All are dependent, directly or indirectly, on the advisory about beggars and vagrants issued by the Senate of Basel sometime in the fifteenth century. This advisory was transcribed, probably in 1475, by Johannes Knebel, then chaplain of the Cathedral of Basel. Because Brandt published *Narrenschiff* in 1494 when he was living in Basel, and because many details in *Narrenschiff* come from the advisory, D. B. Thomas has surmised that Knebel drew Brandt's attention to the advisory (*The Book of Vagabonds*, 11). "Cocke Lorelles Bote" seems to have been inspired either by *Narrenschiff* or *Shyp of folys*. The *Liber Vagatorum* depends on the Basel advisory for both substance and form; much of it is taken verbatim from the advisory, which is available to us in volume 1 of Heinrich

Rogues, Shepherds, and the Counterfeit Distressed 73

Schreiber's *Taschenbuch für Geschichte und Alterthum in Suddeutschland* (Freiburg, 1839), 330–43.
12. Thomas, ed., *The Book of Vagabonds*, 75–77, 89, 103–5.
13. Ibid., 63–65.
14. Robert Copland, *The hye way to the Spyttell house* (London: R. Copland, 1536?, reprinted in A. V. Judges, *The Elizabethan Underworld* [London: George Routledge & Sons, 1930], 1–25, esp. 7. Copland draws on both *Shyp of folys* and "Cocke Lorelles Bote," but he gives much more space to describing beggars and vagrants than do these earlier works.
15. John Awdeley, *The Fraternitye of Vacabondes. As wel of ruflyng Vacabondes, as of beggerly, of women as of men, of Gyrles as of Boyes, with their proper names and qualities. With a description of the crafty company of Cousoners and Shifters. Whereunto also is adioyned the .xxv. Orders of Knaves, otherwyse called a Quartern of Knaues. Confirmed for euer by Cocke Lorell.* (London: 1575; reprinted in *Awdeley's Fraternitye of Vacabondes, . . .*, ed. Edward Viles and F. J. Furnival [London: published for the Early English Text Society, 1869; rpt. 1975]). Furnival and Viles argue persuasively that this book was first published in 1561 (i–iv). Thomas Harman, *A caueat or warening for common cursetors vulgarely called Vagabones* (1567; Harman refers to this earliest extant copy as "the second edition"), ed. Viles and Furnivall, 19–91; Thomas Dekker, *The belman of London bringing to light the most notorious villanies now practised in the kingdome* (N. Okes for N. Butter, 1608).
16. Robert Burton, *The Anatomy of Melancholy*, pt. 1, sec. 2, memb. 4, subs. 6 (Oxford: J. Lichfield and J. Short, 1621), 202–11, esp. 209.
17. "1 Edw. VI.c.3. "An Acte for the Punishment of Vagabondes and for the Relief of the poore and impotent Persons." *Statutes of the Realm . . . from Original Records and Authentic Manuscripts*, 9 vols. (1801–1822), vol. 4, pt. 1, p. 5. This particular statute, sometimes called the "slavery act," set as punishment for any unemployed person who refused to work that he or she be declared a vagabond, branded on the chest with a burning iron in the shape of the letter V, and made a slave for two years; the statute was soon repealed on the grounds that the punishment was so severe that few would enforce it—though as A. L. Beier notes, "the first proposal of the 'Considerations delivered to the Parliament' of 1559 was the revival of the slavery act of 1547 against vagrants." "Vagrants and the Social Order in Elizabethan England," *Past and Present*, 64 (1974) : 3–29, esp. 27.
18. Richard Grafton, *A Chronicle at large . . . of the affayres of Englande . . .* London: 1569). Two volumes in one. 2:1320–22.
19. 5 Eliz. c. 3 "An Acte for the Releif of the Poore," *Statutes of the Realm*, vol. 4, pt. 1, p. 411.
20. 14 Eliz. c. 5 "An Acte for the Punishement of Vacabondes, and for Releif of the Poore and Impotent"; 39 Eliz. c. 3, "An Acte for the Releife of the Poore"; c. 4, "An Acte for the punyshment of Rogues, Vagabonds, and Sturdy Beggars"; 1 Jac. I. c. 7, "An Acte for the Continuance and Explanation of the Statute . . . intituled An Acte for Punishmente of Rogues, Vagabonds, and Sturdie Beggars [39 Eliz. c. 4]"; 7 Jac. I. c. 4, "An Acte for the due execucion of divers Lawes and Statutes heretofore made against Rogues, Vagabonds, and sturdy Beggars and other lewde and idle persons." (*Statutes of the Realm*, vol. 4, pt. 1, pp. 590–98; vol. 4, pt. 2, pp. 896–99; vol. 4, pt. 2, pp. 899–902; vol. 4, pt. 2, pp. 1024–25; vol. 4, pt. 2, p. 1159.) The parliament that passed 7 Jac. I. c. 4 was held in 1609–10. *The Winter's Tale* is thought to have been written in 1610 or early 1611; Simon Forman saw a performance of it on 15 May 1611 at the Globe.
21. For Awdeley and Harman, see note 15.

22. Viles and Furnival, *Fraternitye of Vacabondes,* 36–37.

23. For the argument that Harman's lost original version and the (expanded) earliest extant version were both published in 1567, see F. J. Furnival, preface to Viles and Furnival, *Fraternitye of Vacabondes,* iv.

24. See, e.g., 12 Ric. II, c. 7–10, "Punishment of wandering beggers," *Statutes of the Realm,* vol. 2, p. 58.

25. John Stow includes in his account of the year 1572 the following summary of that year's Parliament:

"In this Parliamente, for so much as the whole Realme of England was excedinglye pestered with Roges, vagaboundes & sturdye beggers . . . it was enacted that all persons above the age of 14 yeares, being taken begging, vagrant, & wandring misorderly, should be apprehended, whipped, and burnt through the gristle of the right eare, with a hot Iron of one inche compasse. . . ."

In the margin appear the words "Roges burnt through the eare." (*A summarye of the Chronicles of Englande from the first comminge of the Brute into this Land, unto this present year of Christ, 1573* [London: Thomas Marshe, 1573], fol. 430.)

Holinshed's 1577 *Chronicles* (fol. 1862) reproduces this passage verbatim, and lists in the index [sig. K4v, 1st column, 13th entry] "Roges appoynted to be burnt through the eare. 1862.2". Raphael Holinshed, *The laste volume of the Chronicles of England, Scotlande, and Ireland* (London: 1577.) The passage appears in *The Third volume of Chronicles . . . . first compiled by Raphael Holinshed . . . now newlie . . . augmented and continued . . . to the yeare 1586* (London: 1587), 1228. The 1587 index adds as an entry the word "Vagabonds" and cross-references "Roges" and "Vagabonds."

26. 1 Jac. I c.7. *Statutes of the Realm,* vol. 4, pt. 2, p. 1025.

27. *The hurt of Sedition, how grieueous it is to a Commune welth* (1549), sig. E5v. This work was included as an "Admonition" from Sir John Cheke in Holinshed's 1577 *Chronicles,* 1688–89 [1689 is incorrectly numbered 1869], and in Holinshed's 1587 *Chronicles,* 1042–55.

28. Cheke, sigs. E4v-E5.

29. Harrison's *Description* appears as "An Historicall Description of the Islande of Britayne, with a briefe rehearsall of the nature and qualities of the people of Englande . . ." in Raphael Holinshed, *The firste volume of the Chronicles of England, Scotlande, and Irelande . . . .* (London: 1577), fols. 1–125; the section on the poor appears as bk. 3, chap. 5, fols. 106 v–107 r. The *Description* appears as "An Historicall description of the Iland of Britaine . . . Comprehended in three bookes," in Holinshed, *The first and second volumes of Chronicles . . .* London: 1587, 1:1–250; the section on the poor appears as bk. 2, chap. 10, pp. 182–30.

30. Holinshed, *The first and second volumes of Chronicles . . .* London: 1587, 1:183.

31. Ibid.

32. See, e.g., Simon Fish, *A Supplication for the Beggers* (ca. 1529) and *A Supplication of the Poore Commons* (1546), in *Four Supplications,* ed. J. M. Cowper, pp. 1–18, 59–92. See also Robert Crowley who, in 1550, addressed the wealthy as follows:

If you charge them wyth disobedience, you were firste disobedient. For without a law to beare you, yea contrarie to the law which forbiddeth al maner of oppression & extortion, & that more is contrarie to conscience . . . ye enclosed from the pore their due commones, leavied greater fines then heretofore have been leavied, put them from the liberties . . . that they held by custome, & reised theire rentes. . . . if you had loved your contrei, would you not have prevented the great destruction that chanced by the reason of your unsaciable desire? . . . How you have obeyed the lawes in rakeing together of fermes, purchaising and prollynge for benefices . . . . (*The Way to Wealth, wherein is plainly taught a most present Remedy for Sedicion*, in J. M. Cowper, ed., *The Select Works of Robert Crowley* [Early English Text Society, extra series, 15, 1872; rpt. Kraus Reprint, 1975], 130–50, esp. 144–45.)

Crowley again, in his *An information and Peticion agaynst the oppressours of the pore Commons of this Realme*, writes to the wealthy:

> Beholde, you engrossers of fermes and teynements, beholde, I saye, the terible threatnynges of God, whose wrath you can not escape. The voyce of the pore (whom you haue with money thruste out of house and whome) is well accepted in the eares of the Lord. . . . Knowe then that he hath not cauled you to the welthe and glorie of this worlde, but hath charged you wyth the greate and rude multitude. And if any of them perishe thorowe your defaute, know then for certentye, that the bloode of them shall be required at your handes. If the impotent creatures perish for lacke of necessaries, you are the murderers, for you have theyr enheritaunce and do minister vnto them. If the sturdy fall to stealeyng, robbyng, & reueynge, then are you the causers thereof, for you dygge in, enclose, and wytholde from the earth out of whych they should dygge and plowe theyr lyueynge. (J. M. Cowper, ed., *Select Works of Robert Crowley*, 151–76, esp. 161–64.)

33. *A fruteful and pleasant worke . . . called Utopia . . . by Syr Thomas More*. trans. Raphe Robynson (London: Abraham Vele, 1551), sig. C4v.

34. Ibid., sigs. C6v-C8.

35. See, eg., *Certayne causes gathered together wherein is shewed together the decaye of England, only by the great multitude of shepe, to the utter decay of houshold keping* . . . . (1550–53), a petition addressed to Edward VI's council:

> We saye, as reason doeth leade us, that shepe & shepemasters doeth cause skantyte of corne [;] . . . where tillage was wont to be, nowe is it stored with greate vmberment of shepe. . . . [As people are thrown off the land,] whether shall then they go? foorth from shyre to shyre, and to be scathered thus abrode, within the Kynges maiestyes Realme, where it shall please Almighty God; and for lack of maisters, by compulsion dryuen, some of them to begge, and some to steale.
> . . . thre hundred thousand persons were wont to have meate, drinke, and rayment, uprysing and down lying, paying skot and lot to God & to the Kyng. And now they haue nothynge, but goeth about in England from dore to dore, and axe theyr almose for Goddes sake. And because they will not begge, some of them doeth steale, and then they be hanged, and thus the Realm doeth decay. . . .

Four Supplications, (Early English Text Society, extra series, 13, 1871; rpt. Kraus Reprint, 1981), ed. J. Meadows Cowper, 95–102, esp. 95–98, 101–2.

36. Mary E. Finch, "Spencer of Althorp," in *The Wealth of Five Northamptonshire Families. 1540–1640* (Oxford: Printed for the Northamptonshire Record Society, 1956), 38–65.

37. See, e.g., the following stanza of the most popular of all the goliardic lyrics, the "Vagabond's Confession," by the "Archipoeta" in *Vagabond Verse: Secular Latin Poems of the Middle Ages*, trans. Edwin W. Zeydel (Detroit: Wayne State University Press, 61):

> Down the highway broad I walk,
> Like a youth in mind,
> Implicate myself in vice,
> Virtue stays behind,
> Avid for the world's delight

> More than for salvation,
> Dead in soul, I care but for
> Body's exultation.

38. See, e.g., *The Pleasaunt historie of Lozarillo de Tormes*, trans. D. Rouland (London: A. Jeffes, 1586); Henry Chettle, *Piers Plainnes seauen yeres Prentiship* (London: J. Danter, 1595); Nicholas Breton, *A Merrie Dialogue betwixt the Taker and the Mistaker* (London: James Shaw, 1603; published in 1635 as *A Mad World My Masters*); Thomas Nashe, *The Unfortunate Traveler* (T. Scarlet for C. Burby, 1594). See also Robert Alter, *Rogue's Progress. Studies in the Picaresque Novel* (Cambridge, Mass.: Harvard University Press, 1964).

39. Schaar, *The Full-Voic'd Quire Below*, 27.

40. For Mercury as god of eloquence, see Walter F. Otto, *The Homeric Gods* (note 6, above); for Thomas Mann's Felix Krull as the trickster/artist, see Donald Nelson, *Portrait of the Artist as Hermes. A Study of Myth and Psychology in Thomas Mann's Felix Krull* (University of North Carolina Press, 1971), and Alter, *Rogue's Progress*, 126–29.

41. This record of the performance of *The Winter's Tale* at the Globe on 15 May 1611 is found in Forman's manuscript *The Bocke of Plaies and Notes thereof per formans for Common Pollicie*. The record is printed by J. N. P. Pafford in his Arden edition of *The Winter's Tale*, xxi–xxii.

42. Pafford notes that "*coll pixci* (i.e., Colle- or Colt-pixie)" is "a hobgoblin, particularly in the form of a ragged (tattered) colt which leads horses astray into bogs, etc." (xxi). In *Nimphidia: The Court of Fayrie*, (published in *Battaile of Agincourt*, 1627, 117–34), Michael Drayton conflates the "colt-pixie" with Hobgoblin or Puck:

> This Puck seemes but a dreaming dolt,
> Stil walking like a ragged Colt,
> And oft out of a Bush doth bolt,
>   Of purpose to deceive us.
> And leading us makes us to stray,
> Long Winters nights out of the way,
> And when we stick in mire and clay,
>   Hob doth with laughter leave us.
> (Stanza xxxvii)

43. Umberto Eco, *La Struttura Assente* (Milan, 1968; cited by Schaar, 17); Schaar, 17.

44. Schaar, 24.

Speech, Silence, and History in *The Rape of Lucrece*

Joyce Green MacDonald

In AN ANALOGY which underscores his perception of poetry as a distinguishing constituent of the aristocratic life, Puttenham introduces his discussion of figures of poetic ornament by comparing the proper "fashioning of our makers language and stile" with a properly dressed gentlewoman:

> And as we see in these great Madames of honour, be they for personage or otherwise never so comely and bewtifull, yet if they want their courtly habillements or at leastwise such other apparell as custome and civilitie have ordained to cover their naked bodies, would be halfe ashamed or greatly out of countenaunce to be seen in that sort, and perchance do then thinke themselves more amiable in every mans eye, when they be in their richest attire . . . then when they go in cloth or any other plaine and simple apparell.[1]

A judicious application of the figures of poetic ornament resembles, Puttenham continues, a skillful *maquillage*. A badly made poem is as ridiculous an object as would result if "the crimson tainte, which should be laid upon a Ladies lips, or right in the center of her cheekes should by some oversight or mishap be applied to her forehead or chinne" (138).

Puttenham's choice of an elegantly dressed and appropriately made-up lady as metaphor for the nature of an appropriately fashioned poem speaks to the highly gendered nature of Renaissance poetic convention, under whose terms the process of speaking about a woman so often became the process of fixing identities for both female object of desire and masculine speaker.[2] Speech about women eventuated in speaking Woman as a cultural presence, a presence which, despite its positioning at the apex of a triangulated economy of sexual exchange between men, remained fixed and passive—the subject of others' desire and not the mistress of her own.[3] The rhetorical strategies of sixteenth-century poems are thus eloquent not only of their authors' expertise in manipulating the sexual tropes of poetic making, but also of how these tropes are implicated in situating a work within the discourses of gender definition.

Recent criticism of *The Rape of Lucrece* has concentrated on reading the poem's high degree of formal self-consciousness as an index to what it might have to say about sex and the social experience of gender.[4] This work, most of it produced by female scholars, creates a sharp contrast with earlier academic generations' virtually unanimous objections to the poem's highly ornamented language. One critic, concentrating on the heroine's apostrophes to Night, Opportunity, and Time after her rape, assigned the flood of Lucrece's distraught speech to normal "human self-delusion (intensified by a feminine proclivity to self-pity and evasive argument)," asserting that by the "long sermon on lust's dishonor" she "preaches" to Tarquin before the rape, she actually "increases its fascination." Indeed, her desperate attempts to persuade Tarquin not to rape her become an invitation: "as if subconsciously she wished force to work his way, but only after she has had time to excuse herself from responsibility."[5] Wholesale rejections of the poem on the grounds of its rich verbal ornamentation have a way of coming to define the ornamentation in sexual terms. Having dismissed the facile misogyny of earlier discussions of the links between language and gender in *The Rape of Lucrece*, however, modern criticism is increasingly convinced that its seemingly endless deferral of closure is in fact significant as a manifestation of the linguistic resistance of the feminine to incorporation within male master narratives.[6] (Lucrece eventually comes to reject the powers of words properly to name or to help her find a solution to her dilemma: "This helpless smoke of words does me no right".[7]) In such arguments, as well as in Renaissance explications of poetic theory, copiousness appears as a distinctively female property of language, a linguistic property often at odds with social prescriptions of female silence, retirement, and obedience.[8]

My discussion of *The Rape of Lucrece* will consider varieties of female speech and silence as they help shape Shakespeare's familial Roman ethos. Lucrece finds her desperate voice only to encounter its limitations in a poem deeply informed by Renaissance assumptions about silence and segregation as indices of female chastity; contradictions and oppositions between modes of speech and silence mark the boundaries of her crisis. As a Roman wife and Roman mother, Lucrece is wholly consecrated to her duty as steward of her husband's and her sons' honor, a duty bound up with self-imposed separation and enclosure. (In Painter's "Second Novell," the adventurous "yonge Romaine gentlemen" find her literally "in the middes of her house" on the night of their fateful wager.[9]) In sleep, in death, however, her body is mysteriously and multiply voiced: evidencing her chaste perfection yet inviting Tarquin's rape, vindicating her innocence and proving Tarquin's guilt. While the conventional Petrarchanism of the poem's opening produces Lucrece as an emblematic work of art, imagining the "silent war of lilies and of roses" in her complexion (71), the uncontrollable intensity of Tarquin's desire dangerously destablizes this poetic attempt to name her precisely. The poem accomplishes this disruption of formal categories of female description and the kinds of patriarchal male-female relationships they produce and reproduce by heightening the customary language of static perfection to hazardous extremes. On the verge of rape, Tarquin perceives the sleeping Lucrece in idealized, transcendent language more evocative of a tomb effigy than a living woman. Her head is "entombed" between "hills" of her pillow; "like a virtuous monument she lies" (390–91). The rape is a perverted performance of the consequences of Lucrece's ideals of self-sacrifice, as Tarquin escalates the abstraction inherent in Roman languages of female behavior by seeing her as more closely resembling a graven image than a living being. Continuing its presentation of the impact of constructions of feminity and feminine behavior on history, the poem informs us that Lucrece's body alone—first appropriated in the initial wager between her husband and his friends as a prize in a homosocial ritual of display, exchange, and rivalry, and appropriated again in death by Brutus's political opportunism—possesses sufficient eloquence to move the people against the Tarquins' tyranny and force a change in the form of Roman government.

The Rape of Lucrece thus, indeed, suggests a powerful connection between gender, speech (and silence), and power. The poem turns its vision of the special place reserved for Roman women under the powerful system of *pietas* on the pivot of its treatments of its heroine's volubility, so that questions of her silence or of her verbal openness resonate throughout the rape and its aftermath. In mounting his narrative poem on received understandings of the familial structure of Roman society and on contemporary formulations of the social and sexual behavior of aristocratic women, Shakespeare broadens and deepens the meaning of the materials he borrows from Ovid and Livy. He creates a new work with a graver, more rigorous sense both of cultural obligation and of the nature of the bonds between the roles of women and the maintenance of the families on which culture and commonwealth were based.

Both of Shakespeare's major sources place Lucrece's tragedy within a historical frame, but neither of them concentrates as particularly on her fate as he does. Livy treats the rape and suicide as a virtual parenthetical aside in his account:

> For when as Tarquinius Superbus by his prowd tyrannicall demenure, had incurred the hatred of all men: he at last upon the forcible outrage and villanie done by Sex. Tarquinius (his sonne) in the night season upon the bodie of Lucretia; who sending for her father, Tricipitinus, and her husband, Collatinus, besought them earnestly not to see her death unrevenged, and so with a knife killed herself: he I say, by the meanes of Brutus, especially was driven and expelled out of Rome, when he had raigned five and twentie yeares.[10]

Ovid's *Fasti* expands its narrative of Lucrece's plight, but similarly locates its recital within a larger narrative of the Tarquins' deceit and cruelty: Sextus Tarquinius "burned, and, goaded by the pricks of an unrighteous love, he plotted violence and guile against an innocent bed."[11] As he was to do in his Roman plays, Shakespeare endeavors to discover the ethical significances of a political event— here, the Tarquins' exile and the change in the form of government—through linking such events to his exploration of character. Here, though, he alters the usual practice in his Plutarchan plays by choosing so radically to reorient the emphases in his sources, lingering as Ovid and Livy do not over the states of mind of the rapist and especially of his victim. The poem establishes a much more direct link between the rape and the political result than is available in the Roman historians, in an early presentation of Shakespeare's concern with the links between familial and civic bodies.[12]

Lucrece's female body, as has already been suggested, is the primary arena for the poem's classicized development of the relationship between private sexual matters and matters of state. In its foregrounding of the domestic sphere, Shakespeare's *Lucrece* takes its place among other early modern writings on the social signifi-

cance of women's roles as mothers and wives, an extremely popular
mode during a period which, as one modern historian has suggested, may have been undergoing a "crisis in gender relations."[13]
Such a notion of a particular crisis in the relationships between
men and women seems of a piece with the widespread anxiety and
even paranoia about the future of the realm that marked the 1590s,
but also takes on new power given that so much of that anxiety
turned on the old queen's apparent refusal to name an heir and
settle the succession: she had never behaved as a conventional
woman, and the nation now seemed to be on the verge of reaping
the whirlwind. Peter Wentworth used the traditional familial rhetoric of power even in his protestation that the queen's failure to
marry had made it impossible to give that rhetoric a physical embodiment in the shape of heirs of her body: a ruler's responsibility
toward her subjects

> is, to be as gods and natural fathers and mothers: for the resemblance
> that is betwixt the office of God towards man his creature, and parentes
> towardes their Children, is the ground and certaine cause, why these
> high names are communicated and given unto you by the spirit of
> God. . . . As therefore you are our head, shew your self to have dutifull
> care and love to your bodie.

Wentworth appealed to the queen as the "nursing mother" of her
people, describing her subjects as "wee your children."[14]

This notion of the incorporation of hierarchical inferiors—
whether subjects or children—into the loving parental body of state
places itself within common familial representations of the nature
of power and authority in Tudor and Stuart England. Many Marian
exiles consistently used Mary Tudor's sex as a serious proof in
their arguments against the legitimacy of her rule, and even the
defenders of Elizabeth Tudor's right to the throne frequently felt
themselves obligated to explain that her royal blood decontami-
nated the impropriety of a woman exercising authority.[15] Observers
of the queen's success during her lifetime at forging means of coexistence between her sex and her political authority recognized that
at bottom, she was playing no mere game. Gender and gender roles
bodied authority, and declining to contract a marriage was seen as
one way of preserving her power:

> The reigns of women are commonly obscured by marriage; their praises
> and actions passing to the credit of their husbands; wheras those that
> continue unmarried have their glory entire and proper to themselves.

In her case, this was especially more so; inasmuch as she had no helps to lean upon in her government, except as she herself provided . . . no kinsmen of the royal family, to share her cares and support her authority. And even those whom she herself raised to honour she so kept in hand and mingled one with the other, that while she infused into each the greatest solicitude to please her, she was herself ever her own mistress.[16]

For Sir Francis Bacon, the queen's ownership of her body was directly indexed to her maintenance of her power. Marriage inevitably "obscures" the accomplishments of a female ruler, while singleness ensures that her glory will remain as "entire," as uniquely her own, as will her virginal body. Remaining sexually closed denied her heirs of her body, but permitted her entry into public speech.

For nonroyal women, spinsterhood was a less likely resort. Yet, in entering marriage, women also entered a relationship whose rules and practices worked to limit their autonomy in strict and specific ways. Although a woman would retain ownership of any land her family made over to her in her marriage contract, for example, only her husband was legally entitled to any profits from the land. Any "moveables" she took with her into the marriage— clothes, furniture, money—became her husband's property. Since women received money more often than property at marriage, they were immediately placed in a position of economic dependence. The effect of such laws was to give a material presence to an increasingly explicit ideology of gender difference and of the necessity of controlling women.

This connection between theories and practices on the proper position of women within marriage is complicated by its placement within two systems of social hierarchy, that of rank as well as that of gender.[17] It has frequently been observed that prescriptions for the silence, retirement, and obedience that the conduct books deemed proper behavior for wives often varied in rigor according to the social station of the audiences for which a particular book may have been intended. Hence, Heinrich Bullinger's *Christen State of Matrimonye* held that there were reasonable limits to the retirement that his readers among the urban bourgeoisie might seek for their daughters. If the seclusion were too strictly enforced, it was likely "ether to make them starke foles or els to make them naughtes when they shall once come abrode into companye"[18] In contrast, English translations of conduct books more consciously aimed at an elite ideal reader tend to urge markedly more severe restrictions. The *Diall of Princes* advocates wifely submission to the will of husbands, even for "Princesses and greate dames." In fact, the leisure enjoyed by ladies of rank created special emphases to the general prescriptions of seclusion. Not only did staying home spare her husband's finances, since it required a less stylish and extensive wardrobe than excessive gadding about, but it also limited women's exposure to opportunities for mischief and therefore to others' libellous speech: "For if the poore wife, the plebyan, goe out of her house, she goeth for no other cause, but for to seeke meate: but if the riche, and noble woman goeth out of her house, it is for nothing, but to take pleasure."[19] Unsupervised pleasure-taking by beings who were commonly esteemed to be "fraile, spite-full, and given to revenge"[20] unnecessarily exposed women to slander and scandal. Because of this acknowledged moral weakness, wise women would at least attempt to cultivate "shamefastnes, which is the onely defence that nature hath givê women, to keep their reputatiõ, to preserve their gravitie, to mainteine their honor, to advance their praise."[21]

In exploring the possibility of accomplishing this kind of moral exchange between innate feminine frailty and higher spiritual and social purpose, George Wither's theological commentary on the emblems in Rollenhage's *Nucleus* (1613) also works from an assumption of woman's inescapably sexualized nature. According to Wither, a woman's yearning for adornment in fact expresses her desire "to please her *Lovers*, or her *Husband's* Eyes." Under the proper circumstances, this desire can transform her into a "documentall signe" of virtue:

> For, hee may bee thy *Glasse*, and *Fountaine* too.
> His Good *Example*, shewes thee what is fit;
> His *Admonition*, checks what is awry;
> Hee, by his *Good* advise, reformeth it;
> And, by his *Love*, thou mend'st it pleasedly.[22]

While arguing that women are indeed capable of recognizing and seeking virtue, Wither's rhyme also centrally assumes that vanity and seductiveness are such elemental parts of female nature that women will rely on them even in such a spiritual undertaking as practicing the subordination proper to wives. Attempting an ideological recasting of these manifestations of the waywardness of womanhood by linking them to obedience and pliability instead of to willfulness and lust, Wither's argument also works to gender the desire to seduce and to find a compelling functional necessity for it even within his less harshly antifeminist conception of woman.

In social practice, the primacy given to sexual matters in the social construction of female reputation seems often to have subsumed the other categories of appropriate female behavior, so that silence and submissiveness were seen as the behavioral evidence of the chastity which was the keystone of female honor.[23] Conversely, the behavior of willful, talkative women was seen as an index of their proneness to other, more grievous sexual enormities. Since "the honor of women is such a nice and charie thing, that it is not lawful for them to thinke, much less to speake, of many things, which men may freely both talk of and put in practise," one theorist adjured, women intending "to preserve their gravitie, must be silent not only in unlawful, but even in necessary matters, unles it be very requisite that they should speake of them."[24] One writer put his disgust for women who violated rules of silence, retirement, and modesty into a jangling rhyme which makes explicit the connections between public, verbal and private, sexual behavior:

> Maides must be seene, not heard, or selde or never,
> O may I such one wed, if I wed ever.
> O Maide that hath a lewd Tongue in her head,
> Worse than if she were found with a Man in bed.[25]

That social rank was a significant indicator of an individual woman's relative ability to subvene the gendered rule of silence is supported by the large representation of aristocrats among the growing number of Renaissance women whose writings are being rediscovered, or in many cases, discovered now for the first time, and put into circulation.[26] And yet, birth into extraordinary social privilege was not necessarily a prerequisite for the achievement of a public voice; the careers of Renaissance women writers from bourgeois or lesser backgrounds demonstrate both an awareness and a sophisticated and self-conscious manipulation of prohibitions against women's public speech.[27] Still, some surviving evidence suggests that one of the stresses in the unhappy aristocratic marriages in the period may have been the partners' experience of contradiction between adjuration to female obedience and self-effacement on the one hand, and the wife's sense of incomplete acknowledgment of her independent possession of rank and social significance before the formation of her marriage on the other.[28]

In studying women in marriages where aristocratic rank is not an issue, however, troubling possibilities created by the clash between exhortations toward female self-effacement and the will toward speech still present themselves. Setting out to memorialize a loved wife who died young after childbirth, Philip Stubbes's *A Christal Glasse for Christian Women* explicitly praises Katherine Stubbes' silence as exemplary to her sex: "She obeyed the commandement of the Apostle, who biddeth women to bee silent, and to learne of their husbands at home . . . She was never knowne to fall out with any of her neighbors, nor with the least child that lived, much lesse to scold or brawle as many will now a daies for every trifle, or rather for no cause at al." In the interest of praising Katherine Stubbes's absolute "integritie of life," however, her widower describes a woman who carried the injunctions to silence and unworldliness to aggressive extremes. "[S]o solitary was she given, that she would verie seldome or never, and that not without great constraint (& then not neither, except her husband were in companie) goe abroad with any, either to banquet or feast, to gossip or make merry (as they tearme it) in so much that she hath beene noted to do it in contempt and disdaine of others."[29]

We do not know, because Philip Stubbes does not tell us, whether Katherine Stubbes had some particular physical reason to believe she would not survive childbirth; certainly death in childbed was common enough. At any rate, as soon as her pregnancy became known, he reports, she started telling her husband and friends "not once, nor twice, but many times, that she should never beare more Children: that, that child should be her death, & that she would live but to bring that child into the world." Stubbes, struck by the fact that his wife's prediction of her death did come to pass, takes it as evidence of a special revelation "unto her by the spirit of God."[30] She took to her bed as her pregnancy advanced, and prayed for death: "I thinke it long to be with my God, Christ is to me life, and death is to me advantage."[31] She rejected even her pet dog as a meaningless vanity before making her profession of the Protestant faith and asking her husband not to mourn her. She died at the age of nineteen after four years of marriage.

Although Philip and Katherine Stubbes were proto-Puritan city dwellers, Philip Stubbes' memorial reconstruction of his wife bears resemblance both to conduct books aimed at elite audiences, in its commendation of her extreme retirement from worldly affairs, and to Catholic-authored tracts, which tended to foreground chastity in their disussions of female conduct and character.[32] As the author of *The Anatomie of Abuses* (1583), Stubbes was already known for his disgust at the unnecessary display and boldness of modern habits of dress for men as well as women.[33] *A Christal Glasse for Christian Women*, its very title evoking not only reflection but also the lingering spiritual ideal of virginal female bodies as fragile vessels, *hortus conclusus*, focuses this revulsion from worldly things on gender and sexuality. Her husband's report of Katherine Stubbes's refusal to display herself unnecessarily, her awareness of the dangers of intemperate speech, her careful rationing of her innocent pleasures, consults a broader set of cultural materials in its construction of her virtue than might have immediately suggested themselves to him in terms of class or religion. If, according to these writings about women, modesty is for them "an naturall vertue,"[34] and that "vertue" is as intimately bound as Stubbes believes it to be with the refusal to make an unnecessary spectacle—either verbal or visual—of oneself, the irrefutable evidence offered by pregnancy of the sexual opening of Katherine Stubbes posed a challenge to the integrity and persuasive power of the extension of his Puritan strictures on speech and display to the arenas of sex and gender. An earlier writer of Puritan sympathy, declaring that the "tricksynes" manifest in women's desire to adorn their bodies with "trappynge trinkets so vayne" smacked of "popishe idolatry," warned that such self-displaying impulses were clear signposts on the road to whoredom:

> And loke well, ye men, to your wives trycksynes,
> whyche is to shamefull wyde,
> Or some wyll not stycke, or it be longe,
> to horne you on everye side.[35]

The Puritan ideals attributed to her by her husband and the less specific cultural exposure to the equation of openness with immodesty performed a powerful dual solicitation of Katherine Stubbes.

When the conduct books and the ideologies of womanhood they transmitted advised women to stay at home and "nat medle with matters of realmes or cities," because their own houses are "cite great inough"[36] for any legitimate purpose, their formulaic language encodes this association of social intercourse with illicit sexuality. They also place the home in an analogical relationship with the public world which was the proper province of men; careful stewardship of her household was, for a woman, functionally the same as honorable conduct in the public realm was for men. Geffrey Whitney informs his readers that his emblem of *Uxoria virtutes*, illustrated by a woman standing on the back of a tortoise holding a chain of keys with her hand at her mouth,

> represents the vertues of a wife,
>> Her finger, staies her tonge to runne at large.
> The modest lookes, doe shewe her honest life.
> The keys, declare shee hath a care, and chardge,
>> Of husbandes goodes: let him goe where he please,
>> The tortoyse warnes, at home to spend her daies.[37]

That at some point her duties toward her household and her obligation to maintain proper vigilance over her sexuality could possibly come into conflict was a terrible irony implicit in doctrines of women's sovereignty. In its concern with speech and silence, and the sexual resonances of both, *The Rape of Lucrece* demonstrates its extreme sensitivity to ideologies of womanhood and to the contradictions they may contain.

Shakespeare's *Lucrece* is a watershed in treatments of the story. Before him, historians wrote about its poliltical lessons and moralists debated the meaning of her suicide; after him, imaginative writers highlight its sexual aspects.[38] Translating Livy, Machiavelli declared that the Tarquins were banished from Rome not because of the rape committed by Sextus Tarquinius, but because his father Lucius Tarquinius "had violated the laws of the kingdom and ruled tyrannically. . . . Hence, if the Lucretia incident had not occurred, something else would have happend and would have led to the same result."[39] Thomas Heywood's *The Rape of Lucrece* (1609) preserves the basic elements of the classical narrative, but alters its emphases by ending with a single combat between Tarquin and Brutus in which they both receive death wounds, instead of with the suicide. Heywood's *Lucrece* also interpolates "severall Songs in their apt places, by *Valerius* the merry Lord among the Roman Peeres" which oddly contrast with Lucrece's misery.[40] Later treatments of or allusions to the Lucrece materials seem to lack Shakespeare's awareness of the bonds between verbal and physical openness, so that they present the places of licit and illicit sexuality in their stories under very different aspects. Heywood's transformation of the legend into a play about Sextus Tarquinius, which ends not with the momentous internal change in the structure of Rome's government but with the triumphal extension of Rome's power over the rebellious "Tuscans," is only one example. Elsewhere, poets attempt to rewrite the Romanized system of value within which

the rape must inevitably appear as disaster. In rebuking the "hated
name / Of husband, wife, lust, modest, chaste or shame" which
impedes a return to a Dionysian golden age, Thomas Carew's "A
Rapture" pictures its Lucrece reading her Aretino and learning

> how to move
> Her plyant body in the act of love.
> To quench the burning Ravisher, she hurles
> Her limbs into a thousand winding curles,
> And studies artfull postures, such as be
> Carv'd on the barke of every neighbouring tree
> By learned hands, that so adorn'd the rinde
> Of those faire Plants, which, as they lay entwinde,
> Have fann'd their glowing fires.[41]

Writing nearly a century after Shakespeare, Nathaniel Lee in *Lucius
Junius Brutus* (1680) spares little concern for Lucrece's suffering
at the hands of Tarquin as he pursues interests in political reform.
The rape becomes only a pretext for his crafty Brutus to rouse the
commons to antimonarchical fury, and Brutus demands as well that
his son Titus renounce his faithful love for Tarquin's illegitimate
daughter to prove his allegiance to his father's political vision. One
hundred years after *Lucrece*, Thomas Southerne's *The Fatal Marriage* (1694) remembers Shakespeare's heroine in the epilogue to
this overwrought tragedy of chastity and faithful love:

> Now tell me, when you saw the Lady dye,
> Were you not puzled for a Reason Why? . . .
> We women are so Whimsical in dying.
> Some pine away for loss of ogling Fellows:
> Nay, some have dy'd for Love, as Stories tell us.
> Some, say our Histories, though long ago,
> For having undergone a Rape, or so
> Plung'd the fell Dagger, without more ado.
> But time has laugh'd those follies out of fashion:
> And sure they'l never gain the approbation
> Of Ladies, who consult their Reputation.
> For if a Rape must be esteem'd a Curse,
> Grim Death, and Publication make it worse.[42]

For Southerne's generation, the idea that rape could be experienced
as a tragedy capable of irrevocably changing the life of a family
and the progress of a state has become the subject for playhouse
joking. In its worldly mockery of Lucrece's suicide, however, the
epilogue also names Lucrece's dilemma: for her, rape is indeed a

powerful "Curse," and the possibility of "Publication" of the fact that she is no longer chaste does compound her fear and shame. The act that Southerne judges as a folly impetuously committed by ladies who are insufficiently attentive to matters of "Reputation" is, in Shakespeare, deemed necessary precisely because of Lucrece's pained devotion to the good names of her husband and sons. His poem can admit of no safe vantage point from which a violated gentlewoman might at her leisure calculate the wisest course of action.

Shakespeare's version distinguishes itself by its presentation of the rape as both a personal and a social disaster, a crime against family, city, and the meaning of Roman history as well as against Lucrece's person. It recognizes that the bodies of men and women lie at the center of the notion of a familial state, and that Tarquin's crime violates the chaste vessel through which patriarchal authority transmits itself. Even before the rape, the poem's Argument tells us that Lucius Tarquinius seized power "after he had caused his own father-in-law Servius Tullius to be cruelly murd'red" (3–4): the rape confirms the Tarquins' defiance of the value of kinship. The *Fasti* specifies that the murder only took place at the instance of Lucius Tarquinius' wife, Sextus Tarquinius' mother Servia Tullia. After having urged her husband to kill her father, the previous king of Rome, she reveled in the murder and the power her husband gained through it by having her coachman drive her chariot across her father's face as he lay dead and unburied in the public streets: "Crime is a thing for kings" (365). This supreme example of un-Roman and unwomanly contempt for the dignity of fathers and families shadows her son's later disregard of his obligations toward his friend Collatine and offers another instance of the way in which the Lucrece materials contain within them hints of later elaborations of the internally contradictory and self-destructive roles played by women in matters of state.

Shakespeare continues to explore the implications of the connection between female chastity and family honor in following Ovid's detailing of Tarquin's threat to kill both Lucrece and one of her slaves and place their bodies together in her bed. In imitating and enlarging upon this Ovidian detail, however, Shakespeare elaborates on its Roman vision of the connections between shame and sexual behavior. Here is the relevant passage in Ovid:

"Resistance is vain," said he "I'll rob thee of honour and of life. I, the adulterer, will bear false witness to thine adultery. I'll kill a slave, and rumour will have it that thou were caught with him." Overcome by fear of infamy, the dame gave way.[43]

While retaining the incident and even the Ovidian pairing of "honour" and "life," Shakespeare markedly personalizes Tarquin's threat. Rather than the vague "rumour will have it" that Lucrece was unfaithful to her husband with a social inferior, Tarquin vows that he will "kill thine honour with thine live's decay" by placing the dead slave in her bed and actively "[s]wearing" to witnesses that "I slew him, seeing thee embrace him":

> So thy surviving husband shall remain
> The scorful mark of every open eye;
> Thy kinsmen hang thy heads at this disdain,
> Thy issue blurred with nameless bastardy;
> And thou, the author of their obloquy,
>   Shalt have thy trespass cited up in rhymes,
>   And sung by children in succeeding times.
>   (516,518–25)

Lucrece's horrified response to Tarquin's threat to inflict a publicly discussed "blemish that will never be forgot" (536) against her posthumous reputation and the good names of her husband and children similarly enlarges upon the Ovidian original. The argumentation comes to a premature end when Tarquin puts out the light and muffles Lucrece's head in her mantle so that she can neither see nor speak as he rapes her. Shakespeare in effect provides a more specific imagining of the sexual crime than Ovid does through verbal dilation on the wretched consequences of Lucrece's unwilling disclosure to Tarquin's "greedy" (368) vision and to the persuasive, delineating powers of public speech and display in making or unmaking her social presence.[44] The "fear of infamy"— of having the fact that another man besides her husband has known her sexually widely spoken of—is what forces Lucrece to yield and ultimately, what causes her to embrace suicide as a solution to her shame.

As noted above, twentieth-century critical scorn for *The Rape of Lucrece's* obsession with speech has concentrated on its impassioned apostrophes to Night, Opportunity, and Time. In arguing that speech and gender are in fact centrally important to the poem's production of Rome as a place where the violation of a respectable matron must resonate in the life of the state, I would like to concentrate instead on a relatively less-observed aspect, its *ekphrasis* of the fall of Troy. Embedded within it narration of Lucrece's changing experiences of her social and sexual objectification, the ekphratic representation of her examination of the "piece / Of skilful painting, made for Priam's Troy" (1366–67) exemplifies the way in which its formal concerns voice its perceptions of gender and history.[45] Shakespeare's elaborate description of Lucrece beholding Hecuba beholding Priam's murder establishes a receding historical vista on the substantive presence of domestic matters in matters of state: the fate of Hecuba, who will suffer the sight of the deaths of her husband, her children, and her civilization, and who will be driven into speechless madness by it, comes to shadow that of Lucrece, who will silence herself in grief and fear over the welfare of her husband and sons. Also present in the Troy tapestry is Helen, whose powerful desirability seemed to so many observers to invite the rape which set into motion the events culminating in the end of a world. George Wither performs this kind of narrative moralizing in his explication of an emblem of two urban gallants fighting while a woman looks out her upper window watching them. The engraving is surrounded by the Latin motto *"Ubi Helena Ibi Troia,"* and the epigraph for his poetic discussion reads *"Where Hellen is, there will be* Warre; / For, *Death and Lust, companions are."*[46] Lucrece's *ekphrasis* rewrites the masculine and historical orientations of epic to find woman—mother, mistress, wife, sexual prey—deeply inscribed within. This gesturing at epic may indeed be initiated with the description of Lucrece's eager contemplation of the tapestry, in which echoes Aeneas's somber discovery of the Troy story carved on the walls of June's temple when he shipwrecks at Carthage in *Aeneid* 1. Like Aeneas, Lucrece weeps to find in the depiction of "Troy's painted woes" (1492) a physical representation of the vastness of her own anguish.

The tapestry depicts Hecuba's face, "a face where all distress and dolor dwell'd," in grief-numbed contemplation of "Priam's wounds,"

> Which bleeding under Pyrrhus' proud foot lies.
> In her the painter had anatomiz'd
> Time's ruin, beauty's wrack, and grim care's reign;
> Her cheeks with chaps and wrinkles were disguis'd:
> Of what she was no semblance did remain.
> Her blue blood chang'd to black in every vein,
>> Wanting the spring that shrunk pipes had fed,
>> Show'd life imprison'd in a body dead.
>
> (1446,1448–56)

The death of her husband, father of her fifty sons, is only the beginning of the grief and rage which will alter Hecuba's human form; *Metamorphoses* 13 tells us briefly that she "lost (after all) her womans shape, and barked all her lyfe / In forreine countrye" (489–90).[47] A fuller description of the Trojan queen's tragic destiny appears later in 13, where she witnesses the death of her daughter Polyxena, who is ritually sacrificed by Neoptolemus at the demand of the shade of his father Achilles; on her death, the Greeks will be granted favorable winds for their voyage home. The post-Homeric accretions of the stories of Polyxena and of Iphegenia, whose father Agamemnon sacrificed her so that the Greeks might have fair winds on the voyage to Troy, complete the framing of the epic story of Troy's fall by episodes turning on the sacrifice of daughters. Ovid uses the Polyxena story to introduce the affective emotion that is his trademark in the *Metamorphoses*, providing Shakespeare's *Lucrece* a suggestive point of connection between the private sorrows of mothers and wives and the larger tragedies affecting world orders. The Ovidian description of Polyxena's death might even furnish a textual model for Lucrece's carefully histrionic public Roman suicide, as she expresses concern for her mother's suffering, excites the pity and admiration of the priest who will perform the execution, and, bearing "too the verry latter gasp a countenance devoid of feare," fell with "a care such parts of her too hyde / As womanhod and chastitie forbiddeth too bee spyde" (571–73).[48]

After bewailing the death of her daughter, Hecuba thinks to take some comfort in the survival of her last, son, little Polydorus, who has been delivered into the safekeeping of Polymnestor, King of Thrace. But on the way to the waterside where she will be carried back to Greece as Ulysses's slave, she discovers Polydorus's body, torn by the "mighty wounds" (644) inflicted by his cruel guardian, and the sight drives her mad. Pretending that she wishes to give him a sum of gold she had hidden for Polydorus' use, she persuades Polymnestor to accompany her away from the main body

> And beeing sore inflamed with wrath, caught hold uppon him, and
> Streyght callyng out for succor to the wyves of Troy at hand,
> Did in the traytors face bestowe her nayles, and scratched out
> His eyes: her anger gave her heart and made her strong and stout.
> (671–74)

As the shocked Thracians pelt Hecuba and the other Trojan women with stones, her rage transforms her flesh: "And as she opte her chappe / Too speake, in stead of speeche she barkt" (681–82).

Her own sorrow and frenzy over the senseless destruction of her family are powerful enough to rob Hecuba of her humanity, to send her off "howling in the feeldes of Thrace" (685). The outrages she suffers as mother and wife are the losses whose signs Lucrece observes and responds to in the painter's representation of her: "Of what she was no semblance did remain." Like Hecuba, she has endured the violation of the family bonds whose existence gave her place and meaning, and she finds in Hecuba's image the will to voice her own outrage:

> "Poor instrument," quoth she, "without a sound,
> I'll tune thy woes with my lamenting tongue,
> And drop sweet balm in Priam's painted wound,
> And rail on Pyrrhus that hath done him wrong,'
> And with my tears quench Troy that burns so long,
>   And with my knife scratch out the angry eyes
>   Of all the Greeks that are thine enemies.
>   (1464–70)

Lucrece, who has found her identity to this point in silence, chastity, and enclosure, finds herself vowing to speak the "woes" of one who is doubly voiceless—both because the Hecuba who inspires her is only a "painted" image of a real woman, and because the legendary queen was involuntarily metamorphosed into a howling animal.

Hecuba's loss of voice and her reduction to a subhuman state figure in other imitations of Ovidian texts than The Rape of Lucrece. Perhaps ironically, given my own argument here on the centrality of speech and enclosure in Shakespeare's poem, these later references to Hecuba tend also to emphasize her voicelessness, although to rather different effect than I believe presents itself in Lucrece. Cooper's Thesaurus, for instance, omits any reference to a physical transformation, noting instead that after all her losses, "she finally waxed madde, and did byte and stryke all men that she mette, wherfore she was called dogge, and at the last was hyr selfe kylled with stones by the Greeks." George Sandys's Ovid's Metamorphoses English'd is conventionally pious about Hecuba's fall from glory:

Shee having lost by violent death so many of her valiant sonnes, seene her husband slaughtered before the Altar of Jupiter, Cassandra ravish't in the Temple of Minerva, Astianar throwne from the top of a tower, Polixena sacrificed on the tombe of Achilles, fallen from the greatnesses

of birth, and the glory of Empire, to that contempt and poverty, that
none would have accepted her as a Servant, had shee not beene cast by
lot upon *Ulisses:* which affords a sad consideration of humane instability, and may abate their pride, and confidence who too much insult in
prosperity; high fortunes confining steepe praecipitations.[49]

Sandys continues his interpretation, though, by addressing the specific meanings of Hecuba's transformation into a dog. Careful on
the one hand to undercut the persuasive power of Ovid's fantastical account by characterizing her metamorphosis as "feigned," he
nevertheless also asserts that her change "was not only derived
from her contemptible condition, but from the acerbity and fury of
her sorrow, expressed in revilings and execrations: for which they
threw so many stones at her, as buried her under their burden."
Finishing his account of Hecuba's place in the *Metamorphoses,*
Sandys adds that "there is a place called *Cynosema,* which signifies
the tombe of the Bitch," known as Hecuba's grave.[50]
Alexander Ross's *Mystagogus Poeticus Or the Muses Interpreter*
is more explicit than Sandys in connecting Hecuba's particular
transformation to her intemperate and unwomanly speech:

And truly, not unfitly may the impudent railing speeches of some
women be compared to the barking of dogs; neither is there any thing
more like barking Cur, then a railer, or scold, which if they would duly
consider, they would be more moderate in their tongues, and circum-
spect of their words.[51]

Again characterizing the metamorphosis as "imaginary," such as
afflicts those "disturbed" men who "imagine themselves to be
Wolves and Dogs," Ross rejects the notion of metamorphosis and
insists that "Hecuba was still a woman, though she seemed to her
self to be a dog." He cites Euripides's *Trojan Women* in support of
his view that "she was so bold and violent in her mouth," and
suggests that the stories say she became a dog "because the
Grecians used her like a dog . . . being impatient of her railing
tongue."[52]
Sandys' linkage of Hecuba's change to her verbal expression of
her grief and Ross's notion of her "violent" mouth are both formed
by an early-modern sensibility of the appropriateness of silence to
womanhood.[53] Ross is especially vehement on Hecuba's inappropriate volubility:

When *Jupiter* had sent the rain-bow, to perswade *Priamus* to go to
Achilles and redeem *Hectors* body from him, promising his assistance,

his Wife *Hecuba* would have diswaded him from going, under pretence, that *Achilles* was cruel and in no ways to be trusted; yet *Priamus* would not hearken to her, but preferred *Jupiters* command to her advice. I wish *Adam* had been so wise as to prefer Gods commands to his wifes counsel: too many women like *Hecuba*, stick not to counsel their husbands in things contrary to *Gods* laws: and too many husbands are so uxorious as to hearken to their wives, and prefer their foolish counsels to the wisdom of God.[54]

In looking at Hecuba gazing aghast on her husband, Lucrece examines a tapestry of bereavement in which also figure the deaths of the queen's last children, the extinction of her seed as well as of her civilization. ("At once both Troy and Priam fell," remarks Golding's Ovid.[55]) Concern for the good names of her husband and children was, of course, uppermost in her mind as she faced Tarquin's assault. Reading the moment where Hecuba experiences the last losses which will push her beyond the limits of human reason and human speech, Lucrece finds a voice for them both; but in finding a voice in which to speak both her fury and Hecuba's, she also locates herself within a story which would be read and reread as exemplifying the perils of female speech.

Given the poem's guiding assumption of the existence of mutually constitutive bonds between the family and the state, Lucrece's position as mistress of her husband's household already gives her considerable cultural presence. However, *Lucrece's* use of the Troy *ekphrasis* as demonstration of its insistently historical definition of the rape carries within the stories of Hecuba and Helen inconsistencies and ambivalences strong enough to destabilize the *ekphrasis'* value as the heroine's point of entry into coherent narration of the tragedy that has befallen her.[56] Commentators read Hecuba's violence against men—however justified it may be—as a provocation; in response to her demonstrative anger, she is punished by madness. Lucrece's own guilty identification with Helen's image in the tapestry further attests to this internal contadiction in commentators' remarks on the Trojan women. Depsite her innocent possession of the "wounderfull beauty" which spurs men to commit any transgression in order to possess her, Helen is nonetheless "the onely occasion of the tenne yeres syege, and finall destruction of the moste famous cities of Troye."[57] The stories about the fates of Hecuba and Helen as they figured in the fate of Troy simultaneously narrate those ladies' responsibility to the strictures governing their gender; foregrounded at the appropriate moments within the epic

tradition, they are additionally judged by their nonfulfillment of
their social contracts as women, mothers, and wives.

The poem's will to historicize the rape also functions to differen-
tiate male and female capacities for authoritative speech. Tarquin
finds himself struggling for words as he plans the rape of his
friend's wife, finally settling on the military vocabulary belonging
to his public role as the heir of the Tarquins. He vows "invasion"
(287); his heart, the "alarum striking" (433), gives his lust "the hot
charge: (434); his hand climbs "the round turrets" (441) of her
breasts. Compelling her to submit, his speech "like a trumpet:
sounds "a parley" (470–71) before he scales the "never conquered
fort" (482) of her body, "to make the breach and enter this sweet
city" (469).[58] Although he claims to be compelled by desire for
Lucrece, he describes her effect on him in terms which more obviously oppose him to Collatine in the civic and martial world than
they link him to her: the sight of her beauty breeds in him "new
ambition" to oust Collatine from his seat on the "fair throne" (411;
413) of her body, for example. Aware that in surrendering to the
impulse to rape his friend's wife he will forfeit all claims to Roman
nobility, he implies that the enormity of the crime he contemplates
and the depth of the moral abdication it requires manifests his
possession of a superheroic indifference to the obligations and re-
sponsibilities of order ("Crime is a thing for kings").[59] Under the
terms of this military language and the unitary identity of Roman
men, the rape demonstrates his possession of the same traits of
daring and initiative which are valued in his public life.

To be sure, a certain amount of self-persuasion is necessary before Tarquin can successfully eroticize his aggression and rivalry
with Collatine. Before he can attack Roman familial institutions
through committing the rape of Lucrece, he must first conquer his
own best instincts and loyalties. His "will" (417) proves stronger
than either his "reason's weak removing" (243) or his "frozen conscience" (247), so that his "servile powers" (295) triumph over his
mind. Indeed, this triumph seems to be produced through his rhetorical willingness to manipulate his standing as Collatine's friend
and as Lucrece's superior to secure his goal. He does not merely
threaten her with sexual assault, but also invokes the entire power
of his presence—a man, a warrior, a governor—in Roman culture
as a weapon to use against her. The poem describes Tarquin's theatrical threats from Lucrece's perspective:

> he shakes aloft his Roman blade,
> Which like a falcon tow'ring in the skies,
> Coucheth the fowl below with his wings' shade,
> Whose crooked beak threats, if he mount he dies:
> So under his insulting falchion lies
>   Harmless Lucretia, marking what he tells
>   With trembling fear, as fowl hear falcons' bells.
>
> (505–11)

After the rape, Lucrece attempts to express her sense of desolation through invoking the civic purpose she knows has been destroyed.

> My honey lost, and I, a drone-like bee,
> Have no perfection of my summer left,
> But robb'd and ransack'd by injurious theft.
> In thy weak hive a wand'ring wasp hath crept,
> And suck'd the honey which thy chaste bee kept.
>
> (836–40)[60]

As a woman, the language of civic order is not properly hers to begin with. As Tarquin's sexual victim, she is no longer privately chaste, and therefore also becomes incapable of her indirect public performances of familial and civic virtue. As does Tarquin, Lucrece, too, ultimately despairs of the powers of rational speech and analysis to resolve her crisis. Betrayed by the authority of stories to shape experience, forced into reliance on foreign vocabularies by her violent exile from the sanctity of her seclusion, faced with the loss of her customary significances within her family and household, Lucrece chooses suicide as the welcome and literal end to this voiceless oblivion.

Perhaps ironically, the sudden shock of her histrionic public suicide—so at odds with her previous identity as a proper Roman matron, so astonishing to her husband and father—is what returns her to the shelter of her cultural role. In death, Lucrece restores her relationship to her family, even as she commits this ultimate defiance of the rules of privacy and female enclosure:

> "O," quoth Lucretius, "I did give that life
> Which she too early and too late hath spill'd."
> "Woe, woe," quoth Collatine, "she was my wife,
> I owed her, and 'tis mine that she hath kill'd."
> "My daughter!," and "My wife!" with clamors fill'd

The dispers'd air, who holding Lucrece' life,
Answer'd their cries, "My daughter!'" and "My wife!"
(1800–1806)

In a formula that acknowledges the incongruity of the action which
restores her propriety, Ovid salutes her as a "matron of manly courage."[61] In death, she finally achieves persuasive eloquence as politic
Brutus delivers an interpretation of her life and her death which
resists all undoing, all contradiction. Incorporating her again within the course of Roman history, he uses her body as a speaking
emblem of the republican virtue whose source the Tarquins have
insulted. His audience vows with him to "show her bleeding body
thorough Rome, / And so to publish Tarquin's foul offense" (1851–
52)—thus making incontrovertibly public the sexual and domestic
segregation to which she devoted her life. Renouncing speech and
history, Lucrece is nonetheless appropriated for the purposes of
both. The conclusion of the poem speaks the contradictions and
perils inherent in Renaissance productions of doctrines of female
sovereignty.

Notes

1. George Puttenham, *The Arte of Englishe Poesie*, ed. Gladys Doidge Willcock
and Alice Walker (Cambridge: Cambridge University Press, 1936; rpt. 1970), 137.

2. See, for example, Ann Rosalind Jones and Peter Stallybrass, "The Politics
of *Astrophil and Stella*," *SEL* 24 (1984): 53–63; Maureen Quilligan, "Feminine
Endings: The Sexual Politics of Sidney's and Spenser's Rhyming," in *The Renaissance Englishwoman in Print: Counterbalancing the Canon*, ed. Anne M. Hasel-
korn and Betty S. Travitsky (Amherst: University of Massachusetts Press, 1990),
311–26; and Mary Ellen Lamb, *Gender and Authorship in the Sidney Circle* (Madison: University of Wisconsin Press, 1990).

3. Nancy Vickers writes persuasively about the presentation of the feminine
as the object of descriptive masculine speech in "'The Blazon of Sweet Beauty's
Best': Shakespeare's *Lucrece*," in *Shakespeare and the Question of Theory*, ed.
Patricia Parker and Geoffrey Hartman (New York: Methuen, 1985), 95–115.

4. Besides Vickers, see Heather Dubrow, *Captive Victors: Shakespeare's Nar-
rative Poems and Sonnets* (Ithaca: Cornell University Press, 1987), 80–168;
Katharine Eisaman Maus, "Taking Tropes Seriously: Language and Violence in
Shakespeare's *The Rape of Lucrece*," *SQ* 37 (1986): 66–82; Robin Bowers, "Incon-
ography and Rhetoric in Shakespeare's *Lucrece*," *ShakS* 14 (1981): 1–21; Nancy
Vickers, "'This Heraldry in Lucrece's Face'" *Poetics Today* 6 (1985): 171–84; and
Tita French, "'A Badge of Fame': Shakespeare's Rhetorical *Lucrece*," *EIRC* 10
(1984): 97–106. Patricia Parker's brilliant *Literary Fat Ladies: Rhetoric, Gender,
Property* (London: Methuen, 1987), ranges far into Shakespeare and eighteenth-
century literature, but 8–17 and 126–32 are particularly relevant to a discussion
of the rhetorical construction of gender in *Lucrece*.

5. Roy Battenhouse, *Shakespearean Tragedy: Its Art and Its Christian Premises* (Bloomington: Indiana University Press, 1969), 19, 16. Bowers cites these and other dismissive passages on p. 1 of her essay.

6. One useful theoretical exposition of this argument is Mary Jacobus, "Is There a Woman in this Text?," *NLH* 14 (1982): 117–54.

7. *The Rape of Lucrece*, line 1027. All Shakespeare quotations are from *The Riverside Shakespeare*, ed. G. Blakemore Evans et al. (Boston: Houghton Mifflin, 1974), and hereafter will be cited parenthetically in the text.

8. See Parker, *Literary Fat Ladies*, 26–31; Ann Rosalind Jones, "Nets and Bridles: Early Modern Conduct Books and Sixteenth-Century Women's Lyrics," in *The Ideology of Conduct: Essays on Literature and the History of Sexuality*, ed. Nancy Armstrong and Leonard Tennehouse (New York: Methuen, 1987), 39–72; and Lynda E. Boose, "Scolding Bridles and Bridling Scolds: Taming the Woman's Unruly Member," *SQ* 42 (1991): 179–213.

9. William Painter, *The Pallace of Pleasure* (New York AMS Press, 1967), 1:18.

10. *The Romane History Written by T. Livius of Padua*, trans. Philemon Holland (London, 1600), 2.

11. Trans. Sir James George Frazer (London: William Heinemann, 1931), 113.

12. Stephanie H Jed's stimulating *Chaste Thinking: The Rape of Lucretia and the Birth of Humanism* (Bloomington: Indiana University Press, 1989), is primarily concerned with fifteenth-century Italy and barely mentions Shakespeare's Lucrece at all, but I have still found it immensely suggestive for the present study of the links between constructions of gender and constructions of historical and social meaning. Jed is concerned with the transmission of the written records out of which later readers can establish such meaning. Informed by philological and etymological methods, she makes a connection between chastity and "castigation," the process through which early Renaissance editors and scholars produced their pure versions of ancient texts, and also narrowed the meanings of Lucrece's rape and suicide. She argues that the historical uses made of Lucrece's rape— especially the belief that it was significant only in that it provided a pretext for the change in Roman regimes—provide a prime example of the way in which the humanistic rediscovery of the past and modern generations' own practices in reading the Renaissance and classical past are themselves deeply implicated in the erasure of women from records of history and culture. In telling and retelling the story of rape and the consequent triumph of republican virtue, Renaissance humanists effectively removed Lucrece and made Brutus the hero of the newly philologically chaste narrative. Jed's observation that the authority of received history may "discourage us from questioning the literary structures within which we work" (5) speaks both to the resourcefulness of the rhetorically informed feminist criticism I acknowledge in n.4 above in affirming the connection between gender, genre, and text, and to my discussion, below, of the barriers Lucrece encounters in attempting to read the Troy tapestry and thus to define herself as a historical actor.

13. David E. Underdown, "The Taming of the Scold: the Enforcement of Patriarchal Authority in Early Modern England," in *Order and Disorder in Early Modern England*, ed. Anthony Fletcher and John Stevenson (Cambridge: Cambridge University Press, 1985), 122.

14. *A Pithie Exhortation to her Majestie for Establishing Her Successor to the Crowne* (London: 1598), 6, 8.

15. Paula Louise Scalingi reviews much of this material in "The Scepter or the Distaff: The Question of Female Sovereignty, 1516–1607," *The Historian* 41 (1978): 59–75. Two books by Retha M. Warnicke, *Women of the English Renaissance and*

Reformation (Westport, Conn.: Greenwood Press, 1983), esp. 47–63, and *The Rise and Fall of Ann Boleyn: Family Politics at the Court of Henry VIII* (New York: Cambridge University Press, 1988), offer useful discussions of the practices of sixteenth-century queenship. Louis A. Montrose, "'Shaping Fantasies': Figurations of Gender and Power in Elizabethan Culture," *Representations* 1 (1983): 61–94; Leah S. Marcus, "Shakespeare's Comic Heroines, Elizabeth I, and the Political Uses of Androgyny," in *Women in the Middle Ages and Renaissance: Literary and Historical Perspectives*, ed. Mary Beth Rose (Syracuse: Syracuse University Press, 1986), 135–54; and Pamela Joseph Benson, "'Rule, Virginia': Protestant Theories of Female Regiment in *The Faerie Queene*," *ELR* 15 (1985): 277–92, are three useful discussions of literary representations of the cultural phenomenon of powerful women.

16. "On the Fortunate Memory of Elizabeth Queen of England," in James Spedding, Robert Leslie Ellis, and Douglas Denon Heath, eds., *The Works of Francis Bacon* (Boston: Brown & Taggard, 1860), 11:450. Philippa Berry, *Of Chastity and Power: Elizabethan Literature and the Unmarried Queen* (London: Routledge, 1989), is concerned with the strategies developed by Renaissance English authors for addressing the problem of how most gracefully to implicate a virgin queen in the literature and social practices of courtship.

17. See Susan Dwyer Amussen, *An Ordered Society: Gender and Class in Early Modern England* (Oxford: Basil Blackwell, 1988), esp. 102–4.

18. Trans. Miles Coverdale (London: 1541), n.p.

19. Trans. Sir Thomas North (London: 1577), f.90.

20. Peter de la Primaudaye, *The French Academie*, trans. T.[homas] B.[owes], (London: 1586), 503.

21. Edmund Tilney, *A Briefe and Pleasant Discourse of Duties in Mariage, called the Flower of Friendshippe* (London: 1586), n.p.

22. In *A Collection of Emblems, Ancient and Moderne* (London: 1635), 91.

23. While my discussion here is fairly closely focused on female sexual behavior as an indicator of social reputation and on the links between sexual openness and female speech, I am not entirely following Lawrence Stone's influential conclusions about rigidly patriarchal Renaissance families first formulated in *The Family, Sex and Marriage in England, 1500–1800* (New York: Harper & Row, 1977). Keith Wrightson, *English Society 1580–1680* (London: Hutchinson, 1982), esp. 90–104, argues that patriarchal and companionate marriage historically coexisted and bases his case on a much broader base of English evidence than does Stone's concentration on the aristocracy. Ralph Houlbrooke, *The English Family, 1450–1700* (London: Longman, 1984), denies Stone's thesis of fundamental change in the pattern of English families from patriarchal to more companionate models, the change occurring sometime during the enlightenment. Alan Macfarlane, *Marriage and Love in England, 1300–1840* (Oxford: Oxford University Press, 1986) marshals comprehensive English evidence to argue the existence of companionate, affective family bonds since the medieval period. Alice Clark, *Working Life of Women in the Seventeenth Century* (London; Routledge, 1919; rpt. 1982), emphasizes the range of public, commercial activities that nonaristocratic women engaged in, and their social consequences.

24. de la Primaudaye, *French Academie*, 517.

25. Peter Stallybrass cites Robert Tofte's marginal gloss in his translation of Bernardo Varchi's *The Blazon of Jealousie* (London: 1615) in his important essay, "Patriarchal Territories: The Body Enclosed," in *Rewriting the Renaissance: The Discourses of Sexual Difference in Early Modern England*, ed. Margaret Ferguson,

Maureen Quilligan, and Nancy J. Vickers (Chicago: University of Chicago Press, 1986), 126.

26. Besides Mary Ellen Lamb on the women of the Sidney-Herbert circle, see Barbara Lewalski,; *Writing Women in Jacobean England* (Cambridge, Mass.: Harvard University Press, 1993).

27. See Ann Rosalind Jones, *The Currency of Eros: Women's Love Lyric in Europe, 1540–1620* (Bloomington: Indiana University Press, 1990), esp. 1–7 and 11–35, on the adaptive strategies displayed in women's texts.

28. See Lawrence Stone, *The Crisis of the Aristocracy, 1558–1641* (Oxford: Clarendon Press, 1965), 660–64; and Alice T. Friedman, "Portrait of a Marriage: The Willoughby Letters of 1585–1586," *Signs* 11 (1986): 542–55. Lewalski's account of the career of Ann Clifford, Countess of Dorset and Montgomery, 125–51, is particularly suggestive of how women could experience patriarchal institutions both as a source of pride and a source of social frustration.

29. Philip Stubbes, *A Christal Glasse for Christian Women* London, 1592, 2.

30. Ibid., 4.

31. Ibid., 5.

32. Ruth Kelso, *Doctrine for the Lady of the Renaissance* (Urbana: University of Illinois Press, 1956), was one of the first scholars to note the pervasiveness of adjurations to chastity in the conduct books, and to discuss how this advice contributed to the cultural formation of English gentlewomen. Margaret Lael Mikesell, "Catholic and Protestant Widows in *The Duches of Malfi*," *Renaissance and Reformation* 19 (1983): 265–279, believes that Catholic-authored works tended to value chastity more than Protestant-authored tracts, which she believes more often advance obedience as the cardinal virtue for women.

33. E.g., "So that when they have all these goodly robes uppon them, women seeme to be the smallest part of themselves, not naturall women, but artificiall Women, not women of flesh & blod, but rather puppits, or mawmets of rags and clowtes compact together" (n.p.).

34. George Whetstone, *An Heptameron of Civill Discourses* (London: 1582), 119.

35. Charles Bansley, *A Treatyse Shewing and Declaring the Pryde and Abuse of Women Now A Dayes* (London: 1550). Ralph Houlbrooke, *Church Courts and the People During the English Reformation, 1520–1570* (Oxford: Oxford University Press, 1979), cites an equally suggestive incident of a man who, haled before an ecclesiastical court on the charge that he had called his neighbor a whore, attempted to excuse himself by explaining that he hadn't meant a "whore of her body," but "a whore of her tongue" (80).

36. Juan Luis Vives, *Instruction of a Christian Woman*, trans. Thomas Paynell (London, 1540), E 2.

37. *A Choice of Emblemes*, ed. Henry Green (London; 1866; rpt. New York: Benjamin Blom, 1967), 93.

38. I began thinking about the embedded and antecedent texts of *The Rape of Lucrece* after first reading Ian Donaldson's *The Rape of Lucretia: A Myth and Its Transformations* (Oxford: Clarendon Press, 1982). Donaldson's study, which traces treatments of the Lucrece story from Livy through the eighteenth century, persuasively demonstrates both the extraordinary vitality of the narrative in western cultures and the relationships betwen versions of Lucretia's life and death and changing interpretations of Roman value. He discusses Shakespeare's *Lucrece*, 40–56. His broader comparative anaylysis is usefully complemented by the attention of Stephanie Jed to the material and social circumstances under which the Lucrece story was transmitted specifically in Renaissance Italy.

39. Niccolò Machiavelli, *The Discourses of Livy*, trans. Leslie J. Walker, S.J. (London: Routledge & Kegan Paul, 1950; rpt. London: Routledge & Kegan Paul, 1975), 3:468–69.

40. See, for example the bawdy catch performed by two Roman nobles and a comic servant after the rape: "Did he take the Lady by the thigh man? . . . And now he came somewhat nie man. . . . But did he do tother thing man? . . . And at the same had he a fling man." Heywood's play was evidently a popular one, being printed four more times after 1609; I cite the fifth edition, including authorial emendations, of 1638, from *The Dramatic Works of Thomas Heywood* (London: 1874; rpt. London: Russell & Russell, 1964), 5:161, 233.

41. In *The Poems of Thomas Carew, With His Masque Coelum Britannicum*, ed. Rhodes Dunlap (Oxford: Clarendon Press, 1949), 52.

42. In *The Works of Thomas Southerne* (Oxford: Clarendon Press, 1988), ed. Robert Jordan and Harold Love; 2:84. Donaldson discusses Southern's play, 87–88. For further treatments of the Lucrece materials, see Laura Bromley, "The Lost Lucrece: Middleton's *The Ghost of Lucrece*," PLL 21 (1985): 258–74; Saad El-Gabalawy, "The Ethical Question of Lucrece: A Case of Rape," *Mosaic* 12, no. 4 (1979): 75–86; and Harriet Hawkins, "Myth and Morals," EIC 34 (1984): 79–87.

43. Frazer, 115.

44. In the biographical and place-name supplement to his *Thesaurus Linguae Romanae et Britannicae* (London, 1565), Thomas Cooper's discussion of Lucrece's rape also emphasizes her fear of public shaming as a reason for yielding to Tarquin: "For feare of . . . shamefull reproch and infamie, rather than for dreadde of death, as after appeered, she suffered the violence of the wicked advouterer." As though conscious of the power of adultery, even forced adultery, in making and unmaking female reputation, however, Cooper finds it necessary to end his entry by adding that "the example of Lucrece shoulde never be a cloke for light women to excuse the unfaithfull breach of wedlocke" (n.p.).

45. The general bibliography on *ekphrasis* in Renaissance poetry is not as large as I expected it to be. I use the term here as James A. W. Heffernan does in his useful discussion, "Ekphrasis and Representation," NLH 22 (1991): 297–316, to refer specifically to "the verbal representation of graphic representation" (299). Heffernan finds that true *ekphrasis* is distinguished by its impulse to establish a narrative for its description of a static image, a characterization which certainly holds true for the Troy ekphrasis in *Lucrece*; to his remarks I would add that graphic images of events or characters in the Troy story, while physically stable, often carry unstable and fluctuating sets of interpretive associations, so that the image offers what may turn out to be only an uncertain opportunity for fixing narrative meaning. Other discussions I have drawn on in this section include Jean H. Hagstrum, *The Sister Arts: The Tradition of Literary Pictorialism from Dryden to Gray* (Chicago: University of Chicago Press, 1958; rpt. 1987), and John Hollander, "The Poetics of Ekphrasis," *Word and Image* 4 (1988): 209–19.

46. *Collection of Emblems*, 27. Judith Dundas, , "Mocking the Mind: The Role of Art in Shakespeare's *The Rape of Lucrece*," SCJ 14, no. 1 (1983): 13–22; S. Clark Hulse, "'A Piece of Skilful Painting' in Shakespeare's *Lucrece*," ShS 31 (1978): 13–22; Elizabeth Truax, "'Lucrece! What Hath Your Conceited Painter Wrought?'," *Bucknell Review* 25, no. 1 (1980): 13–30; and A. Robin Bowers, "Emblem and Rape in Shakespeare's *Lucrece* and *Titus Andronicus*," SIcon 10 (1984–86): 79–96, all discuss the Troy tapestry's meaning in the poem. Robert Miola, Shakespeare's Rome (Cambridge, England: Cambridge University Press, 1983), discusses the Troy *ekphrasis*' roots in *Aeneid* 1–2 and *Metamorphoses* 12, 30–36.

47. I cite Arthur Golding, The .XV. Bookes of P. Ouidius Naso, entytuled Metamorphosis (London: 1567; rpt. London; Centaur Press, 1961); here, line 261.

48. This emphasis on the propriety of Polyxena's death survives in George Sandys's Ovid's Metamorphoses English'd (Oxford: 1632), which notes that "then when shee fell, shee had a care to hide / What should be hid; and chastly-decent dide" (435). In their concern for inscribing Roman and female senses of propriety in this moment of death, Sandys and Golding may be following Fasti, whose description of Lucrece's death also includes this implied connection between posture and chaste decency: "Even then in dying she took care to sink down decently: that was her thought even as she fell" (117).

49. Sandys, Ovids, 447.

50. Ibid., 448.

51. Alexander Ross, Mystagogus Poeticus (London, 1648), 157.

52. Ibid., 158.

53. Hecuba's transformation into a barking dog is missing from at least three medieval treatments of the Troy materials. The Laud Troy Book, ed. J. Ernst Wülfing (London: EETS, 1902) and The Gest Hystoriale of the Destruction of Troy, ed. George A. Panton and David Donaldson (London: EETS, 1869 and 1874) place Hecuba's madness and stoning after Polyxena's death but omit any mention of a transformation. The Seege or Battayle of Troy, ed. Mary Elizabeth Barnicle (London: EETS, 1927) omits Hecuba's madness entirely and skips right from Polyxena's death to Helen's return to Menelaus. The strange image of a "violent" mouth recalls Houlbrooke's report of the woman with the whorish tongue, or Tofte's assertion that a maid with a "lewd tongue" is virtually the same as a fornicator. In all three cases, the open mouth (and the associated vaginal orifice) which these unruly women inappropriately show the world becomes the focus of critiques of their violations of gendered behavior.

54. Ross, Mystagogus Poeticus, 159.

55. Metamorphoses 13.488.

56. Compare my position here with that of Battenhouse, who asks of the poem's portrayal of Lucrece's act of reading, "With how much self-understanding is she capable of reading? Her shallowness as an explicator of great art can then become for us both amusingly pathetic and a caveat for explicators like ourselves" (23).

57. Cooper's supplement. He notes that Paris's seizure of Helen was the second rape she suffered: she was first abducted "at the age of nine yeres by Theseus." For further discussion of treatments of the stories of Helen and their relation to woman's place in generic traditions, see Götz Schmitz, The Fall of Women in Early English Narrative Verse (Cambridge: Cambridge University Press, 1990), 223–41; and Mihoko Suzuki, The Metamorphoses of Helen: Authority, Difference, and the Epic (Ithaca: Cornell University Press, 1989).

58. Maus discusses Tarquin's language of Siege, "Taking Tropes," 67–68.

59. See Sam Hynes, "The Rape of Tarquin," SQ 10 (1959): 451–53.

60. Virgil's Georgics IV was probably the best-known classical precedent of the beehive-commonwealth analogy. Other usages in Shakespeare include Henry V, 1.2.183–204.

61. Fasti 119.

The Case of Eleanor Cobham: Authorizing History in *2 Henry VI*

NINA S. LEVINE

W<small>HEN</small> B<small>UCKINGHAM</small> in *2 Henry VI* interrupts the royal party at St. Albans with news of the arrest of Eleanor, Duchess of Gloucester, his report concisely articulates a familiar narrative, one which links female aggression with witchcraft and treason.[1] This is the tale that his "heart doth tremble to unfold" (2.1.162):

> A sort of naughty persons, lewdly bent,
> Under the countenance and confederacy
> Of Lady Eleanor, the Protector's wife,
> The ringleader and head of all this rout,
> Have practic'd dangerously against your state,
> Dealing with witches and with conjurers,
> Whom we have apprehended in the fact,
> Raising up wicked spirits from under ground,
> Demanding of King Henry's life and death,
> And other of your Highness' Privy Council,
> As more at large your Grace shall understand.
>
> (163–73)[2]

The effectiveness of Buckingham's narrative is demonstrated at once by Gloucester's response: "I banish her my bed and company," he declares of his wife, "And give her as a prey to law and shame, / That hath dishonored Gloucester's honest name" (193–95). Eleanor is promptly tried and sentenced and at the close of act 2 is led away to a life of exile on the Isle of Man.

As it inscribes the duchess's treason within the familiar narrative of virago-witch-traitor, Buckingham's report gains a certain authority, for the characters onstage and perhaps for some members of Shakespeare's London audience, many of whom may have followed the accounts of the recent witchcraft-treason trials in Scotland in

1590–91. The familiarity of Buckingham's report indeed invites the audience to participate in what Annabel Patterson has described as an "Elizabethan cultural practice" of linking past and present events in an "ideological chain."[3] The association between Eleanor's crime and recent events might work, then, to validate the authenticity of Buckingham's charges as well as to reaffirm the universality of the authorizing narrative itself. But Buckingham's account is not the only version of the duchess's crime presented in *2 Henry VI*. His brief report is contained within Shakespeare's own "report" on the duchess, a presentation that in many ways challenges both the facts of Buckingham's account and the narrative pattern authorizing it. For though Shakespeare's Eleanor does indeed desire the crown and consort with necromancers, as Buckingham charges, she also is the victim of what we might call political entrapment: her ambitions are exploited and even manipulated by her husband's enemies to further their own power over the Lancastrian state.

That Shakespeare presents Eleanor's crime as overdetermined or at least doubly determined—she is, after all, both aggressor and victim—complicates our understanding of the relationship between this play and the culture in which it was produced. This relationship is, of course, mediated by any number of factors, by theatrical practices and the individual agency of its author, for example, as well as political and ideological debates. Without diminishing the importance of other "determining" literary and cultural forms, this paper focuses on gender in Shakespeare's representation of Eleanor, in part because this issue has received little critical attention but also because it has particular resonance in Elizabethan England, with a woman on the throne.[4] What, we might ask, is the relationship between Shakespeare's representation of Eleanor's crime and contemporary ways of thinking about powerful women? Does the play call into question the validity of the patriarchal paradigm for defining and controlling women? Or does it reinforce it by dramatizing the dangerous consequences of Eleanor's desires? Is there a relationship between these issues and the ideological contradiction generated by Elizabeth I's reign?

Although these kinds of questions are central to this paper, I shift the focus away from a subversion-containment binary, with its tendency to privilege moments of resolution, and turn instead to the conflicts and instabilities that traverse these resolutions.[5] In this regard, Jonathan Dollimore's call for a materialist feminist criticism that "follows the unstable constructions of . . . gender and patriarchy back to the contradictions of their historical moment"[6] offers a useful starting point. Such an approach to Shakespeare's handling of Eleanor is complicated, however, by the double or, to be more accurate, multiple locus of the "historical moment" in the history play. For while England in the early 1590s constitutes one historical locus for *2 Henry VI*, earlier moments associated with Shakespeare's chronicle sources also contribute to the composite portrait of Eleanor that emerges on the Elizabethan stage. What follows in this paper is an attempt to address Shakespeare's complex and contradictory representation of Eleanor from a number of historical moments, from the fifteenth to the late sixteenth century, and to raise questions about the extent to which representations of Eleanor's crime have been shaped by, and themselves shape, political and ideological struggles.

I

If fifteenth-century accounts are any indication, Eleanor Cobham's crime was a national sensation: her story appears in every extant fifteenth-century English chronicle and in popular ballads as well.[7] Her rank and position alone may explain the attention given her case: as the wife of Humphrey, Duke of Gloucester, protector during the minority of Henry VI, Eleanor occupied the highest position among women in England. She was, as one ballad puts it, "amonge alle women magnyfyed."[8] In 1441, however, she was accused of conspiring with necromancers, of plotting against the king's life so that she and her husband might assume the royal seat. Two of her three accomplices were executed while the duchess herself was sentenced to life in prison, where she died eighteen years later.[9] Her spectacular fall from power inevitably received a good deal of public attention: according to contemporary accounts, she was forced to walk through the crowded streets of London, dressed in a gown of penitence, a wax taper in her hand.

That a peeress should be charged with necromancy and treason was not without precedent, however. Twenty-two years before, Henry IV's widow, Queen Joan of Navarre, had been accused of using necromancy in an attempt against the life of her step-son Henry V, but the differences between the two cases are instructive. Never officially charged or brought to trial, Queen Joan was kept under house arrest for three years before her liberty and property were restored by the king in 1422.[10] By contrast, Eleanor Cobham was subjected to both civil and ecclesiastical examinations, forced to undergo public penance and humiliation, and sentenced to a life of exile. Her case was also significant in prompting a change in English law when parliament, soon after her sentencing, clarified the legal status of peeresses accused of treason or felony: they now would be judged by the same judges and peers of the realm as their male counterparts.[11] This statute had the result of increasing the penalties for female felons, for while ecclesiastical courts typically imposed sentences of public penance, the civil court alone could request a death sentence. The case of Eleanor thus resulted in equalizing the legal status for peeresses of the realm: they, too, could be given death.

That Eleanor's story was first recorded by her enemies, by Yorkist chroniclers in their accounts of the reign of Henry VI, clearly shapes the facts of the narrative that found its way into Shakespeare's Tudor sources. It is not surprising, perhaps, that the legal issues raised by Eleanor's trial receive little or no attention in the fifteenth-century chronicles; nor is there mention of a political context or of a link between her fall and her husband's political decline. Instead, these accounts make much of her involvement in sorcery and necromancy—she is said to have admitted to several of the charges against her—and locate the motive for her treason in her ambition and pride. By suppressing political motives altogether, in a move that would seem to be at odds with the political nature of her crime, these accounts authorize their censure by translating her political desires into a moral framework, one that is in some cases reinforced by a misogynistic discourse. For example, one of the most detailed fifteenth-century accounts, found in a manuscript that had belonged to John Stowe, concluded that the duchess's "pride, fals couetise and lecherie were cause of her confusioun. Othir thyngis myghte be writen of this dame Alienore, the whiche atte reuerence of nature and of wommanhood shul not be reherced."[12]

Another strategy for representing Eleanor's crime was to place the duchess alongside other traitors and heretics who were brought to justice during Henry VI's reign. In one London chronicle a brief account of the duchess's crime and punishment is followed with reference to the fighting in Smithfield between an armorer and his servant and the rise and fall of Jack Cade.[13] In *An English Chronicle* Eleanor's story is preceded by an account of two heretics, a priest who was burnt for heresy and a blaspheming vicar.[14] Linked with heretics and traitors in a chain that effaces differences of gender and class, Eleanor would appear to illustrate yet another case of dangerous treason that must be punished. The issue of gender is raised, however, in the "Lament of the Duchess of Gloucester," a fifteenth-century ballad written by a London citizen and still being sung in Shakespeare's day. Here, the lamenting duchess confesses her "gret offence" and draws this moral for her listeners in the poem's echoing refrain: "Alle women may be ware by me."[15]

Suggestions of the political maneuvering behind the accusations and trial begin to appear in the sixteenth-century Tudor chronicles. Robert Fabyan's account, first published in 1516, retains the familiar story of Eleanor's crime and punishment but prefaces it with a short but telling paragraph on the Duke of Gloucester's enemies who, he writes, "left nat tyll they hadde brought hym vnto his confucion."[16] Published in 1548, Edward Hall's chronicle, generally agreed upon as the principal source for *2 Henry VI*, follows a similar strategy of suggesting the political context for Eleanor's crime. Masterfully brief, Hall compresses his account of the crime and punishment into one sentence that neatly contains the treasonous offense:

> For first this yere, dame Elyanour Cobham, wyfe to the sayd duke, was accused of treason, for that she, by sorcery and enchauntment, entended to destroy the kyng, to thentent to aduaunce and to promote her husbande to the croune: vpon thys she was examined in sainct Stephens chappel, before the Bisshop of Canterbury, and there by examinacion conuict & iudged, to do open penaunce, in. iij. open places, within the citie of London, and after that adiudged to perpetuall prisone in the Isle of Man, vnder the kepyng of sir Ihon Stanley, knyght.[17]

Arrested alongside the duchess were her "ayders and counsailers" who at her request practiced sorcery with the intention of killing the king. The brevity of Hall's text suggests that justice was carried out with dispatch: Margery Jordan was "brent in smithfelde," Roger Bolingbroke was "drawen & quartered at tiborne," Southwell died before his execution, and John Hume "had his pardon."

Without elaboration or commentary, then, Hall narrates the story of Eleanor's fall with a spareness that belies both the importance of the duchess as the protector's wife and the heinous nature of her plot to kill the king and place her husband on the throne. Given his lengthy treatment of the trial of Joan of Arc only a few pages before, this brief account of Eleanor's offense is hardly characteristic of a writer whose prose Geoffrey Bullough has described as "prolix and often cloudy; he could not compress."[18] Hall's deceptively simple narrative is complicated, however, by its context. For Hall places the brief tale of Eleanor as a conclusion to a lengthy presentation of the Duke of Gloucester's complaints against Cardinal Winchester, complaints which bring to a head the long-standing political struggle between the duke and the cardinal. After documenting Gloucester's accusations, Hall asserts that "secret attemptes were aduaunced forward this season, against the noble duke Humfrey of Glocester, a farre of, whiche in conclusion came so nere, that they bereft hym both of lyfe and lande, as you shall hereafter more manifestly perceyue." Hall here begins his story of the duchess. But while Hall suggests a connection between the cardinal's "injury" and the duchess's fall, he avoids any direct criticism of the charges against Eleanor.

The Tudor text that most clearly asserts the political basis of Eleanor's fall is John Foxe's widely read *Acts and Monuments*, a text that has been put forth as a source for Shakespeare's Gloucester but not, surprisingly, for Eleanor. In the first edition of *Acts and Monuments*, Foxe had cited the case of the duchess to illustrate how persecutors "began now to execute their cruelty upon women."[19] But in the 1576 edition, and in all subsequent editions, Foxe extended his original mention to include a lengthy defense answering Alan Cope's objection to his treatment of Eleanor Cobham in the first edition. The charges against the duchess are, he asserts, "a matter made, and of evil-will compacted, rather than true indeed."[20] Raising a series of objections to the charge of treason against Eleanor, Foxe considers political as well as religious motives, mentioning, for example, the "grudge kindled" between the duke and the cardinal. Foxe then concludes his defense of Eleanor by proposing an alternate tradition to the one informing earlier accounts.

Using historical examples, Foxe carefully documents a tradition in which charges of witchcraft are exploited for political gain. "The frequent practices and examples of other times may make this also more doubtful," he writes of Eleanor's treason, "considering how many subtle pretences, after the like sort, have been sought, and wrongful accusations brought, against many innocent persons."[21] Foxe validates his argument with examples, citing, for instance, the false charge laid to "the queen and Shore's wife, by the protector, for enchanting and bewitching his withered arm." In the portrait of the Duke of Gloucester that follows, Foxe links Eleanor's fall directly with the presentation of Gloucester's objections to Cardinal Winchester. Clearly interpreting what was implied in the earlier

Tudor chronicles, Foxe concludes that "the said duchess may appear, more of malice than of any just cause thus to have been troubled."[22] Foxe's revisionist history raises questions, then, about the authority of a ruling ideology that would define enemies of the state as witches. Far more politically sophisticated than Hall's presentation, and certainly more radical, Foxe's defense clearly asserts the political basis of the accusations against Eleanor Cobham.

II

That Shakespeare's Tudor sources contained traces of political and ideological bias from the earlier Yorkist accounts certainly provides one explanation for the play's double-voiced presentation. The possibility that Foxe's account is also a source offers another. But whether Foxe was a source for Shakespeare's Eleanor—and I argue that he was—setting his defense alongside other Tudor accounts offers a way of understanding Shakespeare's strategy for representing Eleanor's crime. Like Hall, Shakespeare inscribes the duchess's crime within the familiar stereotype of the virago-witch-traitor, casting her ambition as unnatural and dangerous. Yet, like Foxe, he calls into question the authority of this model, suggesting that the duchess's crime is determined not only by her ambition but by political struggles as well. In staging the crime itself, which should offer proof of her guilt, and at the same time qualifying the circumstances of that crime in ways which undermine that "proof," Shakespeare could be said to exploit what Robert Weimann has referred to as the "bifold authority" of the Elizabethan stage. The theatrical conventions of an upstage *locus* and a downstage *platea*, Weimann argues, allowed authority to be represented both as an object and as a process of authorization. Generating a dissonance between "authorities represented" and "authorities representing,"[23] in this case between the representation of Eleanor's crime and the conspirators acting as agents in that representation, Shakespeare calls attention to ways in which authority may be constructed.

Shakespeare's initial characterization of the duchess would appear, of course, to validate long-standing anxieties about ruling and unruly women. Almost a caricature of a dominating female, Shakespeare's Eleanor begins by imperiously urging her husband to take the throne, and we quickly see that "in this place most master wear no breeches" (1.3.146), to borrow a phrase from the duchess herself.

"Put forth thy hand, reach at the glorious gold," she commands, only to mock her husband's manhood: "What, is't too short? I'll lengthen it with mine" (1.2.11–12). Gloucester provides the moral gloss, advising his wife to "banish the canker of ambitious thoughts" (18), yet his "troublous" dream of his staff "broke in twain" (26) gives form to his fears. Gloucester's civic impotence, the play suggests, has its origins in his marital impotence, in his failure to command his wife. True to the stereotype of the virago-witch, the duchess chafes at the limitations imposed on her sex in terms that anticipate those of Lady Macbeth[24]:

> Were I a man, a duke, and next of blood,
> I would remove these tedious stumbling-blocks,
> And smooth my way upon their headless necks;
> And, being a woman, I will not be slack
> To play my part in Fortune's pageant.
>
> (1.2.63–67)

Denied the means of power available to her husband, the duchess turns to witchcraft.

It could be argued, then, that Shakespeare's portrait of Eleanor, particularly at the beginning of the play, authorizes patriarchal assumptions linking female domination with witchcraft and the subversion of patriarchal authority in the family and state. Yet while Shakespeare here dramatizes the familiar paradigm of virago-witch-traitor, at the same time he significantly alters our understanding of it by qualifying the duchess's behavior in this scene with the framing soliloquies of York and Hume, soliloquies which show the duchess to be an unwitting pawn in a larger and far more dangerous conspiracy to take the crown. The duchess makes her entrance immediately after York's lengthy speech in which he voices his grievance against the king and vows that with "force perforce I'll make him yield the crown" (1.1.258). The duchess's desire for "King Henry's diadem" in the scene that follows thus parodies (or "boys" to be more precise) York's imperialist desire to possess "fertile England's soil." For it is York, finally, and not the duchess, who with a grotesque literalness will realize her desire to "smooth my way upon their headless necks" (1.2.65). The duchess does indeed "play" her part in "Fortune's pageant," but on Shakespeare's stage it is a part set down for her by her husband's enemies, as the ambidextrous Hume confides to the audience at the close of this scene (1.2.97–99). The framing soliloquies thus circumscribe the duchess's ambition, containing it within larger and more dangerous plots to undermine the monarchy. Rather than validating the paradigm of virago-witch-traitor as a universal truth, then, Shakespeare's presentation, like Foxe's, suggests instead that this familiar narrative has in fact been exploited, and to some extent constructed, by gentlemen conspirators as a means by which they themselves will subvert the state.

Shakespeare's staging of the conjuring scene raises similar questions about authority and representation by presenting and at the same time qualifying Eleanor's participation with witchcraft and treason. Shakespeare's chronicle sources are very clear about Eleanor's involvement. Hall's account makes Eleanor the initiator of the plan to "destroy the kynges person." Her accomplices undertook their sorcery, Hall writes, "at the request of the duchesse."[25] Consistent with Hall is the conjuring scene of the 1594 Quarto, which begins with Eleanor instructing Hume on his part:

> Here sir *Iohn*, take this scrole of paper here,
> Wherein is writ the questions you shall aske,
> And I will stand vpon this Tower here,
> And here the spirit what it saies to you,
> And to my questions, write the answeres downe.
>
> (1.4.1–5)[26]

The fearless duchess who in *The Contention* directs the scene of conjuring becomes in *2 Henry VI* a passive observer. In *2 Henry VI* the conjuring is, as Hume puts it, a "performance" (1.4.2), paid for by the duchess who takes her place "aloft," as audience to Bolingbrook's "exorcisms."

The scene indeed exposes itself as theater as Bolingbrook, and not the duchess, acts as stage manager, directing his players: "Mother Jordan, be you prostrate and grovel on the earth . . . John Southwell, read you; and let us to our work" (10–12). Bolingbrook's fears about the duchess's courage, absent from the chronicle accounts and from *The Contention*, further qualify the extent of her involvement. "I have heard her reported to be a woman of an invincible spirit," Bolingbrook confesses to Hume, "but it shall be convenient, Master Hume, that you be by her aloft, while we be busy below" (6–9). Bolingbrook, after all, must ensure that the scene is set for the duchess's arrest, and before the spirit rises, he advises her to "fear not" for "whom we raise, / We will make fast within a hallow'd verge" (21–22). His words might apply just as well to the "raising" of Eleanor. Never a real threat to the monarchy, it seems, the duchess too is made "fast," securely contained within the circle of conspiracy drawn by Gloucester's enemies. By foregrounding the master plot of the cardinal, Shakespeare radically alters the "fact" of the duchess's witchcraft as it will be reported by Buckingham. The duchess does, to be sure, consort with spirits to learn of the king's death, though she is conspicuously silent during the ceremony itself. But when framed by the machinations of the cardinal and York, the conjuring scene appears as a trick or as York himself describes it, "a pretty plot, well chosen to build upon" (56). By presenting the crime itself as a kind of play-within-a-play, Shakespeare exploits the capacities of the Elizabethan stage in a way that reduces the virago-witch-traitor to an object and, finally, shifts the location of authority away from Eleanor and onto her enemies.

Another alteration Shakespeare makes in his sources that undermines the authority of the charges against the duchess is the substitution of a prophesying spirit for the wax image commonly found in stories of the duchess's fall. Hall had described how the duchess's accomplices, following her instructions, "had deuised an image of waxe, representyng the kynge, whiche by their sorcery, a litle and litle consumed, entendyng therby in conclusion to waist, and destroy the kynges person, and so to bryng hym death."[27] Shakespeare's exchange of a prophesying spirit for a wax image is significant, for rather than conspiring to kill the king, the duchess in *2 Henry VI* is guilty of what would appear to be a lesser crime, that of inquiring into the king's future.[28] The raising of a spirit is, of course, far more spectacular on stage than a diminutive wax figure, but theatrical reasons alone do not fully account for the change this revision makes in the nature of the duchess's crime.[29]

Talking heads and wax images may also have produced specific local resonances for an Elizabethan audience that could have contributed to Shakespeare's choice. For instance, one scholar has argued for the inclusion of the prophesying spirit by locating a source for this play in the 1562 trial of the Pools and Fortescue who, when accused of conspiring against the queen, confessed that they conversed with a spirit not to plot against the queen but only to find out about her death.[30] But there were several recent cases of treason linked to wax images that might also have served as a source for the play. One particularly well-known case of image-making during Elizabeth's reign—Ben Jonson remembered hearing rumors about it—concerned three images of wax discovered in Windsor in 1578. According to the Spanish ambassador Mendoza, "the centre figure had the word Elizabeth written on the forehead" and all three were pierced with pig bristles.[31] Another case, not of

treason but of a wife's attempted revenge on the men who had
denied her husband a promotion, is recorded in London in 1590
when Mrs. Dewse was arrested for fashioning in wax "pictures" of
her husband's enemies and then sticking them with pins.[32] In the
highly publicized trials in Scotland in 1590 and 1591, witches
were charged with conspiring the death of James VI by melting a
wax image of the king over a fire.[33]

Given the prominence of wax images in recent cases of treason
against both Elizabeth I and James VI, Shakespeare's choice of a
prophesying spirit over a wax image might have been shaped in
part by a desire to diminish the seditious resonance of this scene
on the Elizabethan stage. But whatever the reason, the exchange
has the effect of diminishing the duchess's culpability. By suppressing the wax image that in the chronicles materially demonstrates the duchess's treason—and on the Elizabethan stage might
help to link Eleanor's crime to recent cases of witchcraft and treason—Shakespeare weakens rather than reinforces the ideological
chain that constructs the witchcraft-treason paradigm as universal
and transcendent.

III

As the questions posed by the wax image suggest, contradictions
within and among the chronicles do not fully account for Shakespeare's ambivalent construction of Eleanor. That Shakespeare
should enact an "exorcism" on the London stage in the early 1590s,
not long after the trials in Scotland had concluded, invites specula-
tion about relationships between past and present cases of treason
and witchcraft, to be sure. That the play links treason and witchcraft with the issues of gender and power generates other questions.
To what extent does Shakespeare's representation participate in the
debate over women wielding power, particularly as it was framed in
the 1590s as the queen entered her sixties and anxieties about the
succession began to increase? That the most likely heir to the
throne also figured prominently in the treason-witchcraft trials
in Scotland raises even more questions about the play's local
resonance.

Like the case of Eleanor Cobham a century and a half before, the
treason-witchcraft trials conducted in Scotland between November
1590 and May 1591 were clearly political, carried out in large part
to incriminate the Earl of Bothwell, who had been found guilty of

treason in 1589 but had not yet been sentenced.[34] During the course
of the trials more than three hundred witches were said to have
conspired against James VI by raising storms at sea as the king
returned from Denmark with his bride and attempting to consume
his life by melting his image in wax. More than one hundred were
actually examined in trials, frequently presided over by the king
himself. The political emphasis of these trials, as Christina Larner
points out, linked them not with the more recent type of witchcraft
accusations directed against obscure persons, but with an older
type, "in which the accusation of witchcraft was used, sometimes
cynically, as a means to convict, or make popular the convictions,
of a particular person."[35] Nor did the political motives of these
trials remain undetected. In 1591 the English ambassador, Robert
Bowes, who was himself implicated in the charges at one point,
wrote that the witches confessed things "farre more strange then
trewe" in order to gain favor with the king and so reduce their
sentences.[36] Public opinion in Scotland, moreover, appears to have
favored Bothwell, as a letter received by Burghley in 1591 from
an "intelligencer" in Scotland indicates: "notwithstanding off the
heynous crymis laid to his [Bothwell's] chairge, yitt I assuir yowr
honour all Scotland doith allow of his libertie."[37]

It is the English "reading" of these trials that would be the most
useful, of course, in mapping the political resonance of Shakespeare's representation of Eleanor. The English monarchy supported the attack on Bothwell, whose outspoken sympathy for
Mary Stuart and continued involvement in Catholic causes made
him no friend to England.[38] Unofficial reactions may be more difficult to assess, but we do know that James VI himself attempted to
influence public opinion with the 1591 publication of *Newes from
Scotland*, a pamphlet in which Shakespeare's audience could have
read about the trials of the North Berwick witches. Carefully tailored for English readers, *Newes* offered a sensational account, both
titillating and gruesome, designed to enhance the king's standing
in England by presenting him as the enemy of the devil and "the
Lords annointed."[39] Larner has suggested, however, that while
James used the trials to fashion his own particular myth of kingship
for his subjects, his enthusiasm for prosecuting witches also had
the potential to work against him in England, a possibility that may
have led him to justify and qualify his position in subsequent
years.[40]

That Shakespeare in *2 Henry VI* foregrounds the politics shaping
Eleanor's crime and punishment may not be so surprising, then,

given the political nature of recent events in Scotland. What is less clear, however, is the extent to which the play's emphasis on politics offers a critique of Stuart policy. Might the ambivalence of Shakespeare's representation of Eleanor's crime bring into the open contradictions in English attitudes toward events in Scotland, on the one hand reflecting the monarchy's support for curbing Bothwell's power but on the other eliciting the mixture of fascination and horror that the English might have felt about the large number of "witches" who were brought to trial in the process? For though Bothwell was at the center of the trials, most of those actually convicted were women. As one historian has remarked about the trial of Barbara Napier, "it was easier to attack a woman of lower rank than a man of Bothwell's stature and importance."[41] Did the association of women, treason, and witchcraft raised by these trials also draw attention to a dissonance between Jacobean and Elizabethan ideology?

Shakespeare's reluctance to insist too loudly on the equation between female aggression, witchcraft, and treason might be understood in part as deference to his monarch, a woman ruler who had herself been accused of conjuring and conspiring against the state shortly after her sister's accession to the throne. As Lily B. Campbell has pointed out, the charges brought against Elizabeth in 1555 recall many of the details of the case against Eleanor Cobham; not only is the charge of necromancy and treason brought against a woman of high rank—and the specific charge of calculating the monarch's nativity—but the suspicion of entrapment is also voiced in some quarters.[42] John Harington, for example, points to the role of Bishop Gardiner: "Lastly, the plots he laid to entrap the Lady Elizabeth, his terrible hard usage of all her followers, I cannot yet scarce think of with charity, nor write of with patience."[43] On the basis of these and other parallels, Campbell has argued for a specific link between the accusations against Elizabeth and George Ferrers' tragedy of Elianor Cobham, first published in the 1578 edition of the Mirror for Magistrates. Although Ferrers' poem is not usually considered a source for 1 Henry VI, surely Shakespeare must have been familiar with it: both texts provide evidence of entrapment by the cardinal and present the issue of Eleanor's witchcraft in political rather than moral or religious terms.[44]

My concern is not with arguing for a one-to-one relationship between Eleanor's case and the early trials of Elizabeth I, however. Nor is it with establishing the Mirror for Magistrates as a source for 2 Henry VI. As useful as topical references and sources may be in giving us access to forces that may have shaped Shakespeare's presentation, I want to avoid a critical practice that fixes meaning and so limits our understanding of the interplay between texts and the culture in which they are produced. What I do want to give attention to is the relationship between Shakespeare's strategies for representing Eleanor Cobham—for defining and controlling the unsettling figure of "the woman on top"—and the instabilities and contradictions generated by Elizabeth I's gender. In this regard, Shakespeare's handling of the scene of Eleanor's containment is significant in its reworking of the familiar virago-witch-traitor paradigm. For though Shakespeare, like his chronicle sources, foregrounds the capture of the aggressive woman—the duchess is led offstage under guard—he again offers a challenge to the validity of the very emblem of containment that he stages. The ambivalence and unease surounding Shakespeare's handling of Eleanor's containment suggests that traditional ways of handling "the unruly woman," particularly one of high rank, had become problematic in Elizabethan England with a woman on the throne.

In the patriarchal model, concisely illustrated by John Knox's attack on female rule in 1558, the containment of the unruly woman is essential to the well-being of the state. Knox in fact authorizes his seditious call for rebellion against the monarch by citing her unruliness: "They oght to remove frome honor and authoritie that monstre in nature: So call I a woman cled in the habit of man, yea, a woman against nature reigning above man."[45] If the female ruler is, as Knox believes, "the subversion of good order, of all equitie and justice," then removing her from office should bring a restoration of order and justice. With the arrest of Eleanor, however, Shakespeare significantly disrupts this familiar paradigm in a move that might be more in tune with the ruling ideology of the Elizabethan state: for in *2 Henry VI* the containment of Eleanor leads not to the restoration of order in the state but rather to its collapse. Revising the facts and the chronology of his sources, Shakespeare directly links Gloucester's death with his wife's fall, and without the good Duke Humphrey to protect the nation, civil strife soon breaks out.

Shakespeare further disrupts traditional models of power by casting the enemies of the witch-traitor as enemies of the monarchy. The familiar patriarchal model tended to glorify the hero who succeeded in restoring order to the state. *Newes from Scotland*, for example, concludes by pointing out to its readers that James VI's struggle with demonic forces gives proof of the divine sanction of his reign: "And trulie the whole scope of this treatise dooth so plainely laie open the wonderfull prouidence of the Almightie."[46] That Shakespeare should cast the conspiring York as the "hero" who triumphs over the subversive female, a choice that involved rewriting chronicle history, calls into question the model of power that derives its authority from a myth of patriarchal domination. In Shakespeare's version of English history, the unruly female is contained not by a divinely sanctioned hero nor by a civilized code of law, but by the forces of anarchy, by York and Winchester who operate outside the law. Despite York's mouthing concern for "the King and commonweal" (1.4.43) as he makes the arrest, the capture of the witch-traitor in *2 Henry VI* is anything but a patriotic act. In *2 Henry VI*, I suggest, Shakespeare contests the universal truth of the patriarchal paradigm by dramatizing a specific, historic case in which "containment" ironically not only fails to preserve the state but is in fact used to subvert it.

Yet while the play exposes the virago-witch-traitor as a seditious construct, manipulated to undermine the state, one might argue that it nonetheless offers a critique of the politically ambitious woman. Does Shakespeare have it both ways, we may ask, on the one hand reinforcing patriarchal assumptions by casting Eleanor's ambitions as unnatural and dangerous, but on the other pulling back from the seditious implications of a universal equation between female aggression and treason? In this regard, Shakespeare's handling of Eleanor's final moments on stage may be telling. The scene of Eleanor's open penance in the London streets lends itself to a sympathetic treatment. Her rich robes exchanged for a white sheet, the duchess here resembles not the unruly female but another Renaissance stereotype, that of the patient, long-suffering heroine. The situation invites us to pity the fallen woman and to regard her public disgrace, along with her husband, with "tear-stain'd eyes" (2.4.16). But though the duchess may look the penitent with her sheet and taper, she refuses, in the end, to take her place as the silently suffering female. Instead, she chides her husband for his passivity, making him a party to her disgrace, and warns him to beware of York, the cardinal, and Suffolk. That the duchess here goes too far in her accusations is underscored by her husband's gentle censure—"thy greatest help is quiet" (67)—a remark that prompted Samuel Johnson to conclude that "the poet has not endeavoured to raise much compassion for the duchess, who indeed suffers but what she had deserved."[47]

Does Shakespeare thus accommodate patriarchal ideology for the

Elizabethan stage, reworking the familiar story of Eleanor Cobham so as to side-step potentially seditious issues evoked by a display of female power without completely overturning traditional assumptions about women, power, and national order? To be sure, the play weakens the "ideological chain" that would demonize all powerful women, but it nonetheless raises the specter of the dominant female and suggests that while she may not always be a witch, her unnatural involvement in politics does in the end pose a danger to the state and may be exploited by the crown's enemies. While refashioning England's patriarchal history for the Elizabethan stage, Shakespeare's strategies of "accommodation" give shape to a social and political unease not uncharacteristic of the 1590s, a decade in which court factionalism was on the rise, anxieties about the succession began to surface once again, and the nation faced serious economic and military problems. But whether *2 Henry VI* in fact intervenes in particular local debates, Shakespeare's staging of English history clearly reminds his audience of the problems implicit in representation and authority as his revisions work again and again to question the authority of chronicle "fact" and so to foreground the instabilities and pressures intersecting and giving shape to the play of history.

Notes

I would like to thank Molly Rothenberg and J. L. Simmons for their comments on earlier drafts of this essay.

1. For discussions of the ideological basis of witchcraft accusations, see Christina Larner, *Witchcraft and Religion: The Politics of Popular Belief* (Blackwell, 1984), who defines the stereotypical witch as "an independent adult woman who does not conform to the male idea of proper female behaviour" (84); Catherine Belsey, *The Subject of Tragedy: Identity and Difference in Renaissance Drama* (London: Methuen, 1985), 185–91; and Peter Stallybrass, "*Macbeth* and Witchcraft," *Focus on "Macbeth,"* ed. John Russell Brown (London: Routledge & Kegan Paul, 1982), 189–209.

2. All quotations from *2 Henry VI* are from *The Riverside Shakespeare*, ed. G. Blakemore Evans (Boston: Houghton Mifflin, 1974).

3. Annabel Patterson, *Shakespeare and the Popular Voice* (London: Blackwell, 1989), 39.

4. *2 Henry VI* itself has received little critical attention and the figure of Eleanor even less. Recent studies of the history plays that do take up questions of gender have noted the misogynistic resonance of the association between Eleanor's ambition and the charges of witchcraft and treason, but none have considerd the extent to which the play destabilizes the authority of this stereotype: see Barbara Hodgdon, *The End Crowns All: Closure and Contradiction in Shakespeare's History* (Princeton: Princeton University Press, 1991), 61; Phyllis Rackin, *Stages of*

History; Shakespeare's English Chronicles (Ithaca: Cornell University Press, 1990), 173–74n; and Irene G. Dash, *Wooing, Wedding, and Power: Women in Shakespeare's Plays* (New York: Columbia University Press, 1981), 170–74.

5. Jonathan Dollimore, "Introduction: Shakespeare, Cultural Materialism and the New Historicism," *Political Shakespeare: New Essays in Cultural Materialism*, ed. Dollimore and Alan Sinfield (Ithaca: Cornell University Press, 1985), and Louis A. Montrose, "Professing the Renaissance: The Poetics and Politics of Culture," *The New Historicism*, ed. H. Aram Veeser (New York: Routledge, Chapman and Hall, 1989), both offer critiques of the subversion-containment debate generated by recent work in Shakespeare and Renaissance studies.

6. Dollimore, "Introduction," 11.

7. Ralph A. Griffiths, "The Trial of Eleanor Cobham: An Episode in the Fall of Duke Humphrey of Gloucester," *Bulletin of the John Rylands Library* 51 (1969): 381.

8. "Lament of the Duchess of Gloucester," *Political Poems and Songs Relating to English History*, vol. 2, ed. Thomas Wright (1861; Krause, 1965), 206.

9. According to Keith Thomas, *Religion and the Decline of Magic* (New York: Scribner's, 1971), the cases of Roger Bolingbroke and Margery Jourdemain are among the six recorded instances of executions for witchcraft in England between the time of the Norman conquest and Reformation (454n).

10. A. R. Myers, "The Captivity of a Royal Witch: The Household Accounts of Queen Joan of Navarre, 1419–21," *Bulletin of the John Rylands Library* 24 (1940): 263–84.

11. Griffiths, "Trial," 399; see also S. B. Chrimes and A. L. Brown, eds., *Select Documents of English Constitutional History, 1307–1485* (New York: Barnes & Noble, 1961) 276–77.

12. *An English Chronicle*, Camden Society Publications, no. 64, ed. John Silvester Davies (London: Camden Society, 1856), 60.

13. *Chronicle of the Grey Friars*, ed. J. G. Nichols (London: Camden Society, 1852), 18–20.

14. *English Chronicle* 56–57.

15. "Lament," 205–8.

16. Robert Fabyan, *The New Chronicles of England and France*, ed. H. Ellis (London: 1811), 614. Geoffrey Bullough, *Narrative and Dramatic Sources of Shakespeare*, vol. 3 (London: Routledge & Kegan Paul, 1960), places Fabyan's chronicle in the tradition of the London chronicles whose details "often reveal the City's attitude to great personages, e.g. they favour Humphrey of Gloucester and are hostile to Richard III" (5).

17. Edward Hall, *The Union of the Two Noble and Illustre Famelies of Lancastre and Yorke* (1548), ed. H. Ellis (London: 1809), 202. Contractions have been expanded silently in all quotations from Hall.

18. Bullough, *Narrative, 11"*.

19. *The Acts and Monuments of John Foxe*, vol. 3 (New York: AMS, 1965), 704.

20. Ibid., 707.

21. Ibid., 708.

22. Ibid., 711.

23. Robert Weimann, "Bifold Authority in Shakespeare's Theatre," *Shakespeare Quarterly* 39 (1988): 414.

24. M. M. Reese, *The Cease of Majesty: A Study of Shakespeare's History Plays* (London: Edward Arnold, 1961), 185, notes the similarities between this scene (1.2.1–16, 61–67) and *Macbeth* (1.5.16–31).

25. Hall, *Union*, 202.

26. For variants, see Andrew Cairncross, ed. *The Second Part of King Henry VI*, The Arden Shakespeare (1957; London: Methuen, 1985), 186–87; Cairncross points to the differences between F and Q in the treatment of Eleanor in this scene to support his claim that variants in F are the result of the political censorship of Q (xxvi–xxvii).

27. Hall, *Union*, 202.

28. Thomas, *Religion*, writes that the 1563 witchcraft statute tended to blur distinctions in degree by making it a felony "to invoke *evil* spirits for any purpose whatsoever" (442). The same act, however, considered witchcraft a capital offense only if it actually took a human life. Larner, *Witchcraft*, suggests that the populace did not automatically accept the 1563 definitions of witchcraft, citing the case of Barbara Napier in Scotland in 1591: "One of the reasons . . . why the jury were reluctant to convict was that the clause in the 1563 Act which imposed death merely for consulting witches had never before been enforced and that, therefore, it was felt hard to execute her" (12).

29. Robert Rentoul Reed, Jr., *The Occult on the Tudor and Stuart Stage* (Boston: Christopher, 1965), 117, argues for dramatic reasons governing Shakespeare's substitution.

30. Charles Tyler Prouty, "Some Observations on Shakespeare's Sources," *Shakespeare Jahrbuch* (Heidelberg), 96 (1960): 73. For a discussion of the Pool case, see George Lyman Kittredge, *Witchcraft in Old and New England* (Cambridge: Harvard University Press, 1929), 260–61.

31. Both Jonson and Mendoza are cited in Kittredge, *Witchcraft*, 88; Kittredge devotes a chapter to "Image magic and the like" and gives a full account of threats against Elizabeth, 87–90.

32. Kittredge, *Witchcraft*, 89. For a fuller account, see *Gentleman's Magazine*, 209 (October 1860): 380–85.

33. Larner, *Witchcraft and Religion* , 9. See also *Daemonologie (1597)*, ed. G. B. Harrison (New York: Barnes & Noble, 1966), 45–46 for King James's description of how witches can take lives "by rosting of the Pictures" of wax over a fire.

34. For discussions of the Scottish treason-witchcraft trials, see Larner, *Witchcraft and Religion*, 3–22 and Helen Stafford, "Notes on Scottish Witchcraft Cases, 1590–91," *Essays in Honor of Conyers Read*, ed. Norton Downs (Chicago: University of Chicago Press, 1953).

35. Larner, *Witchcraft and Religion*, 10.

36. Stafford, "Notes," 105.

37. Ibid., 117.

38. Ibid., 107.

39. G. B. Harrison, ed. *King James the First: Daemonologie (1597), Newes from Scotland (1591)* (New York: Barnes & Noble, 1966), 29.

40. Larner, *Witchcraft and Religion*, 13–14.

41. Stafford, "Notes," 108.

42. Lily B. Campbell, "Humphrey Duke of Gloucester and Elianor Cobham His Wife in the *Mirror for Magistrates*," *Huntington Library Bulletin* 5: 144–48.

43. Ibid., 148.

44. Bullough writes that "there seems no reason to suppose that Shakespeare was indebted to *A Mirror for Magistrates* in this play" (92).

45. John Knox, *The First Blast of the Trumpet against the Monstruous Regiment of Women* (1558), *The Works of John Knox*, ed. David Laing (1855; New York: AMS, 1966), 416.

46. Harrison, *Newes*, 29.

47. Johnson's "gloss" on 2.4.67 is cited in Cairncross, *Second Part*, 60.

"O Me, the Word Choose!": Female Voice and Catechetical Ritual in *The Two Gentlemen of Verona* and *The Merchant of Venice*

LORI SCHROEDER HASLEM

WHENEVER WOMEN MEET privately and talk, says Simone de Beauvoir in *The Second Sex,* they construct a "counter-universe" which privileges female values not normally accorded a place within a patriarchal-valued universe.[1] To explain the purpose of such private conferences, de Beauvoir borrows a metaphor from the theater. "Confronting man," she says, "woman is always play-acting," but "with other women, a woman is behind the scenes . . ., polishing her equipment . . ., getting her costume together, preparing her make-up . . . before making her entrance on the stage."[2] And yet, when de Beauvoir's metaphor of women being behind the scenes is counterbalanced with her notion of a privately empowered female universe, a considerable paradox emerges, a paradox which de Beauvoir herself acknowledges.[3] For if the understanding among the conferring women themselves is that they are always and eventually to reject female-dictated values in favor of adopting the usual female roles of a patriarchal drama, then the female "counter-universe" really operates more as a "sub-universe," and what passes for female counteraction is ultimately revealed as an illusion of counteraction.

In a related way, Dale M. Bauer studies ways in which female values are both voiced and silenced in several nineteenth-century American novels, but does so by involving Bakhtinian concepts. Thus instead of identifying an apparent paradox whereby women both counteract and support the male realm, Bauer considers

122

whether female voices in these novels participate in what Bakhtin calls a truly open, dialogic community—that is, one in which both dominant and countercultures speak out with legitimate and never fully reconcilable voices—or to a closed, monologic community stamped with final ideological consensus.[4] Bauer contends that in literary works which use feminist dialogic—even those which close with "typically romantic resolutions"—the women in the text

> assert their otherness not by surrendering, but by forcing their language into the context/contest of the dominant languages. That is, not by erasing but by highlighting their otherness can they do battle with patriarchal codes.[5]

Bauer's and de Beauvoir's observations both raise the question of what women in a patriarchal world—fictional or real—truly gain by asserting their values, whether privately (in the margins) or publicly during a period of Bakhtinian "carnival."[6] Any answer, as they both suggest, hinges on what becomes of the countervalued female voice upon closure, upon a return to a patriarchal community or with the schematic romantic closure of much early literature. But if one considers de Beauvoir's point alongside Bauer's, the matter begins to sound rather like the proverbial dilemma of the cup being half empty or half full. When closure involves initially disruptive female values nevertheless giving way to male values, has the disruption been erased or highlighted? Has female counteraction "behind the scenes" been a true counteraction or an illusion of counteraction?

To explore such questions further I want to ground them in a couple of Shakespeare's romantic comedies where the achievement of harmonious, monologic closure is ostensibly central. In *Two Gentlemen of Verona*, I will argue, the private talk of female characters operates not only dramaturgically as a compelling illusion of counteraction to the patriarchal-valued world of the plays but also ideologically as an occasion for exorcising female values and thereby gaining romantic closure. With *Merchant of Venice*, I will contend, the cup is instead half full: while the main of the play works dramaturgically toward a surrender of the female counteractive realm, in act 5 Shakespeare also reasserts and revalues the female voice and thus allows for a dialogical resonance not possible at the close of *Two Gentlemen*. In other words, as Bauer might put it, female values ultimately defer to male values at the romantic close of each play, but Shakespeare comes closer to highlighting female "otherness" in *Merchant* and to erasing it in *Two Gentlemen.*

Much of the work completed on female friendship and communication in Shakespeare does indeed center on the "otherness" of the female world of the play. Juliet Dusinberre argues that not only Shakespearean but all Elizabethan drama is largely about "excit[ing] interest in what a woman's conscience would dictate to her if she were freed from subjection to the male conscience."[7] But while Dusinberre maintains that in Shakespeare this other, female conscience is placed largely with heroines who suffer tragic "isolation" and "solitary sorrow,"[8] other feminist scholars—noting not only the existence of female communicative networks within the plays but also the complicity of the bond that such communication and friendship create—have stressed that Shakespeare's heroines are anything but isolated. Carolyn Asp points to a "conspiracy of women" that tends to "organize itself around female desire."[9] Carol Thomas Neely argues for the importance of the friendship between women that "dominates" the final scene of *Othello.*[10] And Carole McKewin, who examines numerous plays where women converse privately, draws upon de Beauvoir to describe the realm of female discourse as a place where "women together can express their own perceptions and identities, comment on masculine society, and gather strength and engage in reconnaissance to act in it."[11]

In broaching the matter of what female complicity does or does not gain for certain Shakespearean women, I will begin by focusing on a single and recurrent form of female conversation in the plays, namely, a ritualized catechetical comparison of men as potential lovers and/or husbands. Throughout Shakespeare's plays women frequently enact versions of the ritual when they discuss and debate the relative worth of specific men. Just after Emilia sharply criticizes Othello to Desdemona, the two women join in praising the virtues of Lodovico. The Nurse tells Juliet that Romeo is a "dishclout" compared to Paris. The ladies of *Love's Labor's Lost* ridicule the comparative worth of each suitor's love letter. Cleopatra's "girls" protest to her that her former lover Caesar is at least as worthy and valiant as Antony. And act 2 of *The Taming of the Shrew*—presenting a more sadistic twist on such moments of female bonding—opens with Kate binding Bianca's hands and demanding that she tell "Of all thy suitors . . . / Whom thou lov'st best" (2.1.i.9).[12] But when the catechetical ritual is played out to its fullest—as it is in *Two Gentlemen of Verona* and *Merchant of Venice*—it involves one woman naming a series of men while the other woman responds to each in turn with an evaluation. In its fullest form, the ritual culminates with the women agreeing upon and selecting the choicest man available to the heroine, and I call the ritual "catechetical" not only because of its question-and-answerlike format but also because the whole of the ritual implies that the man to be selected has somehow been predetermined, pre-sanctioned by the women. As during the saying of catechism, the ladies' answers come off as rather routine, as though the ritualized process of naming the selected man is more central than is an actual debate over the merits of several men.

That variations of the ritual occur with some regularity in Shakespeare is perhaps of sociohistorical as well as literary significance. In *Friendship and Literature: Spirit and Form*, Ronald Sharp argues that rituals are basic to all friendships and that especially among women exchanges of secrets and other intimate matters are "highly ritualized and conventionalized activities."[13] It is not really surprising, then, that female characters in Shakespeare—and in other later English Renaissance drama—frequently talk together about men and sex. Still, as Linda Woodbridge warns, the women of the drama are indeed literary depictions and so we cannot know how accurately they reflect the behavior of actual women. Perhaps, as Diane Bornstein says of the courtesy books of the Middle Ages and as Woodbridge says of later drama, the frequency with which women are depicted as gossiping together is but evidence of men's (and perhaps especially the male authors') fears—and fancies—that women talk almost exclusively about men when outside of their company.[14]

Whether or not Shakespeare is projecting subconscious fears and fancies with these ritualized female exchanges, his conscious aim probably goes beyond a desire to replicate faithfully the private discussions of female contemporaries. For the usual position of such talk in the plays demonstrates Shakespeare's understanding of the dramaturgical use (especially in the comedies) of having two or more women in league against whatever obstacles—whether psychological or social—impede one or more of the women involved.[15] Shakespeare put the private female alliance to particular dramaturgical use by implementing a well-worn theatrical trope (or "theatergram," as Louise George Clubb has termed it) that dates back to Roman comedy: the young woman in love paired with a female confidante, encourager, and/or messenger.[16] In *As You Like It*, Rosalind's female confidante is a cousin. But more frequently Shakespeare's women have maids or waiting-women for confidantes, as with Julia and Lucetta (*Two Gentlemen of Verona*), Portia and Nerissa (*Merchant of Venice*), Desdemona and Emilia (*Othello*) Juliet and the Nurse (*Romeo and Juliet*), Hermione and Paulina (*Winter's Tale*). Sometimes the maids offer actual assistance in helping their ladies to their lovers (as does Juliet's Nurse), but more often the maids offer the kind of psychological and emotional support found in de Beauvoir's notion of counteruniverse.

In both *Two Gentlemen of Verona* and *Merchant of Venice* such a counteruniverse is suggestively constructed by the catechetical ritual's reversal of more traditional, patriarchal literary structures—found often, for example, in fairy tales—in which the woman is the chosen and not the chooser, the object rather than the subject. Yet within larger structures operating in these plays, I will argue, such choice is only *temporarily* privileged, thus seeming to credit female choice without actually legitimizing it. The female communicative realm is posited as one which must be passed through successfully (i.e., to the satisfaction of the women involved) before a love relationship betwen the hero and heroine can be achieved in the play at large. But a key movement toward romantic closure in each play also involves the heroine's eventual dropping of the pretended empowerment she experienced during private talk with her waiting-woman.

Ostensibly, it is during the catechetical ritual in act 1 of *Two Gentlemen* that Julia discovers for herself that she has feelings for Proteus, feelings which her maid first helps to illuminate and then encourages. Julia initiates the ritual: "But say, Lucetta, now we are alone, / Wouldst thou then counsel me to fall in love?" (1–2). Lucetta seems willing enough to take part in the exchange, and so they proceed:

> *Jul.* Of all the fair resort of gentlemen
> That every day with parle encounter me,
> In thy opinion which is worthiest love?
>   *Luc.* Please you repeat their names, I'll show my mind
> According to my shallow simple skill.

(1.2.4–8)

Julia then lists the names—the fair Sir Eglamour, the rich Mercatio, the gentle Proteus—and Lucetta obligingly recounts in turn each man's virtues and failings. When Julia asks Lucetta about her hesitation to criticize Proteus along with the others, the maid answers simply that she thinks Proteus is best because he seems to love Julia best. All of this talk—and some intervening witty stichomythia between the two ladies—culminates in Lucetta's revelation that she has all along carried a love note for Julia from Proteus. Rather unexpectedly, Julia turns quite testy, and the catechetical ritual abruptly ends as Lucetta—at Julia's angry behest—departs with the letter.

The rest of the scene presents a Julia torn between an impulse to behave like the properly scornful courtly mistress (as Silvia does elsewhere in the play) and an impulse to admit and embrace her own inclinations toward Proteus. Julia's struggle between these two impulses is figured outwardly in her ambivalent behavior toward Lucetta, who encourages her to entertain advances from Proteus. One moment Julia welcomes Lucetta's information and advice; the next she chides the maid for impertinence. As such, the tenuous nature of their communicative bond becomes itself the focus of the scene and acts as a kind of gauge for Julia's vacillating feelings not only toward Proteus specifically but also toward the more abstract question of what role she as a woman ought to play in a love relationship.[17] In varying her responses to Lucetta, Julia in effect tries on the two roles she might play before Proteus: should she be cold and disdainful or warm and aggressive? No sooner has Lucetta returned and have the two women engaged in more witticisms regarding the probable content of the letter than Julia grows testy once again. Before it is over, Julia again dismisses her maid, shreds the letter, and throws it to the wind—a gesture she regrets almost immediately. Significantly, it is with one impulse that she breaks off communication with Lucetta and more literally breaks up the communication (the letter) from Proteus. Equating the torn communication between the women with Julia's torn feelings regarding Proteus, Shakespeare suggests that it is only by mending her communicative relationship with Lucetta that Julia can gain an understanding of herself and her feelings for Proteus.

As Julia chides herself one more time and begins to gather the torn scraps of the love letter, Lucetta reappears and the two reach a quiet understanding on their way in to dinner. Some directors have closed this scene with the two women together picking up the pieces of the shredded letter, a gesture which underscores the idea that by reconstructing the communication from Proteus Julia simultaneously refortifies her bond with Lucetta and reconciles her former ambivalence toward how to play her role with Proteus.[18] With this reconciliation, Lucetta is transformed from a perceived antagonist into the very "table wherein all my thoughts / Are visibly character'd and engrav'd" (2.7.3–4). For her part, Julia gains a private, female-dictated sanction to pursue her relationship with Proteus in an unconventional, noncourtly way—by disguising herself as a page and undertaking a journey to Proteus.

If, as Carole McKewin says, Shakespeare's women talk together as a way of gathering strength to oppose the strictures of identity placed on them by masculine society, then surely Julia—with Lucetta's help—is initially quite successful in opposing the rules of social decorum and female identity which govern the world of the play. For when Julia dresses up like a page, codpiece and all, she seems once and for all to be throwing off the role of the cold, disdainful courtly mistress, a role which the two gentlemen clearly expect their ladies to play. Apparently, then, the scene involving catechetical ritual has empowered Julia not only to choose her lover but also to respond to him in the way that *she* deems suitable.

But at this point in the play we are still in the realm of private female choice, and the authority Julia gains when conversing privately with Lucetta is subsequently shown to be only an illusion of such authority. As Julia moves out of the female into the male-dominated realm of discourse, male values—and thus male choices—increasingly hold sway. Warning Julia that disguising herself as a page might not have the desired effect on Proteus ("I fear me he will scarce be pleas'd withal" [2.6.67]), Lucetta reminds us that women's bold private resolutions are customarily downplayed when the women move into and perform in the ostensibly more important public realm. But Julia has been too emboldened by her exchanges with Lucetta to fear that her audience—her Proteus— might not receive her well in whatever form she has decided to appear. Having once left Lucetta behind, though, Julia both symbolically and actually leaves behind her license of authority. For when she arrives in Milan only to discover that Proteus has quite abruptly shifted loyalties to Silvia, it is made stingingly clear to Julia that her choice in Proteus depends entirely on his continuing his choice in her. Ironically, then, Julia's private choice to play an aggressive role precipitates her having to play a passive role, to work behind the scenes in her disguise as the page Sebastian. In this state of "active passivity," as Anthony Lewis calls it, Julia prefigures other Shakespearean heroines who are "outwardly active and yet harbor within a stultifying vision of themselves as passive, or dead, buried beneath male clothes and frozen in time."[19] As involved in the plot as Julia is throughout the rest of the play, she can in fact do little more than wait and hope to be chosen—indeed, rechosen—by Proteus in the end.

That Julia is reduced from subject to object, from being the chooser (in the private, female realm) to be the chosen (in the male realm) becomes most painfully obvious at the problematic close of the play, whereupon Valentine—wanting to demonstrate his forgiveness of Proteus's overtures toward and attempted rape of Silvia—offers up Silvia, trophylike, to prove his sincerity to Proteus. At this moment, both Julia (still disguised) and Silvia are utterly powerless. It is as though they are indeed behind the scenes—with no equipment left to polish—observing the male-centered drama in which they play no active part.

Thus disempowered, Julia swoons. And it is only at this significant moment, when Julia's very body emblematizes the degree to which her earlier insistence on self-assertiveness has collapsed, that the love relationship with Proteus becomes possible. It becomes possible precisely because the swoon, as Catherine Belsey puts it, "reaffirms [Julia's] femininity."[20] As she falls back into her proper position as object, Julia can only wait for Proteus to repent of his shabby behavior and choose her once again. Indeed, both she and Silvia are noticeably quiet in the play's final moments, a quietness which emphasizes how far we have moved from a legitimization of the saucy, impertinent voice of Lucetta. The female communicative bond is in effect discarded, erased, en route to achieving the male-female love relationship, an "achievement" which is marked by Julia's loss of the authority she exercised during the earlier female conversation. Thus while the play seems to privilege female choice in the earlier acts—in the scene of catechetical ritual between Julia and Lucetta and in Julia's decision to undertake a solitary journey with a new-fashioned identity—the whole of the play suggests that female choice gives way inevitably to male choice.

Seemingly at the center of many of Shakespeare's romantic comedies is the necessary transformation of the hero: a witty, wise, and devoted heroine must educate her erring lover on the nature of true love and its place in the achievement of community.[21] The scheme which I have just outlined, however, suggests, that there is perhaps likewise an education for some of the comedic heroines whom Julia prefigures (Viola, Rosalind, Portia). The young lady must learn that playing at unconventionality is acceptable only insofar as she agrees that there will be an eventual return to patriarchal norms.[22] Within such a design, female autonomy becomes but a temporarily granted frivolity. As Dale Bauer, drawing on Foucault and others, spells out so lucidly,

> Inclusion [in a community] requires playing by the rules of the commu-
> nity, although rejecting the rules can also be part of the game; resistance
> can be appropriated . . ., depending on whether that resistance can be
> manipulated or reabsorbed into community.[23]

And surely Julia's resistance to conventional authority is appropriated by and reabsorbed into the community in just such a way.

I want now to consider whether Portia's various resistances to
patriarchal norms in *Merchant of Venice* are as fully reabsorbed
into the play's emerging community as Julia's are. What I will suggest is that in *Merchant* there is also a dramaturgically oriented
surrender of female values but that because Shakespeare invests
Portia with a wilier and more enduring form of Julia's resistance
and because he reasserts the private female communicative bond
in the final scene of the play, female values in the end continue to
do dialogic battle with patriarchal codes.

Once again it is quite early in the play (act 1, scene 2) that the
catechetical ritual between the lady and her waiting-woman (here
a gentlewoman) appears. As with Julia and Lucetta's communication in *Two Gentlemen*, Portia and Nerissa's talk apparently helps
to resolve the heroine's ambivalent feelings toward the role she as
a woman can play in the patriarchal society of the play. Where Julia
at first struggles with the courtly expectation that she spurn all her
suitors, Portia struggles with the marital determination left by her
father, namely, that she must marry the first man to choose the one
casket (out of three—gold, silver, lead) in which the father has
placed his daughter's picture.

The scene of female catechetical ritual opens with Portia com-
plaining of world-weariness. Nerissa chides her lady for being sad
when there is much in which to rejoice, but Portia protests that—
being in a position where she may exercise no choice—she has
good reason for sadness:

> O me, the word choose! I may neither choose who I would,
> nor refuse who I dislike; so is the will of a living daughter
> curb'd by the will of a dead father. Is it not hard, Nerissa,
> that I cannot choose one, nor refuse none?
>
> (1.2.22–26)

In the scene of catechetical ritual that follows, once again the form
rather than the content of the communication is foregrounded. Although the scene between Julia and Lucetta works through ruptures

in communication toward a bond of complicity, the scene between Portia and Nerissa opens with an established bond of complicity which allows the two women to behave privately as they could not publicly—unless, of course, they were disguised as men. In short, Nerissa and Portia are rather literally polishing equipment behind the scenes, rehearsing the process of hearing, considering, and judging that later in the play—when they are indeed disguised as men—they will be able to perform.

Portia and Nerissa are established confidantes from the start of the scene, but because Nerissa takes up the defense of Portia's dead father's edict—"Your father was ever virtuous, and holy men at their death have good inspirations" (27–28)—the waiting-woman does become a kind of antagonist against whom Portia can realize her frustrations. "Over-naming" the several suitors—the Neapolitan prince, the County Palentine, the French lord, the young baron of England, the Scottish lord, and the young German of royal lineage— Nerissa becomes a sounding board for Portia's discontent. Each of these suitors Portia rejects in turn, for reasons ranging from the Neapolitan's penchant for talking about his horse to the German's habitual drunkenness. Nerissa culminates the list by naming "a Venetian, a scholar, and a soldier"—Bassanio (113). Just as Lucetta spoke in favor of Proteus to Julia, so Nerissa boldly recommends Bassanio to Portia—"He, of all the men that ever my foolish eyes look'd upon, was the best deserving a fair lady" (117–19). But quite unlike Julia, Portia concurs immediately with her waiting-woman's opinion of Bassanio: "I remember him worthy of thy praise" (120). Thus a scene which begins with Portia lamenting her lack of choice turns into one in which Portia's choice—sanctioned by Nerissa—is the only determining factor. Nerissa drops her role as pseudo-antagonist and once again becomes confidante and advisor. The special communicative relationship with Nerissa has allowed Portia to reverse her situation psychologically within the patriarchal-governed world in which she feels caught. And of course Portia's emergence as an astute judge of her suitors antici- pates her subsequent wisdom in judging.

Again, the instance of catechetical ritual seems to subvert patri- archal values by suggesting that the important first step toward a realization of the Bassanio-Portia relationship is arriving at the private female sanction of Bassanio. However, Portia's choosing of Bassanio is of no real consequence. It only seems to be. In fact, the suggestion is that by channeling the expression of her desire into the private catechetical ritual Portia has somehow purged herself

of the need to choose in actuality. For throughout the course of act
2, she stands by submissively as each man in a virtual parade of
suitors chooses from the caskets. She must defer to male choice first
by obeying her father's edict and then by trusting to the individual
intellect and instincts of any qualified man who wants even to try
to choose the right casket. Of course the irony of surrendering all
power of choice to those whom Portia considers to be her intellectual inferiors is not lost on her:

> O, these deliberate fools, when they do choose,
> They have the wisdom by their wit to lose.
>
> (2.9.80–81)

But when Bassanio chooses the leaden casket, Portia's language
softens. She rewards his success by giving him a ring and by committing her "gentle spirit" to be "directed" by him, her new lord,
governor, and king (3.2.163–65). One must not overlook, moreover,
that Bassanio's maintenance of the ring is to be the emblem of *his*
continued choice in Portia.

So here, as in *Two Gentlemen*, the dramaturgical position of the
catechetical ritual suggests that when the female characters privately exercise choice they are *only* playing roles—or else are only
rehearsing for playing roles—which are quite at odds with those
they must play later in the "real" show before the men. That is,
both Julia and Portia, for all their behind-the-scenes rehearsals of
unconventionality, end up playing a more conventional female role.
With Julia, the illusion of female authority is shattered almost as
soon as she leaves the world of private female talk; even her male
disguise gains her little. With Portia, who brings her female confidante with her on her journey to Venice and includes her in the
playacting, the illusion lasts much longer. Portia's authority is ostensibly achieved privately with Nerissa but also publicly when
the two disguise as men. After all, when undercover as judge and
clerk, Portia and Nerissa not only decide the dispute between Shy-
lock and Antonio but also manage to exact the rings from Bassanio
and Gratiano.

And yet even this feat shows not that Portia has achieved any real
authority but rather that she has gained control over the emblem of
Bassanio's choice in her. Portia can manipulate Bassanio's power
to choose—or rather, she can seem to manipulate his power to
choose by shifting ownership of the ring—but that is not the same
thing as gaining such power for herself. Moreover, as Catherine

Belsey says of the court scene, Portia is only "invested with authority . . . on the condition that she changes her clothes and speaks
with the voice of a man."[24] That female authority is validated only
when it is exercised privately with other women or publicly in
male disguise also makes clear that *unqualified* public female authority is not a viable option in the world of the play. Accordingly,
by the end of act 4 of *Merchant*, where the disguised Portia riddlingly asks Bassanio, "I pray you know me when we meet again"
(4.2.419), one senses that the inevitable uncloaking of Portia
will bring an even fuller acknowledgment of her relinquished
autonomy.

A main ideological thrust in both *Two Gentlemen* and *Merchant*,
then, is that in a happily romantic world it is somehow "safe" for
women to be empowered with choice when conversing privately
or to play at making choices when publicly disguised as men so
long as their pretenses of authority are ultimately made known and
rejected. In fact, these manifestations of pretended female choice
are presented as valuable because they engage the heroines in the
processs of learning—through role-playing—that women may publicly perform only certain roles and may only privately indulge
certain desires.[25] Marianne Novy has noted that when the former
playacting of female characters is revealed at the end of the comedies "no shadow falls on the celebration" whereas the exposure of
female pretense tends to prompt great anxiety in the tragedies.[26] I
suggest that this is true of *Two Gentlemen* and *Merchant* exactly
because the women's dropping of male roles symbolizes the volun-
tary (in the case of Portia) or constitutionally unavoidable (in the
case of Julia) surrender of female claims to unconventional, male-
centered forms of power. Although the plays end with obvious emphasis on what the hero has learned, there also is an unspoken
emphasis on and celebration of what the heroine has learned,
namely, that in some sense she either wants or needs to drop the
pretense of being other then conventionally "female."

To say Shakespeare acknowledges that unqualified female choice
is not a viable option in the romantic world of each of these plays,
however, is not to say that Shakespeare himself fully endorses such
an outlook. The question must be, as Erickson puts it, how "heavily
invested" Shakespeare is in the "patriarchal solution of his characters," how ironic and critical his stance is toward the purportedly
happy ending.[27] Indeed, I have been tracing the ways in which Julia
and Portia similarly come to put away disruptive desires to choose
for themselves, but in view of what happens in act 5 of *Merchant*,

one can by no means level Shakespeare's treatment of these two heroines. In a significant dramaturgical way, Portia toward the end "dwindles into a wife," to appropriate Belsey's turn of phrase.[28] But it is also in act 5—during what Belsey elsewhere calls "a coda to the main plot"—that Shakespeare reasserts the female voice and reprivileges the private female communicative bond he established in act 1.[29] With the play's final scene, female values seemingly about to be erased are instead highlighted and given legitimate status in the ongoing dialogics of the play.

It is hard to miss Shakespeare's great emphasis on musical harmony—including the mythical music of the spheres—in the play's final scene, and the metaphor seems naturally to refer to the resolution of the love relationships.[30] And yet there are two very different ways to construe the condition of harmony, both of which inform the play's final scene. While on the one hand harmony may be said to constitute a whole, a single blending of multiple parts, on the other hand harmony is its parts, a correspondence between multiple entities, a nexus of relationships. And in the final scene of Merchant, I maintain, the juxtaposition of these two ways of hearing harmony attaches metaphorically to the dilemma of female values being either erased or highlighted. As such, the dilemma becomes whether in the end the female "voice" sounds as a distinguishable entity—a distinct other—or whether it is utterly subsumed by the whole of the romanticized close.

To describe harmony as a never fully blended relationship among multiple voices is in a sense also to articulate Bakhtinian literary theory. In fact, Bakhtin uses the lyrical metaphor itself to indicate the "problems" of truly dialogic—indeed polyphonic—literature:

> The image of polyphony and counterpoint . . . points out those new problems which arise when a novel is constructed beyond the boundaries of ordinary monologic unity, just as in music new problems arose when the boundaries of a single voice were exceeded.[31]

For Bakhtin, in dialogic literature individual voices remain disparate even in closure; they are "linked rather then merged."[32] Essentially because of such "linkage," moreover, the meaning of each voice (indeed the meaning of all language) is for Bakhtin unfailingly relational. That is, the meaning of each voiced expression "lies on the borderline between oneself and other."[33] Or, as David Carroll explains it, any two voices "exist, function, and take shape only in their interrelationship, and not on their own, the one apart from the other."[34] Every voice is defined—but also continually re-defined—by its interaction with, its dialogue with, "other" voices.

In the final scene of *Merchant*, Shakespeare first presents such an interrelational view of harmony, or polyphony, when Portia enters and notes at length that all things become significant only in respect to their surroundings. Context, she observes, is all:

> *Por.* Music, hark!
> *Ner.* It is your music, madam, of the house.
> *Por.* Nothing is good, I see, without respect;
> Methinks it sounds much sweeter than by day.
> *Ner.* Silence bestows that virtue on it, madam.
> *Por.* The crow doth sing as sweetly as the lark
> When neither is attended; and I think
> The nightingale, if she should sing by day
> When every goose is cackling, would be thought
> No better a musician than the wren.
> How many things by season season'd are
> To their right praise and true perfection!
>
> (5.1.97–108)

Portia's observation that meaning is determined relationally reca-pitulates the main plot, in which justice and mercy gain meaning in terms of each other. But it also bespeaks her special position as a woman who has several times in the play shifted her own context and has thus shifted the perceived meaning—the perceived au-thoritativeness—of her "voice." She shifts out of a patriarchal con-text when enacting the catechetical ritual with Nerissa; she shifts back into a patriarchal context during the casket scene; she shifts back out of it again when playing Balthazar. Along the way, she has realized how differently "seasoned" she was in Bassanio's eyes (and maybe in her own) as she shifted her context, a realization which prompts her to shift contexts one more time as Bassanio and Gra-tiano return without the rings.

When Portia scolds Bassanio for giving her ring to "some woman" (5.1.208), she enjoys apparent female authority by posing as the wronged wife. In assuming this role, Portia is not necessarily shifting out of a patriarchal context, of course, nor is she necessarily achieving any kind of real authority. For the scold was a negative fixture in early modern misogynistic literature, where abusive words afforded wives only "a semblance of power."[35] A more com-pelling reason for hearing male and female voices as distinguish-able and resilient "others" in the romantic harmony of the final

scene comes when Portia resecures her relationship with Nerissa
and in a sense carries on a private conversation with her right
there in front of the husbands. Portia shifts out of a patriarchal
context at the same time that she remains in it.

The two women communicate with each other mainly by using
double entendre: they swear their marriages will be consummated
only when they see the rings again; they accuse the men of giving
the rings to women; they threaten to go to bed with the judge and
clerk and then admit they already have. And so Portia and Nerissa's
way of communicating in this final scene recalls the earlier catechetical ritual in that once again the two women are asserting an
authority they privately understand they will not publicly achieve.
They know that as soon as the pretense of their feigned accusation
is dropped they will assume less authoritative roles as wives. But
the very fact that in the final moments of the play Shakespeare
highlights private female communication as a powerful and ongoing force suggests that the female voice, that female authority itself,
will continue to assert itself—even when it has to insinuate itself
to do so.

I say "insinuate" because Shakespere implies, somewhat paradoxically, that although the unconventional assertion of female authority is mainly relinquished in the play's final moments, it is not
yet entirely put away—as it surely is put away in the final moments
of *Two Gentlemen*. That is, the stipulation at the end of *Merchant*
remains, as it did with the close of *Two Gentlemen*, that female
choice can only be validated when women are in private or when
they temporarily play at being men. Still, Portia's *in cognito* conversation with Nerissa suggests that the women will not only continue
to work, as de Beauvoir would say, behind the scenes but also that
they will never completely abandon their subversive backstage
work when it is time to perform in the patriarchal drama. That
Portia and Nerissa in this scene talk privately and publicly at the
same time, in fact, demonstrates just how much more verbally skillful—and thus how much more potentially subversive—these conversing women have grown since the earlier catechetical ritual. To
apply de Beauvoir's formulation, the women seem to have finessed
operating backstage and onstage simultaneously.

Thus Shakespeare at least in part casts the achieved harmony
between the men and women as dialogic rather than monologic by
implying that women will keep on talking and subverting. However, the dialogics of the play's close are even more complex than
this. For by the end of the play it is also increasingly difficult to

identify Portia and Nerissa's voices themselves as singularly or exclusively "female," especially as they riddlingly scold their husbands about the rings. That is, as Belsey notes, "the full answer to the riddle of the rings is that Portia has more than one identity."[36] Throughout the play much of Portia's language and behavior indicates that she has all along possessed these multiple identities (some "male," some "female"), but

> her marriage in conjunction with her Venetian journey (and the deferred consummation confirms them as inextricable) invests her with a new kind of polysemy. The equivocations and doubles [sic] entendres of Act 5 celebrate a sexual indeterminacy, which is not in-difference but multiplicity.[37]

Any purportedly seamless romantic closure, then, is also strained by the suggestion that what it is to be male and what it is to be female will itself continue to be contextually determined. Indeed, in view of Portia's record of shifted identities, one has to recall the earlier riddle and wonder whether Bassanio can ever entirely "know" Portia as they meet again and again. At the very point of the play's resolution—conventional in part as it is—it also becomes possible to glimpse romantic harmony as an ongoing set of never fully blended "male" and "female" voices, as a series of dialogic moments which keep shifting the relationship between femininity and masculinity and thus keep shifting the meaning of gender itself in a patriarchal world.[38]

And so one reaches the important final matter of Shakespeare's own stance toward gender issues in these two romantic comedies. Claire McEachern, in a very well-informed essay, eschews the common polarization of Shakespeare as either affirming patriarchy or rejecting it. Because patriarchy is itself not monolithic but "founded in a profound contradiction," she recommends instead a focus on historical shifts and progressions in notions of and responses to gender.[39] For as she points out, not only in Shakespeare but also in Renaissance culture itself,

> the subversive impulse of a play (or a person) is not always re-subjugated to the orthodoxy of power, but is instead an agent of change.[40]

McEachern therefore proposes analyzing Shakespeare "in the act of reading, in his sources, his culture," an approach which would, she contends, "take the measure of Shakespeare's difference from his patriarchal culture in his examination of it."[41] To conclude my arguments on the position of female voices in *Two Gentlemen* and *Merchant*, I wish to unite Bakhtinian thought with McEachern's approach to suggest the value of examining Shakespeare in the act of reading, in his own plays, his culture and especially his own perceptions of that culture. By Shakespeare's "reading" here I mean his engaging in what Bakhtin calls the "great dialogue."[42] That is, according to Bakhtin, it is possible for an author to have a dialogic relationship with his or her own characters, provided that the characters are invested with autonomous consciousness and that these characters' perceptions and the author's own perceptions "participate with equal rights."[43]

I contend that to examine Shakespeare's relationship to these two comedies is to discover an author who is in dialogue with—and whose own perceptions are thus being redefined by—both the patriarchal and the subversively feminist voices of his characters. More precisely, by moving from Shakespeare's representation of private female talk in *Two Gentlemen* to that in *Merchant*, I believe, one can see—or perhaps *hear* is the better verb—Shakespeare initiating such an author-character dialogue. While his dialogue with Julia is less than fully valid by Bakhtinian standards, one cannot but feel that it is in Julia's temporarily assertive voice, in conjunction with Lucetta's, that Shakespeare begins to hear and eventually to converse with the more autonomous voices of Portia and Nerissa. And it is the very initiation of this conversation, I maintain, that serves as the "agent of change" McEachern mentions. For this author-character conversation not only gains a legitimate voice for Portia and Nerissa at the end of an otherwise patriarchal dramatic scheme but also partially redefines for Shakespeare himself—at least for the dialogic moment—the nature and viability of romantic closure itself.

Notes

1. Simone de Beauvoir, *The Second Sex*, ed. and trans. H. M. Parshley (New York: Knopf, 1971), 542.

2. Ibid., 543.

3. De Beauvoir sums up the paradox as follows: "[Women] band together in order to establish a counter-universe, but they always set it up within the frame of the masculine universe. Hence the paradox of their situation: they belong at one and the same time to the male world and to a sphere in which that world is challenged. . . . Their docility must always be matched by a refusal, their refusal by an acceptance" (ibid., 597).

4. Dale M. Bauer, *Feminist Dialogics: A Theory of Failed Community* (Albany:

SUNY Press, 1988), 8–9. Bauer is careful to note that Bakhtin's formulation of dialogism refers to a competition between cultures whereas Bauer herself casts dialogism in gendered terms (10–11). For Bakhtin's explanation of dialogic voices being ultimately unreconcilable, see Mikhail Bakhtin, *The Problems of Dostoevsky's Poetics*, ed. and trans. Caryl Emerson (Minneapolis: University of Minnesota Press, 1984), 26.

5. Bauer, *Feminist Dialogics*, 10.

6. For Bakhtin, literary "carnival"—which is rooted in early modern social practice—is a limited period during which subversive cultures rise up, and thus inevitably speak up, in a revelatory public debunking of dominant strictures. See Mikhail Bakhtin, *Rabelais and His World*, trans. Helene Iswolsky (Cambridge: MIT Press, 1968; Bloomington: Indiana University Press, 1984).

7. Juliet Dusinberre, *Shakespeare and the Nature of Women* (New York: Barnes & Noble, 1976), 93.

8. Ibid.

9. Carolyn Asp, "Subjectivity, Desire, and Female Friendship in *All's Well That Ends Well*," *Literature and Psychology* 32, no. 2 (1986): 60.

10. Carol Thomas Neely, "Women and Men in *Othello*: 'What should such a fool / Do with so good a woman?'" in *The Woman's Part: Feminist Criticism of Shakespeare*, ed. Carolyn Ruth Swift Lenz, Gayle Green, and Carol Thomas Neely (Urbana: University of Illinois Press, 1980), 225.

11. Carole McKewin, "Counsels of Gall and Grace: Intimate Conversations between Women in Shakespeare's Plays," in *The Woman's Part* (see note 10), 118–19.

12. All citations of Shakespeare's plays are to *The Riverside Shakespeare*, ed. G. Blakemore Evans et al. (Boston: Houghton Mifflin, 1974).

13. Ronald Sharp, *Friendship and Literature: Spirit and Form* (Durham: Duke University Press, 1986), 64.

14. Diane Bornstein, "As Meek as a Maid: A Historical Perspective on Language for Women in courtesy books from the Middle Ages to *Seventeen Magazine*," in *Women's Language and Style*, ed. Douglas Butturff and Edmund L. Epstein (Akron: Conference on Language and Style, 1978), 135; Linda Woodbridge, *Women and the English Renaissance: Literature and the Nature of Womankind, 1504–1620* (Urbana: University of Illinois Press, 1984), 237.

15. See McKewin, "Counsels of Gall and Grace."

16. Louise George Clubb, "theatergrams," in *Comparative Critical Approaches to Renaissance Comedy*, ed. Donald Beecher and Massimo Ciavolella (Canada: Dovehouse Editions, 1986), 19.

17. See McKewin, "Counsels of Gall and Grace," 121.

18. One production which concludes the scene in this way is the BBC film of *Two Gentlemen*, directed by Don Taylor.

19. Anthony J. Lewis, *The Love Story in Shakespearean Comedy* (Lexington: University of Kentucky Press, 1992), 6.

20. Catherine Belsey, "Disrupting Sexual Difference: Meaning and Gender in the Comedies," in *Alternative Shakespeares*, ed. John Drakais (London: Methuen, 1985), 179.

21. Cf. Lewis, *The Love Story*, 7, 151–52.

22. On the capitulation of comedic heroines to subordinate roles, see esp. Linda Bamber, *Comic Women, Tragic Men: A Study of Gender and Genre in Shakespeare* (Stanford: Stanford University Press, 1982); Lisa Jardine, *Still Harping on Daughters: Women and Drama in the Age of Shakespeare* (Brighton: Harvester Press, 1983); and Carol Thomas Neely, *Broken Nuptials in Shakespeare's Plays* (New Haven: Yale University Press, 1985).

23. Bauer, *Feminist Dialogics*, xi.

24. Catherine Belsey, *The Subject of Tragedy: Identity and Difference in Renaissance Drama* (London: Methuen, 1985), 195.

25. Here I differ from Bamber, who contends that "in the comedies, the women tend to avoid making choices" (see note 22, p. 114). My feeling is that at least in the cases I study here the women do indeed choose but do so in a patriarchal-approved, channeled way that in fact bespeaks the inconsequence of their choices.

26. Marianne Novy, "Shakespeare's Female Characters as Actors and Audience," in *The Woman's Part* (see note 10), 256.

27. Peter B. Erickson, *Patriarchal Structures in Shakespeare's Drama* (Berkeley: University of California Press, 1985), 35.

28. Belsey, "Disrupting Sexual Difference," 187.

29. Catherine Belsey, "Love in Venice," in *Shakespeare Survey*, no. 44, ed. Stanley Wells (Cambridge: Cambridge Univesity Press, 1992), 42.

30. See, e.g., C. L. Barber, *Shakespeare's Festive Comedy: A Study in Dramatic Form and its Relation to Social Custom* (Princeton: Princeton University Press, 1959), 187.

31. Bakhtin, *Problems of Dostoevsky's Poetics*, 22.

32. Ibid., 26.

33. Mikhail Bakhtin, *The Dialogic Imagination*, trans. Caryl Emerson and Michael Holquist (Austin: University of Texas Press, 1981), 293.

34. David Carroll, "The Alterity of Discourse: Form, History and the Question of the Political in M. M. Bakhtin," *Diacritics* 13, no. 2 (Summer 1983): 71.

35. Jardine, *Still Harping*, 107.

36. Belsey, "Love in Venice," 48.

37. Ibid.

38. Belsey describes this point in the play as "a specific cultural moment when the meaning of marriage is unstable, contested, and open to radical reconstruction" ("Love in Venice," 48).

39. Claire McEachern, "Fathering Herself: A Source Study of Shakespeare's Feminism," *Shakespeare Quarterly* 39 (Fall 1988): 273.

40. Ibid., 271.

41. Ibid., 272.

42. Bakhtin, *Problems of Dostoevsky's Poetics*, 71.

43. Ibid.

Shakespeare and the Government of Comedy: *Much Ado about Nothing*

Marta Straznicky

Over the past decade, many Renaissance literary scholars have been at work theorizing and demonstrating the ways in which texts accommodate and resist the political imperatives of their times.[1] While these studies vary considerably in scope, emphasis, and perhaps especially in their conception of how literary texts interact with broader social structures, they have tended to gravitate toward texts that are overtly political in content: in Shakespeare studies, this means almost exclusively the histories and tragedies, and the comedies primarily to the extent that a play foregrounds issues of government.[2] Accordingly, while *Measure for Measure* and *The Tempest* have received their due share of political criticism,[3] most of the other comedies, and especially the Elizabethan ones, have gone practically unnoticed.[4] To my mind, this generic bias may be traced to the theory of power that informs much new historicist writing, the theory that power is a sort of possession owned by or at least centered in the person of the monarch and that it has "effects" that may be charted along a more or less direct trajectory running from the sovereign to any number of members in the social body.[5] This view has taught us a great deal about the representation of power in Shakespeare's "political" plays, in plays that are engaged in direct and intensive ways with the conflicts and struggles surrounding rulership, but we have learned very little about the range of power relations represented in and by the comedies, in plays, that is, which generally keep state matters offstage.[6]

The little political criticism there is of the comedies tends to reduce all power relations in the plays into evidence for the monarch's determinate influence on representation. Assuming that drama is "a vehicle for disseminating court ideology," and that the dramatist "aimed at ingratiating himself with those in power" (39), Tennenhouse argues that the primary political work of Shakespeare's romantic comedies is the deliberate glorification and mystification of the aristocracy (42). Similarly, John Drakakis writes, at the tail end of an article that does not explicitly connect play to governmental power, that the comic ending of *Much Ado*, in which honor is mythologized and bastardy demonized, was "necessary" given that England's monarch "was both the public epitome of virgin 'honour' and . . . the bastard child of Henry VIII" (81). In both accounts, literary discourse is understood as subordinate to state power, with the result that nongovernmental restraints on literary design (such as dramatic convention, economic imperative, or authorial disposition) are difficult to consider apart from monarchic needs.

More importantly, such a limited conception of the political obscures the representation of nongovernmental power relations in the plays themselves. Consider, for instance, the power dynamic at work when an impoverished knight is outwitted by two bourgeois wives, or when the rhetorically sustained egotism of four young scholars is punished with a year-long sentence of charity work, or when a pompous steward is tricked into assuming a ridiculous posture by, among others, his social inferiors. Outwitting, punishing, and tricking is familiar business in the comedies, a business at whose heart is an unequal distribution of power. Yet the received theory of power as unilaterally the possession of the monarch or the ruling class can do little to help us understand its operation, for it cannot explain the dynamic by which wit, luck, ingenuity, and sheer resourcefulness enable some characters to triumph over others in the comedies.

*   *   *   *   *

How, then, is the power to triumph distributed in the comedies and to what end? On what grounds does triumph or failure occur? The first task in working out some useful answers to these questions is to expand our notion of power itself, and here I should like to draw on the work of Michel Foucault. In his later publications and interviews, when Foucault was working intently on the social construction of subjectivity, he abandoned the common notion that power is an instrument of state repression, that it is a kind of class-based marker of difference between those who have it and those who don't. Instead, Foucault began to think of power as the very fabric of social existence, as a kind of relation *between* individuals rather than a force that is exercised *over* individuals. Consequently, Foucault repeatedly insisted that if we are to understand fully the work of power in social relations, we must not restrict the inquiry to state institutions; we must instead begin to reconstruct the particular, concrete ways in which a society's systems of control are put into operation in "ordinary" social intercourse:

> We need to cut off the king's head . . . . To pose the problem in terms of the state means to continue posing it in terms of sovereign and sovereignty, that is to say, in terms of law. If one describes all these phenomena of power (discipline, normalization, surveillance) as dependent on state apparatus, this means grasping them as essentially repressive.[7]

Foucault's objection to a legalistic and sovereigntist understanding of power is that it obscures the ways in which the exercise of power makes possible specific forms of knowledge and subjectivity. That is, Foucault suggests that power *does* more than prohibit; it creates a restricted field of knowledge and action in which specific modes of subjectivity are made available and through which a given society's disciplinary codes are maintained. The important idea here is that power is a mode of production, and that this production is the work of a whole matrix of force relations in a given society rather than of a single-handed and single-minded sovereign.[8]

Foucault's nonsovereigntist theory of power can help to illuminate both a vast network of power relations in Shakespeare's comedies and the ways in which they are engaged in the production of normative social values. Arguably, this is not a ground-breaking discovery, for the conservative bias of Shakespeare's comedies has often been asserted by critics of widely varying ideological persuasions.[9] But what Foucault's categories—power, action, knowledge, production—highlight is the extent to which this conservatism is maintained through a matrix of power relations that in fact precludes any kind of unilateral exercise of sovereignty. In Shakespeare's comedies, power is distributed so as to frustrate a whole range of self-interested behaviors that, while not unequivocally assigned to any particular class or gender, tend to be exhibited most frequently by those who are "in power," aristocratic men. The pattern of distributing and differentiating kinds of power, then, is not so much identifiable with particular characters (or subjects) as it is with particular behaviors (or practices).

*   *   *   *   *

This (re)distribution of power in the comedies resembles an important strain of Renaissance political language, the discourse of tyranny which is found both in statecraft treatises and in Tudor tyrant tragedies.[10] Shakespeare's comedies, in working out distinctions between successful and unsuccessful power plays, between just and unjust authority, use a rhetoric of difference that is remarkably similar to these other kinds of overtly "political" writing. As Rebecca Bushnell has shown, the major intellectual project of the discourse of tyranny is to establish fundamental semantic distinctions between legitimate and illegitimate authority, between king and tyrant, always with a view to justifying one's resistance to a "tyrannous" regime (46). The rhetorical figure most commonly used in making these distinctions is antithesis, Puttenham's "Quarreller,"[11] and there are many examples of highly elaborate catalogues of the antithetical qualities of just and unjust rulers. For instance, Jean Bodin's *Six Bookes of a Commonweale* (1606) has a passage of more than fifty prose lines detailing "The greatest difference betwixt a king and a tyrant":

> a king conformeth himselfe unto the lawes of nature, which the tyrant at his pleasure treadeth underfoot: the one of them respecteth religion, justice, and faith; whereas the other regardeth neither God, faith, nor law: the one of them referreth all his actions to the good of the Commonweale, and safetie of his subjects; whereas the other respecteth nothing more than his owne particular profit, revenge, or pleasure: the one doth all his endevour for the enriching of his subjects; whereas the other seeketh after nothing more, than by the impoverishment of them, to encrease his owne wealth.[12]

What's at stake for Bodin and for the many other writers who labored to establish differences between just and unjust authority is the maintenance of a transgressive political space from which state power can be resisted without endangering the fundamental value of an ordered society. The rhetoric of difference and the theory of resistance that often accompanies it is thus an antiabsolutist voice in Renaissance political language,[13] a voice that throws into doubt ideas about the omnipotence of state power that have been so predominant in new historicist criticism. Authority in these works—and in Shakespeare's comedies, as I go on to argue—is not absolute unto itself. Rather, it is qualified by a set of criteria which are intended to ensure that communal objectives are always being served.

Underlying the drive to differentiation is also the fear of another kind of political instability, the fear that if careful distinctions between kings and tyrants are not made nothing would prevent kings from turning into tyrants and nothing would prevent subjects from resisting the authority of lawful kings. As Bodin puts it, the joining of "these two incompatible words together, *a king a tyrant*: [is] so daungerous a doctrine [that it] hath bene the cause of the utter ruine and overthrow of many most mightie empires, and kingdomes" (220). The ideology of difference, then, is vital to the preservation of civilized human society,[14] and those who carry its torch light the way to such values as stability, harmony, and order.

What distinguishes a king from a tyrant in Bodin's passage, and in the discourse of tyranny generally, is the source and use of power: the king's power derives from an external source such as divine law or popular consent and is directed toward the good of his people, while the tyrant's power is self-authorizing and self-directed. In *The French Academie* (1586), la Primaudaye bluntly sums up the distinction in terms of personal will:

> As it properly belongeth to a royall estate to governe and to rule subjects, not according to the sensuall appetite, and disordered will of the Prince, but by maturitie of counsell, and by observation of lawes and of injustice: so it agreeth with a tyrant to raigne by his absolute will, without all regard either of lawes, or of the precepts of justice.[15]

The emphasis here on moral as opposed to legal criteria of just rule is almost inevitably accompanied in many Renaissance pro-resistance treatises by a strong egalitarian, even populist, undercurrent.[16] In contrast with the painstaking establishment of difference between king and tyrant, we find a number of strategies that are recurrently deployed in *erasing* difference between sovereign and subject. John Ponet, whose *A Shorte Treatise of Politike Power* (1556) was immensely influential in reviving resistance theory during Mary's reign, balances personal will against natural law in a way that explicitly dissolves the difference between ruling and subordinate classes:

> It is also a principle of all lawes grounded on the lawe of nature, that every man should use himself and be obedient to that lawe, that he will others be bounden unto. For otherwise he taketh awaye that equalitie (for there is no difference betweene the head and foote, concerninge the use and benefite of the lawes) wherby commonwealthes be maintened and kept up. (44)[17]

Another source of equalization in the discourse of tyranny is the Protestant shift of authority from an exclusive ecclesiastical hierarchy to a universally available scriptural tradition, as in Christopher Goodman's belief, in *How Superior Powers Oght to Be Obeyd* (1558), that we recognize the legitimacy of a king "by [God's] worde, which he hathe now left to all men to be the ordinarie means to reveale his will and appoyntment" (49). Finally, and perhaps most commonly, many theorists invoke a long tradition of constitutional arguments in favor of limiting sovereignty. In *Of Wisdome* (1612), Pierre Charron argues that a tyrant is to be resisted on the grounds that "he is not master of the state; but only a gardian and a suertie . . . . he is not his owne man, neither is the state his, but he is the states."[18]

This kind of "levelling" thought in the discourse of tyranny shares much with comedy's means of empowering certain practices. We find that illegitimate authority is defined as self-serving and is, over the course of the play, either overturned or reformed through the agency of characters acting on behalf of goals that are explicitly defined as communal.[19] A general observation about the role of genre in the representation of power relations may be made here. The characteristic structural trait of comedy, the movement from social conflict to order (however strained or incomplete that movement may be in any particular play), facilitates and accommodates distinctions between legitimate and illegitimate power that are anchored in the notion of communal approval. Like the statecraft treatises, the comedies utilize a rhetoric of difference to distinguish between just and unjust authority that is grounded in a value system which privileges group survival. One could say, then, that literary design "governs" the representation of social relations in a very specific way, and that Shakespeare's comedies—behaving in a manner analogous to disciplinary codes—distribute power so as to promote a particular kind of social equilibrium.

*   *   *   *   *

In what follows, I will expand this observation by considering to what effect one kind of power, language, is distributed in *Much Ado About Nothing*. In this play, as in many of the comedies, language figures as a Janus-like mediator of contesting wills, as a kind of double-edged sword investing characters of opposing interests either with supremacy or with the power of subversion, depending upon the extent to which they advance the welfare of the community. The discursive and rhetorical conventions of language, then, are depicted in the comedies as being independent of the governing will of any individual character, and even of a ruling class. This disconnection of the power of language from character and class is the precondition for an alternative differential of linguistic success, a differential that seems to be driven primarily by the requirements of genre-specific values that may usefully be summed up in the moral concept of charity.

Interestingly, "charity" figures prominently not only in the comedies but also in Renaissance linguistic theory.[20] In the sixteenth century, linguistic exchange is understood as intersubjective and language is consequently theorized in terms of relationship and agency. Pierre Charron writes that "It is the great Intermedler and Huckster: by it we trafficke, *Merx a Mercurio*, peace is handled, affaires are managed, Sciences and the good of the spirit are distributed, it is the band [sic] and cement of humane society" (44). Furthermore, these relational concepts of verbal exchange carry the weight of an ethical frame of reference, so that to speak is necessarily to perform an action with moral consequences. "The mouth of a wicked man," for instance, "is a stincking and contagious pit, a slanderous tongue murdereth the honour of another, it is a sea and Universitie of evils, woorse then fetters, fire, poison, death, hell" (Charron 44).

Extending from a long tradition of patristic skepticism about rhetoric, this moralistic understanding of language takes its points of reference from the biblical poles of Babel and Pentecost, in a sense the loci of damned and redeemed semiosis.[21] Representing the fundamental fracture of human community, the linguistic chaos visited upon the builders of Babel is a figure of human pride; conversely, the multilingual skills bestowed upon the disciples at Pentecost represent the restoration of human community through the Word, through the message of charity. Accordingly, evil uses of language are represented as socially disruptive while good uses of language are socially instructive: "The toong is the best and worst thing that is . . . . It serveth us to profit and instruct others, and by the same also we hurt and corrupt others" (De la Primaudaye 130).

Here we may also begin to note how linguistic relations are inherently relations of power, how both the establishment and disruption of human community through language involve—to invoke Foucault—limiting and structuring the field of actions of one's audience. In fact, this sharing of a power function by both good and evil linguistic practices threatens to undo the pride/charity opposition that is otherwise so carefully maintained, for the same vocabulary of violence often serves to depict the relationship between speaker and hearer in both proper and improper uses of language. Without specifying the speaker's moral position, Charron describes the experience of speech from the perspective of the recipient:

> it is a powerfull master, an imperious commander, which entreth the fortresse, possesseth it selfe of the possessor, stirreth him up, animateth, exasperateth, appeaseth him, maketh him sad, merrie, imprinteth in him whatsoever passion, it handleth and feedeth the soule of the hearer, and makes it pliable to every sense. (44)

In this passage, simply to listen is virtually to risk self-annihilation. The flip side of this exchange is described by Charron toward the end of his work, again without any kind of explicit moral qualification: "As Brasidas drew from his owne wound the dart wherewith he slew his enemie: So passion being conceived in our heart, is incontinentlie formed into our speech, and by it proceeding from us, entreth into another, and there giveth the like impression which wee our selves have, by a subtle and lively contagion" (549). It may not be obvious that the "subtle and lively contagion" Charron describes here is in fact the "exquisite communication" known as eloquence, a much valued, although much debated, form of expression in the sixteenth century. Charron glances only fleetingly (and belatedly) at the possibility that eloquence may be made to serve "pernicious designments" (550). Other defenses of eloquence insist that it be accompanied with wisdom, in which case the power of violent domination is justified, but the vocabulary remains curiously unchanged. In this vein, Henry Peacham declares with exhilaration that "so mighty is the power of this happy union—I mean of wisdom and eloquence—that by the one the orator forceth and by the other he allureth, and by both so worketh, that what he commendeth is beloved, what he dispraiseth is abhorred, what he persuadeth is obeyed and what he dissuadeth is avoided; so that he is, in a manner, the emperor of men's minds and affections."[22] Thomas Wilson is even more explicit about the force relations underlying verbal practice as he celebrates, in the preface to *The Arte of Rhetorique* (1553), the power of eloquence to ensure social stability:

> Who woulde digge and delve from morne till evening? Who woulde travaile and toyle with the sweate of his browes? Yea, who woulde for his kynges pleasure adventure and hasarde his life, if witte hadde not so wonne men, that they thought nothing more nedefull in this world,

nor anye thing wherunto they were more bounden: then here to live in their duty, and to traine their whole lyfe accordynge to their callynge.[23]

Rather ironically, Wilson's guide to rhetoric promotes itself as an aid to those who would shed their ignorance and join the ranks of the civilized, those who lack other means of access to the "witte" that sustains a fundamentally unequal social system. In other words, Wilson's program of rhetorical training could well lead to revolution, for if he teaches his figures well enough, those of his pupils who are marginal to the center of power could conceivably infiltrate and subvert it. Such an outcome is of course not imagined—and almost certainly not intended—by Wilson himself, but the implication of his twin belief in the inherent power of language and the possibility of widespread access to it is potentially unsettling.

Turning to Shakespeare's comedies, one could say that that potential is realized, for the plays repeatedly represent the conquest of verbally sustained and self-serving supremacy by members of officially disempowered social groups. As in Renaissance linguistic theory, the characteristic abuse of language to achieve superiority in the comedies is, although it manifests itself in various kinds of behavior, a symptom of pride. The men of Padua, for instance, deprive women of voice by vigorously defending constricting notions of marriage and female identity which perpetuate the vanity and protect the interests of the dominant sex. In *Love's Labour's Lost*, Navarre and his academic cohorts pride themselves upon their conquest of baser human passions, setting themselves both apart from and above the uninitiated. They do so, significantly, in martial terms, figuring their vows as entry into combat. Similarly, in the many playlets contrived in *Much Ado About Nothing*, verbal fashioning is a direct means of retaliation for personal injury. Throughout the comedies, words are repeatedly described as weapons, language is a veritable battlefield, and discourse a means of enforcement.

In many of the comedies, however, the abusers of language are ultimately ineffectual and language is reclaimed for the betterment of the comic community. This reversal is made possible—indeed even probable—by a genre that puts into action the view that language is inherently relational, that it always speaks of an other, always implies an other, and so implicitly endows the other with voice.[24] As Foucault has observed, "Discourse transmits and produces power; it reinforces it, but also undermines and exposes it, renders it fragile and makes it possible to thwart it."[25] When the men of Padua label Katherine a shrew, they license her speech; when Navarre mentions the "mere necessity" of the princess's visit, he inscribes her in his not-so-sovereign voice; when he brings Beatrice and Benedick to conformity, Don Pedro authorizes his own subversion. This extension of the power of voice to the other is not, however, controlled by any of the characters; it is a condition, a given, of linguistic exchange as it is represented in comedy. Although she rightly argues that Shakespeare was by and large skeptical about the powers of language, Anne Barton inadvertently makes this point. The limits of language, she writes, "are never, in fact, far away from the tragic vision of life."[26] Just so. The unreclaimed breaking of bonds and triumph of isolation belong to the domain of tragedy, and one might expect language to fail in such circumstances. The inverse argument, then, would hold for comedy: the avowed inadequacy and potential degeneracy of language is overcome, surpassed, somehow contained, and its bonding power is reinstated as a condition of the comic community.[27] The power of voice, the power to effect change by using language in ways not sanctioned by the regnant authority, the power verbally to point up the injustice of the dominant rhetoric is successfully appropriated, then, by those characters whose system of values is essentially in line with that of the community. Mimicking the moral dichotomy of sixteenth-century linguistic theory, Shakespeare's comedies thus accommodate an oppositional space from which group interests may demand audience, authority, and allegiance.

* * * * *

In *Much Ado About Nothing*, that oppositional space is occupied, in due time, by Benedick and Beatrice, a maverick pair of "wit-crackers" who have dominated both stage and page at least since Charles I wrote "Benedik and Betrice" against his copy of the play.[28] The persistence of this domination, even though Claudio and Hero are better suited to the currently popular study of patriarchy,[29] suggests that it may, as the term "dominate" implies, have something to do with the play's representation of power relations. In other words, it may be that Benedick and Beatrice come to dominate the play not because they are more witty, more fully developed, more successful than any of the other characters, but because the values they represent are approved by the play as a whole.[30] Indeed, one may reverse the point to claim that *because* they represent values set in opposition to those of their declining social circle, they are more witty, more fully developed, more successful.

Thinking in terms of "more" and "less" helps to elucidate the differential of success that is at work in the play, a differential that in fact emerges from a seemingly ubiquitous pattern of verbal practice. More than one critic has noticed the prevalence of "fashioning" in the play, and it is by now a commonplace that the "nothing" of the title is, in Elizabethan pronunciation, a pun.[31] More specifically, nearly all the characters in *Much Ado about Nothing* are involved in verbal plotting which, with remarkable consistency, reveals a single power dynamic.[32] For all of the play's self-appointed rhetoricians, devising a verbal trap is a means of repairing injured self-esteem and regaining dominance. For the victims, vulnerability to a particular trapping method discloses weaknesses and culpabilities that are "outlawed" by the government of comedy.

Don John's initial attempt to gall Claudio serves as something of a paradigm for all of the play's subsequent plots. Don John's motive is clearly revenge, a desire to disrupt the male alliance against which he defines himself: we know about his attempted subversion of Don Pedro and its subsequent containment, and we also know that he resents Claudio's military success. On both counts, Don John figures himself as inversely related to Messina's "Men's Club": his military esteem declines as Claudio's mounts ("that young start-up hath all the glory of my overthrow" [1.3.62–63]), and the celebratory mood at Leonato's feast is proportionately related to his defeat ("their cheer is the greater that I am subdued" [1.3.67–68]). Don John's plot to "build mischief" (1.3.43), then, is an undisguised attempt to reassert the power he has lost through regular political channels.

The play takes little interest in the precise effect Don John expects his plotting to have; the general direction is obviously toward splintering his conglomerate enemy, an outcome that fails to materialize. From the perspective of dramaturgy, however, Don John's plot reveals the operative strategies and ideological foundations of Messinan society, and the precise reason for the failure of the plot is thus worth considering. Don John's intended target was not, as Claudio's offputting conclusion about the "witch" beauty might lead us to believe, Hero; the lie was actually aimed both at Claudio and at his brother, Don Pedro, a member of the ruling aristocracy whose desire for Hero would, in any event, be difficult for Claudio to oppose. Later in the play, when Don John targets his brother and competitor indirectly through slander against a woman—when, that is, the charge carries a threat against the patriarchy from a person whose power is actively suppressed—the men's response will differ considerably. Their almost congenital mistrust of women and their far too easy trust—especially where matters of women's transgression are concerned—in words are the very qualities upon which Don John ventures his success.

A similar power dynamic may be seen in Hero's gulling of Beatrice, where the plotter's motive is at least partially the recovery of dominance, and success is assured by the victim's unselfconscious vulnerability. Ursula and Hero's eagerness to see Beatrice "greedily devour the treacherous bait" (3.1.28) may be read as an attempt to overturn her dominance of female discourse elsewhere in the play. Certainly Hero takes full advantage of her captive audience in using decidedly harsh terms:

> But Nature never fram'd a woman's heart
> Of prouder stuff than that of Beatrice.
> Disdain and scorn ride sparkling in her eyes,
> Misprising what they look on, and her wit
> Values itself so highly that to her
> All matter else seems weak. She cannot love,
> Nor take no shape nor project of affection,
> She is so self-endeared.
>
> (3.1.49–56)

This attack upon Beatrice's vanity strikes exactly the right key. It articulates and denounces the isolationist "humour" that divides her from the social circle upon whose approval she actually depends. Furthermore, Beatrice's vanity nurtures another censured quality in the play—false interpretation. Not only are her eyes regularly "[m]isprising what they look on" (3.1.52), but she "spell[s] . . . backward" (3.1.61) all men, regardless of their value, and generally "never gives to truth and virtue that / Which simpleness and merit purchaseth" (3.1.69–70). Inadvertently confirming Hero's charges, Beatrice responds not with self-defense but with a commitment to reform, notably intensifying the proverb "When your ear tingles people are talking about you,"[34]

> What fire is in mine ears? Can this be true?
> Stand I condemn'd for pride and scorn so much?
> Contempt, farewell, and maiden pride, adieu!
> No glory lives behind the back of such.

And, Benedick, love on, I will requite thee,
Taming my wild heart to thy loving hand.

(3.1.107–12)

To anticipate somewhat the conjunction here of taming and love is significant, as is the promise of change. Beatrice will eventually accept patriarchal restrictions on individualism, but in the play's scheme of values and power distribution, this is commendable and comes with a pay-off: once Beatrice conforms to the patriarchal norm, she is endowed with a voice that enables her to critique that norm, taking over as she does so the comic values that are so obscenely abandoned by the play's conventional patriarchal relationship.

The power dynamics at work in Don John's first villainy and in the taming of Beatrice are also brought into play in *Much Ado about Nothing*'s climactic incident, the slander of Hero. Even before Hero is apparently proven guilty, the sequence of hostile fashionings characterizing the latter half of the play is underway. Deliberately assuming a posture of (mock) deference, approaching his brother with a judicious "If your leisure served, I would speak with you" (3.2.73), Don John's proffering of secret knowledge enables him to invert the power relation, drawing Don Pedro and Claudio into his circle of influence in calculatedly foreboding terms:

If you dare not trust that you see, confess not that you know. If you will follow me, I will show you enough; and when you have seen more, and heard more, proceed accordingly.

(3.2.108–11)

In each successive plot that emerges from this one, the plotter uses language to reassert a personal power that is either deemed threatened or actually challenged. Don Pedro and Claudio's response to the information they have received, information which has been given largely in terms of impending personal injury, sets off the round of counteractions. Acutely perceptive of the dangers posed by a sexually liberated woman, Claudio and Don Pedro are completely preoccupied with strategies of defense rather than with assessing the nature of the threat. They hurriedly devise the scenario in which they will reassert their authority over the transgressive woman, should she be guilty (the condition is already a premise), and leave no room in their machinations for handling the villainy of Don John and Borachio, should they turn out to have lied (a possibility left unimagined). What begins as an unfounded suspicion rises with alarming speed to the status of a *fait accompli*, and the three soon chime together in agonized platitudes that point up the fundamental similarity of their visions:

> *D. Pedro.* O day untowardly turned!
> *Claud.* O mischief strangely thwarting!
> *D. John.* O plague right well prevented!
>
> (3.2.120–22)

If all that Claudio and Don Pedro are eventually deemed guilty of is "mistaking," then mistaking is a weighty offense indeed.

The vengeful streak in Claudio's behavior is ill-disguised. Deeply offended as he is, the theatrics Claudio stages in the church scene, to say nothing of his callous behavior following the "death" of Hero, bespeak far more than a thwarted love; they strongly suggest the need to reassert power over the woman who has shamed him. Just as he has the power to enhance Hero's status by marrying her, so he has the power to damage her status by refusing to marry her. It is a power he flaunts with disconcerting confidence, quite out of key with his usual shy, awkward behavior. Posing as the well-intentioned bridegroom, making technical objections to the phrasing of the ceremony, asking rhetorical questions, indulging in self-righteous moralizing, and taking Don Pedro's carefully positioned cue, Claudio arrives at the substance of his charge thoroughly rehearsed:

> There, Leonato, take her back again.
> Give not this rotten orange to your friend;
> She's but the sign and semblance of her honour.
> Behold how like a maid she blushes here!
> O, what authority and show of truth
> Can cunning sin cover itself withal!
>
> (4.1.29–35)

The last two lines may well serve as the motto of the play, and Claudio would do well to pause over them. But he is far too caught up in being the injured party and, perhaps because it is a move unscripted by his mentor, entirely overlooks the evidence Hero puts forward. Hero responds to Claudio's incriminating "one question" in pointedly unadorned language: "I talk'd with no man at that hour, my lord" (4.1.77–86), but her testimony here, even though it is given with the due deference of a "my lord," is scarcely heard, apparently because it does not accord with the "truth" of sense experience, but at least as much because Hero's guilt is already assumed.[35]

Convinced by the authority of princely testimony and straitened under the pressure of subversion (seemingly by Hero; overtly by Claudio), Leonato is the next to seize upon his daughter's guilt, revealing as he does so the absurd conditions which underwrite his "love":

> Why had I not with charitable hand
> Took up a beggar's issue at my gates,
> Who smirched thus, and mir'd with infamy,
> I might have said, 'No part of it is mine;
> This shame derives itself from unknown loins'?
> But mine, and mine I lov'd, and mine I prais'd,
> And mine that I was proud on—mine so much
> That I myself was to myself not mine,
> Valuing of her.
>
> (4.1.131–39)

The frantic incantation of "mine" betrays Leonato's primary concern. Not surprisingly, then, his subsequent willingness to follow the friar's instructions for shaming Claudio is motivated by the opportunity to recover his authority. Significantly, this is the one playlet which fails to enhance the power of the plotter. Leonato and Antonio's furious attack upon Claudio and Don Pedro is met with stunning disregard and mockery. Although it clearly points to the waning rulership of Leonato, this nearly farcical episode, in which all social rules are flouted, more importantly underlines the nature and degree of Claudio and Don Pedro's "mistaking," and considerably undermines the success of the comic harmony at play's end.[36] That Shakespeare has chosen to illustrate yet another aspect of ill-behavior at this late stage of the play, when the truth is moments from being disclosed, would seem to be a significant constructional move. In their merciless taunts of the "old man" and the sense of self-righteousness with which they receive news of Hero's death, Claudio and Don Pedro are virtually divested of sympathy and authority.

With the confession of Borachio firmly supporting his right, Leonato launches two further plots against Claudio in an effort to regain his power:

> Possess the people in Messina here
> How innocent she died; and if your love

> Can labour ought in sad invention,
> Hang her an epitaph upon her tomb,
> And sing it to her bones, sing it tonight.
> Tomorrow morning come you to my house,
> And since you could not be my son-in-law,
> Be yet my nephew.
>
> (5.1.275–82)

Under the pressure of his own guilt, Claudio willingly abandons self-direction and vows to "dispose / For henceforth of poor Claudio" (5.1.288–89). As required, he hangs an epitaph on Hero's tomb,[37] and silently defers to Leonato's authority at the nuptial:

> Claud.   Sweet, let me see your face.
> Leon. No, that you shall not till you take her hand,
>   Before this friar, and swear to marry her.
> Claud. Give me your hand before this holy friar.
>   I am your husband if you like of me.
>
> (5.4.55–59).

It is only after this final self-surrender that Claudio discovers his good fortune.

But there is a notorious sense of dissatisfaction with the conclusion of what is ostensibly the play's main plot. Claudio seems not to have had enough time to consider the weight of his offences, and he gets off rather lightly with the claim that "sinn'd I not / But in mistaking" (5.1.268–69).[38] Furthermore, his exclamation following the disclosure of Hero's innocence is highly dubious:

> Sweet Hero! Now thy image doth appear
> In the rare semblance that I lov'd it first.
>
> (5.1.245–46)

If Hero is merely restored to the same position in Claudio's affections that she held before the crisis, then we may well expect another round of difficulties.[39] Within the confines of their plot, the sins of the offenders are not worked out and loom rather large over the play's conclusion.

One reason for our dissatisfaction with the "comic" conclusion of Much Ado's main plot is that there is a striking similarity between its two moral camps: the machinations of Don John, who is necessarily demonized by the others, are no different in kind from those of Don Pedro, Claudio, and Leonato. All of the play's main characters are plotters, and their plots are all fashioned so as to bolster their own power. In the subplot, however, the play does make use of a rhetoric of difference that labors to distinguish between kinds of verbal practice. Accordingly, it is here, in the relationship between Benedick and Beatrice and, more importantly, in their demarcated difference from the main plot characters, that any satisfactory comic closure must be sought.

Before going on to unfold this argument, let me first return to an earlier observation: in Shakespeare's comedies—as in the Renaissance discourse of tyranny—the rhetoric of difference maintains a distinction between individualist and communalist practices that underlies the distribution of power and that (ideally) enables the play to arrive at a conclusion in which communal stability is affirmed. The outlawing of certain overtly self-enhancing practices, just as the outlawing of certain modes of rulership in Renaissance political writing, can thus be framed as the promotion of social order. Accordingly, the momentum of comedy is in the direction of reformation rather than revolution, with most energy being invested in the recuperation of social values that are so often represented as corrupt early in the play.

In *Much Ado about Nothing*, that recuperation is entrusted to Beatrice and Benedick, but not before they themselves are "reformed." What we find, then, is a sort of double rhetoric of difference that first pits the two wits against social norms, the comic value of which is never in question, and then pits them—once they have accepted those norms—against an evidently corrupt social circle. Opposing as vehemently as they do the value of marriage, and following the Messinan habit of using language to bolster personal superiority, Benedick and Beatrice are obviously poised for a fall. Berated by Antonio and warned by Leonato that "thou wilt never get thee a husband, if thou be so shrewd of thy tongue" (2.1.16–17), Beatrice ingeniously turns the fault into a virtue, claiming that her resultant maidenhood is a ticket to heaven where she hopes to keep merry company with other bachelors (2.1.19–45). This display of wit dazzles Antonio, who fails to find an effective rejoinder and turns instead to Hero, the docile, submissive female, with great expectations: "Well, niece, I trust you will be ruled by your father" (2.1.46–47—we may assume an emphasis on you). But Beatrice is not so easily silenced; answering in Hero's place, she strikes back with a mockery of filial deferance that cuts deeply into patriarchal prerogative:

Yes, faith, it is my cousin's duty to make curtsy and say, 'Father, as it please you': but yet for all that, cousin, let him be a handsome fellow, or else make another curtsy and say, 'Father, as it please me.'[40]

(2.1.48–52)

A moment later, Beatrice scores again with her outright rejection of servitude to "a piece of valiant dust" (2.1.56–57). This time she establishes her independence from Messinan cultural norms so firmly that Leonato surrenders the last word and turns, with what could easily be defensiveness, to his daughter for affirmation of his shaken supremacy: "Daughter, remember what I told you: if the Prince do solicit you in that kind, you know your answer" (2.1.61–62).

With much less self-assertion—perhaps because as a male he is already invested with the privilege of speaking—though with no less conviction, Benedick assumes an analogous antimatrimonial pose in which he, too, appears as a free-wheeling individualist:

That a woman conceived me, I thank her: that she brought me up, I likewise give her most humble thanks: but that I will have a recheat winded in my forehead, or hang my bugle in an invisible baldrick, all women shall pardon me. Because I will not do them the wrong to mistrust any, I will do myself the right to trust none: and the fine is, for the which I may go the finer, I will live a bachelor.

(1.1.221–28)

Distinguishing his future from normative cultural expectations, Benedick revealingly insists upon the power of personal agency: "I thank," "I . . . give," "I will have," "I will not do," "I will do," "I may go," "I will live." In comedy's economy of power relations, however, such antisocial dominance is not sustainable. Paradoxically, if either Benedick or Beatrice are to enjoy supremacy, they must first overcome their aversion to marriage.

As it turns out, Don Pedro's plan for a dual gulling is perfectly apt, for it wagers success on the likeness—and likely mutual attraction—between Benedick and Beatrice. Beatrice's thinly disguised concern for the well-being of Benedick ("I pray you, is Signior Mountanto returned from the wars or no?" [1.1.28–29]) is matched by his inadvertently slipped judgment of her beauty: "there's [Hero's] cousin, and she were not possessed with a fury, exceeds her as much in beauty as the first of May doth the last of December" (1.1.176–79). Furthermore, that the two form a coalition against the values of the others is auspicious. The one thing they agree upon early in the play is their mutual "humour" (1.1.120), which will save not only themselves but also their respective sexes from injury: while Beatrice feels that Benedick's "hard heart" is "[a] dear happiness to women, they would else have been troubled with a pernicious suitor" (1.1.116; 118–20), Benedick hopes Beatrice's "cold blood" stays cold so that "some gentleman or other shall scape a predestinate scratched face" (1.1.120; 124–25). Slim as it is, the evidence promises a celebration of the very institution which both wits initially flout.

In broader terms, the underlying bond between Benedick and Beatrice increasingly takes over the comic values which are abandoned by the play's main plot.[41] The strategy Don Pedro adopts is ideally suited to his two victims: both are taken in by the self-enhancing verbal ostentation they themselves practice, and, ironically, by the fear of public censure. Even though Benedick and Beatrice pose as social rebels, their power feeds on the social attention their subversive opinions attract. By fashioning his strategy to play upon a combination of romantic affection and exalted self-regard, Don Pedro is assured a victory.

The defeat of Beatrice and Benedick into matrimony, as it were, is the requisite for the play's second set of differentiations, differentiations that also pit individualism against community but that locate the reformed wits on the "winning" side. The terms of this second rhetoric of difference are most clearly articulated in the scenes following Claudio's accusation against Hero. A moral chasm opens as soon as the charge is brought forward, splitting the characters in terms of their willingness to accept Claudio's "evidence." The friar, for instance, immediately perceives that the very blush denounced by Claudio is indeed "the sign and semblance of her honour," and wagers his credibility on that fact. That his subsequent plot for bringing Claudio to repentance fails to materialize has been read by some critics as an undercutting of his presumptuous authority.[42] But surely the friar assumes no less than an audience might, that if Claudio truly loves Hero he will recant the minute "he shall hear she died upon his words" (4.1.223), and Claudio's failure to show any sign of remorse accordingly reflects worse on him than on the friar.[43] Furthermore, the opinion of the friar has the weighty backing of Beatrice, who responds to the slander of Hero with a scathing attack on the male prerogative in matters of truth:

Princes and counties! Surely a princely testimony, a goodly count,
Count Comfect, a sweet gallant surely! O that I were a man for his sake,
or that I had any friend would be a man for my sake! But manhood is
melted into curtsies, valour into compliment, and men are only turned
into tongue, and trim ones too.

(4.1.314–20)

The issue here, for Beatrice and for all the others, is the validity of
evidence, and the skepticism with which she receives the evidence
of "princes and counties" points up in one stroke the classist and
sexist bias of "truth" in the play. Opening as it does with a messenger's report, and proceeding through a whole series of hermeneutic
scenarios, *Much Ado* is clearly just as concerned with the nature
of interpretation as it is with fashioning. And as with fashioning,
interpretive activity involves the exercise of power and thus has
two moral faces in the play: self-interested interpretation (most
obviously, Claudio and Don Pedro's easy acceptance of Don John's
"evidence," but also incidents like Benedick's "reading" of Beatrice's unwillingness to summon him to dinner at 2.3.248–52), and
charitable interpretation (the friar's giving Hero the benefit of the
doubt, for example, or Benedick's suspension of judgment). If we
recall the power that is attributed to rhetoric in the Renaissance,
skepticism about linguistic evidence, about the truth value of someone's "word," appears to be a sort of counterforce, a way of guarding
against the loss of independent judgment to which an audience is
potentially susceptible. In this context, Beatrice and Benedick's
faith in Hero's innocence, held as it is against the testimony of their
social superiors, figures as a power of resistance, a power at whose
basis is a commitment to justice.[44]

Accordingly, while the fortuitous discovery and thematic coun-
terpointing of the Watch[45] obviously undermine the authority of
Messina's ruling males, it is Benedick and Beatrice who are granted
the fullest powers of subversion and whose reign over the play's
conclusion lightens the otherwise unrelieved tragic weight of the
offense against Hero. Unlike Claudio who reaffirms, through his
own submission, Leonato's authority, Benedick usurps that authority by openly defying Leonato's instructions regarding the comple-
tion of the marriage ritual, and deftly overturns the authority of
Don Pedro whom he now counsels with his own advice:

Bene. Let's have a dance ere we are married that we may lighten our
own hearts and our wives' heels.
Leon. We'll have dancing afterward.

Bene. First, of my word! Therefore, play, music. Prince, thou art sad;
   get thee a wife, get thee a wife!

(5.4.116–22)

Assuming in addition the punitive function of authority by promising to attend to the villain in due time, Benedick goes on to preside
over the dance with which the play concludes.[46] His exuberant
confidence is everywhere apparent and may reasonably be shared
by Beatrice. That Beatrice is silent during the close of the play as
Benedick virtually takes upon himself—and renews by so doing—
patriarchal authority is, at one level of understanding, not to be
overlooked. But in the play's own terms of reference, it is clear that
the reason for Benedick's successful supremacy in the conclusion,
the source of his authority and of whatever degree of comic renewal
may be claimed for the play (Don John continues to threaten), is in
his connection with Beatrice, in his having surpassed the dangers
and limitations of individualism.[47]

Ironically nurtured by the very crisis that irreparably damaged
the comic tone of the main plot, the connection between Beatrice
and Benedick enables, by means of its difference from the more
conventional romantic relationship in the play, a reformation of
patriarchal gender relations.[48] Above all, it posits mutuality of charity (of husband and wife, but also of all members of the social
body if we remember that marriage is a metaphor for society in the
Renaissance) as the keystone of a just society.[49] Both the mutuality
and the reformative value of their relationship are displayed by
Benedick and Beatrice in the last theatrical practice of the play.
Apparently brought to recognize their mutual affection yet again
by the goading of the others, the last encounter of Beatrice and
Benedick may actually be a playlet of its own (the only one they
stage) which, like the other playlets, reasserts their authority by
deriding the presumptions of their victims:

Bene. Do not you love me?
Beat.   Why, no, no more than reason.
Bene. Why then, your uncle, and the Prince, and Claudio
   Have been deceiv'd—they swore you did.
Beat. Do not you love me?
Bene.   Troth, no, no more than reason.
Beat. Why then, my cousin, Margaret, and Ursula
   Are much deceiv'd, for they did swear you did.
Bene. They swore that you were almost sick for me.
Beat. They swore that you were well-nigh dead for me.

(5.4.74–81)

The sincerity of this exchange is suspect: the patterned syntax and repeated emphasis on the others' testimony and mistakenness suggest a prior rehearsal. Furthermore, Benedick's exaggerated response to the discovery of their respective (strategically planted?) love letters reinforces the sense of an ongoing charade:

> *Bene.* A miracle! Here's our own hands against our hearts. Come, I will have thee, but by this light I take thee for pity.
> *Beat.* I would not deny you, but by this good day I yield upon great persuasion, and partly to save your life, for I was told you were in a consumption.

> (5.4.91–96)

It is difficult not to read these lines as in some sense a display before the others; a display, significantly, which returns to them some of the independence they championed before their defeat by those whom they now dominate. Like Kate and Petruchio, who seem in many ways to have been draft versions of Beatrice and Benedick, *Much Ado about Nothing*'s witty couple stand apart from their social circle in their moment of triumph.[50] Their ability to do so underscores the "power of love" in Shakespeare's comedies.

*   *   *   *   *

And yet the effects of that power are anything but evenly distributed: Foucault's notion of a ubiquitous power, when read through Shakespeare's comic conclusion, would seem to warrant some skepticism.[51] Stepping back from the play, rejecting the play's own account of its ending, we notice that Benedick's magisterial orchestration of events *repeats* rather than reforms the discursive practices through whose subversion his own domination was won. Most obviously, Benedick silences Beatrice—with a seemingly innocuous kiss that actually divests her of the oppositional power with which mouths are invested in this play—and promises to devise "brave punishments" for the escaped Don John. On both counts, Benedick performs an act of subordination which bolsters his own authority as the "reformed" patriarchal male: independent women and bastards undermine the security of the patriarchy's cardinal institution. The triumph of "group" interests at the end of the play, then, is in fact the triumph of politically determined exclusions the legitimacy of which is purchased under the banner of communal welfare.

The exclusions that facilitate comic celebration constitute in large measure the "governing" function of comedy, for their inscription of a code of conduct that privileges the general entails severe restrictions on the behavior of particular individuals. As Stephen Orgel has written, the most individual comic characters are eccentric, and their eccentricity posits an irrepressible norm: "if they cannot ultimately be accommodated to that norm, they will ultimately be expelled by it".[52] In sixteenth-century comic theory, we repeatedly find that this ethical imperative is, in turn, the legitimating trait of the genre. For Whetstone, comedy is a "scowrge of the lewde," for Lodge, it "restrayn[s] the unbridled cominaltie," for Harington, it "make[s] men see and shame at their owne faults," and for these and other writers, comedy's ability to perform "the good amendment of men by discipline and example" (Puttenham 25) makes it a powerful force of social control.[53] But in order for comedy to perform its work successfully, it must risk representing the vices it aims to correct, and it must ensure that those vices are placed in an unambiguously antithetical relation to their moral opposites. The rhetoric of difference, then, is integral to the "scowrging" work of comedy, as Whetstone notes in his dedication of the two parts of *Promos and Cassandra*: "The effects of both are good and bad: vertue intermyxt with vice, unlawfull desyres (yf it were posible) queancht with chaste denyals: al needeful actions (I thinke) for publike vewe. For by the rewarde of the good the good are encouraged in wel doinge: and with the scowrge of the lewde the lewde are feared from evill attempts" (58–59).

But Whetstone's parenthetical "yf it were posible" underscores the brittleness of comedy's reformative project, the potential collapse of its moral oppositions. The fact that vice is graced with representation introduces the possibility that its powers will slip from axiological control.[54] And indeed, the many critical debates regarding the subversive nature of Shakespeare's comedies attest to the reality of the danger.[55] Although the very notion of a comic restoration involves some sense of surpassing corruption, of setting out in a new direction, to restore is also to move backwards, to reinstate a wrongfully disturbed social order. This is the double vision that comedy shares with the discourse of tyranny, where resistance to present authority is justified on the basis of past covenants, be they sacred or secular. In both kinds of writing, the impulse to criticize flirts with anarchy, and the requisite demonizing of existing power leaves in its wake an infinitely repeatable strategy of resistance. Because of this doubleness, this irreducible ambivalence, the "real" political work of the comedies, their role in maintaining or subverting sixteenth-century social structures, can only be determined in the context of contemporary interpretations.[56] In the absence of such interpretations, it is we who must decide the ambivalence, and so risk saying more about the work we make comedy perform than about the work it performed in its own time.

Notes

I would like to thank Professor Irena R. Makaryk for her wise and patient guidance during the initial stages of research for this essay and for providing a model of professionalism long after. I would also like to acknowledge the financial support of the Social Sciences and Humanities Research Council of Canada.

    1. In the area of Renaissance drama, the main studies in this trend are Michael D. Bristol, *Carnival and Theater: Plebeian Culture and the Structure of Authority in Renaissance England* (New York: Methuen, 1985); Jonathan Dollimore, *Radical Tragedy: Religion, Ideology and Power in the Drama of Shakespeare and His Contemporaries* (Chicago: University of Chicago Press, 1984); Jonathan Goldberg, *James I and the Politics of Literature: Jonson, Shakespeare, Donne and Their Contemporaries* (Baltimore: Johns Hopkins University Press, 1983); Stephen Greenblatt, *Shakespearean Negotiations: The Circulation of Social Energy in Renaissance England* (Berkeley: University of California Press, 1988); Steven Mullaney, *The Place of the Stage: License, Play, and Power in Renaissance England* (Chicago: University of Chicago Press, 1988); Leonard Tennenhouse, *Power on Display: The Politics of Shakespeare's Genres* (London: Methuen, 1986); and Robert Weimann, *Shakespeare and the Popular Tradition in the Theater: Studies in the Social Dimension of Dramatic Form and Function*, ed. Robert Schwartz (Baltimore: Johns Hopkins University Press, 1978). The full range of political criticism of Shakespeare is surveyed by Walter Cohen, "Political Criticism of Shakespeare," in *Shakespeare Reproduced: The Text in History and Ideology*, ed. Jean Howard and Marion F. O'Connor (London: Methuen, 1986), 18-46.

    2. The main exceptions to this pattern are Louis Adrian Montrose, "'The Place of a Brother' in *As You Like It*: Social Process and Comic Form", *Shakespeare Quarterly* 32 (1981): 238-54; and John Drakakis, "Trust and Transgression: The Discursive Practices of *Much Ado About Nothing*," in *Post-structuralist Readings of English Poetry*, ed. Richard Machin and Christopher Norris (Cambridge: Cambridge University Press, 1987), 59-84.

    3. On *Measure for Measure*, see David Aers and Gunther Kress, "The Politics of Style: Discourses of Law and Authority in *Measure for Measure*," *Style* 16 (1982): 22–37; Jonathan Dollimore, "Transgression and Surveillance in *Measure for Measure*," in *Political Shakespeare: New Essays in Cultural Materialism*, ed. Jonathan Dollimore and Alan Sinfield (Manchester: Manchester University Press, 1985), 72–87; and Gordon Ross Smith, "Renaissance Political Realities and Shakespeare's Measure for Measure," *Proceedings of the PMR Conference* 7 (1982): 83-92. On *The Tempest*, see Francis Barker and Peter Hulme, "'Nymphs and Reapers Heavily Vanish': The Discursive Con-texts of *The Tempest*," in *Alternative Shakespeares*, ed. John Drakakis (London: Methuen, 1985), 191–205; Paul Brown, "'This thing of darkness I acknowledge mine': *The Tempest* and the Discourse of Colonialism," in *Political Shakespeare*, 48-71; Thomas Cartelli, "Prospero in Africa: *The Tempest* as Colonialist Text and Pretext," in *Shakespeare Reproduced*, 99–

115; and Deborah Willis, "Shakespeare's *The Tempest* and the Discourse of Colonialism," *Studies in English Literature* 29 (1989): 277–89.

4. A rough estimate of this bias may be found in the MLA computerized bibliography, the most recent edition of which gives 184 entries for power and/or politics in the histories, 60 in the tragedies, and 22 in the comedies and romances combined. The obvious proviso to my claim is that I am excluding—as does the MLA from its category of "politics"—the many recent feminist studies of the sexual politics of the comedies (e.g., Marilyn Williamson, *The Patriarchy of Shakespeare's Comedies* [Detroit: Wayne State University Press, 1986].) Interestingly, most of this work has been done by female critics, whereas new historicist and materialist studies of the "political" plays are predominantly by males. This gender/genre connection strangely replicates the often denounced distinctions underlying Linda Bamber's *Comic Women, Tragic Men: A Study of Gender and Genre in Shakespeare* (Stanford: Stanford University Press, 1982). See, however, the recently published collection of articles edited by Valerie Wayne, *The Matter of Difference: Materialist Feminist Criticism of Shakespeare* (New York: Harvester Wheatsheaf, 1991), which takes a major step toward the integration of feminist and materialist critical practices.

5. That theory is best exemplified in the work of Greenblatt, *Shakespearean Negotiations*, who has devised a widely influential "subversion/containment" model of authority which posits that the monarch deliberately permits various subversive cultural practices so as to maintain control over them. Several recent studies, however, have demonstrated persuasively that Greenblatt's model fails to account for the variety of populist strategies that enabled writers to stand outside the subversion-containment dynamic. See, for example, Bristol, *Carnival and Theater*, and Annabel Patterson, *Shakespeare and the Popular Voice* (Oxford: Blackwell, 1990). But even for these critics, power is charted along a sovereign/subject axis, obfuscating other, nongovernmental contexts for the exercise of power.

6. The idea of a *range* of power relations is important here, for I do not mean to imply that the comedies' patriarchal commitments, by now indispensable to our understanding of the plays, are in any way not political. What I do want to suggest is that the representation of power in Shakespeare's comedies is not confined to sexual politics, and that the current theory of power used by new historicism is not up to the task of examining it.

7. Michel Foucault, *Power/Knowledge: Selected Interviews and Other Writings 1972–1977*, ed. Colin Gordon (New York: Pantheon, 1980), 121, 122.

8. See Michel Foucault, "The Subject and Power," afterword to *Michel Foucault: Beyond Structuralism and Hermeneutics*, by Hubert L. Dreyfus and Paul Rabinow (Sussex: Harvester, 1988), 208–26, for the fullest articulation of these ideas.

9. The most influential of the celebratory conservative readings of the comedies are perhaps Northrop Frye, *A Natural Perspective: The Development of Shakespearean Comedy and Romance* (New York: Columbia University Press, 1965) and C. L. Barber, *Shakespeare's Festive Comedy: A Study of Dramatic Form and Its Relation to Social Custom* (Princeton: Princeton University Press, 1959), but their findings are also supported by those critics who seek to expose the injustices at the basis of comic conservatism: e.g., Elliot Krieger, "Social Relations and the Social Order in *Much Ado About Nothing*," *Shakespeare Survey* 32 (1979): 49–61; and Williamson, *Patriarchy*.

10. See Rebecca Bushnell, *Tragedies of Tyrants: Political Thought and Theater in the English Renaissance* (Ithaca: Cornell University Press, 1990), for a study of

the discursive connections between these two kinds of writing. In this section of the paper, I am indebted to Bushnell's analysis of the rhetoric of difference in tyrant tragedies and Renaissance political language generally.

11. See Bushnell, *Tragedies of Tyrants*, 49, on Puttenham's account of antithesis as an "inherently unruly" figure.

12. Jean Bodin, *The Six Bookes of a Commonweale* (1606), ed. Kenneth Douglas McRae (Cambridge, Mass.: Harvard University Press, 1962), 212.

13. On sixteenth-century resistance theory, see Richard L. Greaves, "Concepts of Political Obedience in Late Tudor England: Conflicting Perspectives," *Journal of British Studies* 22, no. 1 (1982): 23–34; and Donald R. Kelley, "Ideas of Resistance before Elizabeth," in *The Historical Renaissance: New Essays on Tudor and Stuart Literature and Culture*, ed. Heather Dubrow and Richard Strier (Chicago: University of Chicago Press, 1988), 48–76. On ideas of resistance in Shakespeare, see Richard Strier, "Faithful Servants: The Praise of Disobedience," in *Historical Renaissance*, 104–33.

14. Bushnell, *Tragedies*, has an excellent analysis of the bestial qualities attributed to the tyrant in Renaissance political discourse (50–56).

15. Peter de la Primaudaye, *The French Academie* (1586) (rpt.; New York: Hildesheim, 1972), 628.

16. On the conflict between moral and legal criteria of just authority in Renaissance political discourse, see Bushnell, *Tragedies*, 36. Interestingly, it is the moral criteria that are found in the comedies, while the histories and tragedies are far more preoccupied with genealogy and other legalistic aspects of legitimacy.

17. John Ponet, *A Shorte Treatise of Politike Power* (1556), reproduced in *John Ponet, Advocate of Limited Monarchy*, by Winthrop S. Hudson (Chicago: University of Chicago Press, 1942), 44. The body metaphor is frequently used as a levelling device. Christopher Goodman, *How Superior Powers Oght to be Obeyd* (1558) (New York: Columbia University Press, 1931) writes that kings ought not "to bringe the rest of the members in cotempte and bondage, but to comforte them, defende them, and norishe them as members of the same bodie" (149). More spectacularly, John Ponet puts the health of the whole body ahead of permanent bodily integrity: "Common wealthes and realmes may live, whan the head is cut of, and may put on a newe head, that is, make them a newe governour, whan they see their olde head seke to have his owne will and not the wealthe of the hole body, for the which he was ordained" (61).

18. Peter (Pierre) Charron, *Of Wisdome* (1612) (rpt.; New York: Da Capo Press, 1971), 490.

19. These goals, however, are also the goals of the patriarchal state. This potentially troublesome equation will be addressed later in the essay.

20. See Jane Donawerth, *Shakespeare and the Sixteenth-Century Study of Language* (Urbana: University of Illinois Press, 1984) and Marion Trousdale, *Shakespeare and the Rhetoricians* (Chapel Hill: University of North Carolina Press, 1982) on the relation of Shakespeare's works to sixteenth-century linguistic theory.

21. On the biblical frame of reference in sixteenth-century linguistic theory, see Margreta De Grazia, "Shakespeare's View of Language: An Historical Perspective," *Shakespeare Quarterly* 29 (1978): 374–88.

22. Henry Peacham, *The Garden of Eloquence* (1577) (rpt.; Menston: Scolar Press, 1968), sig. Aiii.

23. Thomas Wilson, *The Arte of Rhetorique* (1553) (rpt.; Delmar, N.Y.: Scholars' Facsimiles and Reprints, 1977), sig. Aiii.

24. See Goldberg, "Shakespearean Inscriptions: The Voicing of Power," in

Shakespeare and the Question of Theory, ed. Patricia Parker and Geoffrey Hartman (New York: Methuen, 1985), 116–37 on the related idea that "Authority in the Shakespearean text is a matter not of having a voice but of voicing" (119).

25. Michel Foucault, *The History of Sexuality, Volume 1: An Introduction*, trans. Robert Hurley (New York: Vintage/Random House, 1980), 101.

26. Anne Barton, "Shakespeare and the Limits of Language," *Shakespeare Survey* 24 (1971): 20.

27. On the word as bond trope in Renaissance literature generally, see Douglas J. Canfield, *Word as Bond in English Literature from the Middle Ages to the Restoration* (Philadelphia: University of Pennsylvania Press, 1989).

28. Even in the seventeenth century, King Charles was not alone in his judgment. In 1613 The Lord Chamberlain's accounts record payment to John Heminge for "*Benedicte and Betteris*," almost certainly an alternative title for "*Much Adoe abowte Nothinge*," which is also mentioned (A. R. Humphreys, Introduction to *Much Ado About Nothing*, by William Shakespeare, ed. A. R. Humphreys [London: Methuen, 1981], 34). In 1640 Leonard Digges deemed the characters capable of filling the theaters, and Sir William Davenant's hybridization of *Much Ado* and *Measure for Measure* into *The Law Against Lovers* (1662) omits the Hero and Claudio plot altogether (F. H. Mares, Introduction to *Much Ado About Nothing*, by William Shakespeare, ed. F. H. Mares [Cambridge: Cambridge University Press, 1988], 10–11).

29. Carol Cook, "'The Sign and Semblance of Her Honor': Reading Gender Difference in *Much Ado About Nothing*," *PMLA* 101 (1986): 186–202, and Jean E. Howard, "Renaissance Antitheatricality and the Politics of Gender and Rank in *Much Ado About Nothing*," in *Shakespeare Reproduced*, devote considerable attention to the main characters in their studies of patriarchal power structures. See also Janice Hays, "Those 'soft and delicate desires': *Much Ado* and the Distrust of Women," in *The Woman's Part: Feminist Criticism of Shakespeare*, ed. Carolyn Ruth Swift Lenz, Gayle Greene, and Carol Thomas Neely (Urbana: University of Illinois Press, 1980), 79–99, who makes Claudio the central figure in a psychoanalytic reading of the play.

30. Although he does not deal directly with authority, John Traugott, "Creating a Rational Rinaldo: A Study of the Mixture of the Genres of Comedy and Romance in *Much Ado About Nothing*," *Genre* 15 (1982): 157-81, studies the relationship of *Much Ado*'s plots in a similar fashion, proposing that the Hero-Claudio plot is a tragicomedy whose comic potential is underscored by the Beatrice-Benedick plot. Traugott also views the latter as dominant and redemptive.

31. Paul A. Jorgensen, "Much Ado About *Nothing*," *Shakespeare Quarterly* 5 (1954): 287–95, was the first to deal at length with the title's pun on "noting," followed by Dorothy Hockey, "Notes, Notes, Forsooth . . . ." *Shakespeare Quarterly* 8 (1957): 353–58. Since then, referring to the pun has become something of a commonplace. David Ormerod, "Faith and Fashion in *Much Ado About Nothing*," *Shakespeare Survey* 25 (1972): 93–105, discusses at length the use and function of the word "fashion" in *Much Ado*, and points out that the play has the highest concentration of the word in the entire canon (94). The connection between "fashioning" and the pun on "nothing" has, of course, to do with the play's interest in the production and interpretation of meaning. This topic is treated, in three widely differing contexts, by Cook, "Sign and Semblance"; Anthony B. Dawson, "Much Ado About Signifying," *Studies in English Literature* 22 (1982): 211–21; Drakakis, "Trust and Transgression"; and Krieger, "Social Relations."

32. That fashioning has harmful, material consequences is reinforced by the play's frequent use of violent imagery to express the power of words. For instance,

not only do Beatrice and Benedick fight a "merry war," but Benedick also views his position as that of a "man at a mark, with a whole army shooting at me. She speaks poniards, and every word stabs" (2.1.230–32). The same may be said of many other verbal exchanges in the play. According to Cook, this real power of language is a male prerogative: the act of reading is an act of supremacy reserved for men, while being read is emasculating. But Cook fails to trace the full pattern of interpretive activity in the play. Each of the characters is, at some point, both read and reading, both acted upon and acting against, and it is the measure of *difference* between characters' motivations as they read—rather than simply their gender—which reveals the play's moral appraisal of their action. Arguably, all acts of reading in the play are acts of supremacy; this is not, however, to say that all acts of reading are the same.

33. William Shakespeare, *Much Ado About Nothing*, ed. A. R. Humphreys (London: Methuen, 1981), 1.3.62–63. All references to the play are to this New Arden edition.

34. Quoted by Humphreys, Introduction to *Much Ado*, 3.1.107n.

35. In this light, the emphatic use of Hero's testimony earlier in the play as the primary evidence in gulling Benedict appears to have been nothing more than an officially sanctioned female utterance.

36. Although some critics have favored Claudio in the past (see esp. T. W. Craik, "*Much Ado About Nothing*," *Scrutiny* 19 [1952-53]: 297–316; J. Kerby Neill, "More Ado About Claudio: An Acquittal for the Slandered Groom," *Shakespeare Quarterly* 3 [1952]: 91–107; and Charles T. Prouty, *The Sources of "Much Ado About Nothing"* [New Haven: Yale University Press, 1950]), it is now generally accepted that his character is more despicable than need be, and that the excess represents a deliberate dramaturgical move. Even Shakespeare's use of his sources points in this direction, for all of Claudio's counterparts were invested with more motivation and more honorable behavior in the matter of the challenge against Hero. "It seems unlikely," writes Mares, "in view of this systematic departure from the tendency of well-known analogues, that Claudio was intended as a particularly admirable or sympathetic character" (Introduction to *Much Ado* 5-6).

37. But, as Cook points out, even in the tomb scene, with Claudio presumably seeing the error of his ways, Hero is voiceless while Messina's old order is reestablished: "Claudio's placement of the epitaph on her tomb explicitly dramatizes the silencing of the woman's voice, the substitution of the man's" ("Sign and Semblance" 199).

38. Curiously, Claudio's unexpiated guilt does not seem to concern his fellow characters nearly as much as his audience. Ursula brings news that "the Prince and Claudio [have been] mightily abused, and Don John is the author of all" (5.2.90–91), and Leonato decides that while Margaret "was in some fault for this," Claudio and Don Pedro are innocent because they "accus'd her / Upon the error that you heard debated" (5.4.2–4).

39. This kind of circularity is precisely what leads Cook to denounce the ostentatious harmony of the play's conclusion: "whatever conversion or movement the play offers is notably incomplete, for while the sexual conflict points in an illuminating way to the question of gender differences and what is at stake in them, their relation to subjectivity and authority, the play cannot resolve its contradictions from within its own structures of meaning" ("Sign and Semblance" 186).

40. Still, this most explicit of Beatrice's verbal subversions of the patriarchy is double-edged. While her mockery expresses the supremacy of the daughter's desire over the father's will, the very tone and manner of her challenge reinforce the ultimate supremacy of the patriarchy. In broader terms, Carol Thomas Neely,

"Constructing the Subject: Feminist Practice and the New Renaissance Discourses," *English Literary Renaissance* 18 (1988): 5–18, finds much the same paradoxical pattern in the development of female characters in Shakespeare's comedies: "by attaining the verbal superiority, and taking themselves off the pedestal, by asserting their desires and acting on them, Shakespeare's maids are moving toward and necessitating their subordination as wives—their domestication by silence, by removal of disguise, and by giving themselves, their possessions, and their sexuality to the husbands" (6).

41. I disagree, then, with Carl Dennis, "Wit and Wisdom in *Much Ado About Nothing*," *Studies in English Literature* 13 (1973): 223–37, who reads a parallel movement of both plots from one way of knowing (wit) to another (wisdom). Given the inverse relationship of the two plots, the decline of one and the rise of the other (in terms of comic value), tracing any parallel movement would seem to be mistaken. Certainly the terms in which Dennis sets up his argument fail to account for the complex meaning of "knowing" in the play: rather than moving on a single axis from wit to wisdom, the play seems to combine the two moves by endorsing, finally, the love (i.e., wisdom) of the play's ineducable wits. A similarly erroneous pattern is traced by Ormerod ("Faith and Fashion"), whose terms of reference are "fashion" and "faith," with comic value being invested ultimately in the latter at the expense of the former. I would maintain, however, that the play seems to insist upon the coexistence rather than mutual exclusiveness of "faith and fashion" or "wit and wisdom." See also Drakakis's post-structuralist account ("Trust and Transgression") of the play's polarities.

42. See esp. Harry Berger, Jr., "Against the Sink-a-Pace: Sexual and Family Politics in *Much Ado About Nothing*," *Shakespeare Quarterly* 33 (1982): 302–13; Cook, "Sign and Semblance"; and Howard, "Renaissance Antitheatericality," all of whom, significantly, find the play's concluding harmony less than resounding.

43. But one may be tempted to speculate on the authority of the friar, given the possibility that Shakespeare himself played the part (Mares, Introduction to *Much Ado*, 19).

44. It is surely no accident that Benedick suspects Don John in the affair, and following the challenge to Claudio, Benedick's announcement to Don Pedro that "I must discontinue your company" (5.1.16–87) explicitly sets him apart from Messina's censured "Men's Club." (The phrase is borrowed from Berger, "Against the Sink-a-Pace" 305.)

45. Although they do not figure prominently in my analysis, the subplot characters obviously parody the linguistic habits of their superiors. More extensive treatment of Dogberry, who certainly merits study—though his utter ineffectuality has excluded him from my look at power relations—may be found in John A. Allen, "Dogberry," *Shakespeare Quarterly* 24 (1973): 35–53. The linguistic habits of the Watch do, however, point out the largely independent capacity of language to convey truth even where its transmission is hopelessly mismanaged.

46. That the dance dramatizes the restoration of social order no longer goes without saying. The play's other mention of dance is not auspicious (though Beatrice's metaphor for marriage is given during her tenure as a social rebel), and if the masquing episode also represents social harmony, its promise for the future is ominous indeed. In general, the reassessment of the meaning of dance—and often of Shakespeare's comic closure as a whole—has been carried out by critics committed to exposing Shakespeare's patriarchal investiture. In connection with *Much Ado About Nothing*, see Berger, "Against the Sink-a-Pace"; Cook, "Sign and Semblance"; and Howard, "Renaissance Antitheatericality."

47. For readings which emphasize the value of Beatrice's love in the play's

conclusion, see Crick, "Much Ado About Nothing," *Use of English* 17 (1965): 323–27; Barbara Everett, "Much Ado About Nothing," *Critical Quarterly* 3 (1961): 319–35; and Hayes, "Those 'soft and delicate desires'." For counterpositions, see Berger, "Against the Sink-a-Pace"; and Cook, "Sign and Semblance."

48. This thematic and dramatic symmetrical inversion of the two plots has been noted, among others, by Geoffrey Bullough, ed., *Narrative and Dramatic Sources of Shakespeare*, 8 vols. (London: Routledge, 1957–75): "The plots relating to the two pairs are parallel and antithetical: whereas Hero and Claudio are brought together at the beginning with almost excessive ease, and are then almost fatally separated by mistrust, deception and false report, Beatrice and Benedick, separated at first by mistrust, are brought together by deception and false report" (2.74). The plots intersect and reverse directions in the play's crucial scene, 4.1.

49. On mutuality as a virtue in Shakespeare's comedies, see Marianne L. Novy, "'And You Smile Not He's Gagged': Mutuality in Shakespearean Comedy," *Philological Quarterly* 55 (1976): 178–94.

50. Cook's argument that Beatrice and Benedick do not "represent a challenge or an alternative to Messina's limitations," that "even their irony cannot create [another world], for it participates in the assumptions that shape Messina" ("Sign and Semblance" 200), is true insofar as it refers to the ideological commitments of the play, but in terms of the way the play represents its own conclusion, it is important to notice that, at least in the subplot, a striking and necessary change has taken place.

51. In this connection see Nancy Hartsock, "Foucault on Power: A Theory for Women?" in *Feminism/Postmodernism*, ed. Linda J. Nicholson (New York: Routledge, 1990), 157–75, on the limitations of Foucault's understanding of power for explaining women's oppression and for theorizing political change.

52. "Shakespeare and the Kinds of Drama," *Critical Inquiry* 6 (1979): 121.

53. See, respectively, G. Gregory Smith, ed., *Elizabethan Critical Essays*, 2 vols. (Oxford: Oxford University Press, 1904), 1.59, 1.81, 2.210.

54. At least one writer responds to this difficulty by shifting responsibility for moral correctness to the reader. In William Webbe's opinion, a "lacivious disposed personne" will mistake vice for virtue, while the "warie and skylful" are never in danger of misinterpretation (*Elizabethan Critical Essays*, 1.253).

55. Perhaps the best example of such debates is the contest over the political work of *The Taming of the Shrew*. Critics who argue that Katherine's concluding speech extolling wifely submission is either parodic or playful (and hence subversive) include John C. Bean, "Comic Structure and the Humanizing of Kate in *The Taming of the Shrew*," in *The Woman's Part: Feminist Criticism of Shakespeare*, ed. Carolyn Ruth Swift Lenz, Gayle Greene, and Carol Thomas Neely (Urbana: University of Illinois Press, 1980), 65–78; J. Dennis Huston, *Shakespeare's Comedies of Play* (New York: Columbia University Press, 1981); Alexander Leggatt, *Shakespeare's Comedy of Love* (London: Methuen, 1974); and Novy, "Patriarchy and Play in *The Taming of the Shrew*," *English Literary Renaissance* 9 (1979): 264–80; the case for a "straight" speech (and hence one that reinforces the patriarchal domination of men over women) is made by Richard A. Burt, "Charisma, Coercion, and Comic Form in *The Taming of the Shrew*," *Criticism* 26 (1984): 295–311; Peter B. Erickson, *Patriarchal Structures in Shakespeare's Drama* (Berkeley: University of California Press, 1985); Coppélia Kahn, "*The Taming of the Shrew*: Shakespeare's Mirror of Marriage," *Modern Language Studies* 5, no. 1 (1975): 88-102; Valerie Wayne, "Refashioning the Shrew," *Shakespeare Studies* 17 (1985): 159–87; and Marilyn Williamson, *The Patriarchy of Shakespeare's Comedies* (Detroit: Wayne State University Press, 1986).

56. I would suggest that the only recoverable political work of the comedies is the work it is made to perform in interpretation. Foucault writes that interpretation is the act of filling a text's "enunciative poverty," and this strikes me as a useful way of thinking about the things interpretation does *to* a text. In settling meaning, in supplying signification, interpretation puts a text to work. Without the evidence of Renaissance interpretations, then, the "original" political work of the comedies remains radically inaccessible. In this connection, Ralph Cohen's receptionist approach to genre, which seeks to historicize the *purposes* of generic classification in both the sixteenth and twentieth centuries, is extremely promising ("History and Genre," *New Literary History* 17 [1986]: 203–18).

The Failure to Mourn in *All's Well That Ends Well*

LYNNE M. SIMPSON

> Mourning over the loss of something that we have loved or
> admired seems so natural to the layman that he regards it as
> self-evident. But to the psychologists mourning is a great rid-
> dle, one of those phenomena which cannot themselves be
> explained but to which other obscurities can be traced back.
> —Sigmund Freud, "On Transience"

FOR COPPÉLIA KAHN, Shakespearean romantic comedies examine the issue of grief; however, she places this concern in terms of Blos's outline of adolescent development as biphasal and characterized by mourning:

> Confronted with the great imperative of finding someone to love, the
> adolescent must give up the strongest love he has known thus far, his
> love for his parents. To give it up, he must mourn them, and in mourn-
> ing them, he has recourse to the usual mechanism of mourning: he
> identifies with them, or one of them.[1]

Her analysis is illuminating but limited by making largely symbolic that which occurs literally—the death of a parent. Shakespeare is not merely symbolic; he does not simply equate the loss of a parent with the death of childhood. Incomplete, unwhole (and frequently unwell) families characterize the Shakespearean canon. Helena's substitution in *All's Well That Ends Well* of Bertram for her dead father has been so successful it produces guilt. A central issue for me is Helena's inability to mourn: "How mightily sometimes we make us comforts of our losses!" (4.3.62–63).[2]

To win Bertram, Helena numinously cures the dying king of France despite "all the learned and authentic Fellows" that counted him incurable (2.3.12). The procreative power associated with the cure will restore a dying man with not only life but virility; "your dolphin is not lustier" than the king after Helena's tender ministrations (2.3.26). The king may "lead her a coranto" (2.3.43) but will not keep the maid for himself as in the other "problem comedy," *Measure for Measure*. In the economics of risk taking, the "tax of impudence" and "fee" (2.1.169,188) for failure is her death, but Helena also perceives that failing would mean a ruined reputation:

> A strumpet's boldness, a divulged shame
> Traduc'd by odious ballads; my maiden name
> Sear'd otherwise . . .
>
> (2.1.170–73)

Susan Snyder rightly notes the oddness of staking sexual identity on the cure; yet, this seems apropos to me at both a literal and psychological level.[3] I take the terms of Helena's venture as central to her self-definition and to our understanding of the play. Honor is at stake, and "the honor of a maid is her name" (3.5.12). Feminine honor in the Renaissance means chastity (counterpointed throughout by the juxtaposition of male honor in the Italian war).[4] Furthermore, her virginity is de rigueur—part of the fairy tale element and a prerequisite of her power to heal. Yet "maiden's name" should not only be read as virginity; after all, she means it literally. Helena heals through virginity as well as patriarchal sanction:

> With that malignant cause, wherein the honour
> Of my dear father's gift stands chief in
>   power,
> I come to tender it and my appliance.
>
> (2.1.110–12)

"Sear'd" evokes the image of cauterization, a treatment associated with the healing of an external abscess like the king's fistula. Worth noting that Shakespeare infrequently uses "sear," but when he does, it occurs in the context of usurped royal title and position. For example, Anne in *Richard III*, lamenting both her dubious status as queen and marriage to a usurper, cries:

> O would to God that the inclusive verge
> Of golden metal that must round my brow
> Were red-hot steel, to sear me to the brains!
>
> (4.1.58-60)

At the sight of Banquo's ghost, Macbeth recalls the prophecy with horror: "Down! The crown does sear mine eyelids" (4.1.113).[5] In *All's Well* no one steals a crown; however, in terms of this play, knowledge is power:

> Many receipts he gave me; chiefly one,
> Which, as the dearest issue of his practice,
> And of his old experience th' only darling,
> He bade me store up as a triple eye,
> Safer than mine own two . . .
>
> (2.1.104–8)

Rare and precious as "a triple eye," the cure handed down from father to daughter is not unlike a royal diadem. As "th' only darling," the inherited cure is imagined—like Helena herself—as an only child.

Be careful what you wish for . . . you just might get it. From a psychoanalytical point of view, wanting "a baby from the father" is normal: obtaining it spells trouble. (Shakespeareans who disbelieve Freud should refer here to *Pericles*.) For Freud, the castration complex in females signals the onset of the Oedipal complex and not its resolution as with the male.[6] A wish for a baby with the father replaces the absent penis:

> Not until the emergence of the wish for a penis does the doll-baby become a baby from the girl's father, and thereafter the aim of the most powerful feminine wish. . . . Often enough in her combined picture of 'a baby from her father' the emphasis is laid on the baby and her father left unstressed.[7]

"A baby from her father" is realized in the cure—and this baby is highly "emphasized." Regarded as more valuable than Helena, it is also the mainspring of the plot. Two substitutions will occur. By the resolution of the play, impregnation by Bertram replaces "the baby from her father." This pregnancy will in turn be obtained by exchanging a hymen for a wedding ring.

One could imagine a Freudian arguing—given the passage from "Femininity" I cited—that Helena has a particularly resilient case of penis envy judging from her "masculine" pursuit of courtship. Feminist studies celebrate this character for actively pursuing the male love object, a gender reversal of the norm of patriarchal courtship.[8] Albeit, no gal's perfect. Sans the self-conscious femininity and coyness that characterize her namesake and predecessor in *A*

Midsummer Night's Dream, Helena has been similarly taken to task (by feminists and nonfeminists) for her own spaniel-like devotion.

David Scott Kastan argues that as a "shadow of a wife," Helena "is forced to admit once again that her notion of love as something that can be earned—either by healing the King or by satisfying the conditions—is inadequate."[9] Barbara Hodgdon in a psychoanalytic study finds that "denied as both virgin and wife, she is nothing."[10] Her self-sacrifice, faulty masochism, and humiliation are the result of ambivalence over willful desiring; Helena's name alone connotes the sexuality of Helen of Troy rather than the idealized chastity of her double in the play, Diana. Richard P. Wheeler, though locating his discussion on the Oedipal anxieties of Bertram, fascinatingly compares Helena to Shakespeare himself:

> In Sonnets 71 and 72, Shakespeare contemplates his own death as a means of freeing the friend from the shame of his overreaching love; Helena, in a sonnet, announces her impending death as a means of freeing Bertram from her "ambitious love": "He is too good and fair for death and me; / Whom I myself embrace to set him free" (III.iv.16–17).[11]

For Wheeler, Helena suffers from what Freud describes as idealization in love in which "the object has, so to speak, consumed the ego."[12] Snyder locates the gaps between Helena's self-assertion and self-abnegation in her success, noting the embarrassed and self-denigrating language when she chooses among the king's courtiers.[13]

Descriptions of Helena's suffering through her trials range from self-abnegation to the loss of ego, suggesting, in my opinion, a psychological dilemma: guilt. Expected from one who emerges a winner from an Oedipal battle, and yet the fact that she accepts the substitute for the father in Bertram would seem to argue a successful conclusion—in Freudian terms—to her Oedipal complex.

Freud cautions in "Femininity" that while the wished-for baby is emphasized, the father is "left unstressed." Helena inherits the cure used to win Bertram from her father "on's bed of death" (2.1.103). Helena cries after being reminded of "her education" which "she inherits" (1.1.36–37)—in short, her father's medical knowledge. Yet the tears she sheds are not simply for the dead father:

> I think not on my father,
> And these great tears grace his remembrance more
> Than those I shed for him. What was he like?

> I have forgot him; my imagination
> Carries no favour in't but Bertram's . . .
>
> (1.1.77–81)

Forgetting a father? No wonder she feels guilt as long as she assumes the utter substitution of Bertram for her father.

But after all, mourning finally must end. Freud notes that there is nevertheless something mysterious about its passing, which he acknowledges in mourning's "spontaneous end":

> Mourning, as we know, however painful it may be, comes to a spontaneous end. When it has renounced everything that has been lost, then it has consumed itself, and our libido is once more free (in so far as we are still young and active) to replace the lost objects by fresh ones equally or still more precious.[14]

Mourning the lost object is followed by reparation through the choice and idealization of a new object. Bertram certainly is an idealized love for Helena; however, has she truly renounced everything that has been lost? On the contrary, in seeking a substitute, she in effect denies the death of the father by "forgetting" him despite the prominent and constant reminders by those around her. Hans W. Loewald, in exploring the relation of the termination of analysis to the mourning process, concludes, "Such denial is the opposite of mourning":

> Loss of a love object does not necessarily lead to mourning and internalization. The object lost by separation of death may not be mourned, but either the existence or the loss of the object may be denied.[15]

In using the inherited cure to obtain the desired love object, Helena must re-remember the father:

> Th' ambition in my love thus plagues itself:
> The hind that would be mated by the lion
> Must die for love . . .
>   . . . .
> But now he's gone, and my idolatrous fancy
>   Must sanctify his relics. (1.1.88–90, 95–96)

Despite her protestations to the contrary, Helena's glaringly imprecise use of the masculine pronouns (which occurs not only in this soliloquy but throughout the remainder of the scene) betrays an unconscious admission that the substitution of Bertram for the father has been incomplete. "Idolatrous fancy" refers not only to

Helena's ambitious love for Bertram, above her in social station, but also its improper replacement for the father.

"Sanctification" of the father's memory will occur first in the appropriation of his cure to secure the love object. Should we interpret this cure as divine or secular? Lafew offers the first report: "They say miracles are past; and we have our philosophical persons to make modern and familiar, things supernatural and causeless" (2.3.1–3). In the king's cure, it would seem, is that unlooked-for modern miracle, allowing Lafew to hearken back to a mystical past. The public report of the broadsheet ballads apparently sides with him: "A showing of a heavenly effect in an earthly actor" (2.3.23)— a suitably ambiguous headline not unworthy of *The National Inquirer*. Do we witness a heavenly outcome or does "effect" here mean only an impression produced by an artifice or manner of presentation? Inquiring minds want to know. Helena tells the countess that if the king accepts her aid, "his good receipt / Shall for my legacy be **sanctified** [emphasis mine] / By th' luckiest stars in heaven" (1.3.239–41). Only after successfully curing him does she insist, "Heaven hath through me restor'd the king to health" (2.3.64). Helena, by announcing divine sanction, asserts patriarchal approval—a fatherly benediction—of her choice of Bertram.

Sanctification next requires forgiveness—Helena must forgive herself for forgetting the father, for forgetting "a maiden's name" in seeking a married one. We might argue that her choice of a love object alone guarantees self-imposed penance for this guilt, as the critics uniformly harangue Bertram. The inimitable Dr. Johnson, for example, complains in his *Prefaces*:

> I cannot reconcile my heart to Bertram; a man noble without generosity, and young without truth; who marries Helena as a coward, and leaves her as a profligate; when she is dead by his unkindness, sneaks home to a second marriage, is accused by a woman whom he has wronged, defends himself by falsehood, and is dismissed to happiness.[16]

G. K. Hunter points out that Shakespeare rewrites Boccaccio in such a way as to "depress Bertram in our estimation."[17] Or as Carolyn Asp recently put it, "The frog prince remains a frog until the end and the princess chooses to overlook his slimy skin."[18] The plot tests Helena's resolve in an unconsummated marriage in which prince not-so-charming runs off to an Italian war and the pursuit of the chaste (happily) Diana.

Helena's trials for her failure to mourn are enacted publicly through her tribulations with Bertram, but at a more profound level, are self-imposed and internal tests. She stages her own death, symbolically substituting herself for her father in paying for the cure:

> And though I kill him not, I am the cause
> His death was so effected. Better 'twere
> I met the ravin lion when he roar'd
> With sharp constraint of hunger; better 'twere
> That all the miseries which nature owes
> Were mine at once.
>
> (3.2.115–20)

Not hyperbole for Helena because obtaining Bertram was at the cost of a father—being the inadvertent cause of Bertram's death would be psychically unbearable. From the beginning, "the hind that would be mated by the lion / Must die for love"; now, however, a substitution is envisioned: her life for Bertram. She in turn flees in what I take to be a genuine renunciation of Bertram: "He is too good and fair for death and me; / Whom I myself embrace to set him free" (3.4.16–17). Her "death" marks the end of the sanctification.

For Helena, totally orphaned, restoration must necessarily occur outside the family structure in order to reconstitute it. She harbors a fear of "a divulged shame" in obtaining the love object (2.1.170). Hence her insistence that "The Count Rossillion cannot be my brother," that Bertram "must not be my brother" (1.3.150,154). Helena repeatedly must deny a potential surrogate mother in the countess because of the taboo (see 1.3.134–62). Incestuous prohibition allies with social stratification as he is above her in class.

Helena's wooing has an atypically frank sexual component which psychologically exacerbates her guilt over the pursuit of Bertram, a pseudo-brother. Parolles charges that she is "meditating on virginity" (1.1.108); as the following bawdy exchange between the two makes clear, she rather contemplates its loss. Helena envisions a siege of virgins against would-be seducers (1.1.110–31). Although this is a common topoi, I would argue that for Helena, the real war is internal: "How might one do, sir, to lose it to her own liking?" (1.1.147).

> *Parolles*: Will you do anything with it [virginity]?
> *Helena*: Not my virginity; yet . . .
>
> (159–61)

Although the break in the line may be attributed to textual corruption, the ellipse richly suggests daydreaming about the loss of maidenhead—not with Parolles but "one that goes with him" (1.1.97). Her later cryptic remark to Parolles reveals this longing: "'Tis pity . . . That wishing well had not a body in't / Which might be felt" (1.1.175,177–78). Yes, she hopes Bertram is well, but the real wish is for gratified desire. Helena's stress on losing her virginity in the opening scene suggests to me heightened awareness of anatomical distinction. The real complaint contained in the war metaphor of assault is feminine passivity: what active role may a woman play when biologically speaking, virginity must be "taken?"

The bed tricks problematize for many critics the moral virtue of Helena and, in *Measure for Measure*, of Isabella. In both plays, the third act concludes with similar riddles whose punning, repetition, and simple rhyme scheme (a a b b) seek dispensation:

> Let us assay our plot; which, if it speed,
> Is wicked meaning in a lawful deed,
> And lawful meaning in a lawful act,
> Where both not sin, and yet a sinful fact.
>
> (3.7.44–47)

Helena seeks sanctification or "not sin," countering Bertram's proposed adultery with his marital duty to her. After they marry, she begs—though unsuccessfully—a kiss, trying to engage him sexually (2.5.86). The bed trick expedites her own wish fulfillment of sexual consummation. A woman demands her love-choice with no less than a king to support her: this is the troubled prerogative of the Shakespearean father who chooses his daughter's husband.

Critics note the parallels of *All's Well* to Shakespeare's *Venus and Adonis*.[19] Helena's own successful pursuit of the love object recalls the myth of the goddess's conquest of Adonis. Yet the tragic ending of the legend is relevant as well. At the death of Adonis by the wild boar, Venus mixes nectar with his blood to create the red anemone, or wind flower, as annual memorial of the spectacle of his death and her grief. Part of Helena's guilt directly relates to the cure's high cost: "If knowledge could be set up against mortality" (1.1.28–29) rather than be its price.

This drama of death and forgetting, memory and forgiveness, will be repeated in the conclusion of the play. The King of France claims to forgive Bertram for his part in her supposed death in language that echoes Helena's earlier soliloquy:

> We are reconcil'd, and the first view shall
>   kill
> All repetition. Let him not ask our pardon;
> The nature of his great offence is dead,
> And deeper than oblivion we do bury
> Th' incensing relics of it.
>
> (5.3.21–25)

Relics now serve only to incense as they are devoid of true forgiveness (or sanctification in the earlier terms of her soliloquy). The king recalls rather than forgets Helena's death—indeed, the pardon fails to mask the obvious aggression indicated by his word choice of "kill" and "bury."

Restitution must be made. The king concludes that Bertram's prior love for Maudlin "strikes some scores away / From the great compt" (5.3.56-57). But before he consents to a second marriage, the king reproaches Bertram for the next ten lines (57–66) concluding ironically, "Be this sweet Helen's knell, and now forget her" (5.3.67). Bertram's subsequent exposure by Diana and her mother are his punishment for mistreating Helena. But of course Helena is not dead, and whether or not Bertram is sorry is finally anyone's guess. The name of Maudlin must clearly be emblematic, but which does it mean—effusive sentimentality or the tearful repentance of the Magdalene? Shakespeare will restage this scene in earnest in *The Winter's Tale* so that the genuinely repentant Leontes need not marry some version of a Maudlin.

II

All's Well sings its own funeral dirge for the dead; it hearkens back to a "golden age" when the Count Rossilion and Gerard de Narbon lived and the king was young and well. This nostalgia establishes a discrepancy between the values of that court and the present one with it dubious involvement in a foreign war as well as the errant behavior of Parolles and Bertram.

In Painter's *Palace of Pleasure*, Shakespeare's most likely translation of Boccaccio, Bertram's father dies followed by Giletta's. Shakespeare presents the death of both fathers simultaneously. "Succeed thy father," the countess tells Bertram; "hold the credit of your father," Lafew counsels Helena. Helena and Bertram are doubles—split aspects of one grieving ego.

For Bertram, impending departure from the mother specifically causes him to "weep o'er my father's death anew" (1.1.3–4). Separation signals potential loss of restoration in that he overvalues the surviving parent. Rather than seeking reparation through marriage and a family of his own, only the apparent death of his wife allows him to return home to his mother and 'mother'land ["Till I have no wife I have nothing in France"] (3.2.74).

Note simply Bertram's jealous and peevish interruption of the countess's consolation of Helena (1.1.55). Hunter is right in arguing that Lafew's comment in the subsequent line is meant to call attention to Bertram's rudeness. [20] I find it significant that the interruption occurs precisely at the start of the countess's lecture on proper mourning (1.1.47–54). Perhaps Bertram too feels the momentary sting of guilt in crying over the ensuing separation from the mother rather than for the dead father.

Bertram's response to the king's panegyric of his dead father underscores the difficulty in being torn between remembrance and a longing for forgetfulness:

> His good remembrance, sir,
> Lies richer in your thoughts than on his
>   tomb;
> So in approof lives not his epitaph
> As in your royal speech.
>
> (1.2.48–51)

The distance between presence and absence is measured by "royal speech" and silent "epitaph." The good will not be interred with the bones. Neither the countess (who equates Bertram with a "second husband") nor the king allow Bertram to forget his father. In *Hamlet* the Ghost returns from the dead with royal speech for the edification of the son; here the king—surrogate father—who has "both sovereign power and father's voice" (2.3.54) quotes directly the words of the former count:

> "Let me not live," quoth he,
> After my flame lacks oil, to be the snuff
> Of younger spirits, whose apprehensive
>   senses
> All but new things disdain; whose
>   judgements are
> Mere fathers of their garments; whose
>   constancies
> Expire before their fashions."
>
> (1.2.58–63)

The king identifies with the dead father and expresses his own thanatos: "This he wish'd / I, after him, do after him wish too" (64–65).

"Mere fathers" (1.2.62)—fathers apparently too easily forgotten—
are at odds with ungrateful whelps.

Bertram ostensibly desires nothing if not to be a dutiful son to
mother and dead father; however, he has his share of Oedipal difficulties as his note to his mother reveals. Although he has wedded
Helena, he has "not bedded her"—in short, as he closes the note,
"My duty to you" (2.2.20–21, 24). For Bertram succeeding the father, as Wheeler aptly demonstrates, results in Oedipal anxieties
much as holding the credit, the knowledge of Narbon, does in Helena.[21] Like Helena, he seeks a ready substitute—the King of France.
Bertram, too, knows what is expected: "You're loved, sir," he replies
to the King (1.2.68). But the transference of love is not so easy.
Observe Bertram's difficulty with actually rendering dutiful service; he resents being grounded, unable to go outside and play war
with the rest of the boys. To add insult to injury, he is told whom
to marry and saddled with a wife beneath him in station and a
pseudo-sister, one who "had her breeding at my father's charge"
(2.3.114).

In a play proliferate with fathers—dead and alive—it is no doubt
significant (a "meticulous analogy" as Harold C. Goddard put it)
that Parolles's exposure as a traitor occurs at precisely the same
time as Bertram seduces Helena.[22] R. B. Parker notes Shakespeare's
insistence on time in the overlap of the exposure of Parolles's cow-
ardice and treachery between 10 PM and 1 AM (4.1.24) and the bed
trick which occurs from midnight to 1 AM (4.2.54–58, 4.3.28–29).[23]
Bertram identifies with Parolles and merges narcissistically with
one who mirrors him as the pre-Oedipal parent once did. Identification to recover what is lost grows out of Freud's pioneering conception of the "substitute" in which narcissistic affections such as
Bertram displays for Parolles are a "substitution of identification
for object–love."[24] Lafew tells the countess her son was misled by
"a snipp'd taffeta fellow there, whose villainous saffron would have
made all the unbak'd and doughy youth of a nation in his colour"
(4.5.1–4)—the opposite of the Count de Rossillion's exemplar. Potential corrupter of no less than an entire generation, Bertram lays
to rest yet another father in Parolles.

Bertram has an easier time serving the Duke of Florence where
he earns a triumphal war record and is able—at least on the battlefield—to live up to the standard of honor set by his father. Again
the inherent gender distinction in the Renaissance's conception of
honor provides for different motives and potential redress in Bertram. He dukes it out to win dad's approval. She "dies" symboli-

cally but also figuratively in the loss of her maidenhead (read chastely).

The countess laments, "In delivering my son from me, I bury a second husband" (1.1.1.). Giving birth (to a son or to a cure) is equivalent to the death of the father. The clown parodies the larger action of the play as he comments on Bertram's first flight from a substitute father:

> *Clown.* . . . your son will not be kill'd so
> soon as I thought he would.
> *Count.* Why should he be kill'd?
> *Clown.* So say I, madam—if he run away, as
> I hear he does; the danger is in
> standing to't; that's the loss of men, though
> it be the getting of children.
>
> (3.2.36–41)

Bertram flees Helena in terms that suggest an internalization of the play's larger fear that a birth signals the death of a father: "show me a child begotten of thy body that I am father to, then call me husband" (3.2.57–58). Bertram will not "die" to replace the father as Helena does; rather the play assures his well being from the countess's first line to Helena's care-taking in the conclusion.

Fleeing the father as well as the mother as well as the sister in Helena, Bertram's seduction of Diana clearly represents a necessary break with his paternal past. The ring he finally relinquishes "downward hath succeeded in his house / From son to son some four or five descents / Since the first father wore it" (3.7.23–25). Bertram accepts his own mortality associated with fatherhood and renounces a family romance recreation of the dead father. In moving outward from the bonds of immediate family, Bertram's pursuit of Diana enacts the frequently difficult biblical stricture that a man shall leave his father and his mother (symbolized in his earlier flight from France) and cleave unto his wife (Genesis 2:24). The marriage ceremony may now occur without incestuous taboo:

> Here, take my ring;
> My house, mine honour, yea, my life be thine,
> And I'll be bid by thee.
>
> (4.2.51–53)

Bertram's submission finally allows a posture not unlike Helena's self-sacrifice. While she has been forced to remember the father, he now is able to mourn and move forward; he symbolically walks away from the gravesite in surrendering "his monumental ring" (4.3.16). All will come full circle like the ring itself. The father will be properly remembered in the begetting of children as the son becomes father in the conclusion of the play.

Yet Diana is hardly his wife, and Bertram's "abstract of success" in Italy includes having "buried a wife, mourn'd for her" (4.3.83, 85). The touching tribute the supposedly dead Helena receives from the countess and her retainers juxtaposes Bertram's callousness (see 4.5.7–16). His homecoming deflates the prior heroism through his association with Parolles (4.5.1–6) and by "a patch of velvet on's face" which may or may not hide a syphilic scar rather than a war wound (4.5.90–92). The ring he offers Diana in his version of the wedding ceremony is suitably mocked but never reduced to parody. Helena (through Diana) has given him her own ring, a token from her surrogate father, the King of France. By possessing it, he stands accused of foul play in relation to her death; however, all's well that ends well, as Helena insists (twice). Bertram may be forgiven, redeemed through Helena's resurrection.

At the end Helena, no longer a "shadow of a wife" but a living, pregnant one, is absolved of her denial, her failure to mourn. She is not only given a husband but another mother in the countess: "O my dear mother, do I see you living?" (5.3.313). A "living" mother has been substituted for a dead father, a mother she was earlier forced to deny to preclude incest. Sanctification must occur first as the countess's earlier lines make clear:

> Why not a mother? When I said "a mother",
> Methought you saw a serpent. What's in "mother"
> That you start at it?
>
> (1.3.134–36)

The mother may be re–found only after Oedipal guilt is resolved. The post-Edenic world signals a fall from grace otherwise and a breaking of taboo. No freedom from original sin in a world of lapsed fathers; only if Gerard de Narbon had lived then he "would have made nature immortal, and death should have play for lack of work" (1.1.19–20).

III

All's Well enacts a search for identity through separation with family ties and creating them anew: "As we are ourselves, what things are we!" Viola in *Twelfth Night* prefigures Helena in that both women—after the death of their fathers—pursue the love object with implied patriarchal sanction. At the Captain's first mention of the duke, Viola implies posthumous endorsement: "Orsino! I have heard my father name him" (1.2.28).[25] Shielded by her adopted masculine attire and defined as moldable and frail, she passively woos Orsino. She courts Olivia for him and simply hopes, much like Helena, that all's well that ends well:

> Disguise, I see thou art a wickedness,
> Wherein the pregnant enemy does much.
> How easy is it for the proper false
> In women's waxen hearts to set their
>   forms!
> Alas, our frailty is the cause, not we,
> For such as we are made of, such we be.
> How will this fadge? . . .
> . . . .
> O time, thou must untangle this, not I,
> It is too hard a knot for me t'untie.
>
> (2.3.26–31, 39–40)

Again the issue is identity in a fallen world, one beset by the "pregnant enemy." Compare the line "For such as we are made of, such we be" to "As we are ourselves, what things are we!" Viola's conception of identity seems, like her, more passive, more fatalistic. Identity in *All's Well*, though equally problematic, allows more room for invention in its open-ended questioning. This tension between action and passivity can be felt in the plays' opposing stances toward mourning.

The Countess Olivia would seem to be the picture of grief, a woman ravaged by the recent loss of a father and a brother. Yet her grief is largely posturing—a picture indeed, one she willingly unveils for Cesario (1.5.236–38). This act of removing the black veil signals the end of an affected mourning in which Olivia would "water once a day her chamber round / With eye offending brine" (1.1.29–30) and abjure "the company / And sight of men" (1.2.40–41). These are but the trappings and the suits of woe. The idea of sincerity in mourning is a classical commonplace in both Seneca and Plutarch. In *All's Well* Helena's grief needs to be established as genuine:

> *Count.* No more of this [crying], Helena; go to, no more; lest it be rather thought you affect a sorrow than to have—
> *Hel.* I do affect a sorrow indeed, but I have it too.
>
> (1.1.47–50)

Her response is Hamlet's; however, while both are genuine, Hamlet mourns for his father while Helena, as her soliloquy at the end of the scene reveals, grieves over the impending departure of Bertram (see *Hamlet* 1.2.89–100). Still, the two are not unrelated:

> In everyday life, many of us tend to cut short a farewell, perhaps in order to diminish the embarrassment, the ambiguity, and the pain, even though we may be torn between the grief of separation and the eager anticipation of the future awaiting us. Others seem to wish to prolong the farewell; yet it is not the farewell they want to prolong but the presence of the beloved person so as to postpone the leave taking as long as possible. In both cases an attempt is made to deny loss: either we try to deny that the other person still exists or did exist, or we try to deny that we have to leave the beloved person and must venture out on our own. Either the past or the future is denied.[26]

Feste in his role as critical commentator reduces Olivia to a "fool" by recognizing her posturing in grief (see 1.5.64–70). Yet I think it is most in his lyrical and haunting song that he serves as spokesperson for the play's overarching conception of bereavement:

> Come away, come away death,
> And in sad cypress let me be laid.
> Fie away, fie away breath,
> I am slain by a fair cruel maid:
> My shroud of white, stuck all with yew,
>   O prepare it.
> My part of death no one so true
>   Did share it.
>
> Not a flower, not a flower sweet,
> On my black coffin let there be strewn:
> Not a friend, not a friend greet
> My poor corpse, where my bones shall be
>   thrown:
> A thousand thousand sighs to save,
>   Lay me, O where
> Sad true lover never find my grave,
>   To weep there.

$$(2.4.50–66)$$

The song seeks to prevent mourning, and as lover's complaint, simultaneously sings its own threnody, providing in itself a lasting memorial. We recall Viola's famous image of "Patience on a monument, / Smiling at grief" (2.4.115–16). The act of smiling at once seems to deny grief while the image of the funerary monument relentlessly remembers the dead.

Remembering the dead—not forgetting as in *All's Well. Non accettare sostituti!* I am reminded of Il Camposanto di Pisa. This stark white cemetery, rumored to contain dirt from Calvary brought back by the Crusaders, was nearly destroyed by an Allied bombing. Its crumbling frescoes by The Master of the Triumph of Death and broken Roman sarcophagi lie in their ruined splendor even more powerful and moving in their tribute. One statue stands out: "L' Inconsolabile." She never smiles.

Hunter, in editing *All's Well*, locates the difficulty of critical interpretation in the play's very language. He finds "an attempt to express complex thought within the limits of normal syntax and versification" which will not be solved stylistically until the romances with their "extremely loose parenthetical syntax."[27] In the romances, however, the dead are resurrected most astonishingly. Unlike *The Winter's Tale*, here we as audience know that all's well because Helena is still alive. We are finally in a "normal" world rather than in the realm of romance. Despite the fairy tale elements of the play, no one returns from the dead.

Notes

1. "The Providential Tempest and the Shakespearean Family," in *Representing Shakespeare*, ed. Murray M. Schwartz and Coppélia Kahn (Baltimore: Johns Hopkins University Press, 1982), 218–19. Kahn utilizes Peter Blos's work in *On Adolescence: A Psychoanalytic Interpretation* (New York: Free Press, 1962).

2. All citations of *All's Well* are from the Arden edition, ed. G. K. Hunter (London: Methuen, 1967).

3. "*All's Well That Ends Well* and Shakespeare's Helens," *English Literary Renaissance* 18, no. 1 (Winter 1988): 68.

4. See R. B. Parker's "War and Sex in *All's Well That Ends Well*," *Shakespeare Survey* no. 37, ed. Stanley Wells (Cambridge: University Press, 1984). Parker pursues G. Wilson Knight's argument in *The Sovereign Flower* (London: Methuen, 1958) that the play is based on a conflict between masculine and feminine ideas of honor. Parker argues that the ideas of war and love modify one another: Bertram must abandon war to accept his sexuality while Helena must give up her self-abnegation in love by demonstrating increased aggression.

5. Citations of *Richard III* and *Macbeth* are from *The Riverside Shakespeare*, ed. G. Blakemore Evans (Boston: Houghton Mifflin, 1974).

6. All citations are from *The Standard Edition of the Complete Psychological Works of Sigmund Freud*, ed. James Strachey (London: Hogarth Press, 1953–74), "Anatomical Sex Distinction," 19:256.

7. Freud, "Femininity," 22:128.

8. Carolyn Asp concludes, "By the play's end she [Helena] has come to value and depend on the world of women whose power Bertram, with some humility

is forced to acknowledge. Her success argues for a reevaluation of the patriarchal denigration of female desire and a reconsideration of that desire's power and validity in the social order," "Subjectivity, Desire and Female Friendship in *All's Well That Ends Well*," *Literature and Psychology* 32 (1986): 60–61. Barbara Hodgdon asserts "Shakespeare's text generates an incipient critique of patriarchal systems as well as a model of feminized power" in "The Making of Virgins and Mothers: Sexual Signs, Substitute Scenes and Doubled Presences in *All's Well That Ends Well*," *Philological Quarterly* 66, no 1 (Winter 1987): 66. Susan Snyder finds the conclusion, however, less a feminist triumph than Asp or Hodgdon: "Does *All's Well* really 'change the story?' I don't know. What it does do, I think is to enact . . . the difficulties and conflicts of imagining a woman as active, desiring subject. It doesn't end unambiguously well and has trouble ending at all. That shouldn't surprise us" in "*All's Well That Ends Well* and Shakespeare's Helens," *English Literary Renaissance* 18, no. 1 (Winter 1988): 77.

9. "*All's Well That Ends Well* and the Limits of Comedy," *English Literary History* 52, no. 3 (Fall 1985): 583.

10. Hodgdon, "Making of Virgins," 57.

11. *Shakespeare's Development and the Problem Comedies* (Berkeley: University of California Press, 1981), 62.

12. Wheeler, *Shakespeare's Development*, 65, cf. "Group Psychology and the Analysis of the Ego," 18:113.

13. Snyder, "*All's Well*," 67.

14. Freud, "On Transcience," 14:307.

15. "Internalization, Separation, Mourning, and the Superego," in *Papers on Psychoanalysis* (New Haven: Yale University Press, 1980), 261.

16. *The Yale Edition of the Works of Samuel Johnson*, ed. Arthur Sherbo (New Haven: Yale University Press, 1968), 7:404.

17. Hunter, Arden xxvi.

18. Asp, "Subjectivity, Desire," 48.

19. See especially James Calderwood, "Styles of Knowing in *All's Well*," *Modern Language Quarterly* 25 (1964): 272–94, and Snyder, "*All's Well*," 947–48.

20. Hunter, Arden, 56.

21. See Wheeler's masterful chapter entitled "Imperial Love and the Dark House," *Shakespeare's Development*, 34–91.

22. *The Meaning of Shakespeare* (Chicago: University of Chicago Press, 1951), 2:46.

23. Parker, "War and Sex," 104.

24. Freud, "Mourning and Melancholia," 14:249.

25. All *Twelfth Night* citations are from the Arden edition, ed. J. M. Lothian and T. W. Craik (London: Routledge & Kegan Paul, 1975). For calling this similar sanction to my attention, I am indebted to William Kerrigan.

26. Loewald, "Internalization, Separation," 258–59.

27. Hunter, Arden, lviii.

The Wooing of Duke Vincentio and Isabella of *Measure for Measure:* "The Image of It Gives [Them] Content"

CAROLYN E. BROWN

DUKE VINCENTIO and Isabella of *Measure for Measure* are disturbing characters. They both aspire to live saintly existences, professing to be the epitome of morality and chastity, and yet they engage in what often seem to be unethical, sexually charged acts. A few of their activities repeatedly provoke critical disapprobation and puzzlement. Scholars, for example, are unsettled by two celibate figures, repulsed with illicit sexuality as a "vice that most [they] do abhor, / And most desire should meet the blow of justice" (2.2.29–30),[1] deciding on a sexual remedy—the bedtrick—to disentangle complications. Despite the sanctioning of the "substituted bedmate" as a typical Elizabethan plot device and despite the Duke's whitewashing of it as a plan having "merit," the Duke and Isabella's arranging an act of sexual consummation smacks of pandering.[2] Likewise, when the Duke in act 4, scene 3 lies to Isabella about her brother's safety in order to induce her, in turn, to lie and to announce publicly that Angelo has sexually violated her, the Duke and Isabella involve themselves in additional sexually loaded activities. It seems unethical for the Duke to withhold vital news from Isabella and to place this prospective nun in what should be an "abhor[rent]" situation of declaring herself a "virgin violat[ed]." The Duke's marriage proposal to Isabella also rankles some critics, not only because Shakespeare does not clarify Isabella's response, but also because it seems inappropriate for two chaste characters to contemplate marriage. Moreover, the gesture seems dramatically weak, Shakespeare not having developed a love relationship between Isabella and the Duke. Some critics argue, in fact, that Shakespeare introduces an ill-prepared marriage between the Duke and Isabella to try to resolve complex issues that cannot be answered within the constructs of his play.[3]

But the marriage proposal may not be an unmotivated act or Shakespeare's feeble way of resolving plot complications, and the Duke and Isabella's actions may not be as inscrutable as they first seem. The Duke and Isabella may involve themselves in sexually oriented deeds because, despite their protestations to the contrary, they are presented as having a "feeling for the sport" (3.2.115), as Lucio says of the Duke. Critics are dissatisfied with the protagonists' relationship partially because they expect typical romantic gestures from the Duke and Isabella like those that other Shakespearean characters use to woo each other. But we must always remember that *Measure for Measure* is a peculiar play. Scholars, for example, have long acknowledged the play's "problematical" stature, in particular its aberrant qualities that make it "somehow not quite like the romantic comedies which preceded it," that make it "different, strange."[4] Moreover, the Duke and Isabella are like no other lovers in Shakespearean comedy. In fact, they do not manifest any characteristics of lovers. Rather, they pride themselves on being sexually defunct, on having killed their sexuality. They sing no love songs, exchange no rings, make no professions of love. And yet the play is largely concerned with the libido; Eric Partridge, for example, dubs *Measure for Measure* along with *Othello* "Shakespeare's most sexual, most bawdy plays."[5]

Given these paradoxical factors, we should not be surprised if the relationship of the two protagonists, like the play itself, betrays unusual, aberrant characteristics; if, in fact, it is different, strange, out of the ordinary. Their involvement in the bedtrick and their activities in act 5 may constitute a hidden wooing process and contain a subliminal sexual significance for them. Their relationship may be strange in the sense that it is unwholesome, taboo. Critics have proposed that part of the perplexity, even "unpleasantness" of the play results from the darker, "nightmarish" aspects. And the darkness seems to relate to sexuality, pain, and desecration, and to the infliction of humiliation and physical discomfort. Richard Wheeler, for example, proposes that the play explores an "inherently debasing sexual nature" and that Angelo's "degradation of sexuality can be charted through images that intensify its connections with . . . aggressive, external coercion."[6] The Duke and Isabella's wooing may be difficult to detect, then, because it is complex, disturbed, even cankered, "bent" from the natural course.

Some recent scholarship provides a basis from which we can begin to understand the Duke's "strange" relationship with Isabella. First, critics have observed that the Duke differs from other Shakespearean protagonists in that he seldom acts himself, but is, as Lucio says, a "duke of dark corners" (4.3.150). Because he does not involve himself in life, he has not cultivated the sense of touch but rather the less intimate senses of hearing and seeing. The Duke characterizes himself as an "observer" (1.1.28), a "looker-on" (5.1.315), a spectator, not a participant—qualities that Janet Adelman argues betray his voyeurism.[7] Such a character might well identify with a double—a surrogate, a "substitute," a "deputy"— that is, with Angelo.[8] Because the Duke sees a "soul" like himself in Angelo, a man who shares similar proclivities, the Duke can achieve vicarious pleasure by watching his double's actions.[9] Thus he is an "intolerable snoop," to cite Northrop Frye's epithet for the Duke, and becomes involved in others' lives because, as Richard Wheeler and Bernard Paris argue, "he live[s] vicariously through the experiences of others."[10]

To identify with a surrogate and picture oneself in the substitute's place, one must develop the inner eye, the imagination. Janet Adelman notes a proclivity for fantasizing in the Duke's double: "For Angelo, sexual excitement comes only from the idea of violating virtue, as though the act of 'sweet uncleanness' is sweet only if he can imagine himself literally befouling something clean."[11] One can find a comparable fantastical nature in the Duke, in that his strange images of pain, of a "baby beat[ing] the nurse," of "Liberty pluck[ing] Justice by the nose" and of a father threatening his children with bound-up birch rods (1.3.19–30), can be seen as indicating fantasies of beating in the "fantastical" Duke (3.2.89; 4.3.156). Isabella, too, betrays a subterranean sexuality that clashes with her righteous exterior. Although she roots her appeal to Angelo in act 2 in biblical arguments, critics have noted a subliminal seductive tenor to her words and a secret attraction to Angelo's proposal.[12] She, like the Duke, is portrayed as possessing a vivid imagination and uses images that suggest a strange attraction to sexual subjugation: "Th'impression of keen whips I'd wear as rubies, / And strip myself to death as to a bed / That longing have been sick for" (2.4.101–3). Critics have pointed to the eroticism of pain in these lines, to their "fantastic" quality, and to their masochistic tone.[13]

If we consider these recent lines of criticism when tracing the "love" relationship of the Duke and Isabella, their unusual wooing may become less baffling. I propose that their sexuality is represented in the text as unconscious, hidden from the text's presentation of their conscious minds. In other words, the text shows us an Isabella and a Duke who do not recognize the full significance of their perpetrating the bedtrick, who do not see the sexual subtext of their activities. The Duke meets his female complement in Isabella who, like the Duke, is shown as protecting herself from improper desires by resorting to fantasy and vicarious identification and who is shown as secretly relishing sexual violation.[14] They are presented as wooing each other by deriving vicarious pleasure from arranging and describing to each other the details of the tryst between their doubles—Mariana and Angelo. Hearing about the scene is presented as appealing to their voyeurism, to their ability to "see" the scene in their imagination.[15] The Duke arranges the bedtrick and Isabella accedes in order to facilitate what is described as a fantastical nature. The text, then, suggests their relationship is not based on the senses, but rather on the imagination, on the fantasizing about sexual intercourse.[16] Because they are presented as denying themselves physical sexual contact, they, in what the text presents as an unconscious level, have cultivated the mind into a source of gratification.

Much of the reading of *Measure for Measure* that I present here is psychoanalytic in nature—an approach I will address before I proceed to Shakespeare's text. Recently historicists have called such approaches into question by arguing that the Renaissance conceived of self and identity differently from the way modern psychoanalytic theory defines selfhood. Steven Greenblatt, for example, gives a valuable historical perspective to the subject, arguing that individuals were identified not through "psychic history" but through property, name, and social surroundings. Greenblatt suggests that this difference "renders psychoanalytic interpretations marginal or belated."[17] Leah Marcus notes the influence of these new findings on scholarship of the Renaissance, suggesting that critics are resisting from "reading Freudian assumptions back into the early modern era."[18] Although scholars must consider the beliefs and perceptions of the period when studying Shakespeare's works and recognize that he was undoubtedly influenced by them, they must not, however, become constricted by them, blinding themselves to other possibilities in the literature. To view Shakespeare's characters in light of the humors and faculty psychology and the lore of melancholy of his time does a disservice to the complexity of his characterization and does not explain the fascination readers for centuries have felt for his art. What, in part, has made Shakespeare's art outlive that of many of his contemporaries is that he transcends the limitations of the historical conditions in which he lived to depict characters so complicated that they continue to perplex and captivate audiences and readers. Perhaps the Renaissance conception of identity, furthermore, is not as foreign to us as it might seem at first. Norman Holland addresses this point, suggesting that since 1930 "psychoanalysts have arrived increasingly at a self more like the Renaissance concept in being inextricably involved with its social surround."[19] Greenblatt clarifies that because psychoanalysis is a product of the Renaissance, it cannot be used to explain its origins. Considering that Shakespeare, however, so far surpassed the perceptions of his time and was a product of a period receptive to the study of the mind, psychoanalytic approaches seem particularly suitable to Shakespeare and have made significant contributions to the scholarship of his plays.

It has been suggested that the great writers are masters of intuitive psychology, that their insights into the psyche anticipate those of the clinician by three to four decades, that Freud, for example, "may well have learned more from Shakespeare than he did from his patients."[20] Admirers long before Freud have regarded Shakespeare as a genius of psychological intuition. John Dryden, Alexander Pope, Samuel Taylor Coleridge, and Goethe—just to name a few—have paid tribute to Shakespeare's powers of mimesis and his portrayals of the "mind's realities." Samuel Johnson hails Shakespeare for his "representation of life" and contends that Shakespeare's "reputation is therefore safe till human nature shall be changed."[21] Modern critics continue to make the same observations: Bernard Paris claims "Shakespeare created some of the greatest psychological portraits in all of literature"; Patrick Murray praises "Shakespeare's remarkable understanding of the darker recesses of the human mind, and his equally remarkable anticipation of the discoveries of depth psychology."[22] Shakespeare transcends the limited psychology of his time because he describes a "psychic heritage common to all" human beings.[23] He displays human behavior as it has always existed; the modern world simply is able to describe in impressive clinical terminology what Shakespeare expertly delineated. We may speak in different terms from those Shakespeare might have used, but the human nature he captured has not changed. His plays continue to intrigue us because we see ourselves in his characters; we come to understand ourselves better through an understanding of his dramatic personages. Our age may continue to be perplexed by Shakespeare's plays, in fact, because our knowledge of psychology, despite all its terminology and scientific data and observation, still lags behind Shakespeare's unsurpassable understanding of the mind.

In creating his characters, Shakespeare undoubtedly was influenced by his sources and dramatic conventions of his day. Both the Duke and Isabella have their parallels in Cinthio and Whetstone's stories from which Shakespeare borrowed material for *Measure for Measure*. Following the lore of folktale, Shakespeare models his duke on the legendary type of the disguised providential monarch who spies on his kingdom to more astutely assess it and rectify its defects. Shakespeare also capitalizes on the well-known Renaissance device of the bedtrick to bring his comedy to a "happy" conclusion. But it is the modifications of his source material and the conventions that create the complexity and the psychological profundity. While the bedtrick, for example, might have been a standard device, "Shakespeare turned the bed-trick with a difference and did everything he could to provoke 'inappropriate' and 'modern' responses."[24] Critics have noted that Shakespeare changes his sources so as to give the Duke and Isabella human inconsistencies. The Duke, for example, is not a flawless providential figure, nor is his role minimal like that in the sources. His actions are morally questionable and deceptive. Wheeler, for example, sees Shakespeare giving his duke "deep psychological conflict."[25] Shakespeare, similarly, has changed his heroine: she appears in the sources as a modest, selfless young woman who is willing to sacrifice her chastity to save the life of a family member and who ultimately marries and falls in love with the corrupt judge. Shakespeare adds more depth to his heroine by making her into an austere religious figure who espouses magnanimity but practices mean-spiritedness to her brother when he begs for his life, who declares to be dedicated to the spirit but lies, deceives and seems anchored in worldly concerns of the body. Shakespeare complicates matters by making her a rigid member of the strict order of St. Clare and, thus, unable to enact the simple romantic solution of his sources of marrying the corrupt deputy. *Measure for Measure*, then, seems particularly suitable to a psychoanalytic reading in that its characters are psychologically problematic.

The play has perplexed critics and resisted the most sophisticated critical approaches for many centuries. Rosalind Miles contends that the play "holds today an unassailable position as chief 'problem' among the various plays of Shakespeare which have from time to time earned that title."[26] The psychoanalytic readings that have uncovered the voyeurism, vicarious identification, fantasy, and aberrant sexuality, however, have started to make sense of this play. That the results of these psychoanalytic techniques have been so fruitful and have rendered the play more understandable give credibility to the approach, and it is this approach that I explore further. Critics have long noticed the play's psychological orientation: J. C. Maxwell claims that "the germs of twentieth-century psychological ideas" are contained in the play; Michael Long refers to the intensity of the play's "psychological realism"; Joseph Westlund and G. K. Hunter place *Measure for Measure* alongside *All's Well That Ends Well* in their "call for a psychoanalytic reading"; J. W. Lever refers to the play as a "psychological drama" concerned with the "workings of the psyche."[27] My approach is not particularly Freudian in nature; rather, it enlists modern psychoanalytic theory. My analysis is Freudian only insofar as it explores the conflict between conscious and unconscious motives in the characters, between words and actions, between the manifest and latent meanings of characters' behavior. I do not try to impose a theory on the play, but I look closely at the text itself and refer to psychoanalytic theory only in the footnotes to substantiate what I see articulated in the text itself.

As to what extent Shakespeare would have been aware of the reading that I propose or would have been able to articulate the psychology of his characters as I do is impossible to answer. Nor do I think it should have a bearing on a reading of a Shakespearean play. Studies of artistic creation, inchoate and indeterminate though they must necessarily be, suggest that the artist's unconscious plays a dominant part in the creative process, that not all creative decisions are conscious. Writers portray much more about human behavior than they completely comprehend, and they often serve to be poor interpreters of their own work. K. R. Eissler addresses the dilemma by suggesting that "nothing is more subject to change than the meaning that the creator of a work of art attributes to his own creations. And, in any event, which meaning is the real one—the author's conscious evaluation, or the meaning that the work of art he has created has for his unconscious?"[28] I believe, though, that Shakespeare was largely in conscious control of his art and that he provides many signposts in *Measure for Measure* to lead to the kind of reading I provide. As to whether such a reading would have been accessible to Shakespeare's audience is also debatable, but I think ultimately inconsequential. Although we are now coming to realize that all of Shakespeare's audience was not as unlettered or intellectually unsophisticated as was once thought and, thus, Shakespeare could have expected some of his audience to appreciate his psychological subtlety, it is unlikely that any audience has ever fully grasped a dramatist's meaning. Perhaps many of Shakespeare's complex levels of meaning, moreover, are yet to be performed or simply are not performable. At any rate, we do injustice to Shakespeare's genius to reduce his meaning to what only his audience, or any audience of any time, could or can appreciate. Certainly a close reading of a text, an opportunity largely unavailable to Shakespeare's audience, renders a more in-depth understanding than a viewing of a performance of a play. Given our era's familiarity with psychoanalytic theory, we can better appreciate and detect Shakespeare's understanding of the psyche. But Shakespeare's audience must have been as uncomfortable with certain cruxes in the play as audiences are today, as Shakespeare found subtle ways to make his own audience share some level of his psychological sophistication. In *Measure for Measure*, for example, it is largely the incongruities between the professed spirituality of the Duke and Isabella's words and the worldliness of their actions that lead to a fuller meaning and that have bothered audiences and scholars for centuries. Shakespeare most likely made the audience of his day (as he has made audiences for centuries) suspicious that there is a covert sexual significance to Isabella and the Duke's actions. He accomplishes this by giving a seductive tenor to Isabella's appeal to Angelo to save her brother's life; by making Isabella refuse to sacrifice her own virginity yet eagerly involve herself in Mariana's loss of her chastity; by having Isabella describe in act 5 her reputed sexual violation with great fervor and detail; and by having the Duke repeatedly intervene in other characters' sexual lives. Shakespeare's juxtaposition of the sexual exchanges arranged by Pompey and Mistress Overdone with those instigated by the Duke and Isabella also help the audience to see the similarities of the ascetics to the bawds, to see that the bedtrick may be sexually loaded for the protagonists as they perform the offices of procurers.

The Duke and Isabella are complementary characters in many ways: they both live monastic lives characterized by reclusiveness, cerebral pursuits, gravity, and sexual abstinence. As critics have noted, they both show signs, though, of possessing latent sexual desires that they are trying to repress. The image of repression, in fact, is prominent, with the ubiquitous prison house reinforcing the ambiance of confinement and constriction. But there is a major difference between the two characters: while both are trying to deny their sexual natures, Isabella's repression is more severe and her removal from the world more complete. The Duke is a friar in dress only; he is very much a man of the world, and as the ruler of Vienna, he must ultimately return to an active life in all of its dimensions. Isabella's novitiate habit is for real, not a disguise like the friar garb for the Duke. She does not intend to return to the world; in fact, her flight may suggest a fear of her own desires and of the fleshly temptations in that world that she may not feel strong enough to withstand. Vienna, moreover, shows few if any indications of healthy sexuality for men; the opportunities for women are even fewer. Although Shakespeare impresses us with the sexual rigors of the strict nuns of St. Clare, he has Isabella wish for more constraints on her carnality: "And have you nuns no farther privileges?" (1.4.1). Isabella has resorted to the severest means to repudiate her desires and to prevent herself from recognition of them. Her sexuality is far more submerged than the Duke's, and she seems more fearful of her desires and more determined to keep them from ever surfacing. Her psyche, as Shakespeare presents it, seems much more fragile than the Duke's. If the Duke is to be successful in involving Isabella in his sexual scheme, he must appeal to Isabella's need to deceive herself about her desires.

When the Duke first encounters Isabella, the text presents him in the voyeur position, concealed in "dark corners" and secretly "overhearing" the exchange between Isabella and her brother: he instructs the provost to "bring me to *hear* them speak, where I may be conceal'd" (3.1.52) and later tells Claudio he has "*overheard* what hath passed between you and your sister" (3.1.159–60, italics mine). Informing her brother of Angelo's vile proposal, Isabella in act 3, scene 1 is made to unwittingly woo the eavesdropping Duke with her strangely vivid and attractive depiction of the despoliation—a proposal to which she shows a subliminal attraction. Her indirect approach, in which she repeatedly alludes to the sexual attack, is made to appeal to the voyeurism of the Duke, to his ability to envision the rape. Shakespeare makes his usually contemplative Duke move to action and propose a sexual scheme—the bedtrick. The Duke is presented as creating an opportunity for Angelo to act out his cruel desires and for him to identify with Angelo and secretly gratify a fantastical preoccupation with pain. In arranging for Angelo to consummate his union with Mariana, the Duke is shown to arrange a vicarious union with Isabella, as they envision themselves in their respective surrogate's roles. Although the bedtrick does not allow the scene to be experienced firsthand, it is presented as allowing the Duke to "see" it through his own and Isabella's description of the tryst, to again "hear" of the scene as he does in "overhearing" Isabella's reporting the proposed sexual assault to Claudio.

When the Duke introduces the bedtrick, Isabella readily agrees to the plan for several reasons. His appearance as a friar must surely put her at ease, reassuring her that she is part of a religious establishment in which she has placed her absolute trust. His religious garb serves as a guarantee that what she does is righteous. The Duke also has had the advantage of overhearing Isabella's visit with her brother. This position has allowed him to ascertain the importance to Isabella of protecting herself from a conscious recognition of her subliminal desires. And he plays to her need to protect herself from the latent sexual significance of her actions. Isabella advises him on the importance of self-image to herself: "I have spirit to do anything that appears not foul in the truth of my spirit" (3.1.205–6). She attests to her need to deceive not only others but primarily herself, to convince herself that what she does is good. The Duke's persuasive techniques are all geared to doing just this. Besides predisposing her to accept the plan by tantalizing her with repeated mysterious references to a propitious "remedy" and "cure" (3.1.198; 236) that he will not divulge at once, he couches the cryptic proposal in positive terminology: "merited benefit" and a "rupture that [she] may easily heal" (3.1.235). He repeatedly guarantees that her virtue will remain intact, that she can achieve pleasure without guilt: she will "do no stain to [her] own gracious person"; the plan "keeps [her] from dishonour in doing it"; her honor will remain "untainted" (3.1.201; 237; 254). Isabella accedes in part because the Duke assures her she can continue to see herself as a saint.

The Duke is also persuasive because his eavesdropping on Isabella's conversation with Claudio has permitted him to ascertain Isabella's subliminal desires. He plays to her hidden desires so adeptly because they are so similar to his own. His very first words to Isabella indicate a love interest: "I would by and by have some speech with you: the satisfaction I would require is likewise to your own benefit" (3.1.153–54). The sexual nuance to his words makes him sound as if he is asking for a rendezvous with Isabella, as if their meeting will be mutually "satisfying," erotically "beneficial" or pleasing for both of them. The bedtrick is equated with a tryst for them, with a satisfying sexual experience. Shakespeare obliquely associates "speech" or verbal intercourse with sexual gratification, suggesting their exchange will be based on words, on descriptions of the bedtrick that the Duke is about to broach. The Duke betrays that he projects himself into Angelo's place. While he refers to Angelo as his governmental replacement or "substitute"— "How will you do to content this substitute?" (3.1.186)—his language reveals more about what the text presents as his unconscious motives. Identifying with Angelo, his "substitute" or alter-ego, he is described as receiving "content" from Angelo's actions, from imagining himself as Angelo. The Duke's words indicate a blurring of the distinction between himself and his surrogate. In what is delineated as the world of fantasy, the Duke and Angelo fuse into one. Moreover, he betrays that he thinks of Isabella as his sexual partner, bringing him "content" or sexual pleasure by acting out Mariana's part.

While seeing himself in Angelo, the Duke is presented as encouraging Isabella to do much the same with her own surrogate, Mariana. He is shown to woo Isabella by helping her to identify with Mariana, telling her a story about Angelo's betrayal of Mariana, a story that closely coincides with her own compromising situation with Angelo:

> There [in Mariana's brother's shipwreck] she lost a noble and renowned brother, in his love toward her ever most kind and natural; with him, the portion and sinew of her fortune, her marriage dowry; with both, her combinate husband, this well-seeming Angelo . . . [who] left her in her tears, and dried not one of them with his comfort: swallowed his vows whole, pretending in her discoveries of dishonour: in few, bestowed her on her own lamentation, which she yet wears for his sake; and he, a marble to her tears, is washed with them, but relents not. . . . His unjust unkindness, that in all reason should have quenched her love, hath, like an impediment in the current, made it more violent and unruly.
>
> (3.1.219–30; 240–43)

Although clarifying Angelo's unkindness, the Duke gives a haunting, appealing quality to Angelo's cruelty, not enlisting negative but positive words to describe the betrayal. Instead of describing Angelo's behavior as desertion, for example, he says Angelo "left her in her tears"; instead of calling Angelo "cruel" or "mean," he softens Angelo's insensitivity, claiming that Angelo "dried not one of [Mariana's tears] with his comfort." His language poetic and inviting, the Duke may be making what the text presents as a sub-

liminal appeal to Isabella, attracting Isabella to a situation resembling that in her fantasy of a helpless woman abused by cruel Death
(2.4.101–3). He mentions Mariana by name only at the beginning
of the description; thereafter, he uses the general pronouns "her"
and "she" and makes his description of Mariana's situation general
enough that it could apply to Isabella. For the Duke's description
underscores the two women's similarity: like Mariana, Isabella has
lost, or is threatened with losing, her brother; Angelo has left her
"in tears" as she screamed rebukes at him after he propositioned
her, and he paid no heed to her threats; Angelo declares Isabella
will be shown to be "dishonour[able]" if she reveals his sexual
proposal, for no one will believe her; he "swallows his vows whole"
of honorable intentions and vows to "give [his] sensual race the
rein" (2.4.160); although Isabella continues in her "lamentation,"
Angelo becomes even more "relentless," threatening to "draw out"
Claudio's death "to ling'ring sufferance" (2.4.167) if she doesn't
submit to his will. The Duke also describes Mariana as a woman
aroused by Angelo's unkindness, her love becoming more "violent
and unruly" by the abuse, just as critics have noted a latent attraction in Isabella to Angelo's proposal of rape. Shakespeare seems
to mean for his Duke to excite Isabella with the delineation of a
woman, like herself, being aroused erotically with pain. The Duke's
description encourages Isabella to identify with Mariana, a helpless woman, like Isabella, by whom Angelo would "profit," a
woman who gets excited by "unjust unkindness," as Angelo has
also shown to Isabella.

In outlining the details of the scheme, the Duke speaks as though
Isabella is the actual sexual partner:

> Go you to Angelo; answer his requiring with a plausible obedience;
> agree with his demands to the point. Only refer yourself to this advan-
> tage: first, that your stay with him may not be long; that the place may
> have all shadow and silence in it; and the time answer to conven-
> ience. . . . If you think well to carry this as you may, the doubleness of
> the benefit defends the deceit from reproof.
>
> (3.1.243–49; 257–59)

Only once alluding to Mariana going in her "stead," the Duke
speaks not of Mariana's stay but of "your" or Isabella's "stay" as
though Isabella will consummate the union. The Duke informs Isabella of the fortuitous opportunity to act through her representative: "Mariana will stead up your appointment, go in your place"
(3.1.251). The Duke suggests this situation will protect Isabella
from incriminating herself yet permit her to imagine herself experi-

encing sexual plunder and to act out the preliminary steps as if she were going to comply with a lover's demands. The Duke is shown to help Isabella and himself imagine themselves as sexual partners: he claims it is Isabella's appointment, her place in the bed, not Mariana's, and he identifies himself with Angelo. The word "may" (*OED* 3) in "If you think well to carry this as you may" expresses possibility of action or the opportunity to act. The Duke is portrayed as seducing Isabella by helping her to imagine herself experiencing coitus or "doing it," as the Duke suggestively states: "The cure of it not only saves your brother / But keeps you from dishonour in doing it" (3.1.236–37). Although overhearing Isabella tell Claudio that she would rather die than lose her chastity, the Duke speaks as though she might comply: "How will you do to content this substitute?" The Duke's use of the future "will" allows Isabella and him to envision her complying. The Duke is shown to entice her with the idea of her giving a man sexual "content." Isabella is delineated as responding receptively to these tantalizing tactics, not clearing up the discrepancy but speaking evasively, like her partner, to maintain the possibility of her submission: "I am now going to resolve him" (3.1.188). The word "resolve," not meaning to deny but only to determine a situation, implies rejection. But Shakespeare has the equivocal word help to suggest that Isabella imagines the possibility that the Duke suggests, that she goes to a man, whom the Duke identifies with himself, to "resolve him," to answer and appease his sexual demands. She betrays that she, along with the Duke, thinks of her "doing it" or having "done it": "I had rather my brother die by the law than my son should be unlawfully born" (3.1.188–90). She alludes to the results of intercourse, of her giving birth to a child, as Shakespeare suggests the Duke and Isabella play to each other's fantasies, activating the thoughts of her actually submitting to lust.

The Duke speaks as though they are the lovers and the rendezvous is for themselves, betraying their identification with their surrogates. He refers to Isabella as his sexual partner: "[Isabella may] much please the absent Duke, if peradventure he shall ever return to have hearing of this business" (3.1.202–4). The erotic undercurrent in his language alludes to her "pleasing" or sexually stimulating him, not Angelo. His language suggests a situation with Isabella "pleasing" the Duke or helping him to gratify himself by letting him "hear" about and, consequently, imagine himself and Isabella participating in the sexual coupling. When advising Isabella on the conditions of the meeting, the Duke acts as if he arranges a sexual bout with Isabella for himself, conferring with her on the time, the conditions of the meeting, the location of the tryst: her stay "may not be long"; "the place may have all shadow and silence in it; and the time answer to convenience." Likewise, when the Duke alludes to Isabella's acceding to this plan—"If you think well to carry this as you may"—the word "may" (*OED* 4) implies the granting of permission, the Duke inviting her to accept his proposal as though he asks for himself. Mention of Angelo and Mariana and their parts in the scheme is scanty; rather the Duke and Isabella are made to speak as though they are the actual participants. Both identifying with their substitutes, they are presented as courting each other as if they provide for their own meeting. Because Shakespeare makes them live in the world of fantasy, he has them confuse what happens to themselves and what happens to their surrogates.[29]

The text presents the Duke as wooing Isabella by delineating the bed scene in titillating details, evoking verbal pictures that allow the characters to imagine themselves participating in the scene.[30] Both the Duke and Isabella are shown to imagine the tryst—the time and the length of the visit, the forbidden, clandestine aspects of it—the image coalescing with the depiction of each particular of the event. The Duke verbally seems to take himself and Isabella to the sexual scene and activates their voyeuristic tendencies. He delineates Angelo's attitudes and actions—as though he lives them. He, for example, describes Angelo intractably "demand[ing]" her submission and making "requirings," imperatively ordering her to "fit [her] consent to [his] sharp appetite." The Duke describes not only Isabella's response but also her attitude, playing to her fantasy of adopting a "prone" (1.2.187) or sexually receptive position. He describes her assuming a "plausible obedience," a synonym for "prone," and not just capitulating to Angelo's every demand, "to the point," but acquiescing "plausibly," willingly or seductively. The Duke speaks of Isabella showing a receptivity, an attraction to the attack, agreeing with Angelo "to the point." Shakespeare is possibly suggesting that the image of her sexually acquiescing to his surrogate stimulates the Duke to the "point" or to an erection. Although providing superfluous directions, the Duke designates another possibility: "Haste you speedily to Angelo; if for this night he entreat you to his bed, give him promise of satisfaction" (3.1.262–64). The advice obviously gratuitous, the Duke is presented as reluctant to cease the fantasizing and determined to increase the erotic vividness of the scene. He is made to imagine the vision once more, anticipating Angelo's uncontrollable libido and his peremptory "entreat[y]" or lover's demand that she "lay her body down" so that he can do what he "wills." Speaking once again as if Isabella will actually perform the act, the Duke alludes to Angelo "entreat[ing] you" or Isabella, not Mariana, "to his bed." He describes Isabella in a prone position, giving Angelo "satisfaction" or sexual pleasure, offering herself to Angelo, the Duke's "substitute," with whom he identifies. Under the reputed purpose of preventing any slip-ups in the sexual exchange, the Duke is more precise about the bedtrick than he need be, delineating Angelo's every response and demand. The text presents the Duke and Isabella as making contact with each other's fantasies, their language serving to excite each other through the mind as they are shown to see themselves in the persons of Angelo and Mariana.

Shakespeare makes Isabella eagerly respond to the sexual tenor of the Duke's proposition: "Let me hear you speak farther. I have spirit to do anything that appears not foul in the truth of my spirit" (3.1.205–6). She attests to her "spirit," not just her courage but her ardor, her sexual passion for the Duke and his plan.[31] The sexual subtext suggests she may mean to woo the Duke with her promise to be "spirit[ed]" or sexually lively and active (*OED* 14b). She seems to seduce the Duke with her willingness to perform any sexual act he requires as long as it doesn't foul her body. The bedtrick fouls Mariana directly and fouls Isabella only through vicarious participation. She attests that it is the "speaking" or the verbal descriptions that serve as stimulants and asks him to "speak further" or more intimately. Shakespeare portrays his two characters as having so aroused each other with the verbal foreplay that they show an eagerness to act out their parts and accomplish the real thing, which improves the vividness of their imagining themselves doing "it": the Duke orders Isabella to "haste you speedily to Angelo . . . that it may be quickly" (3.1.267). They seem to hasten the bedtrick not primarily out of concern for saving Claudio's life, which they don't mention, but because they want "it," a word they both use equivocally to denote sexual intercourse. They act as if they are rushing to their own tryst and prod each other to hurry to the rendezvous spot. They are shown to be at a point of almost painful arousal that can only be released through their doubles' actual physical union.

After the Duke's stimulating and graphic talk, it is no wonder that Isabella's language betrays cerebral stimulation; "The image of it gives me content already, and I trust it will grow to a most prosperous perfection" (3.1.260–61). Although she, like the Duke, speaks on two levels and refers to the righteousness or "perfection" of the plan, there seems to be a sexual import in her words, as her language woos the Duke with sexually rich connotations like those in his own language. Isabella picks up yet again on the Duke's suggestive use of "it" to mean, in general terms, sexual intercourse and, in more specific terms, the penis. She attests to the strength of the "image" (*OED* sb.5), the well-focused mental picture that brings her "content" or sexual gratification. The image is so strong that she is described as envisioning the "growth" of the situation to "perfection," imagining not just the preliminary steps but the consummation, the "perfection" of copulation.[32] Her language seems even more graphic and particular than this, for with the verb "grow," Shakespeare could be suggesting that she is attracting the Duke with a verbal picture of "it" or a penis "growing," achieving an erection. Isabella's language betrays that simply hearing about the particulars of the scenario results in sexual excitement, every detail leading to a higher pitch of arousal, as she envisions herself and the Duke achieving a "prosperous perfection."

They arrange the bedtrick to sharpen the erotic imagery of sexual violation. But the escape into fantasy is also a protection from these very desires. The text's presentation of the characters' conscious motives indicates they altruistically surrender themselves to save Claudio's life and assist the shamed woman Mariana. But the presentation of the unconscious indicates they are doing something quite different. The subtext implies that they dedicate themselves to securing sexual pleasure for others as a means of finding self-gratification. Shakespeare makes his two "lovers" into what Anna Freud calls "enthusiastic matchmakers," who become fervently interested in the love life of others, living in the sexual lives of others instead of having erotic experiences of their own and never realizing the full significance of their actions.[33] A line in the play encapsulates much of what this relationship tells us about the theme of the play: "What we do not see / We tread upon, and never think of it" (2.1.25–26). As the Duke and Isabella's relationship illustrates, the play is not so much about what we can see as about what we do not see and what the characters are shown not to see about themselves. A sexuality unlike the "downright way of creation" guides their actions—a sexuality that we and the characters do not think about because we cannot see it. Shakespeare examines how his characters' covert sexuality that resides primarily in the mind involves them in questionable activities and makes them into "seemers," not so much villainous deceivers but self-deceivers.

But Shakespeare makes the Duke better protected from recognition of his desire than he does Isabella. It is the Duke who controls the situation and who arranges for Isabella to act out the incriminating part of the plan. He formulates and articulates the scheme, but it is Isabella who makes it happen, who assumes the active role of visiting Angelo and refining the lurid details. The Duke's role is much more passive as he waits to hear of the success of Isabella's activities. Although the Duke suggests that he will be an equal participant by making the preparations with Mariana—"The maid will I frame, and make fit for his attempt" (3.1.256)—while Isabella makes arrangements with Angelo, in act 4, scene 1 he slyly reveals that he has reneged on his part of the deal: "I have not yet made known to Mariana / A word of this" (49). By revealing his dereliction at the last moment, he tricks Isabella into acting out his part for him, telling Mariana to take Isabella "by the hand, / Who hath a story ready for your ear. / I shall attend your leisure" (4.1.55–57). Isabella has no other alternative but to perform his duties if all of her careful planning is to succeed. The Duke increasingly distances himself from active involvement in the fulfillment of unconscious desires. He maneuvers Isabella into doing what all of her extreme repressive measures are meant to prevent: she translates into action prohibited fantasies and comes perilously close to allowing her instinctual wishes to enter consciousness. Besides wooing Isabella, the Duke in many senses is also trapping her into helping him to fulfill his fantasies without him incurring any guilt or responsibility.

By act 4, scene 1, much of the groundwork for the bedtrick has been completed, Isabella having met with Angelo and made all of the preparations. She has duped him into thinking she intends to comply with his lustful demands. She reports back to the Duke, informing him of the "tokens" between her and Angelo. Isabella declares to be concerned only about helping her brother and shows herself to be a good actress, not making Angelo suspicious that she is disingenuous and plays a cagey game to trap him. In fact, she proves to be too good an actress. She plays too believably the role of a prone, sexual woman, and Shakespeare makes us uncomfortable with her wholehearted involvement in the play acting. She, for example, reports that Angelo "show[ed] [her] / The way twice o'er" (4.1.40–41). She is not portrayed as showing repugnance about her extra activities of letting Angelo "show" her twice. Rather, she has done much more than necessary. The Duke instructed Isabella to inform Angelo that her "stay with him may not be long"; she does this and more. She acts as if she is going to the tryst herself and provides her own excuse for the brevity of her stay: "I have possess'd him my most stay / Can be but brief: for I

have made him know / I have a servant comes with me along"
(4.1.44–46). She, moreover, is shown to outline superfluous details
that do not ensure the bedtrick's "prosperous perfection":

> I have ta'en a due and wary note upon't;
> With whispering and most guilty diligence,
> In action all of precept, he did show me
> The way twice o'er.
>
> (4.1.38–40)

Shakespeare makes her description betray an attraction to the sur-
reptitious planning, to her lover's guilty demeanor and eagerness
to consummate the arrangement, and even to her lover's intonation,
his "whispering," his secrecy. She underscores his "diligence," his
determination to soon enjoy her sexually, dwelling on a man's sexual yearning for her. By making the phrase "with whispering and
most guilty diligence" a squinting modifier, one that can apply
either to Isabella or Angelo, Shakespeare has Isabella unwittingly
attest to her own persistence and enthusiasm to arrange a sexual
exchange, her own "guilty" participation and her whispering the
conditions of the plan.

Furthermore, the erotically loaded description of the way to the
bed betrays the sexual import of her visit:

> He hath a garden circummur'd with brick,
> Whose western side is with a vineyard back'd;
> And to that vineyard is a planched gate,
> That makes his opening with this bigger key
> Which from the vineyard to the garden leads;
> There have I made my promise
> Upon the heavy middle of the night
> To call upon him.
>
> (4.1.28–35)

Critics have noted the strong sexual tenor of her words, Isabella
using the plant, cultivation, and garden imagery, loaded with sexual
import in the Renaissance and particularly in Shakespeare.[34]
Instead of declaring the gate opens with a key, she tortuously
says "his opening" to the gate "is made" "with this bigger key." Although critics have tried to disentangle her words, suggesting the
baffling pronoun "his" is actually a reference for "it," Isabella's
syntax is strained, and she seems to be describing much more than
an entrance to a garden. She speaks of a male agent "opening" an
entrance, of "making" an opening or enjoying a woman sexually.

By using the general pronouns of "he" and "him" throughout her description and not specifically designating Angelo, Isabella is shown to arouse the Duke with erotically charged images of intercourse and to allow him to imagine himself as the unspecified agent who opens the gate of a woman, with whom she identifies herself. Her sensuously graphic description of the scene suggests a delight in being privy to the intimate details, which have stimulated erotic fantasizing.

The painstaking meticulousness of her description is also significant. Shakespeare suggests that the arousal of Isabella's fantasizing powers prevents her from differentiating between reality and fantasy: "In action all of precept, he did show me / The way twice o'er" (4.1.40–41). Since Isabella expresses herself obliquely, we are not sure whether we are to imagine that she bodily followed Angelo through the steps or whether he merely described the scenario for her. Shakespeare does not have her state that Angelo described the way to her but, instead, has her refer to the talk in terms of action: he "show[ed]" her. The equivocal language denotes that Isabella has perhaps so pictured Angelo's words that "precept" has become "action"; words have become the real thing. By making her speak as though Angelo has physically led her through the steps, Shakespeare alludes to his character's highly refined imagination that has permitted her to see her walk the way to the bed; she "saw" the scene by "hearing" Angelo's words. Angelo's recounting the way "twice o'er" to her allows Isabella several times to imagine herself opening the gates, walking through the vineyard and garden, and arriving at a bed of sexual plunder.

By inviting Isabella to go to Angelo and present herself as Angelo's willing lover, the Duke allows both of them to strengthen the possibility that she will yield her virginity. She is shown to no longer just fantasize about making a "promise," as the Duke imagines for her; she in person promises to give herself. This enactment makes her the substitute's lover, arranging a tryst not for Mariana, but for herself, preparing to submit not just in fantasy to the deputy's lust, but in actuality. She is presented as not just imagining herself Mariana; for a short while she actually is the woman who will have sex with the substitute. This acting out helps both the Duke and Isabella to more easily identify with their substitutes and to see themselves in their respective roles. Shakespeare does not have Isabella avoid indelicate references to herself as a sexual partner but, to the contrary, has her speak as though she intends to fulfill her part of the bargain: "There have I made my promise . . .

to call upon him." Her language does not clarify that it is actually Mariana's promise that she makes and not hers at all. Although the Duke alludes to Mariana in "Are there no other tokens / Between you 'greed, concerning her [Mariana's] observance?" (4.1.42–43), Isabella does not continue with the references to Mariana and shows a reluctance to surrender the fantasy of her yielding to a man's "will." Her words surfeited with allusions to herself, she speaks of "my" stay (44), of a servant accompanying "me" (46) and staying upon "me" (47), of "my" going to argue "my" brother's case (47). In showing Isabella act out Mariana's part and identify with Mariana, Shakespeare has her forget in the ardor of her planning the bedtrick that she is not the one who will consummate the plan. For the moment, she and Mariana become one. The text, in fact, suggests Isabella has lived the rehearsal with Angelo as though it were the actual performance. She says "I have possess'd him" (44). While Shakespeare has her mean to explain that she has talked to Angelo and informed him of her intentions, her words are awkward and contain a sexual undercurrent, revealing an arousal at planning the ravishment. She speaks of "possessing" a man or of having a man sexually.[35] For Isabella, discussing and visualizing the rape seem tantamount to living it. The image is so intense that she seems to have envisioned experiencing intercourse and derives "content."

Shakespeare has the subtext indicate that Isabella woos the Duke with these ideas of intercourse, as both of them imagine their participation in the assignation. Just as Isabella lets Angelo "show" her the way twice so that she can luxuriate in the "image of it," the Duke does the same to Isabella: "But shall you on your knowledge find this way?" (36) and "Are there no other tokens / Between you 'greed?" (42–43). The presentation of the Duke's consciousness suggests he selflessly works for others' causes and means to prevent any slip-ups. But Shakespeare makes his prying for more details gratuitous and makes us feel that the Duke does not intend to miss one aspect of the scenario. He is shown to be interested in the "tokens," the intimate details, the little signs and passwords that lovers always share. These superfluous requests betray that Shakespeare may be suggesting that Isabella takes the Duke to the rendezvous in his mind—just as the Duke did to Isabella in act 3, scene 1 when he meticulously outlined the plans for the bedtrick. The Duke makes Isabella's "precepts" into "actions" and sees himself as Angelo, just as Isabella sees herself as Mariana. Shakespeare indicates that his Duke strikingly imagines the scene by having him elicit vivid details. The Duke alludes to the time of the exchange, the night being suitable to an amorous encounter: "The vaporous night approaches" (58). His words denote the hot lust on a cold night; the time will be "vaporous" or steamy and heated (*OED* "vapour" sb. 2). He responds to Isabella's garden imagery of procreation, perhaps envisioning the consummation along with Isabella: "Our Corn's to reap, for yet out tithe's to sow" (76). His language sounds sententious and grave, as he cites biblical aphorisms about sowing the seeds of goodness and collecting tithes. But the sowing imagery has already been established as highly sexual in the play. He, along with Isabella, alludes to the planting of seeds in the garden, of the sexual tillage of the fertile ground, critics having equated the word "tithe" with "tilth."[36]

The meeting between Isabella and the Duke continues to present them as though they are providing for their own encounter, agreeing on the time, the secrecy, the place, the tokens between them. The Duke acts out Angelo's role with Isabella, concurring with her on the tokens of their assignation. Shakespeare has the Duke act like an eager, "diligent" lover, who makes certain that Isabella can find her way to the bedchamber, as if he asks for himself and as if he prepares for his own encounter with Isabella: "But shall you on your knowledge find this way?" Although Mariana is present and she is the key participant, not they, neither the Duke nor Isabella is presented as allowing her to contribute much to the discussion or the planning. Shakespeare suggests that Mariana serves as a cover, a way for his protagonists to be protected from the real significance of their actions, a guarantee that the plans are for Angelo and his fiancée, not for Isabella and the Duke.[37] Shakespeare makes us suspicious of Isabella when he has her usurp Mariana's part, not allowing Mariana to respond to the Duke but speaking for her: "She'll take the enterprize upon her, father, / If you advise it" (66–67). He makes her identification with Mariana so complete that she does not surrender the fantasy of her yielding to the rape. Although hiding behind the reference to Mariana, Isabella acts out Mariana's part and accedes to the Duke's wishes. She requests that the Duke take an active part as well, that he act out Angelo's role and request that she give herself. The Duke responds to Isabella's request, refusing merely to offer his "consent" or agreement with the bedtrick but, rather, adopting the pose of a lover, who "entreat[s]" or begs amorously: "It is not my consent, / But my entreaty too" (68–69). In act 3, scene 1, the Duke has imagined Angelo "entreat[ing]" Isabella "to his bed" (263). Now the Duke is shown to do more than imagine himself saying Angelo's words; he says them himself, asking a woman to submit to his will. Mariana all but disappears from the scene and the bedtrick. The Duke entreats as though he were Angelo; Isabella answers for Mariana and acquiesces to undertake the bedtrick as though she were Mariana. And yet Isabella and the Duke's subterranean, cerebral love affair is hidden under the appearance of their arranging a meeting for two other lovers.

Through words, they are portrayed as erotically exciting each other, "bringing" each other to what will be "done" to Mariana. The "action" of intercourse is experienced through "precepts," and the "image of it brings [them] content." Their relationship is based on pure fantasy, on cerebral stimulation. They imagine the union and go to the scene in their minds. Isabella has envisioned the scene at least twice with Angelo; now she envisions it again with the Duke, whom she identifies with Angelo. Just as Isabella observes the suspenseful steps to the bedroom through Angelo's descriptions, the Duke is made to observe them through Isabella's directions. She reports her "fantastic" sexual experience to the Duke and woos him with images of intercourse. They are never shown to touch physically; rather, they are made to "touch" or caress mentally and "possess" or sexually know each other through images, which become a substitute for intercourse.

In act 5 Shakespeare has the Duke indulge in more "idle dream[s]" (4.1.64) with Isabella. Although the Duke attests to having the most upstanding motives for inducing Isabella to claim she has been sexually violated, Shakespeare compels us to question the Duke's actions in act 5 by making his motives obscure and his behavior unethical. In making the Duke ask Isabella to speak Mariana's part and present herself as a victim of rape, Shakespeare suggests the Duke is creating another sexually provocative situation that embodies his fantasies.[38] Shakespeare may be indicating that the Duke woos Isabella again, allowing her to continue in her vicarious identification with Mariana and to indulge in the "image that brings [her] content," an image of her as a "prone" woman submitting to a man's "intemperate concupiscible lust"—the fantasy that has grown to a "prosperous perfection" in her imagination. The Duke's overseeing her plea in act 5 and allowing her to go at her own leisurely pace may be a way for him to "hear" of the sexual violation again, just as he is shown doing in act 4, scene 1, and to "see" the image of the rape scene in the mind. Serving as the judge of Isabella's pleas, he makes Isabella direct her story of despoliation to him and woo him with the image, as he controls her responses with his questions and demands. Isabella, likewise, is not made to show awareness of the true significance of her actions: she claims to accede to the Duke's plan in order to disclose

Angelo's turpitude and bring him to justice. Although she merely follows the Duke's directions and although before act 5 she protests "to speak so indirectly I am loth" (4.6.1), Shakespeare has her so convincingly perform her part that we feel uneasy with her behavior at the beginning of act 5. That Shakespeare has her histrionically throw herself into the role of violated maiden indicates he means for us to detect a secret delight in Isabella, as she is shown to imagine herself as Mariana and to savor the details of the sexual attack. She refers to the ravishment as "true" not because she is presented as a shameless liar but because she is presented as having so graphically imagined herself in Mariana's place that it is as if the despoliation has happened to her and she speaks of a "true" event. Fantasy has become a substitute for reality.

Isabella repeatedly alludes to the ravishment in erotically rich terminology and is made to excite herself and the Duke with the images. She, for example, daringly suggests the loss of her maidenhood, clarifying that she was "wrong'd" (22), raped or sexually ruined, and no longer deserves the status of "maid" or virgin, her virginity having been "violated." She passes over the truthful aspects of her story in one grand gesture—"How I persuaded, how I pray'd and kneel'd, / How he refell'd me, and how I replied" (96–97)—and rushes to the "vile conclusion," the sexual consummation of a bestial erotic act:

> the vile conclusion
> I now begin with grief and shame to utter.
> He would not, but by gift of my chaste body
> To his concupiscible intemperate lust,
> Release my brother; and after much debatement,
> My sisterly remorse confutes mine honour,
> And I did yield to him.
>
> (98–104)

Although Angelo attributes "strangeness" to Isabella's appeal to discredit her and save himself, there is some truth to his words: she does, indeed, speak "strangely"—passionately and enthusiastically—for a demure novice. The misplaced emphasis on herself and her active participation in the deflowering may be Shakespeare's way of betraying the intensity of her imagining herself as a sexual partner: "*My* chaste body"; "*My* sisterly remorse confutes *mine* honour, / And *I* did yield to him." She underscores not Claudio's supposed death, not Angelo's nefarious proposition, but her complying with a man's fleshly desires.

She, moreover, speaks vividly and with no disgust of a man enjoying her "virginal," unspoiled body: "He would not but by gift of my chaste body" rescind his death orders for Claudio "and I did yield to him." She willingly "yielded" or submitted to a physical assault, "yield" denoting compliance to forceful physical pressures (*OED* 20b), and gave him the present or "gift" of her body, "yield" also meaning to give a favor (*OED* 10).[39] Rather than underscoring the contemptibility of the rapist's appetite, she concentrates on its intensity and ferocity, and her gratuitously descriptive accounting of her attacker's sexual proclivities almost sounds as if the character has actually experienced a man's desires: "his concupiscible intemperate lust." Her synonyms emphasize her attacker's sexual intemperance: his "lust" or animal-like passion is "concupiscible," eagerly desirous, and "intemperate," unbridled and excessive. Her words create the picture of an oversexed, brutal man demanding that she appease his overpowering libido and herself complying with his sexual excesses. Furthermore, that Shakespeare has her speak of not just one wanton instance of coitus but a sexually full night makes us feel that he is suggesting Isabella has visualized the act again and again, savoring the lust-filled evening of love: "But the next morn betimes, / His purpose surfeiting, he sends a warrant / For my poor brother's head" (104–5). Unnecessarily graphic, she claims a man "surfeit[ed]" or excessively indulged his "purpose" or genitals at her expense. Her riveting on the sexual act to the exclusion of all else, her erotically suggestive delineation, and her favorable portrayal of her submission to Angelo's keen appetite—all of these unsettle us and encourage us to believe Shakespeare is suggesting his character's enjoyment in relating the "practice" and her attraction to the image of sexual violation.

The Duke several times alludes to Isabella's erotic arousal at describing the bed scene and to the seductiveness with which she enacts it: "She speaks this in th'infirmity of sense" (50), and her delivery has "the oddest frame of sense" (64). Because the word "sense" recurs throughout the play and, as William Empson clarifies, comes to have the meaning of sexuality,[40] Shakespeare has the Duke suggest that he thinks of Isabella in sexual terms, and that Isabella has aroused him with her story. This story, once again with its paucity of references to Angelo by name, allows the Duke to place himself in Angelo's role. His word choice suggests an attraction to her "frame of sense," her alluring "frame" work or body, and to her story "frame[d]" with "sense" or designed to arouse his passions for her.

At the play's end, Shakespeare has the Duke drop his purely subliminal approach and make a patent sexual overture by proposing marriage to Isabella. This proposal is predicated on the preceding subtextual wooing process during the preparations for the bedtrick. Shakespeare certainly leaves Isabella's response to the Duke's marriage proposal indeterminate, and by doing so he allows for her consent. Many critics have felt quite sure that Isabella does accept, and my reading of the vicarious wooing allows a basis for an affirmative answer from Isabella. But Shakespeare seems deliberately to create uncertainty and discomfort in his audience, for with simply one word of assent from his heroine he could resolve the problem if he means for her to agree. I believe that Shakespeare's text as well as Isabella's psychology, as it has been presented, lead to a strong possibility that Shakespeare means for Isabella to reject the Duke. Although Isabella gives no verbal clues to her decision, the Duke's reaction to her silence adumbrates her behavior:

> If [Claudio] be like your brother, for his sake
> Is he pardon'd; and for your lovely sake
> Give me your hand and say you will be mine.
> He is my brother too: but fitter time for that.
> By this Lord Angelo perceives he's safe;
> Methinks I see a quickening in his eye.
>
> (488–93)

He seems to try to predispose her into accepting his marriage proposal and into overlooking his previous questionable actions, capitalizing on the rejoicing mood and on Isabella's gratitude for Claudio's rescue, and proposing to her immediately upon producing Claudio. That after proposing to her he must add an incentive for her to accept, by stating that Claudio is his "brother too," suggests she may reject him. His cavalier dismissal of the matter— "but fitter time for that"—and dashing to a new topic of Angelo's safety may indicate an attempt to cover up an embarrassing, awkward rebuff from Isabella. That the Duke must proffer his proposal again and that he does so cautiously add more credence to the possibility that Isabella rejects his first suit:

> Thanks, good friend Escalus, for thy much goodness;
> There's more behind that is more gratulate.
> Thanks Provost, for thy care and secrecy;
> We shall employ thee in a worthier place.

Forgive him, Angelo, that brought you home
The head of Ragozine to Claudio's:
The offence pardons itself. Dear Isabella,
I have a motion much imports your good;
Whereto if you'll a willing ear incline,
What's mine is yours, and what is yours is mine.
So bring us to our palace, where we'll show
What's yet behind that's meet you all should know.

(526–36)

By having the Duke express appreciation and felicitation to every character imaginable and make requests that even he admits are needless ("The offense pardons itself"), Shakespeare seems to suggest that his duke is dragging his heels, meandering toward the proposal, as though hesitant to elicit another repulse. The Duke implores Isabella just to listen to him as though he fears she will reject him (as she may have the first time) even before he begins. That he tries to be more persuasive than in his previous proposal (such as couching his new plan in positive words, playing to her self-interests, and promising to do her "good") indicates once again that Isabella is not predisposed to accept and needs prodding. Isabella's second rejection may be suggested by the same silence that marked the first proposal and by the Duke's attempt to cover up: he dashes to another topic and scurries everyone off to his palace as if to avoid another awkward lull in events.

That Isabella would reject him is fully understandable, despite the previous subliminal wooing. Shakespeare may mean her silence to indicate that she recognizes at this point, as do we, that the Duke has lied to her not just once, but several times, and that there was little justification for such deception. Her silence may signal a recognition that her participation in the bedtrick was not necessary nor were her public lies and public shaming about her loss of virginity. Although the Duke promised during the planning of the bedtrick and in act 4, scene 3 that he would bring her "grace" and "general honour" and always protect her "spirit" from stain, she must now realize that he has not kept his part of the bargain, that he has trapped her into staining herself in order to protect himself. He does not protect her during her protest as a "virgin violated" in act 5 but, rather, disbelieves her and sends her to prison as a sinner. He never elucidates the details of the bedtrick beyond Mariana's vague allusions to it; he never vindicates Isabella, never clarifies his vital participation in the bed switch, never assumes responsibility for it. While he has not shielded her reputation, he, on the other hand, has done all he could to enhance his own as a "man divine and holy" (5.1.146): by uncovering Angelo's seeming, reuniting Mariana with the man she loves, and bringing Claudio back from the dead, the Duke looks majestic, "like power divine" (5.1.367), a powerful figure who performs such miraculous acts that he puts everyone "into amazement how these things should be" (4.2.203–4). The Duke has maneuvered her into revealing herself as a sexual woman of the world, certainly not a "thing enskied" and reserved only for a convent, as a woman who could be proposed to as a prospective mate for himself. Shakespeare makes the marriage proposal suggest that the Duke desires to physically consummate their union of the mind. Since abdicating his power to Angelo, the Duke has been shown to take a more active part in realizing his fantasies, not just removing himself and letting Angelo act on his own but participating in arranging the technicalities of a rendezvous. As a result, Shakespeare seems to suggest the Duke's desires have come to the fore and demand much more than vicarious satisfaction or the contentment derived from fantasizing. What he prevented Angelo from doing—fitting Isabella's consent to his "sharp appetite"—the Duke alludes to doing himself, now fully incorporating into his being the side of himself that Angelo represents. And he can do so and still maintain his virtuous public and self-image, for all of his actions have been geared to protecting himself from conscious recognition of the deeper significance of his previous questionable behavior or of the present marriage proposal. As a dispenser of joy and Christian benevolence at the play's end, he ensconces himself in acceptability, disguising his "crabbed" desires behind the guise of a religious and socially sanctioned marriage, presenting himself as a mortal yet virtuous man. He has never aspired, moreover, to be a saint, like Isabella, who renounces the world. In fact, as the ruler of the land he is expected to partake in the social contract, to produce heirs and to embody active not reclusive virtues. For him to live a monastic life as he has in the past makes him suspect, not holy. The advice he gives to the ascetic Angelo applies as easily to himself: "for if our virtues / Did not go forth of us, 'twere all alike / As if we had them not. Spirits are not finely touch'd / But to fine issues" (1.1.33–36). But the situation is quite different for Isabella. It is difficult to believe that Shakespeare means for us to think that his heroine could contemplate marriage with a man who has lied to her, tricked her, and broken his word to her in the most cruel fashion. Such double-dealing and disingenuousness seem hardly the basis for a

216 CAROLYN E. BROWN

life-long commitment, no matter how much the Duke protests he does it for her own good.

The Duke, in addition, has not allowed her to secure either her public or self-image, which he has secured for himself. He has sacrificed her image as a saint to preserve his image as a glorious ruler. Shakespeare presents her as trapped by the Duke into enacting both of their fantasies and into incurring all of the guilt and attention. By tricking her into acting out her fantasies before the whole court as a deflowered, sensuous woman and into speaking untruths, he prevents her from ever returning to the protection of the convent. But, more importantly, by tricking her into accepting partial responsibility for Angelo's fall—"I partly think a due sincerity govern'd his deeds / Till he did look on me" (5.1.444–45)—he forces her to acknowledge what she has been trying desperately to deny from the play's beginning: her unconscious subpersonality. Despite all of the protective measures of vicarious identification, fantasy, and projection, Isabella is made to recognize the latent sexual import of her actions, to recognize that she seduced Angelo and that she engaged in the bedtrick not just to save her brother but also to satisfy her repressed desires. Her actions now appear "foul in the truth of [her] spirit," and there is no way she can delude herself any longer. The Duke proves to be a poor judge of character and, thus, fallible and unlike the providential rulers of Shakespeare's sources. Just as he miscalculates when he thinks that Angelo will pardon Claudio once the deputy satisfies his "sharp appetite" with Isabella / Mariana, he misjudges Isabella's situation, underestimating the importance of sanctity, or at least the semblance of it, to Isabella. Marcia Riefer labels *Measure for Measure* as "Isabella's tragedy" and calls her one of the Duke's "prime victims."[41] With the indeterminate ending and Isabella's stark silence, Shakespeare allows for the possibility that Isabella cannot talk, that she suffers a psychic breakdown with the collapse of her defenses, and that her situation is truly tragic. What Shakespeare may mean to depict is the entering into his heroine's consciousness of all of the forbidden instinctual drives of the unconscious. And this drives Isabella into a deadly silence signifying terror at what she "sees."

Notes

1. All textual quotations are from the New Arden *Measure for Measure*, ed. J. W. Lever (London: Methuen, 1965).
2. Critics are repeatedly disturbed by Isabella and the Duke's participation in

the bedtrick and detect a sexual nuance to their activities: for example, D. R. C. Marsh, "The Mood of *Measure for Measure*," *Shakespeare Quarterly* 14 (1963): 34, suggests that "whatever their motives, [Isabella and the Duke] are performing a bawd's office"; Louise Schleiner, "Providential Improvisation in *Measure for Measure*," *PMLA* 97 (1982): 232, argues that the scheme "gives off a whiff of procurement."

3. Critics have objected to what seems like an unprepared-for proposal: Meredith Anne Skura, *The Literary Use of the Psychoanalytic Process* (New Haven: Yale University, 1981), 244, claims no one "is content with the Duke's last-minute proposal of marriage to Isabella, who does not even reply" and labels the proposal an "arbitrary device" to bring about a happy ending; Joseph Westlund, *Shakespeare's Reparative Comedies: A Psychoanalytic View of the Middle Plays* (Chicago: University of Chicago, 1984), describes the proposal as "very schematic and unrealized" (153) and complains that "we have no reason to think that the Duke has been leading up to [a marriage proposal] all along" (181).

4. The quotations belong respectively to Jean E. Howard, "*Measure for Measure* and the Restraints of Convention," *Essays in Literature*, 10 (1983): 149, and Herbert Howarth, *The Tiger's Heart: Eight Essays on Shakespeare* (Oxford: Oxford University, 1970), 130.

5. *Shakespeare's Bawdy*, 2d rev. ed. (New York: Dutton, 1969), 46.

6. *Shakespeare's Development and the Problem Comedies* (Berkeley: University of California, 1981), 102, 109. For a thorough analysis of the sadomasochistic tenor to the sexuality, consult Carolyn E. Brown, "Erotic Religious Flagellation and Shakespeare's *Measure for Measure*," *English Literary Renaissance* 16 (1986): 139–65.

7. "Mortality and Mercy in 'Measure for Measure,'" in *The Shakespeare Plays: A Study Guide* (Delmar, Calif.: University Extension, University of California, San Diego, and Coast Community College District, 1978), 107. Adelman claims the Duke is "one who voyeuristically sees unseen, lurking everywhere" and designates the Duke's sexuality as "voyeuristic."

8. Nancy S. Leonard, "Substitution in Shakespeare's Problem Comedies," *English Literary Renaissance* 9 (1979): 282, and Robert Rogers, *A Psychoanalytic Study of the Double in Literature* (Detroit: Wayne State University Press, 1970), 72, underscore the "crucial aspect" of "doubling" or "substitution" in the play.

9. The psychoanalytic terminology for this technique is "projective identification," explained by the following: George F. Mahl, *Psychological Conflict and Defense* (New York: Harcourt Brace Jovanovich, 1969), 179, claims that a projector establishes identification when he detects the same unconscious wishes in another person that he is defending himself against; James S. Grotstein, *Splitting and Projective Identification* (New York: Jason Aronson, 1981), 123–24, defines the phenomenon as a "mental mechanism whereby the self experiences the unconscious phantasy of translocating itself, or aspects of itself, into an object for exploratory or defensive purposes."

10. Northrop Frye, *The Myth of Deliverance: Reflections on Shakespeare's Problem Comedies* (Toronto: University of Toronto, 1983), 24; Wheeler, *Shakespeare's Development*, 132; Bernard J. Paris, "The Inner Conflicts of *Measure for Measure*: A Psychological Approach," *The Centennial Review* 25 (1981): 266, argues that it is "a fear of forbidden or conflicting feelings" that makes the Duke "engage in vicarious living."

11. "Mortality and Mercy," 108.

12. Frye, *Myth*, 21; Arthur C. Kirsch, "The Integrity of *Measure for Measure*,"

Shakespeare Survey 28 (1975): 96; Carolyn E. Brown, "*Measure for Measure*: Isabella's Beating Fantasies," *American Imago* 43 (1986): 67–80.

13. Harriet Hawkins, "'The Devil's Party': Virtues and Vices in *Measure for Measure*," *Shakespeare Survey* 31 (1978): 107, underscores the sadomasochistic tenor to her words, "charged with an erotic power that might well evoke a gleam in the eye of the most depraved marquis." Rosalind Miles, *The Problem of "Measure for Measure"* (London: Vision, 1976), 224, alludes to her "fantasies of martyrdom and self-sacrifice." Wheeler, *Shakespeare's Development*, 112, declares that her "repudiation of Angelo's advances is in turn strangely, masochistically eroticized in a vivid fantasy that expresses her own tormented image of sexual contact."

14. Julia Segal, *Phantasy in Everyday Life* (New York: Penguin, 1985), 51–52, and Glenn Wilson, *The Secrets of Sexual Fantasy* (London: J. M. Dent, 1978), 146, explain the "protective" aspects of fantasy and projective identification, Segal claiming that feelings are "perceived in a 'safer' situation—where they can be attributed to others." Seeing the instinct that one wants to repudiate in a representative, one can reassure oneself that it exists elsewhere, not in oneself, and yet gratify it vicariously at the same time.

15. Ian Gibson, *The English Vice* (London: Duckworth, 1978), 314, notes that for people who are excited by beating fantasies, arousal "may as easily arise from seeing, reading or hearing about beatings as from experiencing" the real thing.

16. Wilson, *Secrets*, 178, attests to the role that the mind can play in sexuality: "imagination can comprise a powerful sexual stimulus," and he calls the phenomenon "eroticism by means of the imagination." David Shapiro, *Autonomy and Rigid Character* (New York: Basic Books, 1981), claims that for people aroused by sexual subjugation, sexuality is a "highly ideational matter, far more a product of the imagination than of the senses" (128–29) and that "ideas and images of subjugation, humiliation, pain" are especially erotic (131–32). Robert J. Stoller, *Sexual Excitement* (New York: Pantheon Books, 1979), 127, refers to "cases where the person in the actual scene is unsatisfied or only faintly excited while recollection leads to an orgasm."

17. "Psychoanalysis and Renaissance Culture" in *Literary Theory/Renaissance Texts*, ed. Patricia Parker and David Quint (Baltimore: Johns Hopkins University, 1980), 221.

18. "Renaissance/Early Modern Studies" in *Redrawing the Boundaries: The Transformation of English and American Literary Studies*, ed. Stephen Greenblatt and Giles Gunn (New York: MLA, 1992), 58.

19. "Introduction" to *Shakespeare's Personality*, ed. Norman N. Holland, Sidney Homan, and Bernard J. Paris (Berkeley: University of California, 1989), 4.

20. K. R. Eissler, *Discourse on Hamlet and "Hamlet": A Psychoanalytic Inquiry* (New York: International Universities, 1971), 4.

21. "Dedication to *Shakespeare Illustrated, 1753*" in *Samuel Johnson on Shakespeare*, ed. W. K. Wimsatt, Jr. (New York: Hilling & Wung, 1960), 14.

22. Bernard J. Paris, *Bargains with Fate: Psychological Crisis and Conflicts in Shakespeare and His Plays* (New York: Plenum, 1991), 8; Patrick Murray *The Shakespearian Scene: Some Twentieth-Century Perspectives* (New York: Barnes & Noble, 1969), 34.

23. Alex Aronson, *Psyche and Symbol in Shakespeare* (Bloomington: Indiana University, 1972), 1.

24. Skura, *Literary Use*, 268.

25. Wheeler, *Shakespeare's Development*, 127.

26. Miles, *Problem*, 13.

27. J. C. Maxwell, "*Measure for Measure*: The Play and the Themes," *Proceed-

ings of the British Academy 60 (1974): 199; Michael Long, *The Unnatural Scene* (London: Methuen, 1976), 86; Westlund, *Shakespeare's Reparative Comedies*, 2; G. K. Hunter, "Introduction" in *All's Well That Ends Well* (London: Methuen, 1966), liv; Lever, *Measure for Measure*, lxxv, cxii.

28. Eissler, *Discourse*, 195.

29. Segal, *Phantasy*, 50, explains that "as the inner world of fantasy is likely to confuse what has happened in phantasy with what happened in reality, so it is likely to confuse what happens to self and what happens to other people."

30. Theodor Reik, *Masochism in Modern Man* (New York: Farrar, Strauss, 1941), 46, and 67, specifies that imagining a sexual scenario is important for fantasiers, who often "linger on preparatory activities instead of progressing to genital satisfaction" and "dwell on the details." Shapiro, *Autonomy*, 129, argues that this "ideational" sexuality "may include in the event and even in the fantasy, little actual physical contact or none at all." Stoller, *Sexual Excitement*, 31, explains that "every detail [of the scenario] counts for increasing excitement."

31. Frankie Rubinstein, *A Dictionary of Shakespeare's Sexual Puns and their Significance*, 2d ed. (London: Macmillan, 1989), 250, notes that "spirit" usually applies to men and their sexual potency, or more specifically to the penis or semen. But it can more generally mean sexual passion. In *Shakespeare's Sonnets* (New Haven: Yale University, 1977), editor Stephen Booth also records the sexual submeanings in "spirit" as sexual vigor or ardor (441–42).

32. Wilson, *Secrets*, 78, contends that the "hearing of details can activate fantasizing until [the image] has grown."

33. *The Ego and the Mechanisms of Defense* (New York: International Universities Press, 1946), 132–45. Anna Freud labels the process "altruistic surrender" and cites as an example the case of a girl who has scruples of conscience about sex for herself but who champions other people's gratification in order to secure vicarious fulfillment.

34. Rupin W. Desai, "Freudian Undertones in the Isabella-Angelo Relationship of *Measure for Measure*," *Psychoanalytic Review* 64 (1977): 489, for example, glosses the gate and the little door as symbols of the "vagina, uterus, hymen" and the two keys as the "phallus and the sperm."

35. Partridge, *Shakespeare's Bawdy*, 165 and 131.

36. The explication is recorded in *Measure for Measure: A New Variorum Edition of Shakespeare*, ed. Mark Eccles (New York: MLA, 1980), 193.

37. Shapiro, *Autonomy*, 128, explains that for fantasizers people often serve as "props, an aid to the imagining of a scene of erotic sensuality."

38. Sigmund Freud, "A Child is Being Beaten: A Contribution to the Study of the Origin of Sexual Perversions," in *Standard Edition*, trans. and ed. James Strachey (London: Hogarth, 1955), 17: 179, explains why the fantasier repeats a scenario: "The phantasy has feelings of pleasure attached to it, and on their account the patient has reproduced it on innumerable occasions in the past or may even still be doing so." Similarly much of *Measure for Measure* involves the Duke instigating a series of actions that embody his sexual fantasies.

39. Rubenstein, *Dictionary*, 110–11, suggests the word "gift" can sometimes in Shakespeare refer to genitals or sexual favors.

40. "Sense in *Measure for Measure*" in *The Structure of Complex Words* (Norfolk, Conn.: New Directions, 1951), 274, 276.

41. "'Instruments of Some More Mightier Member': The Constriction of Female Power in *Measure for Measure*," *Shakespeare Quarterly* 33 (1984): 167, 161.

"To the Very Heart of Loss":
Renaissance Iconography in
Shakespeare's *Antony and Cleopatra*

Peggy Muñoz Simonds

S HAKESPEARE'S TRAGEDY *Antony and Cleopatra* dramatizes a mortally dangerous "relationship" between two very glamorous international celebrities at a crucial period in the history of western civilization. As personalities, the two lovers both attract and repel not only each other but scholars as well. Thus literary critics have called Antony everything from a romantic "Herculean hero"[1] and a noble lover[2] to a gluttonous epicurean living only for the pleasures of the flesh.[3] In her turn, Cleopatra, admired by most feminist critics,[4] has been compared by male scholars to the cunning enchantress Circe, who transforms men into animals; to the Whore of Babylon (from the Book of Revelation) who offers a cup of pleasure to all the kings of the world[5]; and to the transcendent pagan goddesses Venus and Isis.[6] Martin Spevack, in *The New Variorum* edition of the play,[7] surveys all these varying attitudes toward Cleopatra among scholars; while the Egyptian queen's seemingly endless fascination for writers, artists, and movie makers has also resulted in a recent popular study entitled *Cleopatra: Histories, Dreams and Distortions* by Lucy Hughes-Hallett.[8]

The two characters undeniably embody all of the above elements and more, since Shakespeare—unlike Plutarch—has portrayed both Antony and Cleopatra as strangely ambivalent personalities. Janet Adelman points out that "*Antony and Cleopatra* insists that we take the lovers simultaneously as very mortal characters and as gigantic semidivine figures."[9] The same critic has also taught us to look for the perspectives that the various characters in a play reveal toward one another. In fact, the very concept of dramatic character, she argues, is rather disconcertingly slippery in this particular Shakespearean tragedy (3–7), since "it is this movement of perspectives rather than the revelations of a psychodrama or the certainties of a morality, which is most characteristic of *Antony and Cleopatra*" (30). Thus, we may find it especially significant that within the text of this particular tragedy we almost immediately find the same ambivalent feelings toward Antony and Cleopatra among the other characters that we have seen among the scholars. Cleopatra, for example, is lavishly praised by Enobarbus but is often called unpleasant names by her lover and other Romans, which suggests that she embodies a certain strange doubleness in her very nature.

In a similar fashion, Antony, much disliked by Plutarch,[10] is described in the play by his friends and enemies alike as both heroic and besotted. Octavius Caesar reports that his old friend and ally has fallen into the mold of a hopeless libertine:

> This is the news: he fishes, drinks, and wastes
> The lamps of night in revel; is not more manlike
> Than Cleopatra; nor the queen of Ptolomy
> More womanly than he; hardly gave audience, or
> [Vouchsaf'd] to think he had partners. You shall find there
> A man who is th' [abstract] of all faults
> That all men follow.[11]

> (1.4.4–10)

But when Caesar wishes Antony back in Rome to fight against Pompey, he warmly commends Antony's bravery and manly endurance as a soldier (see 1.4.56–71). Although Pompey regards Antony as currently no more than an "amorous surfeiter," he also admits that "His soldiership / is twice the other twain" (2.1.33, 34–35). Pompey further observes with relief that "Mark Antony / In Egypt sits at dinner, and will make / No wars without-doors" (2.1.11–13), a suggestion that prolonged idleness has made the hero too soft to fight again. However, the Roman triumvir then delivers a prophetic curse on Antony, a curse which sums up the story of the hero throughout the remainder of the tragedy:

> But all the charms of love,
> Salt Cleopatra, soften thy wan'd lip!
> Let witchcraft join with beauty, lust with both,
> Tie up the libertine in a field of feasts,
> Keep his brain fuming; epicurean cooks
> Sharpen with cloyless sauce his appetite,

That sleep and feeding may prorogue his honor,
Even till a Lethe'd dullness—

(2.1.20–27)

Similar conflicting observations on Antony's character are made throughout the play by others of various social ranks.

Antony thus emerges as a man deemed previously great but now failing in warlike prowess and courage, though one still believed capable of reform and of a return to political preeminence,[12] if he could just make up his mind what he wants. Cleopatra herself compares him to an anamorphic painting with a double image: "Though he be painted one way like a Gorgon, / The other way's a Mars" (2.5.116–17), while canny Maecenas observes after Antony's death that "His taints and honors / Wag'd equal with him" (5.1.30–31).

Through colorful visual pageantry[13] and one spectacular banquet scene after another onstage, Shakespeare's tragedy dramatizes Antony's fall from heroic virtue to helpless sensuality in Egypt. Moreover, the hero's violent moments, during which he wildly displays uncontrolled jealousy and wrath, soon erode much of our sympathy for this man who can no longer control his passions. For the modern reader or spectator, such an insidious change in a once respected personality suggests the presence of some form of addiction, an illness that is always initially caused by the stimulation of the pleasure center in the brain. Indeed, J. Leeds Barroll has argued persuasively that the hero is seduced by all the forms of fleshly pleasures from Gluttony to Lust, and Frank Kermode has described Antony's obvious addiction to the "lavish banquet of the senses" that Cleopatra has so generously laid out for him in Egypt.[14]

More recently, Michael Lloyd hints that Antony is addicted rather specifically to games of chance, which are mentioned over and over again in the play, and which increasingly cause him to become a pawn of the fickle goddess Fortuna. She is here not the stable Roman Fortune of Plutarch but mere chance or hazard.[15] Since worldly pleasure is actually one of the major gifts of Fortuna to her favorites, Barroll and Kermode's emphasis on the importance of Voluptas or sensory pleasure in the tragedy is surely correct, although it is equally clear through the language of the play that Antony is also fatally addicted to gambling itself, probably because of the initial pleasures associated with the arrival of good fortune. In this he is much like the unhappy nineteenth-century heroes of Dostoyevsky's short novel *The Gambler* and of Pushkin's story "The Queen of Spades." Having once achieved good fortune through his own earlier efforts in politics and on the battlefield, Antony now wants to maintain his high position as a world leader through sheer luck rather than through reasonable action. In any case, according to Charles A. Hallett, there are some forty-five uses of the word "fortune" in *Antony and Cleopatra*.[16]

The purpose of the present essay is to build on the above mentioned studies, and others like them, in order to arrive at a Renaissance reading of the tragedy. Using the iconographic approach to Shakespeare's words and stage imagery, I shall demonstrate (1) that a fatally addicted Antony and other characters in the play describe Cleopatra herself in terms of the attributes widely associated with the pagan goddess Fortuna; (2) that Antony's foolish trust in Fortune's continuing love for him allows him to be caught like a fish on a hook baited with female sexuality and beauty and then to be sacrificed to her honor and glory; and (3) that although a bereft Cleopatra attempts in the end to immortalize her own brilliant performance of Fortuna in the great theater of the world as a transcendent artistic work of marble statuary, the play does end tragically—if somewhat ambiguously so—for both the lovers. Caesar removes their bodies from the monument built to honor the Egyptian queen for eternity and buries them together, we know not where. In addition, Shakespeare reminds us that once Antony falls from power the Augustan *pax romana* will be achieved in the Mediterranean world. At this time, the unstable rule of Fortune, a goddess who traditionally entices men and women to evil, will give way to a new temporal era after the Nativity of Christ and to the universal rule of Divine Providence over chance—or so it was believed by most commentators in Shakespeare's time.

To depict here in visual terms the goddess Fortuna and her attributes, I make use primarily of engravings disseminated throughout northern Europe during the Renaissance and of woodcuts from popular emblem books of the period. I see the emblem book as a verbal and visual art form parallel to the drama, although a genre often tending to state meanings directly rather than ambiguously.[17] Emblems can, therefore, be very helpful to us in understanding many intellectual and moral traditions of Elizabethan and Jacobean culture, but, of course, emblems were seldom, if ever, used as direct sources by William Shakespeare. They are offered here only as analogues to ideas either dramatized by Shakespeare or expressed by his characters in *Antony and Cleopatra*. As Adelman argues, "iconography and mythography can provide a context for the play; they can serve to identify those images which the original audience might have felt to be particularly significant and to suggest the range of signification" (100).

I

To begin with, although Cleopatra as a historical personage and as a literary topos herself cannot literally be Fortuna in the play, the dramatic behavior of Shakespeare's seductive character and the fickle goddess of luck do indeed have much in common. Marilyn Williamson correctly observes that,

> Both are wanton, alluring but wavering, changeable women of infinite variety. Both are associated with Isis, with Venus, with a serpent: "He's speaking now, / Or murmuring, 'Where's my serpent of old Nile?' / For so he calls me" (1.5.24–26). And Cleopatra treats Antony very much as Fortune does; he believes himself betrayed by her three times—at Actium, with Thidias, and in the final battle of the play.[18]

Even such invectives as "Triple-turn'd whore" and "false soul of Egypt" (4.12.13, 25) hurled against Cleopatra by her lover are typical of the traditional complaints against the goddess Fortuna voiced by her victims (Williamson, 427). Antony's infatuation with such a dangerous figure in vain hopes of forever retaining her love and her favor gives tragic significance to his subsequent loss of everything—reputation, power, even life itself—in her service.

Renaissance emblems warning against Fortuna as an alluring but exceedingly dangerous mistress were, of course, plentiful. To take just one example, Thomas Combe's *The Theater of Fine Devices* (1593 and 1614),[19] an English adaptation of Guillaume de la Perrière's *Théâtre de bons engins* (1539), contains an emblem on the topos of Fortune's basic deceit that seems particularly relevant to Antony's personal tragedy. The *inscriptio* of Combe's emblem 20 states, "They that follow fortunes guiding, / Blindly fall with often sliding." The *pictura* (fig. 1) shows a winged and blindfolded nude female, who holds out her sail with her right hand to catch the winds and who leads with her left hand a blindfolded bearded man. Even though the man uses a cane, it does not keep him from stepping into a black hole in the ground—meant to represent a ditch—along with his equally blind guide. The emblem implies that Fortune, blind deity of all worldly success, pleasures, and goods, is ultimately a death goddess. Combe's *subscriptio* reads as follows:

EMBLEME XX.

They that follow fortunes guiding,
Blindly fall with often sliding.

You blinded folkes by Fortune set on hye,
Confider fhe is darke as well as ye,
And if your guide do want the light of eye,
You needs muft fall, it can none other be.
When blind do leade the blind,they both do lye
In ditch, the Prouerbe faith, and we do fee:
  And thofe that truft to fortunes turning wheele,
Whē they feare leaft,their fall fhall fooneft feele.

Fig. 1. Blind Fortune leads her blind worshipper into a ditch in Emblem 20 from Thomas Combe's *The Theater of Fine Devices* (London: Richard Fields, 1593 and 1614); reproduced by permission of The Huntington Library, San Marino, California.

You blinded folkes by Fortune set on hye,
Consider she is darke as well as ye,
And if your guide do want the light of eye,
You needs must fall, it can none other be.
When blind do leade the blind, they both do lye
In ditch, the Prouerbe saith, and we do see:
And those that trust to fortunes turning wheele,
When they feare least, their fall shall soonest feele.[20]

The sources of this emblem include not only Boethius's *Consolation of Philosophy* (bk. 2.1) but also the New Testament, specifically Matthew 15:14: "And if the blind lead the blind, both shall fall into the ditch." This double fall into a ditch by both the goddess and her victim sounds much like the stormy love relationship between Antony and Cleopatra in Shakespeare's tragedy, as we shall see.

In addition to direct warnings like the above against Fortuna, the fine arts—and in particular, Renaissance emblem books—provide us with visual examples of at least nine very well-known attributes of the goddess Fortuna. These include (1) her two faces of good and bad fortune, (2) her associations with the sea, (3) a sail with a breeze to fill it, (4) a sphere, (5) a ship's rudder, (6) the dolphin, (7) the wheel, (8) wings, and (9) the inconstant moon. It is significant that Shakespeare's characters in *Antony and Cleopatra* endow the Egyptian queen with all nine of these attributes, suggesting thereby that as high priestess of the Hellenistic goddess Isis-Fortuna, she is in their eyes also the earthly bait of Fortune herself.

First, Cleopatra as a mistress is simultaneously fickle and two-faced, offering both good and bad luck to her followers whenever she pleases. As Lady Philosophy informs Boethius in *The Consolation of Philosophy*,

If you were to wish for a law to control the comings and goings of one whom you have freely taken for your mistress, you would be unjust and your impatience would merely aggravate a condition which you cannot change. If you hoist your sails in the wind, you will go where the wind blows you, not where you choose to go; if you put seeds in the ground, you must be prepared for lean as well as abundant years.[21]

In Shakespeare's play, Antony is well aware of Cleopatra's deceitfulness, admitting ruefully to Enobarbus that "She is cunning past man's thought" (1.2.145), an observation which implies that she has superhuman powers. Moreover, Cleopatra—often referred to as a "gypsy" since the English word comes from "Egyptian"—tells her attendant Charmian to deceive Antony when she sees him: "If you find him sad, / Say I am dancing; if in mirth, report / That I am sudden sick" (1.3.3–5). After Antony's final military defeat, she has Mardian falsely inform her lover that she is dead by her own hand, thereby inciting Antony to commit suicide as well. This dishonest or double-faced aspect of Fortuna, which may partially explain our ambivalent critical responses to Cleopatra, is colorfully depicted in an illumination of *Fortuna Bifrons* (fig. 2) from the French translation of Boccaccio's *Fall of Princes*, an important literary source of *de casibus* stories for the Renaissance in general. Anna B. Jameson was clearly pointing to this two-faced nature of the Egyptian queen when she suggested in 1832 that "What is most astonishing in the character of Cleopatra is its antithetical construction—its *consistent inconsistency*" (quoted in Spevack, 691).

Second, Fortuna is associated with the sea, and rightly so, since the ocean traditionally symbolizes mutability or change. In fact, the figure of Fortuna is frequently illustrated as skimming over the waves on a boat, a wheel, a sphere, or a dolphin, and we can usually see a ship or two in the background of typical woodcuts, such as that from Geffrey Whitney's emblem on Occasion in *A Choice of Emblemes* (fig. 3). As we know, Fortuna and Occasion were often conflated in art and poetry during the Renaissance.[22] In Shakespeare's tragedy, Cleopatra first appears to Antony from the waters of the River Cydnus, reclining in state on her barge in a deliberate and alluring imitation of Apelles's famous painting of the *Birth of Venus* from the sea.[23] Moreover, as Adelman states, "Enobarbus associates the sea with chance and hazard: it suggests fortune itself, that realm in which Caesar is necessarily supreme (147).

Shakespeare's dialogue tells us that Cleopatra also indulges in fishing competitions with her lover, once having had a diver place a salt fish (i.e., a dead one) on her lover's hook under water to make him believe he has caught something or has had good luck. But as we shall see, Antony, himself, is the unlucky fish to be caught.[24] In addition, she twice tempts Antony, whose strongest forces are on land, to do battle against Octavius at sea where she can easily control the disastrous outcome. Finally, according to Frederick Kiefer, Horace, in his *Odes* (1.35.6) termed Fortuna "empress of the ocean" (204). We should note that Cleopatra is called "empress" three times in the tragedy, although her actual political rank is no higher than that of queen.

The third attribute of Fortuna is the combination of a sail and a breeze to fill it, as we can see in Gilles Corrozet's image of Occasion

Fig. 2. *Fortuna bifrons* from the French translation of Boccaccio's *The Fall of Princes* [Ms Hunter 206 (U.1.12)]; reproduced by courtesy of the Glasgow University Library.

Fig. 3. Fortuna-Occasio skimming over her element the sea in Geffrey Whitney, *A Choice of Emblemes* (Leiden: Christopher Plantin, 1586), 181; reproduced by permission of the Folger Shakespeare Library.

(fig. 4). Indeed, as Kiefer points out, "Cicero said of Fortune, 'When we enjoy her favouring breeze, we are wafted over to the wished for haven; when she blows against us we are dashed to destruction.' Both Ovid (*Ex Ponto*, 2.3.21ff) and Seneca (*Hercules Oetaeus*, ll. 692ff.) liken Fortune to a breeze filling the sails of a ship" (Kiefer, 196). In *Antony and Cleopatra*, the word "sails" is mentioned six times, four times at very crucial moments in the play. For example, Enobarbus describes Cleopatra's barge as having purple sails (2.2.193) when she goes down river to meet Antony. During the battle of Actium, Cleopatra deserts Antony's ships and, according to Scarus, "The breeze upon her, like a cow in [June]— / Hoists sails and flies" (3.10.14–15). Scarus continues his account as follows:

Lymage doccafion.

Hafte toy bien toft d'attrapper
L'occafion, quand el' f'auance:
Si tu la laiffes efchapper
Tu en feras la pœnitence.

Fig. 4. Fortune with her sail, from Gilles Corrozet, *Hecatomgraphie* (Paris: Denys Ianot, 1543), sig. Mii verso; reproduced by permission of the Folger Shakespeare Library.

                        She once being loof'd [ready to sail away],
          The noble ruin of her magic Antony,
          Claps on his sea-wing [sets sail], and (like a doting
                                        mallard),
          Leaving the fight in height, flies after her.

                                                      (3.10.17–20)

The above report of Antony's foolishness at sea is a good example
in the play of the tradition embodied in Combe's previously men-

tioned emblem on blind Fortune with her sail leading her blind worshipper to disaster. In Shakespeare's play, Canidius then enters to proclaim, "Our fortune on the sea is out of breath, / And sinks most lamentably" (3.10.24–25). Although Plutarch rationalizes Cleopatra's behavior at Actium as a ploy to facilitate her own escape from Octavius Caesar, Shakespeare offers no explanation for her erratic flight. In the very next scene, the queen, although fickle and irrational by nature, rather coyly asks forgiveness from an addicted Antony: "O my lord, my lord, / Forgive my fearful sails! I little thought / You would have followed" (3.11.54–56).

In Antony's second encounter with Caesar by sea, Scarus observes that "Swallows have built / In Cleopatra's sails their nests" (4.12.3–4), an omen hinting that the gods are with her and that this will be a lucky day.[25] But, continues Scarus, "The auguries say / They know not, they cannot tell, look grimly, / And dare not speak their knowledge" (4.12.4–6). Since swallows can also symbolize "faire-weather friends,"[26] the goddess Fortuna promises here more than she ever plans to deliver. For once again fickle Cleopatra sails away from battle and is then called a "Triple-turn'd whore" (4.12.13) by Antony, who may be referring here to the third or downward turn of Fortune's wheel, the fourth turn bringing defeat and death. This pattern is clearly depicted in an illustration of Fortune contrasted with the very Wisdom (Sapientia) that the hero lacks as a man of action rather than of contemplation. The woodcut (fig. 5) is the title page of Francis Petrarch's *De remediis utriusque fortunae* (1527). At this point in the tragedy, Antony accepts his military defeat with the words, "Fortune and Antony part here, even here / Do we shake hands" (4.12.19–20), for Cleopatra "Like a right gypsy, hath at fast and loose / Beguil'd me to the very heart of loss" (4.12.28–29).

According to Boethius, such betrayal is precisely in the nature of Fortuna, who cannot act otherwise. Lady Philosophy reproves the grieving prisoner in the *Consolatio* as follows:

> "What is it, my friend, that has thrown you into grief and sorrow? Do you think that you have encountered something new and different? You are wrong if you think that Fortune has changed toward you. This is her nature, the way she always behaves. She is changeable, and so in her relations with you she has merely done what she always does. This is the way she was when she flattered you and led you on with the pleasures of false happiness. You have merely discovered the two-faced nature of this blind goddess. Although she hides herself from others, she is now wholly known to you." (bk. 2, prose 1).

✿Senſuyt le premier liure de francois petracque poete florentin/des Reine des de fortune proſpere. Tranſlate de latin en francois.✿

Fig. 5. Fortuna and her wheel are opposed by Sapientia and her mirror on the title page of the French edition of Frances Petrarch's *De remediis utriusque fortunae* (1527); reproduced by permission of the Folger Shakespeare Library.

Fig. 6. Fortuna on her sphere brings both good and bad fortune to mankind in Emblem 1 of Theodore de Bry's *Emblemata Nobilitatis* (Frankfurt: Theodore de Bry, 1592); reproduced by permission of the Folger Shakespeare Library.

"Not know me yet?" (3.13.157) asks Shakespeare's Cleopatra of her doting lover. In *Antony and Cleopatra* the shifting breeze behind Fortune's billowing sail destroys Antony partly because, having deserted his long-suffering and prudent wife Octavia, he now has no Lady Philosophy nearby to offer him intellectual comfort.

Sometimes in iconography the figure of Fortuna stands on a sphere—her fourth attribute—indicating her habit of constantly turning about, as in the *pictura* of an emblem by Theodore de Bry. The same picture also depicts her association with Venus through the scallop shell on which her sphere balances and with the presence of a venomous serpent that usually signifies deceit or fraud (fig. 6). De Bry's motto reads "His Fortvna parens; illis inivsta noverca est" ("To these [on the left side] fortune is a parent; to those [on the right side] a wicked stepmother"), while according to the verse:

> Nunc toto saeuit, nunc ridet ab aethere Phoebus,
> Hic vehitur vitreis, mergitur alter aquis.
> Hinc ostendat opes, hinc fortiter efurit ille:
> Quid nisi Rhamnuntis regna fidemque vides?

(Now Phoebus frowns on everything, now he smiles
        from the heavens;
    This man is carried on the waves, another is plunged
        into the waters.
    Here he offers wealth, there extreme hunger.
    What see you in this but the rule and faith of Nemesis?)[27]

Fortune's association with a globe also suggests her dominance over worldly affairs of every sort. Since the conflict between Antony and Octavius is in fact concerned very precisely with the question of world dominance, there are some forty-three references to the "world" in *Antony and Cleopatra*.

As I have previously suggested, Antony loses the worldly card game against Caesar because he is a compulsive gambler in love with fickle Fortuna, who will not always let him win. In contrast, the cooler Octavius almost always intelligently seizes occasion by the forelock, as many scholars have noted, and thus controls his fortunes through the practice of Machiavellian *virtú* or manliness against the female wiles of the goddess.[28] For example, we observe him showing some temperance during the wild bacchic orgy aboard Pompey's ship and later practicing rational generalship in his conduct of the war against Egypt. As John F. Danby observes, however, Octavius also "falls recognizably into Shakespeare's studies of the 'politician'—the series that begins with Richard III and continues down through Edmund."[29] In any event, for an alert Caesar, Fortuna acts as a sturdy mast, allowing him to trim or hoist the sail at will. Exactly this image of Augustus Caesar together with Fortuna appears in an etching by Rembrandt that was used as an illustration in E. Herckmans' *Praise of Sea-faring* (fig. 7).[30] I suspect that Shakespeare gave us a fairly positive—if Machiavellian—portrait of Octavius in *Antony and Cleopatra* because the propaganda machine of his king and patron, James I of England, was at that time identifying James with Augustus Caesar, Prince of Peace.[31]

Symbol 23 by Achille Bocchi represents bad Fortune with one hand holding her sail and with the other controlling her fifth attribute, the rudder (fig. 8), while good Fortune holds up a cornucopia of flowers and vegetables. Although the motto is "Avrea sors regvm est, et velle, et posse beare" ("The king's fortune is golden, and it wishes to and is able to benefit us"), both the picture and verse of emblem 23—dedicated to Henry, King of France—actually emphasize the double nature of fortune. According to the verse,

Fig. 7. Octavius Caesar and Fortune as a mast in Rembrandt van Rign's etching of "The Ship of Fortune," an illustration for E. Herckmans' *Der-Zee-Vaert Lof,* bk. 3 (White/Boon.111.11/11), of 1633; reproduced by permission of the National Gallery of Art, Washington, D.C.

Augustis olim in thalamis fortuna solebat
   Peni ab Romuleis aurea Principibus,
Nempe id magnanimos Reges insigne monebat,
   Omni vt deberent, at cuperent studio
Fortunare homines, nam ceca, volubilis ille est
   Vulgaris, passim que fauet immeritis.
Verum oculata ipsa, et stabilis, que sceptra gubernat
   Regia cui clauum copia diua tenet.
Ergo si regum fortuna est aurea multos
   Pro meritis posse, et velle beare homines,
Haec Henrice eadem digno tibi Lilia sert
   Aurea qui nostra haec florida secla beas.

(Once, golden fortune used to dwell in the majestic chambers of the Roman emperors. Surely this figure reminded the magnanimous kings that they were obliged and desired assiduously to benefit men. For she is blind and fickle, everywhere favoring the undeserving. But the other is sighted and stable, she who governs royal powers, the goddess of plenty who holds the helm. Hence if the king's fortune is golden, it can and wishes to bless many men for their merits. These golden lilies [*fleurs de lys*] are rightfully yours, Henry, who bless these our prosperous times.)[32]

L   LIB. I.

AVREA SORS REGVM EST, ET VELLE,

ET POSSE BEARE.

Symb. XXIII.

Fig. 8. Fortune with her rudder in Symbol 23 of Achille Bocchi, *Symbolarum . . . Libri Quinque* (Bologna, 1574), bk. 1, p. 21; reproduced by permission of the Folger Shakespeare Library.

Of course the people of a nation do tend to share at least the bad fortunes of their kings, if not always the good, and we can see in Shakespeare's play how Antony's descending fortunes adversely affect his followers. After the desertion of Enobarbus, a much chastened Antony cries out in guilty despair, "O, my fortunes have / Corrupted honest men!" (4.5.16–17).

Shakespeare uses the word "rudder" twice in *Antony and Cleopatra*. During the battle at sea, Enobarbus reports that "Th' Antoniad [Cleopatra's flagship], the Egyptian admiral, / With their sixty, fly and turn the *rudder*. To see't mine eyes are blasted" (3.10.2–4; my emphasis). After losing the sea battle through this shift in his fortunes, Antony berates Cleopatra as follows: "Egypt, thou knew'st too well / My heart was to thy *rudder* tied by th' strings, / And thou shouldst [tow] me after" (3.11.56–58; my emphasis).

A sixth attribute of Fortuna is the dolphin, a sea mammal usually associated with the goddess Venus.[33] Since Nonnus had claimed in his *Dionysiaca* that a dolphin carried Venus on its back to her new home in Cyprus (13.438–44), an unlaced Venus in a red gown sits on a marvelous dolphin throne in a Renaissance painting by Cosimo Tura now in the National Gallery, London (fig. 9). She provocatively holds a branch of cherries in her right hand. Nevertheless, the casual iconographic conflation of Venus and Fortuna during the Renaissance is a well-known phenomenon and clearly occurs in *Antony and Cleopatra* (Kiefer, 158–92).

Although in Shakespeare's play the heroine is at first a representative of Venus, whom she "o'er-pictures" with visual hyperbole as extravagant as her language, she later behaves more and more obviously like the goddess Fortuna during the final acts of the tragedy. Yet Fortune must be as attractive as Venus is to men, or who would follow her? Since the fickle goddess is often depicted by artists in the company of Eros, the little love god himself, we should not be surprised by the presence of the squire named Eros in *Antony and Cleopatra* (4.4), especially during the charming scene concerned with arming Antony for battle. At this time Cleopatra and Eros work together as armorers, while Antony boasts fatuously, "If Fortune be not ours to-day, it is / Because we brave her" (4.4.4–5). The truth, of course, is just the opposite, since Antony entirely trusts Fortune and never braves her until after she has deserted him. We should also be aware that the image onstage of Cleopatra and Eros arming Antony is a direct inversion of the popular Renaissance topos of Venus and Cupid *disarming* Mars, thus providing us with a good reason not to accept the critical

Fig. 9. Cosimo Tura's *Allegory of Venus* depicts the goddess on her dolphin throne; reproduced by permission of the National Gallery, London.

Fig. 10. Gilles Corrozet's Fortune rides the seas with one foot on her sphere and the other on a dolphin in Emblem 41 of the *Hecatomgraphie* (Paris: Denys Ianot, 1543), sig. F vi verso; reproduced by permission of the Folger Shakespeare Library.

interpretation that argues for a transcendent love affair like that of Venus and Mars between Antony and Cleopatra.[34] On the contrary, Shakespeare demonstrates in this play that universal peace cannot occur until both Antony and Cleopatra have met their tragic ends and Octavius Caesar is in full control of the Roman empire.

Emblem 41 in Gilles Corrozet's *Hecatomgraphie* (1543) illustrates Fortuna riding the waves with one foot on a sphere and the other on a dolphin (fig. 10). Henry Green translates Corrozet's epigrammatic dialogue, which discusses the nature of the goddess in general and sums up her many attributes, as follows:

> Tell me, O fortune, for what end thou art holding the broken mast wherewith thou supportest thyself? And why also is it that thou art painted upon the sea, encircled with so long a veil? Tell me too why under thy feet are the ball and the dolphin?
> It is to show my instability, and that in me there is no security. Thou seest the mast broken all across,—this veil also puffed out by various winds,—beneath one foot, the dolphin amid the waves; below the other foot, the round unstable ball—I am thus on the sea at a venture. He who has made my portraiture wishes no other thing to be understood than this, that distrust is enclosed beneath me and that I am uncertain of reaching a safe haven—near am I to danger, from safety ever distant; in perplexity whether to weep or to laugh,—doubtful of good or of evil, as the ship which is upon the seas tossed by the waves, is doubtful in itself where it will be borne. This then is what you see in my true image, hither and thither turned without security.[34]

In Shakespeare's tragedy, Cleopatra admiringly remarks of Antony that "his delights were dolphin-like" (5.2.88–89), thereby alluding to his uncontrollable lust[36] and his own trait of inconstancy, which rivals that of Cleopatra herself. In any case, through the lovers' symbiotic relationship, the dolphin becomes an attribute in the play of both leading characers.

As I have pointed out earlier, Fortune and Amor (Eros) were often close companions in Renaissance literature and art. For example, an engraving by Johann Ladenspelder depicts Venus-Fortuna riding with her sphere on a triumphal car and directing a winged Cupid at whom to shoot his arrow (fig. 11). Indeed, according to Kiefer, Italian and French novellas of the period often linked Fortune with a personification of Love, and sometimes with Death as well. "As a result, the [English] dramatists usually treat Fortune not in isolation but in relation to Love and Death" (Kiefer, 158). The same is certainly true in the tragedy of *Antony and Cleopatra*, where the two leading characters are almost drowning in their physical love for each other but embrace only death in the end.

A seventh major attribute of Fortuna is the familiar wheel, as depicted in Hans Sebald Beham's 1541 engraving of Fortuna, who holds the palm of victory in her right hand the wheel in her left hand (fig. 12). Cleopatra herself mentions the wheel in Shakespeare's tragedy. When Antony is dying in her monument, she hyperbolically exclaims, instead of comforting him, "let me rail so high / That the false huswife Fortune break her wheel, / Provok'd by

Fig. 11. Fortuna as Venus with her son Cupid in an engraving by Johann Ladenspelder; reproduced by permission of the National Gallery of Art, Washington,
D.C.

my offense" (4.15.43–45). It would seem that we are now hearing a
hypocritical priestess of Fortuna rail against her own chosen deity
at this moment, since she herself is directly responsible for Antony's pitiful condition.

Wings are an eighth attribute of the fickle goddess. We see her
winged in Beham's engraving and also in Albrecht Dürer's more
famous engraving of a winged Fortuna, who stands on a sphere
hovering over the world she rules (fig. 13). With her right hand she
offers a goblet of wine like Circe's cup (a major temptation for
Dionysian Antony), but in her left hand she holds the bridle of
Nemesis to indicate that her worshippers must ultimately pay for
whatever they receive from her in the world. This aspect of retribution on the part of Fortuna/Nemesis (see Kiefer, 31–41) is surely a
major theme in Shakespeare's tragedy. In *Antony and Cleopatra*,

Fig. 12. A winged Fortuna holds her wheel and the palm of victory in a 1541 engraving by Hans Sebald Beham (1500–50); reproduced by permission of the National Gallery of Art, Washington, D.C.

Fig. 13. Albrech Dürer's winged "Nemesis (The Great Fortune" (1501/02) stands
on her sphere and holds a cup of wine in her right hand, while the bridle of
Nemesis hangs ominously from her left hand; reproduced by permission of the
National Gallery of Art, Washington, D.C.

Fig. 14. "Fortune is like the Moon" from George Wither's *A Collection of Emblems* (1635). Fortune holds the moon in her left hand; reproduced by permission of the Folger Shakespeare Library.

the heroine thinks of herself as having wings when she tells Proculeius that she will not become a captive of Octavius: "Know, sir, that I / Will not wait *pinion'd* at your master's court" (5.2.52–53; my emphasis), obviously meaning that she will not submit to having her wings clipped by Octavius.

Gabriel Rollenhagen's Fortuna, reproduced by George Wither (fig. 14), is also a moon goddess and as changeable as her ninth attribute, the moon, with which Cleopatra is so often compared in the play. The circular motto is "Fortuna ut Luna" ("Fortune is like the moon"). The goddess holds a waning moon in her left hand as a symbol of where her gifts will finally lead and to remind us that, since the moon goddess controls the ocean tides, she controls as well all the significant occasions in the life of man. Of course, Antony finally recognizes that the moon of Fortuna is in fact his

most deadly enemy when he laments, "Alack, our terrene moon /
Is now eclips'd, and it portends alone / The fall of Antony!"
(3.13.153–54). It is also significant that Antony refers here to a
"fall," a word that often alludes to the fall from Fortune's downward
turning wheel as well as to the fate of the hero in a tragedy after
he has been guilty of *hamartia* (faulty judgment) through *hubris*
(pride) in the eyes of the gods. Antony has clearly been both foolish
and arrogant during most of the play.

Because Shakespeare's characters endow Cleopatra with these
nine attributes of Fortuna in the play, the playwright seems to be
manipulating our responses toward his heroine and making her
not so ambiguous after all. We are to see her in this play as attractive
but very untrustworthy. Furthermore, the association of Cleopatra
with Fortuna by other characters encourages us to reject a romantic
view of the lovers and to believe instead that Antony is really in
love with the element of chance in the universe. In fact he does
behave more in the manner of an irrational gambler—despite his
often "wounded chance" (3.10.35)—than like a wise general and
statesman or "the triple pillar of the world," especially when he
insists on engaging Octavius' forces at sea, against the advice of
his officers.

In contrast, Octavius is proud of his Machiavellian ability to remain calm under stress and to seize Occasion's forelock at exactly
the right moment. On the battlefield he orders his army to

> Strike not by land, keep whole, provoke not battle
> Till we have done at sea. Do not exceed
> The prescript of this scroll. Our fortune lies
> Upon this jump.
>
> (3.8.3–6)

Enobarbus comments on the difference between the two men, when
Antony rashly challenges his younger rival to settle their differences by a duel or a trial by combat:

> I see men's judgments are
> A parcel of their fortunes, and things outward
> Do draw the inward quality after them,
> To suffer all alike. That he should dream,
> Knowing all measures, the full Caesar will
> Answer his emptiness. Caesar, thou has subdu'd
> His judgment too.
>
> (3.13.31–37)

And, shortly before his death, a characteristically jealous and wrathful Antony informs Eros that Cleopatra "has pack'd cards with Caesar's, and false-play'd my glory / Unto an enemy's triumph" (4.14.18–20).

II

Yet Antony has willfully chosen his own bad fortune by allying himself with Cleopatra, who hooks him with love as though he were a game fish and even changes his personality from that of an honest solider to that of someone much like herself. Once addicted to her, Antony becomes as false to others as Cleopatra is to him and a compulsive liar. When Caesar offers him the hand of his sister Octavia in marriage in order to forge a family bond between them, Antony quickly disclaims Cleopatra as an impediment: "May I never / (To this good purpose, that so fairly shows) / Dream of impediment!" (2.2.143–45). Next he promises Octavia to reform himself: "My Octavia, / Read not my blemishes in the world's report. / I have not kept my square, but that to come / Shall be done by the rule"(2.3.4–7).[37] Then in 3.2 he once again swears to Caesar that he will cherish Octavia, but Enobarbus knows better:

> He will to his Egyptian dish again: then shall the sighs of Octavia blow the fire up in Caesar, and (as I said before) that which is the strength of their amity shall prove the immediate author of their variance. Antony will use his affection where it is; he married but his occasion here.
> (2.6.125–31)

A true addiction is, of course, a passionate affair of the heart that is almost impossible to resist, although Pompey wisely observes, just before he himself falls off Fortune's wheel, that "I know not / What counts harsh Fortune casts upon my face, / But in my bosom shall she never come, / To make my heart her vassal" (2.6.53–56).

Antony, in contrast, allows Cleopatra to take any liberties with him that she desires. She boasts that "Ere the ninth hour, I drunk him to his bed, / Then put my tires and mantles on him, whilst / I wore his sword Philippan" (2.5.21–23). This allusion to the affair between Hercules and Omphale draws upon a popular Renaissance satirical topos to signify the emasculation of a military hero by love. When Lukas Cranach the Elder painted a version of the story in 1537, for example, he mischievously included two dead birds in

Fig. 15. "Hercules and Omphale" (1537) by Lukas Cranach the Elder; repro-duced by permission of the Herzog Anton Ulrich-Museum, Braunschweig, Germany.

the upper left corner of the panel to represent the sexual orgasms of the lovers. This oil painting (fig. 15) is actually an emblem, since Cranach included a Latin epigram over the head of the bearded Hercules, who is now dressed comically as a woman by Omphale and her ladies:

> HERCULEIS manibus dant Lydae pensa puellae
> Imperium dominae fert deus ille suae.
> Sic capit ingentis animos damnosa voluptas
> Fortiaque enervat pectora mollis amor.
> (The Lydian girls give tasks to the hands of Hercules;
> He submits to the rule of his mistresses.
> Thus ruinous sensuality enslaves the will of the great one,
> And passion weakens the strong heart by its effeminacy.)[38]

The same topos appears in Henry Peacham's English emblem book *Minerva Britanna* (1612) with a woodcut depicting Hercules dressed as a woman and spinning thread (fig. 16). According to the epigram,

A LCIDES heere, hath throwne his Clubbe away,
  And weares a Mantle, for his Lions skinne,
Thus better liking for to paſſe the day,
With *Omphale*, and with her maides to ſpinne,
    To card, to reele, and doe ſuch daily taske,
    What ere it pleaſed, *Omphale* to aske.

Si temperata ac-
ceſſerit Venus nó   That all his conqueſts wonne him not ſuch Fame,
alia Dea eſt adeo   For which as God, the world did him adore,
gratioſa . Euripi-   As Loues affection, did diſgrace and ſhame
des in Medea.   His virtues partes. How many are there more,
                            Who hauing Honor, and a worthy name,
                            By actions baſe, and lewdnes looſe the ſame.

Propert.

          Quicquid amor iuſſit, non eſt contemnere tutum,
          Regnat et in ſuperos ius habet ille Deos.

Vini

Fig. 16. Hercules spinning in the Emblem "Vis Amoris" by Henry Peacham,
Minerva Britanna (London, 1612), 95; reproduced by permission of the Folger
Shakespeare Library.

Alcides heere, hath throwne his Clubbe away,
And weares a Mantle, for his Lions skinne,
Thus better liking for to passe the day,
With *Omphale*, and with her maides to spinne,
   To card, to reele, and doe such daily taske,
   What ere it pleased, *Omphale* to aske.

That all his conquests wonne him not such Fame,
For which as god, the world did him adore,
As Loues affection, did disgrace and shame
His virtues partes. How many are there more,
   Who hauing Honor, and a worthy name,
   By actions base, and lewdnes loose the same.[39]

Yet at another time in his life, Hercules heroically chose virtue over pleasure and became a demigod.

In contrast to his ancestor and patron deity Hercules, Mark Antony, as a number of critics have remarked,[40] chooses Voluptas over Virtue, and he is quite aware of the dangers implicit in his choice. As early as act 1, scene 2, he admits that "These strong Egyptian fetters I must break, / Or lose myself in dotage" (lines 116–17). When Antony is unable to free himself from the excitement of "chance and hazard" (3.7.47), however, the demigod Hercules ascends mysteriously to the sound of music and leaves him to his self-chosen catastrophe. Although in Shakespeare's *Cymbeline*, another more powerful god—Jupiter—descends to save a hero who has reformed, in *Antony and Cleopatra* Fortuna so completely overcomes the hero's reason that he willingly sacrifices himself upon her altar, running to his death like a bridegroom to his marriage bed, as he himself proclaims, and his patron god abandons him.

In any case, the wise and always diplomatic Octavia, an excellent lady (who is maligned in the play only by a messenger in mortal terror of Cleopatra), might well have saved Antony if he had remained with her. As Danby observes, "Octavia is the opposite of Cleopatra as Antony is the opposite of Caesar."[41] She seems to play the role of Wisdom or Sapientia in antithesis to Cleopatra's apparent miming of Fortuna, and Thidias comments in act 3 that, "Wisdom and fortune combating together, / If that the former dare but what it can, / No chance may shake it" (13.79–81). Moreover, as Boethius discovered in prison, Lady Philosophy alone prepares men and women to overcome Fortune by teaching them through wisdom to control their passions. But Antony tries only half-heartedly to love his wife. Octavia, in turn, is given no specific attributes of Sapientia by the playwright, except the evidence of her calm, thoughtful behavior and the ironic praise of Maecenas: "If beauty, wisdom, modesty, can settle / the heart of Antony, Octavia is / A blessed lottery to him"(2.2.240–43).

Nonetheless, when the Egyptian Soothsayer, a representative of Fortuna, informs Antony that in politics Caesar has more "natural luck" than he does and will beat him at every game in Rome, Antony agrees. He then decides to return immediately to his exotic banquet of the senses in Egypt:

> The very dice obey him,
> And in our sports my better cunning faints
> Under his chance. If we draw lots, he speeds;
> His cocks do win the battle still of mine,
> When it is all to nought; and his quails ever
> Beat mine, inhoop'd at odds. I will to Egypt;
> And though I make this marriage for my peace,
> I' th' East my pleasure lies.
>
> (2.3.34–41)

And back he goes posthaste to Cleopatra-Fortuna, the source of all his physical and psychological pleasures.

The thematic significance for a Renaissance audience of Antony's decision to leave Octavia behind in Rome can perhaps best be understood by examining emblem 51 in the 1593 *Emblematum Liber* by Jacob Boissard (fig. 17). Under the motto "Expers Fortvna est Sapientia" (Wisdom has no part in Fortune"), we see Sapientia reading a book on dry land, accompanied by all her traditional attributes (from the owl to an armillary sphere), while a nude Fortuna sails heedlessly on down the river with her wine jars and her treasure chest aboard. According to the epigram,

> Fortuna dubia haud vehitur sapientia cymba;
>   Nec vanis fulta est indiga divitiis.
> Sed cura vigili et studio solerte parata,
>   In varia rerum cognitione seder.
> (Wisdom by no means sails in doubtful fortune's boat;
>   Nor does it need the support of vain riches.
> But prepared by watchful care and skillful devotion,
>   It stands firm in the knowledge of the mutability of
>   things.)[42]

Perhaps better known to students of English drama is the emblematic title page of Robert Record's *The Castle of Knowledge*

L.I.

Rudolpho Magiftro Medico,

EXPERS FORTVNÆ EST SAPIENTIA.

F Ortuna dubia haud vehitur fapientia cymba;
  Nec vanis fulta eft indiga divitiis.
Sed cura vigili & ftudio folerte parata,
  In varia rerum cognitione fedet.
      F I N I S.

Fig. 17. Wisdom remains on terra firma with her books, while Fortune sails her boat before the wind in Emblem 51 of Jacob Boissard, *Emblematum Liber* (Frankfurt, 1593), 103; reproduced by permission of the Folger Shakespeare Library.

also depicting the fundamental opposition between Sapientia and Fortuna (fig. 18). On the left of a central castle, the figure of Urania (Heavenly Wisdom), holding "The Sphere of Destiny" (an armillary sphere symbolizing Divine Providence) and a pair of compasses (human rationality), stands under the sun of reason on a cube representing stability. On the right hand side of the picture, blind Fortune teeters on her unstable sphere, while holding the bridle of Nemesis in her left hand and the Wheel of Fortune—"whose ruler is ignorance"—in her right hand. The irrational moon shines down upon her. According to the verse,

> Though spitefull Fortune turned her wheele
> To staye the Sphere of Vranye,
> Yet doth this Sphere resist that wheele,
> And fleeyth all fortunes villanye.
> Though earthe do honor Fortunes balle,
> And bytells blynde hyr wheele aduaunce,
> The heauens to fortuen are not thralle,
> These Spheres surmount al fortunes chance.[43]

Part of Antony's bad fortune is that Gluttony and riotous sexuality have already so marred his reason that he is now fortune's fool, despite such native virtues as courage and magnaminity. We should remember, after all, that in early modern England, passionate love itself was considered to be a type of insanity by writers such as Robert Burton. Unwilling to bridle his passions, Antony is ready to be transformed into a beast by act 4 and to be sacrificed to the goddess he has chosen to serve.

In 2.5, Cleopatra compares Antony to a fish (an ancient symbol of the male sex organ), then admits that she is a whore by profession, or one of those women "that trade in love" (2.5.2) and are the bait of pleasure for unwary men (Adelman, 60). She thus requires mood music as food to accompany her sport while fishing for her lover.

> Give me mine angle, we'll to th' river; there,
> My music playing far off, I will betray
> Tawny [-finn'd] fishes; my bended hook shall pierce
> Their slimy jaws; and as I draw them up,
> I'll think them every one an Antony,
> And say, "Ah, ha! y' are caught.
>
> (2.5.10–15)

According to Paul F. Watson, fishing and hunting imagery of this sort derives from Ovid's *The Art of Love* 1:43–50, and when

Fig. 18. Sapientia opposes Blind Fortuna on the title page of Robert Record's *The Castle of Knowledge* (London, 1556); reproduced by permission of the Folger Shakespeare Library.

Boccaccio concludes his influential epic the *Teseida*, he slyly sings of the amorous font where only rarely does one become a good fisherman with profit. Explaining that the vagina is the font, the gloss continues: "Because of too much fishing in the amorous font there are those who get skinned by it."[44]

The sexual implications of fish continued to be playfully used by artists throughout the seventeenth century and early eighteenth century in Dutch genre painting, as we can see by the London National Gallery's "A Woman with a Fish Pedlar in a Kitchen" (fig. 19) painted in 1713 by Willem van Mieris. Here the rabbits are traditional fertility symbols; the fish are allusions to the phallus; the dead birds[45] are as salacious in meaning as the hunting cat at the bottom of the painting; and the unlikely bas relief beneath the shop window depicting the sea nymph Galatea about to mount a lusty dolphin, which has been bridled by *amorini* for her Triumph, has nothing whatsoever to do with chastity. Even the wind instruments played by the tritons and a putto on the bas relief are symbolic of sensory pleasures.[46]

Clifford Davidson notes that a fish is also associated with idleness or the figure of Sloth in Cesare Ripa's *Iconologia*. He quotes from Ripa that "Fish, it was believed, when touched by a net or by hands become so stupified that they cannot escape. Idleness affects the idle in the same way; they cannot do anything."[47]

When Cleopatra asks Enobarbus if she is to blame for losing the battle at sea, Enobarbus sensibly replies, "Antony only, that would make his will / Lord of his Reason" (3.13.2–4), for as Aristotle teaches, only our rationality makes us different from the animals. Even Antony himself finally becomes aware of his descent into bestiality by the third act when he rails at Cleopatra, condemns Thidias to be beaten, and wishes "that I were / Upon the hill of Basan, to outroar / The horned herd!" (3.13.126–28). The *Riverside Shakespeare* annotates this line (deriving from Psalm 22) as a reference to Antony's cuckolding by Cleopatra, but no mistress can cuckold her lover. Only a lawful wife like Octavia can give her husband horns in the eyes of society. On the other hand, Antony is decidedly bullish or beastly at this moment in the play, roaring with impotent fury and jealousy, which indicates that he is under the control of bestial passions. Later in Shakespeare's tragedy, Cleopatra sees Antony as a wild bird or game animal to be snared. As his true captor, she rather sarcastically greets him after battle: "Lord of lords! / O infinite virtue, com'st thou smiling from / The world's great snare uncaught?" (4.8.16–18). Antony is by now sufficiently

Fig. 19. "A Woman with a Fish Peddlar in a Kitchen" (1713) by Willem van Mieris depicts fish as a sexual symbol: reproduced by permission of the National Gallery, London.

dehumanized to become a sacrificial offering to the goddess Fortuna whom he worships so passionately.

As John Holloway has argued, all of Shakespeare's major tragedies include an artistically embedded human sacrifice to some deity or other:

> the tragic protagonist in these plays is one who has moved from a position at the centre of well-ordered human life, to a position in which he is alien to that, in essence opposed to it, allied to what is enemy to it. Parallel with this, the protagonist passes through an ordeal of suffering which brings him from prosperity to death, but it is not death seen merely as one of the fortuitous hazards of life; it is seen from the start as the proper, and over the course of time as becoming almost the chosen, end of life lived as the protagonist has lived it.[48]

In comparison to Shakespeare's Antony, Sophocles' tragic hero Oedipus is described by the Chorus as a hunted animal hiding away in forests and caves from his pursuers but ultimately destined to become a human sacrifice to Dionysus or Bacchus, the Greek god of irrationality, whose ritual dance Antony leads aboard Pompey's ship in 2.7, and whose name he often assumed while drinking.

Renaissance art also takes note of man's descent to the bestial through the machinations of Fortuna. For example, Achille Bocchi has an interesting emblem on Fortuna's deliberate transformation into a beast or monster of another famous warrior, Alexander the Great. The motto of symbol 66 reads "Bellva fit caesae statvit qvi credere sorti" ("He becomes a beast who has decided to trust to blind fate"). The engraving depicts a winged Fortuna with her sail filled with wind (fig. 20). As she steps out of her motorized scallop shell (associating her with Venus), Fortuna replaces the kneeling Alexander's helmeted but severed head with the tripartite head of a monster. Under a second motto stating "Qvam stvlta sit svperbia" ("How Foolish is Pride"), the epigram reads

> Caeca vni Fortuna sibi quos credere adegit,
> Magna ex parte auidos decorus magis atque capaces
> Efficit, hinc olim iussit se, non modo passus
> Dicier Aemathius ivvenis magno Ioue natum.
> Dumque cupit tali gestorum extendere famam
> Nomine: corrumpit potius, six protinus ipsi
> Fortunae totum quise permiserit vltro,
> Vero hominis regno spoliat se prorsus, et ingens
> Bellua fit capitum multorum, luminis expers.

CXLII LIB. III.

BELLVA FIT CAECAE STATVIT QVI
CREDERE SORTI.

Symb. LXVI.

LIB. III. CXLIII

QVAM STVLTA SIT SVPERBIA.

Symb. LXVI.

Cæca vni Fortuna sibi quos credere adegit,   (ces
Magna ex parte auidos decoris magis, atq̃ capa-
Efficit . hinc olim iufsit se , non modo passus
Dicier Aemathius iuuenis magno Ioue natum .
Dumq̃ cupit tali gestorum extendere famam
Nomine : corrumpit potius . sic protinus ipsi
Fortunæ totum qui se permiserit Vltro ,
Vero hominis regno spoliat se prorsus , & ingens
Bellua fit capitum multorum , luminis expers .

Fig. 20. Fortuna transforms Alexander the Great into a beast in Symbol 66 of Achille Bocchi's *Symbolarum . . . Libri Quinque* (Bologna, 1574), bk. 3, 142; reproduced by permission of the Folger Shakespeare Library.

(Those whom she has impelled to trust to her alone, blind Fortune for the most part makes more greedy for honor than they have a right to: hence in olden times she ordered herself; not only the Macedonian youth born from great Jove suffered. When he desired to extend the fame of his deeds under her name she destroyed him instead: That is what happens to one who continually entrusts himself to Fortune of his own accord. Truthfully in the realm of man she ruins him utterly, and he becomes a many-headed monster, deprived of light.)[49]

The point here is the same as that in Francisco Goya's famous etching of a nightmare: "Los Caprichos" or "The Sleep of Reason produces Monsters." Having failed to control his animal passions through his reason, Antony, like Alexander, finally descends to the level of a beast.

When Antony believes in act 4, scene 14, that he has lost the

44   ANDREAE ALCIATI

Fortuna uirtutem superans.

Cæsareo postquàm superatus milite uidit
Ciuili undantem sanguine Pharsaliam:
Iamiam stricturus moribunda in pectora ferrum,
Audaci hos Brutus protulit ore sonos:
Infelix uirtus & solis prouida uerbis,
Fortunam in rebus cur sequeris dominam?

Fig. 21. The virtue of Brutus is overcome when he commits suicide, according to Andrea Alciati in the *Emblemata* (Paris: Wechel, 1534), p. 44; reproduced by permission of the Folger Shakespeare Library.

war and that Cleopatra has committed suicide in order to avoid capture by the Romans, he tries to kill himself by running on his sword, as Brutus had done successfully before him in Shakespeare's *Julius Caesar*. We should note here that emblem 44 (fig. 21) in the 1534 edition of Andrea Alciati's *Emblemata* suggests that suicide is always in the cards for the worshippers of Fortune. Alciati's *inscriptio* introduces the topos as "Fortuna virtutem superans" ("Fortune overcoming virtue"). The *pictura* shows Brutus running on his sword, while the *subscriptio* reads as follows:

> After he was overcome by Octavian's army, he saw
> Pharsalia flowing with the blood of citizens.

Just as he was about to unsheathe his sword
    against his dying heart,
Brutus with audacious mouth
    uttered these words:
Miserable Virtue, caring only for words,
why do you follow Fortune as the
    mistress in events?[50]

Geffrey Whitney's emblem 70 is an adaptation of the same notion. However, Brutus at least achieves his goal of being a Roman who vanquishes himself, while Antony—also overcome by Fortuna—botches even his own suicide. He is then carried mortally wounded to Cleopatra's mausoleum, a symbolic stronghold that she fears to leave since she is determined not to be taken prisoner by Octavius. "Your wife Octavia, with her modest eyes / And still conclusion, shall acquire no honor / Demuring upon me" (4.15.27–29), she assures the dying Antony.

During the incredible stage emblem that follows, the Egyptian queen and her women draw Antony—like a huge fish—up to the second level of the monument. In fact, a fish net might be the most appropriate means for achieving this feat onstage,[51] since Cleopatra speaks irreverently of her final taking of Antony as a sporting event: "Here's sport indeed! How heavy weighs my lord!" (4.15.32). Another Alciati emblem (number 75 in the 1621 edition) describes something rather like this grotesque situation. Under the motto "In amatores meretricum" ("On lovers of harlots"), the woodcut depicts a fisherman wearing a female goatskin disguise and pulling ashore a large bream he has just netted (fig. 22). We should remember, of course, that goatskins were associated both with sexuality and with Greek tragedy itself. According to Alciati's *subscriptio* in translation,

The fisherman, having donned the skin of a shaggy she-goat, has
    added a pair of horns to his own head;
and standing on the edge of the shore he deceives the amorous
    bream, whose passion for the snub-nosed flock [of goats] drives it
    into the nets.
The she-goat brings to mind the harlot; the bream resembles the
    lover, who, poor wretch, caught by an indecent love, perishes.[52]

Antony, caught helplessly in two-faced Fortune's net, also perishes like the amorous bream. But Cleopatra then reminds the audience that the winning general, Octavius Caesar, is no better than the man he has defeated in battle with the help of Fortuna: "'Tis paltry

EMBLEMATVM LIBELLVS.   33

In Amatores meretricum.

Villofæ indutus pifcator tegmina capræ,
Addidit ut capiti cornua bina fuo,
Fallit amatorem ftans fummo in littore Sargum,
In laqueos fimi quem gregis ardor agit.
Capra refert fcortum,fimilis fit Sargus amanti,
Qui mifer obfcæno captus amore perit.
C

Fig. 22. Andrea Alciati depicts the amorous fish caught in a net by a fisherman wearing a goatskin in the *Emblemata* (Paris: Wechel, 1534), 33; reproduced by permission of the Folger Shakespeare Library.

to be Caesar; / Not being Fortune, he's but Fortune's knave, / A minister of her will" (5.2.2–4). However, a few minutes later, she ironically orders Proculeius to "tell him / I am his fortune's vassal, and I send him / The greatness he has got" (5.2.27–29).

In terms of sacred history, the Roman goddess Fortuna is about to give way to the rule of Divine Providence at this point in political history. Octavius Caesar announces that "The time of universal peace is near" (4.6.4.), an allusion to the Augustan peace or the *pax romana* necessary for Christ's Nativity to occur in Bethlehem. From then on the notion of Fortune tends to be transformed philosophically into the notion of Providence as the ruler of human lives. Referring to this important theological change, a few copies of Whitney's 1586 *Choice of Emblemes* contain the emblem "Fato, non fortuna" (Fate, not fortune"), which has the following verse:

> The varying dame, that turnes the tottering wheele,
>   To whome the worlde hathe longe ascribed power,
> To lifte men vp, where they all pleasures feele,
> To throwe them doune, where all their sweete is sower:
>   Whose worshippes longe in euerie coaste weare rife,
>   Euen as the guide, and goddesse of this life.
>
> Yet here, behoulde her diêtie is dash'de,
> And shee subdu'de, and captiue vnto man:
> And nowe, all those that seru'd her bee abash'de;
> And doe confesse that FORTVNE nothinge can:
>   But onelie GOD defendes the mighties seates:
>   And houldes them vp, in spite of Enuies threates.[53]

Whitney's woodcut (fig. 23) shows a courtier or lover with his left hand displaying the laurel branch of victory and his right hand grasping the hand of God, who stabilizes him at the top of the wheel. The courtier's feet rest on the back of a fallen blind Fortune, who is defeated at last by human faith in the superior power of the Judeo-Christian deity. Fortune's wheel can turn no more, or so certain Protestant theologians believed. As Kiefer explains, "Although most Christians tolerated Fortune as a somewhat ambiguous presence within the culture of the late Middle Ages, thinkers of the Protestant Reformation generally did not. In their attitude they resemble the Church Father who so often inspires their writings—Augustine. And, like him, they adopt an antagonistic attitude toward Fortune" (16–17). By having Octavius mention the approaching *pax romana*, Shakespeare seems to agree in this play that Divine Providence will soon become the new ruler of the world after the military defeat of Antony and Cleopatra by the Romans.

III

The entire last act of the tragedy is now given over to Cleopatra's attempts to deify her dead lover and herself, with rather ambiguous results. Her poetic eulogy of the dead Antony in the famous dream speech beginning "His face was as the heav'ns" (5.2.79) is, of course, typical of the hyperbole of tragic endings in the theater.

T H E varijnge dame, that turnes the totteringe wheele,
To whome the worlde hathe longe aſcribed power,
To lifte men vp , where they all pleaſures feele,
To throwe them doune, where all their ſweete is ſower:
  Whoſe worſhippes longe in euerie coaſte weare rife,
  Euen as the guide, and goddeſſe of this life.

Yet here, beholde, her diêtie is daſh'de,
And ſhee ſubdu'de, and captiue vnto man:
And nowe, all thoſe that ſeru'd her bee abaſh'de;
And doe confeſſe that F O R T V N E nothinge can:
  But onelie G O D defendes the mighties ſeates:
  And houldes them vp, in ſpite of Enuies threates.

Conſpicitur nunquam meliore potentia cauſſa,   Ouid. 2. Ponr. 9.
  Quàm quoties vanas non ſinit eſſe preces.
Hoc nitor iſte tui generis deſiderat , hoc eſt
  A ſuperis orta nobilitatis opus.

                              O 3   SINCE

Fig. 23. Divine Providence maintains the courtier at the top of Fortune's wheel in Geffrey Whitney's *A Choice of Emblemes* (Leiden: Christopher Plantin, 1586), 109 (STC 25437.8); reproduced by permission of the Folger Shakespeare Library.

There is also very probably a blasphemous allusion by the Egyptian queen here to the angel of the Book of Revelation as having been her lover.[54] Yet the audience knows, after all, that Antony was no heavenly angel, and Dolabella quickly assures Cleopatra that no such wondrous human ever existed. Nevertheless, Helen Morris has shown real likenesses between the eulogy and Albrecht Dürer's illustration for Revelation 10:1–6,[55] with interesting implications for the underlying Christian meaning of the tragedy. Most commentators believe, however, that Cleopatra is comparing her victim here ("His legs bestrid the ocean, his rear'd arm / Crested the world") to the Colossus of Rhodes, which as a lost monument of antiquity had become a symbol for the Renaissance of Time's decay of monuments (we might call it today the "Ozymandias" topos) in contrast to the art of literature, which was supposed to live on in human memory. In fact, Shakespeare himself made use of this topos in Sonnet 55, where he claims that "Not marble nor the gilded monuments / Of princes shall outlive this powr'ful rhyme." The poet's suggestion that, unlike poetry, marble itself is inconstant ought to be kept in mind when we later consider arguments that Cleopatra is the artistic creator of her own funeral monument through which she achieves immortality.

Peacham's emblem on the topos illustrates the Colossus bestriding the harbor but also holding what Antony clearly lacks: a book and the lamp of knowledge (fig. 24). According to the verse,

> The Monuments that mightie Monarches reare,
> COLOSSO'S statues, and Pyramids high,
> In tract of time, doe moulder downe and weare,
> Ne leaue they any little memorie,
>   The Passenger may warned be to say,
>   They had their being here, another day.
>
> But wise wordes taught, in numbers sweete to runne,
> Preserued by the liuing Muse for aie,
> Shall still abide, when date of these is done,
> Nor ever shall by Time be worne away:
>   Time, Tyrants, Envie, World assay thy worst,
>   Ere HOMER die, thou shalt be fired first.[56]

Ironically, Cleopatra's horror of being played hereafter onstage by a squeaking boy actor is evidently mistaken. The many poetic dramatizations of *Antony and Cleopatra* will actually bring the couple far more fame in the future than either her exaggerated comparison

THE Monuments that mightie Monarches reare,
   COLOSSO'S ftatües, and Pyramids high,
In tract of time, doe moulder downe and weare,
Ne leaue they any little memorie,
     The Paffenger may warned be to fay,
     They had their being here, another day.

Scindétur veftes,
geminæ frangen-
tur et aurum,
Carmina quem
tribuent fama
perennis erit:
Ovid: Amor: E-
leg: 10.

But wife wordes taught, in numbers fweete to runne,
Preferued by the liuing Mufe for aie,
Shall ftill abide, when date of thefe is done,
Nor ever fhall by Time be worne away:
     Time, Tyrants, Envie, World affay thy worft,
     Ere *HOMER* die, thou fhalt be " fired firft.

" Exitio terras
cum dabit vna
dies. Ovid:

Ovid: Eleg:vltim:

     Ergo cum filices, cum dens patiatur aratri
        Depereant ævo, carmina morte carent.
     Cedant carminibus Reges, Regumque Triumphi,
        Cedat et auriferi ripa beata Tagi.

                                      Pro

Fig. 24. Henry Peacham depicts the Colossus of Rhodes as a monument inferior to literature (or the book he holds) in *Minerva Britanna* (London, 1612), 161; reproduced by permission of the Folger Shakespeare Library.

of Antony to an angelic Colossus or her own now vanished funeral monument.

For her death scene, Cleopatra assumes the role and one of the costumes [Vincenzo Cartari depicts two] of the moon goddess Isis-Fortuna (fig. 25), whose earthly representative she most certainly is as queen of Egypt. According to Thomas Allan Brady, in antiquity Isisi was both a civic deity and the goddess worshipped by an important hellenistic mystery cult:

> Not only are the statues and monuments of her worship found in all parts of the Roman Empire and her symbols quite commonly used on rings, gems, pins, and other jewelry, but many grave reliefs and tombs show representations of her symbols, particularly the *sistrum* and the *situla*. The deceased, if a woman, was frequently portrayed on the funeral monument in the costume characteristic of the deity.[57]

Thus John Bowers's argument that Cleopatra consciously attempts by her staged death to transform herself into a decorative funerary statue of marble within her own carefully designed memorial monument is historically very probable. On the Jacobean stage, the monument itself "would have been anachronistically transposed into the sort of native monument whose examples crowded the cathedrals and adorned almost every parish church in England. These were the ornate chantry-chapels which were erected around the actual tombs during the period following the first outbreak of the plague in the fourteenth century."[58] Such chantry-chapels were fortified and could provide sanctuary. Some even had two stories, such as the famous tomb-chapel of Henry V (ca. 1440) that "ushered in a new style by adding a second story as a gallery front."[59]

It seems, moreover, that there were actually two versions of the goddess Isis during the Roman period—the terrestrial and the celestial—as was also true of Venus in Platonic philosophy. Indeed Celestial Isis was discovered by Lucius in *The Golden Ass* by Apuleius to be stronger than ordinary Fortune, "whose threads she unravels."[60] The priest who initiates Lucius, after he has been transformed from an ass back into a man, tells him

> to consider himself as rescued from the sway of Fortuna, that supposedly all-powerful goddess; or, in an alternative formulation of the priest, as having passed from the blind Fortuna into the protection of a Fortuna who is not only herself seeing but the source of light and vision (= knowledge?) for the other divinities. (Solmsen, 95)

Fig. 25. Vincenzo Cartari's two images of the moon goddess Isis-Fortuna in *Le imagini de i dei de gli antichi* (Venice: Vincentio Valgrisi, 1571), 120; reproduced by permission of the Folger Shakespeare Library.

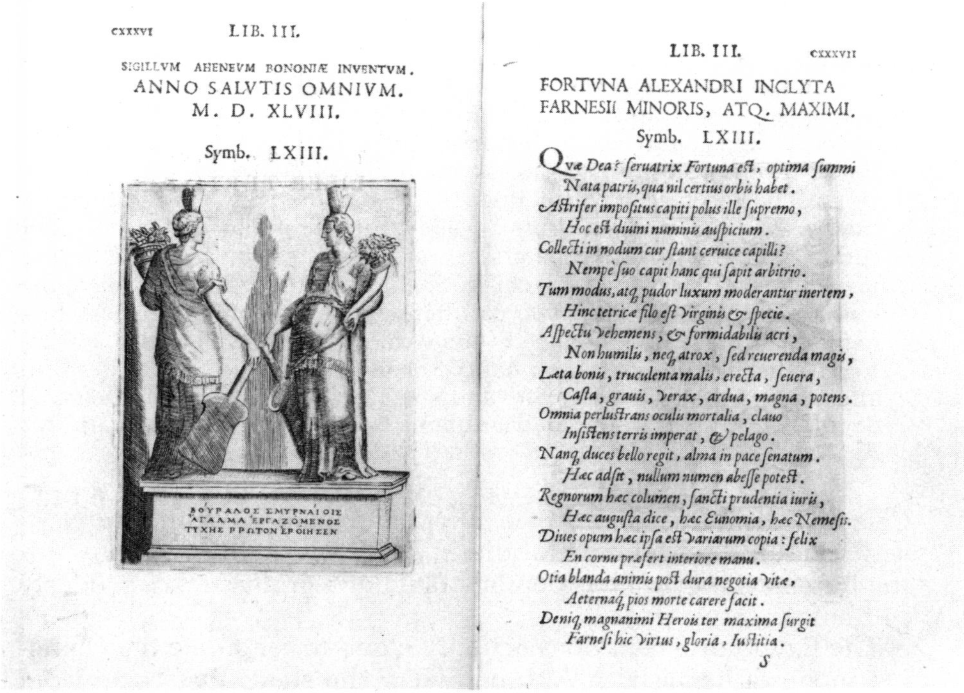

SIGILLVM AHENEVM BONONIÆ INVENTVM.
ANNO SALVTIS OMNIVM.
M. D. XLVIII.

Symb. LXIII.

FORTVNA ALEXANDRI INCLYTA
FARNESII MINORIS, ATQ. MAXIMI.

Symb. LXIII.

Qvæ Dea? feruatrix Fortuna eſt, optima ſummi
Nata patris, qua nil certius orbis habet.
Aſtrifer impoſitus capiti polus ille ſupremo,
Hoc eſt diuini numinis auſpicium.
Collecti in nodum cur ſtant ceruice capilli?
Nempe ſuo capit hanc qui ſapit arbitrio.
Tum modus, atq, pudor luxum moderantur inertem,
Hinc tetricæ filo eſt Virginis & ſpecie.
Aſpectu vehemens, & formidabilis acri,
Non humilis, neq, atrox, ſed reuerenda magis,
Læta bonis, truculenta malis, erecta, ſeuera,
Caſta, grauis, Verax, ardua, magna, potens.
Omnia perluſtrans oculis mortalia, clauo
Inſiſtens terris imperat, & pelago.
Nanq, duces bello regit, alma in pace ſenatum.
Hæc adſit, nullum numen abeſſe poteſt.
Regnorum hæc columen, ſancti prudentia iuris,
Hæc auguſta dice, hæc Eunomia, hæc Nemeſis.
Diues opum hæc ipſa eſt Variarum copia: felix
En cornu præfert interiore manu.
Otia blanda animis poſt dura negotia Vitæ,
Aeternaq, pios morte carere facit.
Deniq, magnanimi Herois ter maxima ſurgit
Farneſi hic Virtus, gloria, Iuſtitia.

S

Fig. 26. Achille Bocchi depicts Earthly Isis-Fortuna with her back to the viewer and Celestial Isis-Fortuna in Symbol 43 of the *Symbolarum . . . Libri Quinque* (Bologna, 1574), bk. 3, cxxxvi; reproduced by permission of the Folger Shakespeare Library.

As far as Shakespeare's *Antony and Cleopatra* is concerned, however, the audience will have to decide for itself whether or not to believe in the validity of Cleopatra's ceremonial transformation from Terrestrial Isis (earth and water) into Celestial Isis (fire and air). Only the latter could provide a foolish and lascivious Antony with immortality.

It so happens that Bocchi published an interesting emblem flattering Alexander Farnese on just such an Isis. It is symbol 63 entitled "The Famous Fortune of Alexander Farnese the Lesser (but also the Greatest)." The picture actually illustrates two Fortunas dressed as Roman matrons and holding both the cornucopia and the rudder (fig. 26). The verse reads in translation,

What goddess? Fortune the preserver she is, best born of the highest father, the world has nothing more certain. That structure [*astrifer*] set on top of her head is the sign of divine power. Why is her hair collected in a roll around her head? Obviously he who is discerning will capture this by his own judgment. As measure and modesty set bounds to idle luxury, so here is an image of a maiden with an ominous thread. With forceful aspect and sharp features, not submissive nor terrible, but rather reverend, propitious to the good, ferocious to the bad, upright, severe, chaste, grave, truthful, intense, great, potent. Surveying all mortal things with her eyes, she rules over land by foot and over sea by her rudder. For she directs generals in war and statesmen in peace. In her presence, no power can be lacking. She is the support of kingdoms, the knowledge of divine law; you call her august, Eunomia, Nemesis. She herself is the rich abundance of the wealthy: see how she displays the fruitful horn with her nearer hand. She gives peace and joy to the soul after the hard struggles of life, and she saves the faithful from eternal death. And finally in the magnanimous heroic Farnese springs up this thrice-great virtue, glory, and justice.[61]

Celestial Isis does insist, on the other hand, that "measure and modesty" should "set bounds to idle luxury," and neither Antony nor the human Cleopatra has demonstrated either measure or modesty in Shakespeare's tragedy.

The Egyptian queen does actually claim to renounce the changing moon of Terrestrial Fortuna, when she states that "now from head to foot / I am marble-constant; now the fleeting moon / No planet is of mine" (5.2.240–41). Is this merely wishful thinking on her part? In any case, Shakespeare seems to imply here for some scholars, including Adelman (155), that with her demise, Cleopatra is in fact metamorphosed into a marble statue of the goddess Isis. Marilyn Williamson states that in the final scene of the play "Cleopatra rises to the occasion: as a creature of the imagination, she sees Caesar's intention [to include her in his triumph] as a threat to the very center of her existence, and she creates in the ritual of her suicide her answering artistic triumph, one that will impress upon human memory *her* interpretation of the story."[62] Anne Barton believes that the transformation will be victorious since Cleopatra accomplishes it "by creating a tableau, still and contemplative in living art, which transfigures and quiets the events in which it was immanent."[63] But Shakespeare himself never tells us in the tragedies what happens to his characters after their deaths, since this is the realm of the deity. At the very least we can say that a work of art in marble (an inconstant material itself, as we have seen), Cleopatra will apparently forever *symbolize* her variable and contrary nature in human memory rather than continuing to act out inconstancy on the stage of the world. She becomes in the recollected image of her suicide, a death "Which shackles accidents and bolts up change" (5.2.6), an artistic icon of that which she has always merely imitated—the goddess Isis-Fortuna in one of her two forms.

Of considerable historical interest in the ongoing Cleopatra controversy is the fact that a gifted female poet of the English Renaissance, Aemilia Lanyer, stated what seems to be the typical seventeenth-century Christian woman's understanding of Cleopatra in her poem *Salve Deus Rex Iudaeorum* (pub. 1611). Contrasting the Egyptian queen's sensual love with the love for Christ felt by her own patroness, the Countess of Cumberland, Lanyer wrote the following verses:

> Great *Cleopatra's* loue to *Anthony,*
> Can no way be compared vnto thine;
> Shee left her Loue in his extremitie,
> When greatest need should cause her to combine
> Her force with his, to get the Victory:
> Her Loue was earthly, and thy Loue Diuine;
>   Her Loue was onely to support her pride,
>   Humilitie thy Loue and Thee doth guide.
>
> That glorious part of Death, which last shee plai'd,
> T'appease the ghost of her deceased Loue,
> Had neuer needed, if shee could haue stai'd
> When his extreames made triall, and did proue
> Her leaden loue vnconstant, and afraid:
> Their wicked warres the wrath of God might moue
>   To take reuenge for chast *Octavia's* wrongs,
>   Because shee enioyes what vnto her belongs.
>
> No *Cleopatra*, though thou wert as faire
> As any Creature in *Antonius* eyes;
> Yea though thou wert as rich, as wise, as rare,
> As any Pen could write, or Wit deuise:
> Yet with this Lady canst thou not compare,
> Whose inward virtues all thy worth denies;
>   Yet thou a black Egyptian do'st appeare:
>   Thou false, shee true; and to her Loue more deere.[64]

Lanyer states quite clearly that the betrayal of one's love was unacceptable behavior to women at this time in England, and I doubt that this attitude toward betrayal has changed since then.

SERVILES ANIMVS REFVGIT GENEROSIOR ACTOS. 4.

Fig. 27. Theodore de Bry sees Cleopatra's death as heroic in Emblem 4 of his *Emblemata Nobilitatis* (Frankfurt, 1592); reproduced by permission of the Folger Shakespeare Library.

In contrast to such a negative view toward the Egyptian queen, Chaucer describes Cleopatra as a good woman willing to sacrifice her body to the worms in order to redeem her Antony,[65] while the Renaissance emblematist Theodore de Bry admiringly portrays her death as heroic in a verse interpreting his fine engraving of "Cleopatra the Egyptian" (fig. 27):

> Actias Ausonias fugit Cleopatra Catenas,
>   Aspide somnifera brachia moras gerens.
> Nec tulit Oenotrii Victoris vincla superbi,
>   Sic vmbram exhorret mens generosa suam.
> [Cleopatra fled the chains of the Italian of Actium,
> Bearing on her arms the asp's deadly bite.
> Nor did she carry the bonds of the proud Roman victor,
> So greatly did her noble spirit abhor his shadow.][66]

Nevertheless, I see neither of these elements in Shakespeare's version of the story. For him, Cleopatra's "courage" consists of finding an easy and painless way to die and by taking a macabre "joy o' th' worm" (5.2.289) before our eyes. Not only does her servant Iras die more bravely before her, but after the queen's death, Charmian must straighten Cleopatra's royal crown, which has ludicrously fallen awry. In addition, the bad fortune earlier predicted by the Sooth-sayer in 1.2 for Charmian comes true indeed, despite all her ser-vices to Cleopatra as Terrestrial Isis and her fervent prayers to Celestial Isis.

Although Cleopatra does indeed consciously attempt by her staged death to transform herself into a decorative funerary statue of marble within her own memorial, Bowers observes that Octavius frustrates the queen's artistic design for her mausoleum by ordering soldiers "to take up her bed, and bear her women from the monu-ment" (5.2.354–55) to another place where Cleopatra will lie next to her Antony (Bowers, 291). Ironically, no one today knows where to find the tomb of Mark Antony and the seductive mistress of both his good and bad fortunes.

In conclusion, we must return once more to the Thomas Combe emblem of Fortuna at the beginning of this essay. In it, like Antony and Cleopatra, the blind goddess and her blind worshipper both fall into a ditch (see fig. 1). Although we cannot be sure that Shake-speare knew this particular emblem, we may be confident that he was very familiar with Matthew 15:14 on the blind leading the blind into a ditch, a biblical passage to which he apparently alludes twice in the tragedy of *Antony and Cleopatra*. Apart from Antony, Cleopatra's most articulate admirer in the play is Enobarbus, who follows Antony's shifting fortunes almost to the end. When this soldier's final desertion is surprisingly rewarded by Antony's gen-erosity, Enobarbus asks in contrition, "I fight against thee? No, I will go seek / Some *ditch* wherein to die" (4.6.36–37; my empha-sis). Later Cleopatra threatens to starve herself to death before she will allow Octavius to exhibit her in his Roman triumph: "Rather a *ditch* in Egypt / Be gentle grave unto me" (5.2.57–58; my empha-sis). One thing is certain: Terrestrial Fortuna, when unopposed by Wisdom, traditionally leads all her adoring worshippers to tragic defeat and death in the end . . . that is, "to the very heart of loss."[67]

Notes

1. See Eugene M. Waith, *The Herculean Hero* (New York: Columbia University Press, 1962), 113–21.

2. See Donna B. Hamilton, "*Antony and Cleopatra* and the Tradition of Noble Lovers," *Shakespeare Quarterly* 24 (1973): 245–51.

3. See J. Leeds Barroll, "Antony and Pleasure," *Journal of English and German Philology* 57 (1958): 709–20.

4. Feminists tend to see the Egyptian queen as a woman of power, who is courageous enough to choose her own lovers and to dominate them and destiny through her art. To cite just a few examples, see Irene Dash, *Wooing, Wedding, and Power: Women in Shakespeare's Plays* (New York: Columbia University Press, 1981), 209–47; Carol Thomas Neely, who sees Cleopatra as an artist in *Broken Nuptials* (New Haven and London: Yale University Press, 1985), 136–65; Mihoko Suzuki, *Metamorphoses of Helen: Authority, Difference, and the Epic* (Ithaca and London: Cornell University Press, 1989), 258–63, where the author argues that by "Allowing heroic Cleopatra to take control of her own representation, Shakespeare allies himself with her energies of difference rather than with political hegemony and the literary tradition that justified that hegemony" (263); and more recently, Evelyn Gajowski, "Antony and Cleopatra: Female Subjectivity and Orientalism" in *The Art of Loving* (Newark: University of Delaware Press, 1992), 86–119. Gajowski sees Cleopatra as partly "a manifestation of a prepatriarchal goddess" associated with snakes (119), although I would add that the later male association of such a goddess with the vice Luxury during the Middle Ages and early Renaissance must also be taken into consideration.

5. See J. Leeds Barroll, "Enobarbus' Description of Cleopatra," *Texas University Studies in English* 37 (1958): 61–78, and Clifford Davidson, "Antony and Cleopatra: Circe, Venus, and the Whore of Babylon," in *Shakespeare: Contemporary Critical Approaches,* ed. Harry R. Garvin (Lewisburg: Bucknell University Press, 1980), 31–55.

6. Plutarch as mythographer conflated the goddesses Venus and Isis in his famous study of Isis and Osiris.

7. See "Cleopatra," 687–99 and "Transcendent Love," 641–47, in *Antony and Cleopatra: A New Variorum Edition of Shakespeare,* ed. Marvin Spevack et al. (New York: The Modern Language Association of America, 1990).

8. (New York: Harper & Row, 1990). See also *Cleopatra,* ed. Harold Bloom (New York: Chelsea House, 1990); Ernle Bradford, *Cleopatra* (New York: Harcourt Brace Jovanovich, 1972); Hans Volkmann, *Cleopatra: A Study in Politics and Propaganda,* trans. T. J. Cadoux (London: Elek Books, 1958); and Ivor Brown, *Dark Ladies* (London: Collins, 1957).

9. See Adelman, *The Common Liar: An Essay on "Antony and Cleopatra"* (New Haven and London: Yale University Press, 1973), 11; cited hereafter in parentheses in text.

10. Plutarch claims that Antony was "to the most parte of men, cruell and extreame. For he robbed noble men and gentle men of their goods, to geve it unto vile flatterers." See Geoffrey Bullough, *Narrative and Dramatic Sources of Shakespeare,* 8 vols. (New York: Columbia University Press, 1964), 5:272.

11. All quotations from *Antony and Cleopatra* are taken from *The Riverside Shakespeare,* ed. G. Blakemore Evans et al. (Boston: Houghton Mifflin, 1974) and are cited hereafter in parentheses in text.

12. Barroll notes that Antony is the only Shakespearean tragic hero who inspires great love in others. See *Shakespearean Tragedy* (Washington, D.C.: The Folger Shakespeare Library, 1984), 272. On the ambiguities of Antony, see also the same author's "Shakespeare and the art of character: a study of Anthony," *Shakespeare Studies* 5 (1969): 159–235.

13. See Minoru Fujita, *Pageantry and Spectacle in Shakespeare* (Tokyo: The Renaissance Institute, Sophia University, 1982), 111–31.

14. See Barroll, "Pleasure," 712, and Frank Kermode, "The Banquet of Sense,"

in *Shakespeare, Spenser, Donne: Renaissance Essays* (London: Routledge & Kegan Paul, 1971), 98–99 n.20.

15. See Lloyd, "Antony and the Game of Chance," *Journal of English and German Philology* 61 (1962): 548–54.

16. See Hallett, "Change, Fortune, and Time: Aspects of the Sublunar World in *Antony and Cleopatra*," *Journal of English and German Philology* 75 (1976): 87. Hallett also observes that "Shakespeare has deliberately drawn for us a constantly shifting world, a world that contains no fixed star by which wandering barks can take their bearings. Impermanence, he stresses, is found on all levels—the natural, the social, the personal. It permeates existence. And for Antony and Cleopatra, there is nothing beyond" (78).

17. On the other hand, I have argued elsewhere that Andrea Alciati, father of the emblem book, was particularly interested in calling our attention to the inner meaning of texts and that his emblems are, therefore, not always easy to interpret. See my "Alciati's Two Venuses as Letter and Spirit of the Law" in *Andrea Alciato and the Emblem Tradition: Essays in Honor of Virginia Woods Callahan*, ed. Peter M. Daly (New York: AMS Press, 1989), 95–125.

18. See Williamson, "Fortune in *Antony and Cleopatra*," *Journal of English and German Philology* 67 (1968): 426–27; cited hereafter in parentheses in text. For other essays on Fortune in the play, see also Raymond Chapman, "The Wheel of Fortune in Shakespeare's Historical Plays," *Review of English Studies* n.s. 1 (1950): 2; Lily B. Campbell, "The Mirrours of Fortune," *Shakespeare's Tragic Heroes* (1930; rpt. New York: Barnes & Noble, 1965), 3–10; Matthew Proser, *The Heroic Image in Five Shakespearean Tragedies* (Princeton: Princeton University Press, 1965), 203–4; and Charles A. Hallett, "Change, Fortune, and Time: Aspects of the Sublunar World in *Antony and Cleopatra*," *Journal of English and German Philology* 75 (1976): 75–89.

19. See Peter M. Daly, "The Case for the 1593 Edition of Thomas Combe's *Theater of Fine Devices*," *Journal of the Warburg and Courtauld Institutes* 49 (1986): 255–57.

20. See Combe, *The Theater of Fine Devices* (London: Richard Field, 1593 and 1614), sig. B8.

21. Boethius, *Consolation of Philosophy*, trans. Richard Green (Indianapolis: Bobbs-Merrill Educational Publishing, 1962), bk. 2, prose 1.

22. See Frederick Kiefer, *Fortune and Elizabethan Tragedy* (San Marino: The Huntington Library, 1983), 206–9. I am much indebted to this fine study.

23. See William S. Hecksher, "The Anadyomene in the Medieval Tradition (Pelagia—Cleopatra—Aphrodite): A Prelude to Botticelli's 'Birth of Venus'," in *Art and Literature: Studies in Relationship*, ed. Egon Verheyen (Durham, N.C.: Duke University Press, 1985), 138–45.

24. See Davidson, *"Antony and Cleopatra,"* 35.

25. On the iconography of swallows, see Peter M. Daly, "Of Macbeth, Martlets and other 'Fowles of Heuen'," *Mosaic* 12 (Fall 1978): 23–46.

26. See Clifford Davidson, *"Timon of Athens:* The Iconography of False Friendship," *The Huntington Library Quarterly* 43 (Summer 1980): 195. Davidson quotes the Renaissance proverb "Swallows, like false friends, fly away upon the approach of winter" (Tilley S1026).

27. De Bry, *Emblemata Nobilitatis* (Frankfurt: Theodore deBry, 1592), 23.

28. See Hanna Fenichel Pitkin, *Fortune is a Woman: Gender and Politics in the Thought of Niccolo Machiavelli* (Berkeley: University of California Press, 1984), 156. In contrast to Machiavelli, whom he influenced, Marsilio Ficino follows Plato in arguing that Fortune may be controlled through the pilot's human

skill when his ship is caught in a *tempestas*, a word synonymous with *fortuna* during the Renaissance. See Edgar Wind, "Platonic Tyranny and the Renaissance Fortuna: On Ficino's Reading of *Laws* IV, 709A–712A," in *Essays in Honor of Erwin Panofsky*, 2 vol., ed. Millard Meiss (New York: New York University Press, 1961) 1:491. Wind adds that "Plato admits that 'fortuna cannot be forced. Any attempt to do so would be a sign of *hubris*, an insult to the inscrutable wisdom of the God who in the end adjusts our chances to our skill. Hence the truly skilful pilot never relinquishes his sense of the ominous. His patience in waiting for the right kind of storm is as important as his ability to ride it" (496).

29. See John F. Danby, *Poets on Fortune's Hill* (London: Faber & Faber, 1952), 143.

30. For a commentary on the etching, see H. Diane Russell, *Eva/Ave: Woman in Renaissance and Baroque Prints* (Washington, D.C.: National Gallery of Art, 1990), 220. I discovered many of my illustrations of Fortuna in this fine catalogue of a National Gallery exhibit.

31. See Jonathan Goldberg, *James I and the Politics of Literature* (Baltimore: The Johns Hopkins University Press, 1983), 43 and fig. 12. Donna Hamilton departs from orthodox new historicist readings of the later plays to make a convincing case that Shakespeare was criticizing the pretensions of King James, while pretending to flatter him, in her study *Virgil and "The Tempest": The Politics of Imitation* (Columbus: Ohio State University Press, 1990), ix–xii; as do I, using the iconographic approach, in *Myth, Emblem, and Music in Shakespeare's "Cymbeline": An Iconographic Reconstruction* (Newark: University of Delaware Press, 1992). See especially "Political Iconography and Irony," 21–25, and "The Iconography of Primitivism in *Cymbeline*," 136–67.

32. Bocchi, *Symbolarum . . . Libri Quinque* (Bologna, 1555), bk. 1, p. 21. English translation by Roger T. Simonds.

33. See Michael A. Jacobsen and Vivian Jean Rogers-Price, "The Dolphin in Renaissance Art," *Studies in Iconography* 9 (1983): 32–33, 37–39. See also Kiefer, *Fortune and Elizabethan Tragedy* (The Huntington Library, 1983), 204.

34. For an interesting discussion of the Venus and Mars theme, see Adelman, *The Common Liar* (New Haven: Yale, 1973), 78–101. However, Adelman does not notice Shakespeare's curious inversion of the theme.

35. Green, *Shakespeare and the Emblem Writers* (London: Trübner, 1870), 262.

36. See *All's Well That Ends Well*—"Why, your dolphin is not lustier" (2.3.26), a comment by Lafew. This is one *in malo* meaning of the dolphin; however, *in bono* the animal symbolizes salvation because of its association with Arion and haste or swiftness. In Rome, according to Ad de Vries, dolphins were connected with "the turning-points at each end of the low wall of the circus, around which the chariots had to turn in the races." These turning points were marked by "metae" or "a group of conical pillars with dolphins on them," where fortunes were told for ordinary women. See de Vries, *Dictionary of Symbols and Imagery* (Amsterdam and London: North-Holland, 1974), 142–43. The word may also refer to "dauphin" in Shakespeare's works, but that meaning is not possible in *Antony and Cleopatra*.

37. Barroll indicates that the same metaphor appears in George Wither's *Collection of Emblemes* (1635), where "we are informed that the square is law and that the bridle is discipline." See "Antony and Pleasure," 719.

38. Translation by Roger T. Simonds. See my essay "The Herculean Lover in the Emblems of Cranach and Vaenius," *Acta Conventus Neo-Latini Torontonensis*, ed. Alexander Dalzell et al. (Binghamton, N.Y.: Medieval & Renaissance Texts & Studies, 1991), 697–710.

39. See Peacham, *Minerva Britanna* (London: 1612), 95.

40. See especially John Coates, "'The Choice of Hercules' in *Antony and Cleopatra*," *Shakespeare Survey* 31 (1978): 45–52.

41. See Danby, *Poets*, 142.

42. Jean Jacques Boissard, *Emblematum Liber* (Frankfurt: 1593), 103.

43. Robert Record, *The Castle of Knowledge* (London: 1556), title page.

44. See Watson, *The Garden of Love in Tuscan Art of the Early Renaissance* (Philadelphia: The Art Alliance Press, 1979), 95. I am indebted to Elizabeth Bassett Welles for calling this book to my attention.

45. For a discussion of the sexual implications of birds in Dutch genre painting, see E. de Jongh, "Erotica in Vogelperspectief," *Simiolus* 3 (1968–69): 22–74.

46. See Emanuel Winternitz, *Musical Instruments and their Symbolism in Western Art* (London: Faber & Faber, 1967), 48–56.

47. See Davidson, "Antony and Cleopatra: Circe, Venus, and the Whore of Babylon," 34–35.

48. See Holloway, *The Story of the Night: Studies in Shakespeare's Major Tragedies* (London: Routledge & Kegan Paul, 1961), 143–44.

49. Bocchi, bk. 3, symbol 66. Translation by Virginia W. Callahan, to whom I am also indebted for the reference to Goya.

50. See Peter M. Daly, Virginia W. Callahan, and Simon Cuttler, ed., *Andreas Alciatus: Index Emblematicus*, 2 vols. (Toronto: University of Toronto Press, 1985), 1, emblem 44.

51. For a discussion of the difficulties in staging this scene, see the New Cambridge edition of *Antony and Cleopatra*, ed. David Bevington (Cambridge: Cambridge University Press, 1990), 43–44, and the *New Variorum Edition*, ed. Marvin Spevack, 785–87.

52. Daly et al., ed. 1, emblem 75.

53. Whitney, *A Choice of Emblemes* (Leiden: Christopher Plantin, 1586), 109. The Folger Shakespeare Library copy (STC 25437.8) has this emblem.

54. See Ethel Seaton, "*Antony and Cleopatra* and the *Book of Revelation*," *Review of English Studies* 22 (1946): 219–24.

55. See Morris, "Shakespeare and Dürer's Apocalypse," *Shakespeare Studies* 4 (1968): 258–61.

56. Peacham, *Minerva Britanna*, 161.

57. See "Isis," *The Oxford Classical Dictionary*, 2d ed (1970).

58. See Bowers, "'I Am Marble-Constant': Cleopatra's Monumental End," *Huntington Library Quarterly* 46 (1983): 284.

59. Ibid.

60. See Friedrich Solmsen, *Isis among the Greeks and Romans* (Cambridge, Mass.: Harvard University Press for Oberlin College, 1979), 94–95; hereafter cited in parentheses in text.

61. See Bocchi, cxxxvi–cxxxvii. English translation by Roger T. Simonds.

62. See Williamson, *Infinite Variety: Antony and Cleopatra in Renaissance Drama and Earlier Tradition* (Mystic, Conn.: Lawrence Verry, 1974), 210.

63. See Barton, "'Nature's piece 'gainst fancy': The Divided Catastrophe in *Antony and Cleopatra*." London: Bedford College, 1973), 20.

64. See Lanier 2, Women Writers' Project, Brown University (6–19–90), 170–71. I am indebted to Boyd Berry for this reference.

65. Although most critics believe Chaucer's story of Cleopatra to be ironic, see also V. A. Kolve, "From Cleopatra to Alceste: An Iconographic Study of *The Legend of Good Women*," in *Signs and Symbols in Chaucer's Poetry*, ed. John P. Hermann and John J. Burke, Jr. (University: University of Alabama Press, 1981), 130–78.

66. De Bry, *Emblemata Nobilitatis*, 147. Translated by Roger T. Simonds.

67. The first section of this paper was presented at the South Central Renaissance Conference, April 1991, in New Orleans, and a version of the completed essay was read and discussed by the Colloquium on Women in the Renaissance on 30 January 1992, at the National Museum of Women in the Arts, Washington, D.C. I am especially grateful to Leeds Barroll and Mihoko Suzuki for their interest in this essay and for their very useful suggestions.

Prospero's Empty Grasp

John S. Hunt

OVER THE COURSE of the last two or three decades, many readings
of *The Tempest* have cast the protagonist's magisterial authority in
a new, harsher light. Affirmations of his godlike attempt to make
his world over in a better image have increasingly given way to
indictments of the self-centered presumption involved in the attempt. Prospero's use of magical power to secure his place on the
island and regain his place in Milan seems less than self-evidently
valuable today. Indeed, it has come to threaten the very notion of
him as virtuous or heroic, on which enjoyment of the play would
seem to depend. "New historicists," reading the play as complicit
in the crime of colonial subjugation, have consummated this growing hermeneutic of suspicion by urging a complete undermining
of the rhetoric whereby Prospero appears the hero of the piece, the
locus for the audience's sympathetic identification and the focus
for its judgments, regarding him instead as a kind of mask for economic and political power, amoral, impersonal, and ruthless.

These critical responses yield dimensions of Prospero's character
that the older, providential conceptions did not. And the play becomes larger and more interesting when one recognizes how thoroughly it has been constructed out of power relations. But the
question of what exactly Shakespeare is doing with Prospero seems
harder than ever to answer these days. If admiring critics, persuaded by the resemblance between Prospero's highly theatrical
enterprise and Shakespeare's own, often insufficiently distinguished the intentions of the character from those of the playwright, many of those who have sought to tear Prospero from his
pedestal have made the obverse mistake of assuming that if the
protagonist's intentions are somehow corrupt then the play is also.[1]
Both approaches are intuitively insufficient to Shakespeare's dramatic medium and the perfect pitch of ambiguity to which he else-

where brought it. If one agrees that the language that Caliban learned from Prospero has benefitted him only by enabling him to curse, it is precisely because, in cursing, Caliban's voice wins one to some conviction of the injustice of Prospero's taking the island from him. Indeed, in usurping Caliban, Prospero makes problematic any moral authority that he derives from himself being the victim of usurpation.

Much of Shakespeare's ambiguity recalls similar ambiguity in Montaigne's essay "Of Cannibals." The figure of Caliban, whose name appears to have been conceived by anagrammatically transposing "cannibal," resembles the natives of the essay in being conceived as a mixture of attractive and abhorrent traits. In considering the non-European, non-Christian Other, Montaigne not only focuses on some bloodthirsty traits, including their practice of eating human beings, historically the most potent weapon in the European's arsenal of devices to demonize those whom they wished to subdue (though Montaigne stops far short of demonization himself). He also flirts, much more recklessly, with the flip side of demonization—nostalgic identification with the Other as an earlier version of the civilized self—so that the Brazilian natives float for a while in his mind as living remnants of humanity's primal, beatific closeness to natural instinct. Finally, neither kind of simplistic evasion of difference describes Montaigne's attitude. With much the eye of a twentieth-century ethnographer he describes in detail the Brazilians' various cultural practices and compares them with European ones; though cannibalism seems offensive to "reason," its horror becomes tame when set beside the European fondness for tearing apart bodies while they are still alive.

Like the simple but elegant culture depicted in the Frenchman's essay, Shakespeare's more brutish, solitary native seems to be an attempt to imagine what human life would have been like prior to the ambiguous march of human civilization. If Caliban is cunning, animalistically impulsive, murderous, ignorant of all cultural refinements and sexual mores, vulnerable to alcohol, and strong-smelling, he also is courageous, alert to beauty, freedom-loving, hospitably generous, unselfconscious, and immune to the blandishments of consumerist materialism. By dramatizing, in his fawning adoration of Stephano, Caliban's manifest personal insufficiency, his need for direction from more complete human beings, the play makes his rebellion against his Italian overlord seem a misguided attempt to circumvent spiritual evolution. But along the way it invites considerable sympathy by evoking his intuitive closeness to the natural resources of the island, and a natural psychological resourcefulness that leads him to resist tyrrany, embrace offered friendship, and throw himself with wholehearted energy into whatever seems to hold the best chances of happiness. This whole plot strand may have been conceived as a response to one of the most arresting social criticisms in the essay "Of Cannibals": Montaigne's anecdote about three Brazilian Indians who travelled to France, saw the economic inequities of the French social classes, and asked their guide with amazement why the poor there did not grab the rich by the throats or burn down their houses. Montaigne does not make out of this incident a call for the downfall of aristocrats or Europeans, and Shakespeare does not stir sentiment for the downfall of Prospero. Both writers accept the inevitability of the dominant power arrangements, while creating a space in which to hear the voices that they suppress, the truths that they exclude.

Shakespeare's most famous borrowing from Montaigne's essay displays the same critical ambiguity. The passage in which Gonzalo envisions a perfect "commonwealth" on the island in terms of the freedom from state power, and the paradisal bounty of nature, enjoyed by human beings in the Golden Age outdoes Montaigne's rhapsody in softheaded idealism (Montaigne dismisses the golden age as an invention of human art, insufficient to the real marvels of nature). And the slightly dotty old man is mocked by the sharp young blades Antonio and Sebastian, who recognize instantly the impossibility of instituting a government without the instruments of coercion that make government what it is. But in between these extremes lies a balance something like the balance beween Montaigne's enthusiasm for primitive humanity and his ethnographic relativism. The duo's annihilating mockery does not obscure the sincere good feeling that motivates Gonzalo as he tries to console the disconsolate Alonso, or their own thoroughly unlikeable malice (here they lack all feeling not only for Gonzalo but for Alonso). Besides good feeling there is a kind of wisdom to Gonzalo's utopian dream, for in painting a providential picture of the island's "abundance" it urges Antonio to accept what he cannot change and savor the good in his "preservation." Furthermore, the vision, despite its naive impossibility, establishes an imaginative counterweight to the harsh politics that prevail in Italy and on the island as well. When one sees Antonio and his brother Prospero in the full swing of action, Gonzalo's vision of commonality without coercion appears more desirable than risible. Antonio's Machiavellian calculation and Prospero's grim little police state both manifestly lack the element of free reciprocity that Gonzalo extols.

In his more brutally assertive way Prospero, too, is a utopian

dreamer, hankering after earthly paradise, and the play lends itself
to even more strongly ambiguous interpretations of his exercise of
power: like Gonzalo's advice to Alonso, it can either be affirmed as
a providential redemption of human limitations or derided as the
vain indulgence of an ego detached from human reality. This essay
will explore both halves of the paradox (which finally, I think,
merge into a single understanding) from the vantage of still another
detail in Montaigne's essay: two sentences that read, "I am afraid
we have eyes bigger than our stomachs, and more curiosity than
capacity. We embrace everything, but we clasp only wind."[2] This
briefly stated image of a human body frustrated with its impotence
will be relatively unfamiliar to most students of Shakespeare's play,
and perhaps was no more than passingly familiar to Shakespeare
himself. But whether or not he consciously used it as a source for
the artistic structures of his final masterpiece, it helps to identify
those structures and to define how the play presents the power
relations that make up so much of its content. Montaigne's image
embodies, and subverts, the Renaissance idealistic notion that human knowledge resembles God's in its capacity to comprehend the
universe and to turn that knowledge into transforming power. In
Shakespeare's hands the image describes how Prospero impresses
upon other characters their inability to master their environment.
But Prospero's magic is itself one of the most notable expressions
of the Renaissance ethos of intellectual mastery, and the lesson
finally applies more forcefully to the teacher than to any of those
whom he presumes to teach. In breaking the grip of others Prospero
discovers how empty his own actually is, opening up new possibilities of mutual dependency, new opportunities for fruitful embrace.
Seen in this light Prospero is the hero of the piece, but a hero
something like the pilgrim in the *Divine Comedy*, who discovers
principles for the happy conduct of human life only in the course
of confronting massive error in his own. Prospero's error is fundamental: he denies life itself, by believing that intellectual control
of experience can substitute for experience. His magical studies,
which are instrumental in securing his material prosperity, finally
stand revealed as the greatest obstacle to his spiritual well-being.

I

In Prospero's words about Caliban, Shakespeare anticipated remarkably well the future language of English-speaking colonialism.
The history of American natives likewise lives in Caliban's experi-

ences: a native living harmoniously with the land extends hospital-
ity to a European traveller; he subsequently becomes the object of
the visitor's missionary zeal to plant European culture on new soil;
failing to conform to the European's cultural codes, he is
demonized as a dirty, ineducable, treacherous, and ungrateful burden on the white man's magnanimity and deprived of his lands
and his freedom; and over time the relation hardens into one of
unremitting, brutal exploitation and punishment. From Shakespeare's limited means—the reports of the wreck of the *Sea-
Venture* off the coast of Bermuda, sixteenth-century English travel
reports, anecdotal information on the Spanish conquests, and the
occasional glimpses that he gained from Montaigne and other con-
tinental writers—he gleaned some essential features of the European encounters with distant cultures.

Still, *The Tempest* hardly makes sense simply as a representation
of colonialism. More elements of the plot do not fit the model
than do. And many details discourage attempts to read the play
colonially: the island exists in the Mediterranean, not the new
world; Prospero and Miranda, and later Alonso and his company
(also, for that matter, Sycorax in her immigration from North Af-
rica) arrive as hapless victims of disaster, not as explorers; Caliban
is not a cannibal, does not possess any of the physical qualities
attributed to the American natives, and is native to the island only
in the strict sense that Sycorax was still pregnant when she arrived;
and the paltry menage of slaves that Prospero maintains only for
the material prosperity of himself and his daughter, and only until
he can manage to return to Italy, falls considerably short of the
Spanish program of pillaging entire civilizations and converting
them into raw material for economic profit. Indeed, it would be
astonishing if *The Tempest* were a consistent representation of colonialism: England lagged far behind Spain in its miserable attempts to colonize Virginia; its attitudes toward the original
inhabitants were still very diverse and uncertain; colonial ideology
lagged so far behind colonial practive even in the greater European
sea powers that no other writer of fiction in Europe had yet produced such a work; the interests of capitalist men of the theater
were hardly identical with those of capitalist colony-builders; and
in no other play did Shakespeare content himself only with representation of topical material.[3]

What *The Tempest* does consistently represent is a world
founded on the idea of mastery—a world where Prospero achieves
(within the confines of the island) supreme mastery, making slaves
even of those who are accustomed to rule. In the 1950s Bernard

Knox argued persuasively that the play owes much to ancient Roman comedy, where "bad" or stupid slaves like Caliban (and also
Stephano, Trinculo, and perhaps Antonio) rebel against their masters, only to be made subject again by the end of the play, and
where "good" or clever slaves like Ariel (and perhaps Ferdinand
and even Miranda?) aid their beseiged masters and are ultimately
rewarded with freedom.[4] Read in this way, Shakespeare's work af-
firms the rigid hierarchical divisions of Elizabethan society much
as Roman comedies had affirmed the still more rigid distinction
between slave and free in ancient society; as in many of his plays,
the patriarchal order is disrupted by usurpation and/or rebellion
only to be righted in a somewhat changed form at the conclusion.
But, as Knox pointed out in the conclusion of his essay, this model
explains what Shakespeare is doing only within clearly "recognizable limits"; in the same speech in which Gonzalo marvels at how
the social order has been restored out of apparent chaos, with Prospero finding "his dukedom / In a poor isle," he adds, "and all of
us, our selves, / When no man was his own."[5] The ancient comic
paradigm cannot account for this Christian language of dying to
the worldly self to be reborn in the spirit—with its urging not
of a particular social order but of universal conditions of human
consciousness. Nor does it make much sense of the utopian logic,
the longing for a more perfect society, that has frequently been
noticed as a thread running throughout the play. Both of these
related forms of idealism make more sense in the context of Renaissance optimism about human possibility—as do the plot elements
which suggest colonial subjection of the cultural Other. Colonialism arose organically, one might even say inevitably, from the equation of knowledge with power that marks Renaissance thought from
its beginning. And looked at in this way, Shakespeare's play does
not offer just one strikingly prophetic response to contemporary
historical practice: it addresses his age's most basic creeds about
the relation of knowing subject to known object.

When Renaissance writers proclaim the "dignity of man," or wax
lyrical on his being created "in the image of God," they mean something different from the medieval belief that the desires of human
beings seek fulfillment beyond the earth, in union with a heavenly
Maker. The increasingly secular aims of the Renaissance coincided
briefly with the firm religious belief of the preceding epoch, before
giving way to seventeenth-century fideism, eighteenth-century de-
ism, and the nineteenth-century discovery that God is dead. Prior
to its dissolution, this fusion of religious and secular consciousness

produced the doctrine that human beings can become *like* God while on earth through their capacity to refashion the materials of experience in forms more perfectly answering to human desire. The soul's relation to God becomes secondary—not in any absolute sense, perhaps, but certainly in terms of what people of the age write about—to the self's relation to its physical and social environment. In literature, in the fine arts, in ethics, in political philosophy, in natural science, attention shifts from how human action, discourse, and production are involved in a static universe organized by divine intentionality, to a sense of the universe as dynamically responsive to the questions that people ask of it. From the discovery that experience is larger than any conception of it, and the equal but opposite realization that consciousness itself organizes that experience, come the Cartesian dualism of subject and object that directs the course of much modern philosophy; ambitious political conceptions stretching from Machiavelli and More down through the Enlightenment thinkers to Marx; experimental innovations that detached natural science from Church Aristotelianism and directed it toward practical results; theories of the artist as genius that got a second lease on life in the Romantic movement; the systematic organization of economic enterprise that has given us banks, corporations, industrial mass production, and efficient harvesting of natural resources—and the voyages of discovery, the colonial conquests, the competitive differentiation of societies denoted by the terms "developed" and "underdeveloped." The Renaissance glorification of the consequences of knowledge can be summed up in the word *mastery*, with its ambiguous sense of intellectual comprehension and economic and political domination. In regarding the human intellect as that which, as much as God or intelligible essences, organizes our universe, Renaissance "man" gave himself the authority to make the universe over in his own image.[6]

Today the bloom is certainly off the rose. The evolution in the connotations of the phrase "the dignity of man" indicates how far our emotional responses to the ideology of intellectual mastery have swung. Instead of indicating the prerogatives of the ruling classes the phrase speaks to us of the claims of the dispossessed; it evokes Caliban's natural indignation at being enslaved and tortured more than Prospero's natural right to enslave and torture him. And yet we are still recording the history of post-Renaissance thought. While colonialism, capitalism, romanticism, socialism, fascism, industrialism, consumerism, scientism all have suffered colossal embarrassments, each of these expressions of the ambitious European mind admits transformation and goes on. Colonialism shifts from Europe to Asia, shifts as well from military subjugation to more sophisticated, primarily economic controls. Fiascos in scientific ambition—the invention of appalling instruments of destruction, ecologically catastrophic engineering projects, industrial pollution—do not produce a moderation of the ambition, but only a determination to perfect it by ameliorating its past mistakes. Abominable failures in the envisioning of political systems, grotesque abuses in the course of developing more efficient wealth-producing economic enterprises shake our faith in can-do thinking, but do not derail it. We live still with that intoxicating myth of intellectual mastery of the unvierse that drove the explorers across the ocean and onto the American continent.

Montaigne is rare for his age in questioning this myth directly and comprehensively. In a famous passage from the "Apology for Raymond Sebond," he asks of man the dignified,

> Who has persuaded him that that admirable motion of the celestial vault, the eternal light of those torches rolling so proudly above his head, the fearful movements of that infinite sea, were established and have lasted so many centuries for his convenience and his service? Is it possible to imagine anything so ridiculous as that this miserable and puny creature, who is not even master of himself, exposed to the attacks of all things, should call himself master and emperor of the universe, the least part of which it is not in his power to know, much less to command?
>
> Presumption is our natural and original malady. The most vulnerable and frail of all creatures is man, and at the same time the most arrogant. . . . he equals himself to God, attributes to himself divine characteristics, picks himself out and separates himself from the horde of other creatures, carves out their shares to his fellows and companions the animals, and distributes among them such portions of faculties and powers as he sees fit. How does he know, by the force of his intelligence, the secret internal stirrings of animals? By what comparison between them and us does he infer the stupidity that he attributes to them?
> When I play with my cat, who knows if I am not a pastime to her more than she is to me? (328–29, 330–31)

While Montaigne has always struck twentieth-century readers as remarkably modern in his experiential skepticism, his habit of affirming only what passes through his protean consciousness, he is also historically conservative in designating intellectual pride as the chief source of man's delusion and unhappiness, and locating well-being in a kind of submission to necessity. The submission is not so much, as in Augustine, to God, but to the conditions of corporeality and mortality in which the creator saw fit to place his creature. "Man must be constrained and forced into line inside the barriers of his order. The poor wretch is in no position really to step outside them; he is fettered and bound, he is subjected to the same obligation as the other creatures of his class, and in a very ordinary condition, without any real and essential prerogative or preeminence. That which he accords himself in his mind and in his fancy has neither body nor taste" (336).

The essay "Of Cannibals" develops this idea of surrender to creaturely experience in terms of the contrast between advanced and primitive civilizations. To Montaigne, the natives that his French source has encountered in South America represent life lived more or less in a state of nature, prior to most of the corrupting effects of human ingenuity. "They are still in that happy state of desiring only as much as their natural needs demand; anything beyond that is superfluous to them"; they possess "the knowledge of how to enjoy their condition happily and be content with it" (156). Europeans, on the contrary, represent the presumptuous tendency of human beings to imagine themselves superior to other creatures. The essay begins with several anecdotes about how ancient Greeks (the original Europeans) encountered armies from Rome expecting to find barbaric ineptitude, only to discover sophisticated military organization. In the sentences that follow, it turns to the modern European encounter with an unexpected new world, and observes that its pretensions to understand the world have been similarly humbled:

> This discovery of a boundless country seems worthy of consideration. I don't know if I can guarantee that some other such discovery will not be made in the future, so many personages greater than ourselves having been mistaken about this one. I am afraid we have eyes bigger than our stomachs, and more curiosity than capacity. We embrace everything, but we clasp only wind. (150)

Just as Europeans have been geographically wrong about what they would find on the other side of the Atlantic, the essay goes on to argue that they are culturally wrong to assume the barbarity of the peoples encountered there. And the references to military conquest just before this passage seem to indicate some awareness of the anticolonialist implications of that position. All of these intentions

come together in Montaigne's picture of the human being as a creature deluded in its ambition to devour experience. His corporeal
image of eyes and hands straining to apprehend what stomachs
cannot comprehend addresses the vacancy in the Renaissance ideology of intellectual mastery. The body's inability to conquer its
environment represents synechdochally or metonymically the
mind's inability to master its experience.

Although Montaigne himself does not explicitly do so, it seems
impossible not to connect this image from the beginning of the
essay with the essay's principal subject, cannibalism. In supposing
themselves endowed with some godlike authority over their environment, human beings view everything outside themselves as matter to be devoured, energies to be tamed. The American natives are
not exempt from this misjudgment, despite their beautiful habit of
"speaking of men as halves of one another" (159). Montaigne takes
pains to point out that their cannibalism is not performed for the
sake of nourishment, but to increase their revenge on their conquered enemies. By not only ingesting their adversaries but pro-
longing the date of execution, treating them well, tempting them
to escape, taunting them with their coming indignity, they seek to
break their spirits. But their enemies do not succumb. Montaigne
recounts a song composed by a prisoner that urges his captors to
come eat him,

> for they will be eating at the same time their own fathers and grand-
> fathers, who have served to feed and nourish his body. 'These muscles,'
> he says, 'this flesh and these veins are your own, poor fools that you
> are. You do not recognize that the substance of your ancestors' limbs is
> still contained in them. Savor them well; you will find in them the taste
> of your own flesh.' An idea that certainly does not smack of barbarity.
> (158).

Cannibalism thus stands as a vivid emblem both of the desire to
subject others to one's will and of the unpleasant realization that
one can never cease being subject *to* others. The body's perma-
nently ambiguous relationship to its environment—as eater and as
eaten—indicates the vanity inherent in presuming to regard other
beings (and, for that matter, the body itself) as things to be conquered and assimilated.

Cannibalism per se echoes only incidentally and faintly in *The
Tempest*: in the image of Prospero's brother as a parasitic vine that
covered his body and sucked out his lifeblood, or in the apparition
of Trinculo's legs and voice projecting from Caliban's robe, which

prompts Stephano to wonder how his friend came to be the excrement of this strange creature ("How cam'st thou to be the siege of this moon-calf? Can he vent Trinculos?").[7] But the play embodies as well as any work of Renaissance literature the yearning to master experience that is expressed in Montaigne's image of human beings as voracious gazers, graspers, and eaters.

The many responses to the island and its inhabitants yield a cross-section of the varieties of this human hunger. At the most benign, there is the lyrical yearning expressed by the native inhabitants. Ariel's memorable visions of walking on the salt wave and living under the blossom that hangs on the bough are matched with Caliban's eloquent appreciation of the island's mysterious sounds, which usher in dreams where "The clouds methought would open and show riches / Ready to drop upon me" (3.3.146–47). The yearning becomes less fine, and less benign, when Stephano joins the revery:

> *Steph.* This will prove a brave kingdom to me, where I shall have my music for nothing.
> *Cal.* When Prospero is destroyed.
>
> (ll. 149–50)

Stephano's response to the music is no more instantaneously acquisitive than Trinculo's initial response to Caliban; he thinks, "A strange fish! Were I in England now, as once I was, and had but this fish painted, not a holiday fool there but would give a piece of silver. . . . When they will not give a doit to relieve a lame beggar, they will lay out ten to see a dead Indian" (2.2.28–34). Of all the Italians, Gonzalo is least contemptible in his responses to this strange new land. After seeing some of Prospero's spirits, whom he supposes human beings, he says, "though they are of monstrous shape, yet note, / Their manners are more gentle, kind, than of / Our human generation you shall find / Many—nay, almost any" (3.2.31–34). And, earlier, the strange properties of the island make him think of it as a place where mankind might make a new start. But his pacific vision is somewhat compromised by his prefacing his remarks with the words, "Had I plantation of this isle, my lord . . . And were the king on't, what would I do?" (2.1.147). Antonio and Sebastian, of course, are much worse. A catastrophic shipwreck does not distract Antonio from the Machiavellian calculation at which he labors singlemindedly and efficiently; quickly realizing that if Ferdinand is dead and Claribel is in Tunis then only the beating of Alonso's heart keeps Sebastian from the possession of the throne, he sets about convincing him to murder his brother—an outcome that will mean Antonio's no longer having to pay tribute to Naples, cancelling the arrangement that he made with Alonso when he sought help in seizing his brother's dukedom.

The play does not suggest that the hunger to master experience expressed in the characters' responses to the island is necessarily wicked or vain. When Ferdinand is cast into the ocean by the shipwreck, his bodysurfing to shore appears, in Francisco's description, an act of heroically beautiful integration with the alien environment:

> I saw him beat the surges under him
> And ride upon their backs. He trod the water,
> Whose enmity he flung aside, and breasted
> The surge most swol'n that met him. His bold head
> 'Bove the contentious waves he kept, and oared
> Himself with his good arms in lusty stroke
> To th' shore, that o'er his wave-worn basis bowed,
> As stooping to relieve him.
>
> (2.1.119–26)

The passage recalls a similar description of a man surviving shipwreck at the beginning of Sidney's *New Arcadia*, much as the praise of a horseman's Centaur-like fusion with his animal in *Hamlet* recalls another such passage in the *Arcadia*.[8] In all four accounts the intelligence and resourcefulness of man, his capacity to suit his mind to the nonhuman Other, make him an object of wonder, a protean delver into the secret nature of things. But the devouring quality in humanity's orientation to its environment poisons the vision of perfection at its root. Shakespeare seems concerned to bring out this distinction between generous and acquisitive wonder, participatory and assimilative union, in Miranda's ecstatic response to the Europeans ("O wonder! / How many goodly creatures are there here! / How beauteous mankind is! O brave new world / That has such people in't!") and Prospero's sardonic correction: "'Tis new to thee" (5.1.181–84). In dealing with people who decouple aesthetic delight from moral responsibility, viewing wondrous things as a source of profit, she must take care not to give herself away.[9]

Montaigne's image of empty grasps and empty stomachs appears most dramatically in the moment when Prospero's magic most clearly manifests the moral purpose of checking this acquisitive impulse. Alonso, Antonio, and Sebastian, "three men of sin" (3.3.53) who have conspired to wrest political authority by force from its rightful possessors, have wandered the island for some time when they encounter a banquet laid out for them by spirits; they spend a long time gazing at the food without attempting to eat it, as they weigh their great hunger against the risk of being poisoned. When they decide to accept the risk and reach for the food, it disappears into thin air, and Ariel appears in the terrifying form of a harpy to reproach them for their wickedness. The men respond by drawing their swords, which Ariel dismisses as an attempt to grasp the air: "You fools! I and my fellows / Are ministers of Fate. The elements, / Of whom your swords are tempered, may as well / Wound the loud winds, or with bemocked-at stabs / Kill the still-closing waters" (ll. 60–64). Only repentance, he says, will remedy the fault that has cost Alonso his son already and will in time produce worse misfortunes. Montaigne's two images of gazing without eating and reaching without grasping are used in this scene to convey the hollow presumption in these men aspiring to political authority that does not belong to them. The image-logic of a body frustrated in its effort to control its environment is completed as Prospero's charms induce a kind of desperate trance in the men, who are "all knit up / In their distractions. They are now in my pow'r; / And in these fits I leave them." (ll. 89–91).

The play begins with a similar visual impression of grasping frustrated by the intractability of air. Like the banquet scene, the spectacular storm scene is produced by Ariel, who later proudly recounts to Prospero all the details of his artistry. But the dialogue and stage directions give no indication of Ariel's presence. The scene has been constructed to show two things: the mariners' powerlessness to control their ship, and the nobles' powerlessness to control the mariners. The audience sees sailors desperately manipulating ropes, and aristocrats desperately giving the boatswain ignored orders.

> What cares these roarers for the name of king? To cabin! Silence! . . . You are a councilor; if you can command these elements to silence and work the peace of the present, we will not hand a rope more. Use your authority.
>
> (1.1.16–17, 21–24)

Of the two groups, the aristocrats are more deluded in thinking that they have some "authority" to exercise in such circumstances. Gonzalo, with his wry insistence that they will not drown because

the boatswain was born to be hanged, and Alonso, by his silent
compliance with the boatswains's commands, display some dim
awareness of the futility of their position; Antonio and Sebastian,
who descend into brawling bawls, show none. Shakespeare's art
here does not, as in the banquet scene, address merely political
authority that has been usurped. It emphasizes the limitations of
political authority itself. After his party survived the wreck of the
Sea-Venture and found Bermuda to be a hospitable environment,
the new governor of Virginia encountered concerted opposition to
his plan of pushing on to Jamestown; the Italian rulers in this scene
are even more powerfully balked by an environment where their
power to control is simply inappropriate.[10] The tempest reduces
the king to asking, twice, "Where is the master?" (ll. 9–10, 12). The
master in this chaotic microcosm is not the captain of the ship, of
whom he inquires, but Prospero, Ariel's "master" (1.2.189).[11]

The literally and figuratively frustrated grasps that one sees respectively in the mariners and their superiors resembles the frustrated efforts of the king's party to grasp first the food and then
their swords; and this action repeats itself throughout the play.
Caliban has crudely attempted to pull Miranda into a sexual embrace and Prospero punishes him for it; Ferdinand reaches for his
sword when Prospero threatens to enslave him, and is charmed
into paralysis; Antonio and Sebastian raise their swords to kill the
king and find him mysteriously awake before they can use them;
Stephano, Trinculo, and Caliban go to kill Prospero and in their
alcoholic state are led through briers and into a stagnant pond,
mired "up to th' chins" in filth; trying again, Stephano and Trinculo
reach for Prospero's rich garments hanging on a clothesline, and
again bring down disaster on themselves. If one pushes the paradigm to a more metaphorical remove, it describes still more events
of the play. Miranda requests more information than her father is
ready to give her and is in a moment laid asleep by his magic;
Ferdinand pursues haunting music about the island and can never
locate its source; Caliban answers the same haunting call in his
dreams and "weeps to dream again"; Ariel and Caliban reach for
their freedom and are disappointed; Gonzalo dreams of possessing
the island and is mocked; Ferdinand yearns for his bride and is
sternly warned not to "break her virgin-knot" before the marriage
is accomplished (4.1.15).

The actions performed on stage are buttressed in the play's language, which is filled with images of confined or paralyzed bodies,
and of consciousness held tightly within the body. The mariners,

"dead of sleep" (5.1.230), are "clapped under hatches" (5.1.231), "stowed" within their ship (1.2.230) which is itself stowed in a "deep nook" (1.2.227). Ferdinand is first described by Ariel "In an odd angle of the isle, and sitting, / His arms in this sad knot" (1.2.223–24). Alonso, wishing that "mine eyes / Would, with themselves, shut up my thoughts," thinks that his son "i' th'ooze is bedded," and wishes to "lie mudded" with him there (3.3.100–102); he and his companions are "all knit up in their distractions" (3.3.89–90); he thinks at the end that "This is as strange a maze as e'er men trod" (5.1.242). Trinculo complains to Caliban of olfactory imprisonment: "Monster, I do smell all horse piss, at which my nose is in great indignation" (4.1.199–200). Prospero rescues Ariel from being imprisoned between the two halves of a "cloven pine" and threatens to "rend an oak / And peg thee in his knotty entrails" (1.2.294–95). He threatens Caliban, whom he keeps "stied" within a "hard rock" with "Side-stitches that shall pen thy breath up" (1.2.326).

All of these visual and readerly images reinforce the main action of the play's plot: Prospero's systematic and effective suppression of the other characters' capacity for action. They also elaborate across the canvas of a five-act play the idea that Montaigne sketches in two sentences: the uncomprehending futility in human beings' impulse to reach out omnivorously into their environment. The characters of *The Tempest* are exceptionally strong-willed, but Prospero's balking of their wills typically shows them that they are fundamentally ignorant about their world. Caliban bases his rebellion on his understanding that Stephano is a god and his liquor "celestial"—two costly errors. Ferdinand thinks he knows his father to be dead (like Alonso his son) and his prospective father-in-law to be hostile; his understanding is deficient on both counts. Antonio convinces Sebastian to kill his brother with the argument that they are far from anyone who can see and balk their efforts—also a mistake. And everyone from Italy supposes (the biggest mistake of all) that Prospero has been safely disposed of twelve years earlier. The states of confinement and paralysis that the vengeful duke inflicts on them seem calculated to drive home their impotence, their smallness in the face of a microcosm infused with godlike omniscience and omnipotence.

The religious overtones in *The Tempest* extend to redemption as well as justice, revelation as well as humbling chastisement. In addition to sketching a picture of people's incapacity to comprehend and control their environment, the play's images of confinement convey a positive, less ego-bound definition of the self's relation to that environment. Shakespeare uses Christian language and symbolism to develop this notion. Gonzalo's words about everyone having found himself "When no man was his own" recall New Testament language about the surrendering of one's life to God. And the metaphor of bodily death and rebirth that accompanies this notion in the Gospels acquires an ineffably beautiful expression in Ariel's song of consolation to Ferdinand. The images of paralyzed bodies that permeate the fabric of the play produce here the symbolic fantasy of a drowned corpse inhabited and reanimated by creatures of another realm. King Alonso loses none of his majesty for being mastered in this way:

> Full fathom five thy father lies;
>   Of his bones are coral made;
> Those are pearls that were his eyes;
>   Nothing of him that doth fade
> But doth suffer a sea change
> Into something rich and strange.
> Sea nymphs hourly ring his knell . . .
>
> (1.2.397–402)

Thinking Ferdinand dead, Alonso in fact longs to be dead with his son on the sea floor, and the ruination of his proud complacency lends itself to Prospero's project of humiliating him into repentance. The song offers an imagistic equivalent of this psychology, and describes it as an avenue onto beauty. The dead king's bodily incorporation with the oceanic element symbolizes a perfect intercourse between self and cosmos, a passage into mystical participation.

But while the play draws on Christian concepts and metaphors to convey the sense of participation in something larger than the self, it does not direct this longing to belong toward a transcendent object. As in all of Shakespeare's plays, it is human community which completes the self (or promises to complete it, or fails to). Sexual unions, the familial relations that result from sexual unions, nonfamilial brotherhoods and sisterhoods, and hierarchic organizations of individuals into bodies politic, define the transcendence of narrowly egoistic selfhood for Shakespeare. In *The Winter's Tale*, his previous work, the sundering of sexes, families, friends, and nations was healed by the marriage of two young heirs—Florizel and especially Perdita representing new blood, a new spring in the cycle of generational seasons, a new chance for the primal unity that motivates human longing. *The Tempest* reenacts this symbology, offering the love of Miranda and Ferdinand as its model for the achieved union of self and other. Their initial encounter presents the love at first sight as a kind of beatific vision, interweaving it with Ariel's singing of "Full fathom five" ("no mortal business," in Ferdinand's estimation) and Prospero's promises to soon grant the fairy's ecstatically longed-for liberty (1.2. 406–8, 420–22). Miranda calls Ferdinand "A spirit," "A thing divine," "nothing natural"; he calls her a "goddess" and in his first address, "O you wonder!," hits the Latin sense of her name (ll. 410, 418, 422, 427). What justifies such language from an audience's point of view is not the attractiveness of the two teenagers but the mutual erotic submission that promises to join them. Prospero, looking on and speaking in asides to the larger audience of watchers, observes that "At the first sight / They have changed eyes" (ll. 441–42); "they are both in either's pow'rs" (l. 451). When Ferdinand is paralyzed and enslaved by Prospero, he greets his paralysis by thinking that he can bear any loss, "Might I but through my prison once a day / Behold this maid. All corners else o' th'earth / Let liberty make use of. Space enough / Have I in such a prison" (ll. 487–94). Later, he totes logs meditating that "most poor matters / Point to rich ends. This my mean task / Would be as heavy to me as odious, but / The mistress which I serve quickens what's dead . . ." (3.1.3–6). The submission that he bears to Miranda, and she to him, in this scene prompts Prospero to exclaim, "Fair encounter / Of two most rare affections! Heavens rain grace / On that which breeds between 'em!" (ll. 74–76). The substantiating telos of Prospero's logic of disempowerment is this: that in the quasi-physical incorporation of one life into another, human beings locate their only true freedom, the freedom to transcend, in some measure, their ego-bound separateness. By a tragicomic paradox, powerlessness to control may convey equal power to enjoy, and acceptance of experiential limitations may free one to realize a fuller kind of selfhood.

II

This has been, so far, largely a descriptive account of a vein of imagery that informs *The Tempest*'s spectacle, thought, and action. The interesting critical questions concern Prospero's place in its logic of disempowerment. As the unmoved mover of all the other characters, to what degree do his intentions coincide with the play's? Prospero thinks of himself as a kind of god, and he seeks not only control but righteous and redemptive control, based on the willing submission of those whom he subjugates. To varying degrees he receives this submission: from Antonio and Sebastian and the minor characters least of all, somewhat more from Ariel and Caliban and Alonso, and from Ferdinand and Gonzalo in full measure. But to what extent does the play validate his claim of superhuman authority? If the audience, too, is meant to bow to Prospero's charms, then Shakespeare's art itself can be accused of casting spells: for the man possessed of extraordinary power his art is self-justifying, superseding all moral and political questions, while for the sheep in his charge happy submission stifles discontent, as religion drugs the masses in Marx, or as the missionary salvation promised through the centuries to American natives presumed to compensate for the destruction of their cultures, the plunder of their wealth, and the loss of their liberty.

The second half of this essay will argue that *The Tempest* forces Prospero to the recognition of an empty grasp more effectively than he does any of the other characters. It supports his socially ordained political authority, but rebukes his ambition to reach beyond ordinary human limitations into a kind of divine self-sufficiency. The seeming fullness of power achieved in his magical art is, finally, a handful of air.

The hollowness appears most obviously in a frustrating disparity between his hopes for magical transformations and mundane imperfections in the human material that he tries to transform. The fearsome madness that Prospero inflicts on Alonso, Antonio, and Sebastian may feed his appetite for vengeful retribution, but it satisfies less well his desire to remake them spiritually. His greatest success, the king's contrition in act 5, proceeds from the repentance which Ariel's display of godlike wrath has called forth. But this magical feat is more a *coup de theatre* than a divine revelation. Alonso's first words after the harpy leaves suggest that he is not so much being epiphanically illuminated as publicly confronted with something foul that he already knows about himself, as Claudius is by Hamlet's play, or as one might be in church: "the thunder, / That deep and dreadful organ pipe, pronounced / the name of Prosper; it did bass my trespass" (3.3.97–99). Antonio and Sebastian do not even display any repentance, here or in act 5. Caliban submits but remains more or less the same. Like Alonso, he speaks in religious terms ("I'll . . . seek for grace"), but he displays no moral or psychological sea-change; nor is it clear exactly how he should.

Only Ferdinand and Gonzalo, who hardly occupy Prospero's category of "men of sin," wax rhapsodic about what they discover on the island, and both, it seems, are already inclined to think this way. Ferdinand does not speak of liberating bondage only in connection with Miranda; of other women that he has known he says that "many a time / Th' harmony of their tongues hath into bondage / Brought my too diligent ear" (3.1.40–42). Gonzalo finds wonder in hardship not only in act 5 but also as he is standing on shore after surviving the shipwreck, and even during the storm. As for the passion between the young lovers, Prospero no doubt learns something important about his prospective son-in-law's character by forcing him to carry firewood, but both Ferdinand and Miranda seem constitutionally inclined to the most abject mutual submission, all magical enslavement aside. And Prospero's strident insistence on banishing sexual lust from the attraction (expressed magically in the wedding masque) makes sense chiefly in terms of his own neurotic preoccupations and his determination to see Miranda married to the Prince of Naples; as a formula for perfection of the relationship of these exemplary lovers, it seems arbitrary, strained, and somewhat unnatural.

The more one thinks about Prospero, the more one questions the superficial impression of him as a superhuman character and begins to see the sleight of hand behind the carny act. Older readings of the play tended to justify his fabulous power by assuming that Prospero's wisdom and beneficence were as godlike as his omnipotence, while some recent criticism has excoriated it for its eurologophallocentric applications. But the play throws a wrench into both machines by boldly outlining the limits of Prospero's much-vaunted powers. Now that we have gotten beyond the defensive need to distinguish Prospero's "white" magic from Sycorax's soul-endangering necromancy, the next step should be to observe that, regardless of how Shakespeare's contemporaries would have understood its ontological and moral status, magical power accomplishes little and impedes Prospero's spiritual development.[12] Many of the practical demands he makes of it are of dubious value: subduing unruly strangers and turning them into domestic help (if carrying logs is good for Ferdinand, why not for Prospero and Miranda?); quieting a curious daughter (would she betray him by blabbing his secrets?); putting enemies out of commission by deranging their wits (how would righteousness and redemption be served if, not restrained by Gonzalo, their "desperate" condition led them to suicide?); mounting elegant theatrical productions (something of this in a moment). Its few real triumphs aside, the magic is often simply a tempting distraction, as it was when Prospero first took it up and lost his dukedom.

If Prospero's magic obliges his practical requirements, it mostly disappoints his ambition of transforming human souls and social relationships. Like the experimental science that for a time it was inseparable from (chemistry coexisted with alchemy and astronomy with astrology, and Sir Isaac Newton wrote with equal seriousness about both magic and physics), Renaissance magic, in Shakespeare's presentation, promises a brave new world but for the most part delivers only more sophisticated means of manipulating the old one. It is amoral, technocratic, and does not (to paraphrase Yeats) enable the possessor to put on God's wisdom with his power. Or one could say (stealing from Auden) that it makes nothing happen: Prospero can suspend action, paralyze bodies, summon music, mount apparitions, influence the weather, and above all inflict pain and anxiety—but unlike the God he superficially resembles he engenders little.[13] His power to dispose all the fundamental forces of nature is expressed allegorically through his controlling Ariel, who has affinity for the elements of air and fire, and Caliban, who comprehends the earth and water of the island. But God's real miracle is accomplished in creating and sustaining life, as Shakespeare suggests in Miranda's anguish for the passengers on the wrecked ship: "Had I been any god of power, I would / Have sunk the sea within the earth or ere / It should the good ship so have swallowed and / The fraughting souls within her" (1.2.10–13). All his providential intentions aside, Prospero's theurgic power is chiefly to subdue and manipulate, as Caliban emphasizes: "I must obey. His art is of such pow'r / It would control my dam's god, Setebos, / And make a vassal of him" (1.2.372–74).

Prospero's magical power not only fails to improve others; it also distances him from others, rendering vain his dreams of spiritual and social regeneration even on the level of his own psychology. His emotional connections are more limited than Hamlet's. Gonzalo is his Horatio: a trustworthy, sexless, personally irrelevant ally hanging about backstage. The other Italians represent a corrupt world which has undone him and stamped him a failure, and which he in turn abominates. Caliban, after the initial friendship spoiled, has been reductively typecast as a stand-in for the treacherous usurpers, one whom Prospero can control utterly.[14] Caliban's dead mother stands in for the other conspicuously absent women in the play, receiving in a virulent form Prospero's characteristic suspicion that men can never be sure who has begotten the children they produce; in unmindfulness of his wife (she is mentioned once, in a backhanded tribute to her chastity), Prospero escapes from sexuality by thinking of himself as both a patriarch and a birth-giver.[15] Miranda is in his opinion presexual, and Caliban's threat to impregnate her allows Prospero not only to enslave him but also to fiercely guard her chastity until she can be advantageously married.[16] Prospero's only real companion, the inhuman Ariel, seems to be as much a reflection of his master's disembodied artistic intelligence as a distinct personality.[17] In all of these ways, Prospero is a dreamer trapped in the nightmare of past experience, a mind painfully detached from the life of the body, a self contemptuously separate from the entanglements of society, a cultivated person cultivating nothing. His magic only exacerbates his distrust, by removing him from the need to depend on others.

One kind of emotional connection, to be sure, sustains Prospero throughout the play: most of his actions are intended for the benefit of his daughter Miranda. His third and fourth lines in the play say so, and however much this motive may coincide with motives of self-advancement, nothing that occurs subsequently really undermines the statement. But his relationship with his daughter seems infected with a kind of joyless self-preoccupation. In the long passage of plot exposition that follows Prospero's declaration of solicitude for Miranda, he interrupts his narrative three times to sharply interrogate her about whether she is paying attention or not. The gratuitousness of such worry is suggested by Miranda's reply the third time: "Your tale, sir, would cure deafness" (1.2.106). One hears a man who cannot easily dispense with his iron control of self and others, even in a long-awaited moment of intimacy with the closest person in his life. Shakespeare provides a visual equivalent of this emotional tension in still another image of an empty grasp. Prospero prepares for the speech in which he tells Miranda her history by having her remove his magical robe:

> 'Tis time
> I should inform thee further. Lend thy hand
> And pluck my magic garment from me. So.
> [Lays down his robe.]
> Lie there, my art. Wipe thou thine eyes; have comfort.
> (1.2.22–25)

Wishing to be for a moment a parent rather than a ruler, Prospero relaxes his grip by asking his daughter to use *her* hands to divest him of what separates them. His remarks first to his robe and then to Miranda testify, as does the action itself, to his divided loyalties. His power alienates him from the very person whom he most uses it for. The disrobing symbolizes the stripping away of one kind of relationship to his environment and the substitution of another.[18] In order to become human with another human being, Prospero must remove that which maintains him in a position of mastery of others.

If his relation to Miranda is somewhat distorted by his need for control, his relations with Ariel and Caliban are horribly mangled. As the gargantuan second scene of the play continues, Prospero occupies the stage without interruption and, after narcotizing Miranda, encounters each slave in turn, answering resistance from them with overwhelming displays of force. The encounter with Ariel, in which the spirit politely points out that his work contract has expired, is as violent a piece of emotional manipulation as Iago's of Othello. Clearly some affection dwells in this relationship, and the abortive rebellion concludes amicably, with Ariel tractably agreeing to "do my spriting gently," and Prospero promising to enforce his servitude for only two days more. But a large part of Ariel's tractability proceeds from terror. Prospero is all fatherly affirmation ("My brave spirit!" "Why, that's my spirit!") as long as Ariel performs all of his commands "to point" (2.1.194), and enjoys it. When his creature turns "moody," however, Prospero's fatherhood turns abusive. He assaults him with insults ("malignant thing!" "my slave," "Dull thing!") and with the sort of humiliating questions that allow only for one-word answers (a perennial favorite of bullies in armies and law courts). He recounts with obsessive relish a history that Ariel knows only too well (a favorite rhetorical gambit of patriarchs everywhere). And he delivers a horrifying threat to reenact the torture from which he originally rescued the spirit.

When Caliban succeeds Ariel on the stage, we meet someone who cannot be cowed so easily by Prospero's rhetorical manipulation. Consequently the threats and the invectives proliferate in the kind of sputtering, deadly earnest rage that marks Lear's damnations of his daughters. A somewhat full sampling from this part of the scene: "Thou earth, thou! Speak!" "Come, thou tortoise!" "Thou poisonous slave, got by the devil himself / Upon thy wicked dam, come forth!" "Thou most lying slave, Whom stripes may move, not kindness! I have used thee (Filth as thou art) with humane care"; "Abhorred slave, / Which any print of goodness wilt not take, / Being capable of all ill!" "thy vile race, / Though thou didst learn, had that in't which good natures / Could not abide to be with": "Hagseed, hence!"; "shrug'st thou, malice?"[19]

When, by the end of this seemingly unending scene, Prospero has feigned distrust of Ferdinand and added him to his menage of slaves, and in the process met Miranda's gentle remonstrance on her lover's behalf with violent condescension—"What, I say, / My foot my tutor?" (ll. 469–70)—our introduction to an emotionally unbalanced policeman is complete. First impressions count for much in the theater as in life, and in this play the protagonist is introduced as a difficult combination of gentleness, honorable ambition, and authoritative mastery, on the one hand, and, on the other, testiness, baseminded aggression, and authoritarian reaction. However effective his power, it appears to cost him even more in tranquility, freedom, and dignity than it does his slaves.[20] Caliban's assessment as he instructs Stephano in how to murder him has the ring not only of resentment but of truth:

> Remember
> First to possess his books; for without them
> He's but a sot, as I am, nor hath not
> One spirit to command. They all do hate him
> As rootedly as I.
>
> (3.2.95–99)

An ordinary foolish mortal without the liberty to acknowledge it to anybody or to claim the indulgence that is its due, Prospero lives far from emotional touch with those whom he commands.

His retrospective tale to his daughter in the second scene establishes a context for understanding this isolation. As a younger man, Prospero was so disinterested in mundane political involvement in the lives of his subjects that he virtually invited Antonio's usurpation. His exposition of the story to Miranda describes how, enjoying his position as Duke of Milan but not the duties associated with the title—preferring contemplation to action, learning to rule, books to people—he entrusted his duties to his beloved brother, and was outraged when Antonio cleverly conspired to become Duke in name as well as deed. Whether one reads Prospero as self-aware or as self-justifying in this account (probably he is some combination of the two), the portrait of a callow mistake emerges clearly. The images that he uses to illustrate his choice resemble the images of confinement and paralysis that attach to his disempowerment of others in the play, and predict his disempowerment at the hands of Antonio. Finding his library a "dukedom large enough" (2.1.110), Prospero was "transported" (l. 76)—, "rapt in secret studies" (l. 77), "neglecting worldly ends, all dedicated / To closeness and the bettering of my mind" (ll. 89–90). The self-containment figured in these metaphors seemed serenely happy to Prospero, superior to the feverish self-advancement of the ducal court—figured as a forest which Antonio managed skillfully, knowing how to advance some aspirants toward the sun and "trash for overtopping" (l. 81) others that struggled too energetically for pre-eminence. The two strains of imagery converge in a way that drives home action's superiority to inaction, when Prospero says that "now he was the ivy which had hid my princely trunk / And sucked my verdure out on't" (ll. 86–87)—the growing vine over-whelming Prospero's paralytically inert form. In retrospect, Pros-pero's self-sufficiency has been ruinously flawed by a narcissistic indifference to other lives, and not at all sufficient to the world of action; in an environment of competition, predation, and coercion, renunciation of power is a recipe for ruin.

The Prospero that we meet in the play has learned well the lesson that no one will provide for his welfare, and his daughter's, if he does not do so himself. But in another way he has learned nothing at all. In turning his contemplative art to practical ends, with a vengeance, in overcompensating for his extreme aversion to politi-cal power with an authoritarian omnipotence that transcends mere politics, in inflicting on others the paralytic helplessness that so traumatized him twelve years earlier (no matter how "providential" the outcome), he merely perpetuates from a position of strength the extreme disjunction of self and other that he ignorantly enjoyed in his library. Instead of occupying a place in a society, with its sustaining network of relationships and its transpersonal rules for maintaining order, he creates and enforces an order out his own will. After the rupture in his initially friendly relations with Cali-ban he trusts no one with the authority that he has achieved in his life, and comes to somewhat resemble Caliban's mother, "the foul witch Sycorax, who with age and envy / Was grown into a hoop" (1.2.258–59). Any real transformation in his spiritual life requires some understanding that will take him out of himself, into other lives—and the play is constructed to suggest the beginning of such understanding.[21]

Like *The Odyssey*, *The Tempest* begins *in medias res*, accom-plishing in the protagonist's conversation with a female interlocu-tor the retrospective summary of a prolonged exile, and then moving into present time that will realize a triumphant return to his homeland. The tragic beginning and the comic conclusion of this action conform to the outlines of Homer's epic romance; other features recall Aristotle's formula for the structure of a tragedy. The disaster has begun with a momentous "error": Prospero's refusal to act his assigned role as Duke of Milan. And the process of recovery begins with a "reversal" in this course of action, coinciding with a "recognition": Prospero's decisions not to seek vengeance and to renounce his magical power, prompted by his awareness that he is deficient in some essential human capacity for feeling. In Aristotle's account the original *hamartia* and the ultimate *anagnoresis* bear no necessary relation to each other. In Shakespeare's play they do. Prospero comes to recognize precisely what he mistook in the beginning and has continued to mistake all along: his dependence on other people, and on his own creaturely experientiality, for spiritual fulfillment. This enlightenment resolves a psychological crisis, and to the extent that Prospero's psychology is the story of the play, the recognition *is* the reversal, generating and encompassing his decisions to pardon his enemies and to forsake his magic. As with Oedipus, on whose story Aristotle chiefly modeled his theory, awareness of a longstanding error instantly transforms the course of a life and the course of the lives arranged around it.

Any humbling recognitions that Alonso and Ferdinand and Caliban acquire in the course of the play pale before what Prospero finally begins to learn about himself. The first glimmer of understanding, an excessively tragic one characterized by self-pity, comes immediately after his climactic humiliation of the "three men of sin," and during what also promises to be a climactic triumph: the spirit-masque offered as a wedding present to Ferdinand and Miranda. Prospero refers to it with false modesty as "Some vanity of mine art" (4.1.41), but he clearly thinks of it as his crowning glory as a magus and a father, as Ferdinand obligingly intuits when he exclaims, "So rare a wond'red father an a wife / Makes this place Paradise" (ll. 123–24). [22] Here more than anywhere his grasp seems full and fulfilling—artful mythology coinciding with "bounteous" nature to create a vision of human life blessed by nurturing female deities. But the perfection is illusory, fragile not only because it is summoned by a charmer's spell but also because it willfully excludes essential realities of human nature. Wedding tributes traditionally urge the joys of procreation, but this one is preceded by Prospero twice (ll. 13–23, 51–54) enjoining Ferdinand to keep his libidinous hands to himself until after the wedding ceremony. In the masque itself, Ceres will not promise her bounty, nor can the singing and dancing begin, until Iris assures her that Venus and Cupid (who assisted Pluto in raping her daughter) will not be attending.[23]

If the shipwreck and the banquet scene showed ordinary human beings that their efforts to control their lives were vain, this final spectacular demonstration of Prospero's magical art ends with the magician himself realizing in a true sense the "vanity of mine art." For after doing his utmost to artfully exclude the element of animal lust, Prospero brings his vision to a crashing halt when he recalls that the chthonic would-be rapist of his own Proserpine cannot be excluded by mere magical tricks. Ruining his own spell by sudden, involuntary speech, he becomes pathetic when he orders the spirits out after they have already, with a "hollow and confused noise," vanished. The tempest that confounded mariners and nobles at the beginning of the play here returns to pound at Prospero's mind.[24] Ferdinand observes, "This is strange. Your father's in some passion / That works him strongly," and Miranda replies, "Never till this day / Saw I him touched with anger so distempered" (ll. 143–45). Prospero apologizes for his behavior by saying,

> Sir, I am vexed.
> Bear with my weakness; my old brain is troubled.
> Be not disturbed with my infirmity.
> If you be pleased, retire into my cell
> And there repose. A turn or two I'll walk
> To still my beating mind.
>
> (ll.158–63)

In the hauntingly beautiful but very bitter lines that precede these, he laments that his magical grasp has held only spirits which are now "melted into air, into thin air":

> And, like the baseless fabric of this vision,
> The cloud-capped towers, the gorgeous palaces,
> The solemn temples, the great globe itself,
> Yea, all which it inherit, shall dissolve,
> And, like this insubstantial pageant faded,
> Leave not a rack behind. We are such stuff
> As dreams are made on, and our little life
> Is rounded with a sleep.
>
> (ll. 151–58)

Prospero's consternation must stem at least in part from frustration over his inability to escape even for a moment the fearful isolation that authoritarian power enjoins upon those who wield it. Kings can never sleep soundly, knowing for a certainty that someone somewhere is sharpening a knife for them, and Prospero at this moment is looking that reality in the face. But the words address a bigger, more inclusive dissatisfaction: the "little," "insubstantial" quality of human life, and his inability to escape this condition through the force of magical art. His vaporous creations can no more substantiate his existence than dreaming castles in the air can build them on the ground. In his excessively despairing summary of life and death, Prospero gets his first glimpse of an important truth—the spiritual incompleteness of human life, its dependency and provisionality—without acknowledging the capacity for connection with other creatures that tragicomically redeems this condition.

For all the marvellous capacities of his "art," Prospero's grasp is finally as empty, as needy of being filled by others, as that of any other character in the play. Indeed he does, as Montaigne says, "clasp only wind." Ariel is the creator who makes things happen within his arena of natural forces, Prospero merely the commander of this astonishing piece of air—and in Prospero's world of human relationships even his derivative authority counts for little.[25] The strongly urged irony of this masque scene is that Prospero, having helped to lay the foundations for a happy union between Ferdinand and Miranda, cannot himself enjoy the bountiful involvement in another life that his theatrical production predicts for them. Like his enemies gazing on a banquet they cannot consume, like Moses gazing from a mountaintop into the promised land he cannot enter, Prospero sees displayed just beyond his reach a treasure that is denied him. The godlike power that he displays in the production of the masque does not yield human fulfillment, but only reveals more starkly the void that underlies each solitary human life. Perfectly comprehensive as his intellectual grasp is in a practical sense, spiritually he feels the same emptiness that keeps Alonso searching throughout the play for Ferdinand and Ferdinand for Alonso, that drives Ferdinand and Miranda into each other's arms, that impels Caliban to search out gods worthy of his devotion and sexual encounters that might people the isle with more Calibans. What Harry Berger calls his "god's-eye view"—the voyeuristic, manipulative detachment that makes him a kind of Wizard of Oz, perpetually pulling levers behind a screen—proves no adequate substitute for a life that is experientially involved with other lives.[26]

Any critical judgment of Prospero is finally a judgment of the *peripeteia*, or reversal, from longstanding tragic animosity to comic reconciliation at the beginning of act 5, when he decides to pardon his enemies and renounce his magical power. Is there really a movement from vengefulness to acceptance here, or does Prospero simply dramatize in a self-congratulatory way his intention to pardon the wrongs done to him, giving as little of his true mind to Ariel as anyone else?[27] And does Prospero really renounce anything, or is his farewell to magic (as most critics today suppose) merely a genial concession to the weakness of those around him now that he has triumphantly achieved his ends and no longer needs it, accompanied by a grandiloquent pat on his own back for his generosity? Both of Prospero's assertions invite suspicion. Many of his previous actions in the play—his reassuring Miranda that "no harm" has come to the people on the ship, his determination to see her married to the son of his enemy, his feigning hatred for the young man while secretly approving his virtue, his effort to induce "repentance" in his adversaries—suggest that he holds a providential, beneficent intention throughout the play. Although his words suggest a man stepping back from the brink of violence, his actions have been those of the pacific idealist who forsook power for bookish dreams. But, at the same time, his renunciation of magic hardly seems equivalent to a renunciation of power. Prospero remains entirely in control through the remainder of act 5: rehearsing his grievances before his enemies while they are still in catatonic arrest, promising Ariel freedom once more as he once more heaps tasks upon him, stage managing the reunion with Alonso and Gonzalo, threatening Antonio and Sebastian sotto voce, revealing Ferdinand and Miranda behind a curtain at an opportune moment, reasserting dominance over Caliban, tweaking Stephano and Trinculo for their failed coup, ordering "auspicious gales" for the trip home as Ariel's final task, then turning to the audience and pleading powerlessness to determine the weather as his authority for demanding a gale of applause from them. This Prospero, far from giving up power as a sentimental interpretation of his words would have it, is exercising power more impressively than he has anywhere else in the play (not to mention his previous life).

Prospero's authoritative control does not contradict or cancel his intention to live peacefully with the Italians. It indicates merely that the young idealist has learned how to make things happen in the world of politics, rather than trying to wish them into being. Political power is not in itself evil. On the contrary it is, with familial love, an indispensable component of the glue that holds human communities together, and Prospero's place is at the head of his dukedom, actively managing its affairs. His behavior in act 5 promises greater success in his second tenure. Having renounced magic, he makes the Italians accept him as Duke by using the ordinary, sanctioned means of human persuasion: moral authority, mutual indebtedness, sympathetic identification, dispensation of favors, intimidation, construction of a public image. King Alonso is made to feel many things: grateful relief at being released from his "distraction" and finding his son alive; impotence at learning that Ferdinand's marriage (unlike the unfortunate Claribel's) has been arranged without him; power at being told that the duchy is his to restore (even while Prospero "requires" it of him); guilt at having conspired to deprive the rightful owner of it in the first place; importance at being one of two heads (soon to be peacefully united) of a newly restored social order; absence of danger from a lesser noble who might be harboring murderous resentment but proclaims instead that when he returns to Milan every third thought will be his grave. Antonio and Sebastian, notoriously silent during a scene of joyful reunion, are made to feel one thing: the threat that their attempted murder of Alonso—which Prospero enticed them into conceiving and then prevented them from executing—can be made public at any time. In all of these ways Prospero retains, and masterfully uses, the traditional tools of politics.

But, if Prospero's renunciations of revenge and magic are not exactly what they seem, then what of the impression of recognition and reversal that Shakespeare was apparently at pains to create in this final scene of the play? One option is to read that too as a piece of stage managed rhetorical manipulation—a phenomenally good one, judging by all the audiences and readers who have been suckered into an indulgent attitude toward the forgiving, undesigning nobleman returning home to die.[28] There is another possibility: that Prospero changes nothing about his public course of action in act 5 but does embark on a significant change in his emotional orientation to the world around him. It has been argued that, while Prospero's *intentions* have been charitable rather than vengeful throughout the play, not until his conversation with Ariel in act 5 do his angry emotions give way to "the *feeling* of charity".[29] Fine as this distinction may sound, it is an important one, answering to the immense chasm between Prospero's public persona and his jealously guarded inner life, and to his difficulty in establishing relationships with other human beings. The actions that he undertakes in act 5 are smoothly consistent with a course of development that begins long before the play and runs through it, and with his conception of himself as impeccably righteous. But the feelings that he expresses to Ariel—rather, his recognition that he is deficient in feeling—follow from the tempestuous upheaval that afflicted him at the interruption of the wedding masque. That tempest, our only direct glimpse of the Prospero within, proceeded from his awareness of the poverty of human life. Having attempted to exclude essential human realities from his grandiose personal paradise, he was humbled by seeing that human beings cannot make a new creation from nothing in this way; they arrive only at nothing.

The conversation with Ariel marks his dawning awareness of the other, saving half of this violent recognition: namely, that compassion for other human beings can fill the void in a life built on airy intentions. Ariel's life is all airy intentionality, but he at least has a keen awareness of what he is missing: "Hast thou, which art but air, a touch, a feeling / Of their afflictions, and shall not myself, / One of their kind, that relish all as sharply, / Passion, as they, be kindlier moved than thou art?" (5.1.21–24). Prospero's declaration that "the rarer action" consists in pardoning evil rather than avenging it invites one to think of him as the New Testament God, weighing mercy against justice, omnipotent punishment against ineffable grace. But there the resemblance ends. The Christian God pardons sin in His creatures because of His superabundant love for them. He so loves the world that He gives His only begotten son to ransom it: the love generates the pardon. Prospero, this exchange implies, pardons partly *so that* he may feel love for his fellow creatures. Or—to construct the analogy somewhat differently—if Prospero is a god prior to this point in the play, it is the testy senile delinquent of the Old Testament that he most resembles. As the Jewish God evolved in time, from a being unfathomably Other than His creations and given to periodic fits of outraged incommensurability, to one that is incarnate in humanity, so Prospero, in resolving to pardon his enemies, moves out of inhuman apartness into some sense of, "touch" with, "feeling" for, others—some perception of "kindness," in the medieval sense of creaturely commonality. Having become godlike through the artistic control of everything in his consciousness and everyone in his environment, he discovers that to be blessed he must rediscover the space between human beings, where selfhood is realized in others.

The Tempest depicts Prospero as a man of personal weakness and insufficiency, locked in hermetic solitude. The magical art which yields him such spectacular practical control of his environment, far from remedying this unhappy self-involvement, only exacerbates it. In renouncing magic as soon as he can safely do so, Prospero seems to be renouncing principally his place behind the Wizard's screen, and trying to relocate himself in his native human community. Far from removing himself from the arena of power relations as he mistakenly did before, he aims to achieve in his own life the connectedness of self and other, the fertile dependency on other lives, that he has helped to foster in Ferdinand and Miranda. In the terms of Montaigne's image, his iron grip opens into a guarded embrace. Shakespeare's stagecraft emphasizes this as soon as the Italians are freed from their paralysis: Prospero affectionately clasps Alonso ("Let me embrace thy body") and then Gonzalo ("Let me embrace thy age, whose honor cannot / Be measured or confined") (5.1.109, 121–22). That he does not embrace the sullen Antonio and Sebastian suggests the risk in such in-armings, just as his earlier warnings to Ferdinand and Miranda not to give rein to their passions until marriage identifies a similar risk in sexual couplings; but only in the vulnerability of such relationships with other people can he find wholeness.

Prospero's relationship to Caliban culminates in another such guarded renunciation of separateness, another tentative affirmation of physical connectedness. Caliban's original sin was sexual. It was his effort to embrace Miranda that originally pricked Prospero to abominate him as a degenerate beast. In offending Prospero's sexual mores, Caliban became not only culturally inscrutable, lacking in the refinements of European civilization, but spiritually degenerate, one of those unsalvageable reprobates whom bodily infirmity infects with wickedness. The initial, failed effort to assimilate the Other gave way to an effort to deny its humanity, by defining it as monstrously animal. The final scene of the play preserves this sense of spiritual difference: Caliban exclaims at the assemblage of European nobility, "these be brave spirits indeed! / How fine my master is!" (5.1.261–62), and resolves to "seek for grace. What a thrice-double ass / Was I to take this drunkard for a god / And worship this dull fool" (ll. 296–98). But any sense of absolute disjunction between this divine European intelligence (authentically embodied in Prospero, and parodied in Stephano) and Caliban's earthy animality dissolves in Prospero's notoriously cryptic final words about Caliban. In saying "this thing of darkness I acknowledge mine,"

Prospero appears—grudgingly, painfully—to give Caliban a place in his own identity, and to do so on just that sexual ground which occasioned the original sundering. Synechdochally reified as a phallic "thing," a body that moves in dark places, Caliban comes finally to represent to Prospero some corporeal aspect of his own being that he has held at arm's length for a long time. In regarding himself less as a duality of controlling mind and uncontrollable "thing," he admits more possibility of seeing other human beings as what the Brazilians would call "halves" of himself.

Prospero's recasting of the terms of power into an ethic of relation rather than disjunction, participation rather than domination, concludes stylishly in the play's epilogue, where he addresses the audience and invites them to embrace him with their approval and good will. Having already made provision for the proper winds to blow he hardly needs what he requests, a tempest. But, like the poor actor begging approval for his show, the solitary wizard reaches out to a community of ordinary human beings, emphasizing his "faint," merely human powers now that he has surrendered his magical control of spirits. The language toward the end of the epilogue is strongly Christian:

> And my ending is despair
> Unless I be relieved by prayer,
> Which pierces so that it assaults
> Mercy itself and frees all faults.
> As you from crimes would pardoned be,
> Let your indulgence set me free.

The speech has mistakenly been read as a *theosis*—a final approach to godhead, a bridging, through faith, of the small gap between rational theurgy and divine mystery—and, at the other extreme, as a perversion of the logic in the Lord's Prayer of charitably pardoning others' transgressions.[30] Neither reading allows the lines the force of their own intention, which is to describe in Christian language a state of reciprocal relation between human beings. The speaker seeks salvation from creatures of his own kind, by giving them the power of granting or withholding affirmation which he has previously wielded. Appealing to his and their common insufficiency and dependency (the basis of all Christian charity), he asks them to enfold him in community. Rather than grasping what he needs, he requests it from the "good hands" of others; rather than commanding the forces of the air with the words of his mouth, he proposes to rely on the "gentle breath" of those who value him.

The *Tempest* has long been read as a romance of rebirth, a symbolic restoration of some kind of primal harmony in human affairs. Long critical tradition has it that, through a providential art that narrows the gap between humanity and divinity, Prospero not only rectifies the injustice of his usurpation as Duke of Milan, but also, by casting various lives into confusion, effects their spiritual renewal in ways normally associated in this period with the operation of divine grace. In this view of the play Prospero's actions affirm the sacredness and also the self-determination of human life by showing how an individual's choices and actions can facilitate salvation, both in a practical and a moral sense. If this traditional understanding of the play is to survive the suspicion that has increasingly been leveled at Prospero, it must begin to acknowledge, as Prospero begins to, that whatever sacredness resides in humanity lies not in the isolated, extraordinary ego, but in the mind's relation to those things—body, community, world—that it defines itself in opposition to. Neither in isolation nor in a steely grip can the protagonist find the spiritual prosperity he desires; the only alternative is the risky openness of an embrace.

Notes

1. Francis Barker and Peter Hulme address this problem in their revisionist reading, "Nymphs and reapers heavily vanish: the discursive con-texts of *The Tempest*," in *Alternative Shakespeares*, ed. John Drakakis (London and New York: Methuen, 1985), 191–205. They are at pains to correct the impression that Prospero's construction of the past is a reliable narration. "Such identification hears, as it were, only Prospero's play, follows only his stage directions, not noticing that Prospero's play and *The Tempest* are not necessarily the same thing" (199). But, while persuasively driving home this wedge—principally by observing that Prospero's dramatic interruption of the wedding masque betrays his anxiety over his colonialist "sub-plot"—Barker and Hulme reject the notion that Shakespeare might be using this interruption, the play's "dramatic climax," to undermine Prospero. "But to speak of Prospero's anxiety being staged by *The Tempest* would be, on its own, a recuperative move, preserving the text's unity by the familiar strategy of introducing an ironic distance between author and protagonist" (203). Such traditional authorial and critical strategies are not to be allowed; for entirely unexplained reasons the play admits "a fundamental disquiet concerning its own functions within the projects of colonialist discourse" (204), while working singlemindedly to suppress that disquiet and authorize Prospero. Thus Shakespeare and Prospero are, after all, pretty much the same, but in a bad way.
2. Quoted from *The Complete Works of Montaigne: Essays, Travel Journal, Letters*, tr. Donald M. Frame (Stanford: Stanford University Press, 1948), 150. All subsequent quotations of Montaigne in this essay identified by page number in this edition, within parentheses. I have used Frame's translation throughout the essay. For these two sentences, Florio writes: "I feare me our eies be greater than

our bellies, and that we have more curiositie than capacitie. We embrace all, but we fasten nothing but wind."

3. These and other weaknesses (as well as strengths) in the new historicist readings of the play as a document in colonialism are skillfully set out in Meredith Anne Skura's valuable critique, "Discourse and the Individual: The Case of Colonialism in *The Tempest*," *Shakespeare Quarterly* 40, no. 1 (Spring 1989): 42–69.

4. Bernard Knox, "*The Tempest* and the Ancient Comic Tradition," in *English Stage Comedy*, ed. W. K. Wimsatt, Jr. (New York: Columbia University Press, 1955), 52–73.

5. Ibid., 73.

6. The original, and still indispensable, exploration of Renaissance knowing as a subjective construct rather than an insight into transcendent realities is Ernst Cassirer's *Individuum und Kosmos in der Philosophie der Renaissance* (1927), trans. Mario Domandi as *The Individual and the Cosmos in Renaissance Philosophy* (Philadelphia: University of Pennsylvania Press, 1963). Also fascinating in this connection is Charles Taylor's *Sources of the Self: The Making of the Modern Identity* (Cambridge, Mass.: Harvard University Press, 1989), part. ch. 8 on Descartes.

7. *The Tempest*, 2.2.111–12. Quoted from the Signet edition of the play, ed. Robert Langbaum (New York: New American Library, 1964). All subsequent quotations from this edition are cited in parentheses within the text.

8. Sir Philip Sidney, *Arcadia* (Harmondsworth, Middlesex: Penguin, 1977), 66, 247–48, and *Hamlet* 4.7.81–90.

9. Miranda can be read allegorically here as emblematic of the natives of the New World (old to them) in their ingenuous encounters with the representatives of the Old (new). Montaigne describes this enthusiasm in his account of the Brazilians who traveled back to France, noting that they are "ignorant of the price they will pay some day, in loss of repose and happiness, for gaining knowledge of the corruptions of this side of the ocean" ("Of Cannibals," 158).

10. See Stephen Greenblatt's wonderfully evocative reading of Strachey's reports of the colonists' experiences, in *Shakespearean Negotiations* (Berkeley and Los Angeles: University of California Press, 1988), 147–58. Greenblatt thinks that "Prospero's magic is the romance equivalent of [the brutal] martial law' (156) that Governor Gates declared in Virginia after crushing the colonists' bid to remain in hospitable Bermuda. But, unlike some less judicious and openminded readers of colonial parallels, he recognizes that the interests of Shakespeare's theater are not identical with those of the Virginia Company: while the play promotes Prospero's power, it also moves "toward forgiveness" (157) and calls authoritarian power into question. The tension need not indicate disingenuous suppression of an authentic anxiety; on the contrary, it may indicate a deliberate critique of power, starting with the Italian nobles in this first scene and moving on to Prospero himself by the end of the play.

11. I am indebted for this observation to David Sundelson, "So Rare a Wonder'd Father: Prospero's *Tempest*," in *Representing Shakespeare: New Psychoanalytic Essays* (Baltimore and London: the Johns Hopkins University Press, 1980), 33–53; see 33–34.

12. See D'Orsay W. Pearson, "'Unless I Be Reliev'd by Prayer': *The Tempest* in Perspective," *Shakespeare Studies* 7 (1974): 253–82. Pearson's scrupulously scholarly exposition of Elizabethan and Jacobean attitudes toward magic brings out the tension between a pagan philosophical understanding of theurgy as making man like God and the Christian rejection of such a position, and between Prospero's conception of himself as godlike and an audience's perception of him

as "unkindly" (257) and ineffective. I agree with Pearson's assessment of the protagonist's profound error: "The final resolution of *The Tempest* comes about not through any sacerdotal ability on Prospero's part to engender a change of character in his victims, but rather because he foregoes his pretensions to godhead and assumes his proper role as man" (273). I do, however, find his insistence on the demonic peril of Prospero's magic, and on Prospero's intention to destroy his enemies physically and spiritually, somewhat forced. A more relaxed, perhaps complementary critique of Prospero's magic is offered in Harry Berger's "Miraculous Harp: A Reading of Shakespeare's *Tempest*," *Shakespeare Studies* 5 (1969): 253–83. Berger attacks the art as an indulgence of the duke's "self-delighting recreative impulse" (256), which "continually distracts him from his ethical purpose, and in one famous instance leads him to forget what goes on around him" (257). Berger speaks of Prospero's intense inwardness, his bitter disillusionment with the world as it is, and for him as for Pearson "the central action of the play [is] Prospero's reinvolvement with human beings after twelve years of magic for magic's sake" (258). For Berger, "Frye, Kermode, Orgel and others who worry over the distinction between white and black magic in their efforts to justify Prospero, miss the more important distinction between magical and nonmagical (ethical, rhetorical, etc.) modes of response to life's problems" (281).

13. See Greenblatt, *Shakespearean Negotiations*, 142–46, for a persuasive development of the notion that "Prospero's chief magical activity throughout *The Tempest* is to harrow the other characters with fear and wonder and then to reveal that their anxiety is his to create and allay" (142). In Greenblatt's view, this inclination is not only an aggressive "dream of power, a dream perfected over bitter years of exile," but "salutary" (143). "The entire action of the play rests on the premise that value lies in controlled uneasiness": so Prospero makes the "swift business" of Miranda and Ferdinand's mutual infatuation difficult, humiliating, tense; instead of merely grabbing his dukedom he puts the usurpers through "an elaborate inward restaging of loss, misery, and anxiety"; and "in the play's most memorable yet perplexing moment [the interrupted wedding masque], the princely artist puts himself through the paralyzing uneasiness with which he has afflicted others" (144). These are penetrating observations, though the suffering seems to me far more efficacious in Prospero's case than in any other character's, and Prospero's paralyzing anxiety seems more suffered than self-inflicted.

14. This observation about the psychological economy of Prospero's abomination of Caliban has been repeated by many critics; as far as I know it was first made by Harry Berger. See "Miraculous Harp," 261: "Caliban is 'all the subjects that he (Prospero) has,' and in kicking him about, Prospero may continually, and securely, re-enact his failure in Milan . . . . His value as a scapegoat exceeds his usefulness as a handyman. . . . Poor Caliban is a platonist's black dream: Prospero feels he has only to lay eyes on his dark and disproportioned shape to know what Evil truly Is, and where."

15. See Stephen Orgel, "Prospero's Wife," in *Rewriting the Renaissance: The Discourses of Sexual Difference in Early Modern Europe*, ed. Margaret W. Ferguson, Maureen Quilligan, and Nancy J. Vickers (Chicago: University of Chicago Press, 1986), 50–64, esp. 50–51, 54–55. Also see Janet Adelman, *Suffocating Mothers: Fantasies of Maternal Origin in Shakespeare's Plays, Hamlet to the Tempest* (New York and London: Routledge, 1992), 237.

16. See Lorie Jerrell Leininger, "The Miranda Trap: Sexism and Racism in Shakespeare's *Tempest*," in *The Woman's Part: Feminist Criticism of Shakespeare*, ed. Carolyn R. S. Lenz, Gayle Green, and Carol T. Neely (Urbana: University of Illinois Press, 1980), 285–94.

17. See Berger, "Miraculous Harp," 255–56. Also see Coppelia Kahn, "The Providential Tempest and the Shakespearean Family," in *Representing Shakespeare*, 217–43. Kahn notes that "The terms of endearment with which he plies Ariel and no one else are wasted on the spirit," who has no human feelings (237).

18. And it seems *only* symbolic. In terms of Prospero's psychology, little changes after this disrobing; he still nags her about not listening, and puts her to sleep when he is done with her.

19. I follow here the arbitrary practice of some editors in giving Miranda's speech (ll. 351–62) to Prospero, on the grounds simply that these lines are utterly out of the character that Miranda elsewhere displays, and utterly in character for Prospero.

20. Hegel (in *The Phenomenology of Spirit*, I believe) and Martin Luther King were later to characterize the master-slave relationship as mutually enslaving, though I have not tracked down either remark.

21. In "Shakespeare's *The Tempest*: The Wise Man as Hero," *Shakespeare Quarterly* 31, no. 1 (Spring 1980), 64–75, Paul A. Cantor observes that, while Shakespeare normally makes plays out of action and passion, this one strongly subordinates elements like the love story and the usurpation stories to the story of Prospero's superior understanding. That is true, but it should be added that the story of Prospero's wisdom moves simultaneously toward two different resolutions: his control of the other characters, and his dawning awareness that his own understanding is deficient—that intellectual mastery has diminished his capacity for emotional presence in other lives.

22. Here again I depart from the Signet text's "a wond'red father and a wise," following Jeanne Addison Roberts' 1978 discovery that in the printing of the first folio the crossbar on the "f" in "wife" broke after only a few impressions, converting it to a long "s" in most copies. See Orgel, "Prospero's Wife," 63–64. As Orgel wryly notes, this inadvertent omission of the female is oddly appropriate to the play—and, one might add, to this scene, where sexual passion is banished from a wedding masque.

23. Spenser's *Epithalamion* does something comparable, but not very similar, in urging the joys of procreative union while banishing Petrarchan erotic passion and the suspicion of sexual infidelity (following Catullus in the latter). But Spenser is distinguishing fruitful kinds of love from unhappy ones, and celebrating sexual delight. Prospero's banishment of Venus and Cupid is not accompanied by any definition of what love should be, or any celebration of sexual union.

24. See the important essay of Karen Flagstad, "'Making this Place Paradise': Prospero and the Problem of Caliban in *The Tempest*," *Shakespeare Studies* 18 (1986), 205–33. Flagstad reads Prospero as a would-be god who tries to rewrite the principles of creation: "The masque is, in short, a 're-vision' in which the loss of perpetual spring—classical mythical counterpart of the Christian Fall of humankind—is effectively reversed. The roles of the gods are altered, contrary elements are purged by expulsion, a revised *mythos* is celebrated: the Rape does not occur; the loss of perpetual spring does not obtain" (209). Caliban is the beast in this Edenic garden, embodying everything that Prospero tries to exclude from his utopian vision; and in giving Ferdinand logs to carry Prospero tries to expel an interior beast from his son-in-law-to-be. Like the most ambitious of the Renaissance magi, who "aspired to nothing less than a recovery of imagined lost powers over the entire created universe," Prospero thinks that his art can reestablish paradise; "Knowledge is power—power enough to nullify a fall which was originally the consequence of partaking from a forbidden Tree of Knowledge" (213).

As this irony would suggest, Prospero's project is doomed to failure. Caliban is inexorable, ineradicable, legitimate; to deny him "is to be at once more, and less, than human" (217). In trying to suppress him Prospero demonstrates his resemblance both to Caliban and to Sycorax, and makes Caliban into a monster who wreaks havoc on his paradise. More, the whole universe seems to recoil on Prospero's effort to remake it, reasserting primal chaos. Drawing upon the elaborate structural symmetry of scenes 1.2 to 4.1 discovered by Mark Rose in *Shakespearean Design*, Flagstad observes that the play's original tempest-chaos in 1.1 is mirrored in Prospero's personal tempest at the interruption of the wedding masque (both concentrically framing the establishment of paradise in 3.1). But this time the tempest is beyond Prospero's control, and aimed at him.

25. See Margreta de Grazia, "*The Tempest*: Gratuitous Movement of Action Without Kibes and Pinches," *Shakespeare Studies* 14 (1981): 249–65, for a cogent distinction between the physical control that Prospero's magic accomplishes and authentic spiritual responsiveness.

26. Berger, "Miraculous Harp," 271.

27. E. M. W. Tillyard was one of the first not to take Prospero's words at face value on this point, in *Shakespeare's Last Plays* (London: Chatto and Windus, 1938). For Tillyard, the remark to Ariel about taking part with his reason against his fury is "a re-enactment of a process now past, perhaps extending over a process of many years": "Prospero does not change fundamentally during the play, though, like Samson's, his own accomplished regeneration is put to the test. If he had seriously intended vengeance, why should he have stopped Sebastian and Antonio murdering Alonso?" (53–54). Harry Berger subjects Prospero to a far more sardonic skepticism, seeing no "change of heart in himself, but a change, a slight adjustment, of role which will make his part in the recognition scene more effective"; by "The rarer action" he means the more stunning theatrical role, and all of his words to Ariel are a kind of rehearsal of the scene he will enact with the Italians ("Miraculous Harp," 272–74).

28. This tends to be the judgment of critics who have approached the play as a document in racism, colonialism, and sexism. See for instance Lorie Jerrell Leininger, "Cracking the Code of *The Tempest*," *Bucknell Review* 25, no. 1 (1980): 121–31. Leininger writes, p. 122: "My own sense of *The Tempest* is that it is in code, that its allegorical and Neoplatonic overlay masks some of the most damaging prejudices of Western civilization, and that a fruitful mode of dealing with the play is to examine the strategies of indirection by which the play dazzles, seduces, or confuses an audience into accepting a selective distribution of justice and mercy, while blocking out some parts of the dramatized material."

29. Herbert R. Coursen, Jr., "Prospero and the Drama of the Soul," *Shakespeare Studies* 4 (1968): 316–33; see 317.

30. For the first reading, see Walter Clyde Curry, *Shakespeare's Philosophical Patterns* (Baton Rouge: Louisiana State University Press, 1937), 196–97. For the latter, see Leininger, "Cracking the Code of *The Tempest*," 128–29.

Distinguishing Shakespeare from Fletcher through Function Words

Thomas B. Horton

Stylometry is defined as the technique of making a statistical analysis of some characteristics of literary style. Often stylometric studies focus on authorship questions, and often they rely on computers to count language features in a text and to perform some kind of statistical analysis on these counts. Computers have been used in stylometric authorship studies since the 1960s, when computers first became available for use by scholars in any field. Many of these studies have been controversial for a number of reasons. Most humanities scholars cannot understand the complexities of mathematical methods, nor are they inclined to trust a scientific approach to their own problems. On the other hand, the practitioner of stylometry may fail to understand fully important textual aspects of the authorship problem that seriously affect the assumptions of the statistical study. For example, evaluating a text's authorship by measuring something associated with punctuation will not be valid if scholars have determined that punctuation was later added or modified by a scribe or printer. The stylometric approach has also raised objections from literary scholars when a scientist has based an analysis on certain textual features that do not seem interesting or significant to the literary scholar. Finally, there have been controversies among the advocates of stylometry themselves regarding the best statistical methods to use or the best textual features to measure.

Not surprisingly, the field of Shakespearean authorship studies has been a frequent battleground for those who strongly advocate stylometry. For the most part, the accepted mainstream of Shakespearean textual scholarship has been unaffected by the results of any statistical authorship study, although a number of articles in the area have been published in journals devoted to computer applications in the humanities. When I began the research described in this paper, my goal was to attempt to evaluate the effectiveness of a number of stylometric techniques on a suitable Shakespeare problem (one for which it might just be possible to arrive at an answer). Another goal was to pay particular attention to the well-established body of knowledge developed by editors, bibliographers, and other Shakespearean scholars.

The possible collaboration between Fletcher and Shakespeare in *The Two Noble Kinsmen* and *Henry VIII* is an excellent test for evaluating the effectiveness of stylometry. Most scholars accept that Shakespeare and Fletcher are the possible authors involved, and that most scenes are probably wholly written by one playwright or the other. There is strong linguistic and stylistic evidence supporting existing attributions that the stylometric results can be measured against. In addition, there are a relatively large number of undisputed plays by both authors that can serve as control samples by which habits of composition can be identified. Finally, there is still some disagreement about the question of collaboration among Shakespearean scholars.

This paper summarizes parts of a large research project that led to my Ph.D. dissertation.[1] In this study, common function words were counted and studied to see if they might be useful in distinguishing Shakespeare from Fletcher (as they have been in other studies). A statistical procedure known as *discriminant analysis* was used with this data, and both the data and procedure were thoroughly evaluated on samples of known authorship to determine the accuracy and limitations of this method for determining authorship. Finally, the procedure was applied to the scenes in *Henry VIII* and *The Two Noble Kinsmen* that contain at least five hundred words. The results indicate that both plays are collaborations and generally support the accepted divisions. However, a number of scenes thought by many to be Fletcher's work resemble Shakespeare more closely in their use of function words.

In order to study the question of collaboration in *Henry VIII* (H8) and *The Two Noble Kinsmen* (TNK), twenty-four Shakespeare and eight Fletcher plays were selected to represent the two dramatists. Of these texts, six were set aside as a *test set*. These were treated as if their authorship was unknown. All procedures that I evaluated were applied to samples from these six plays, and the results were used to judge their effectiveness. The remaining plays (twenty by Shakespeare and six by Fletcher) were used to establish each author's characteristics of composition. These texts are referred to as the *control set*.

At the time this study began, only two editions of Shakespeare's works existed in electronic form. The Riverside edition was not available to scholars at that time, but I was granted access to the quarto and folio texts prepared by T. H. Howard-Hill for the series of concordances published by Oxford University Press. Using early editions led to some problems with regard to experimental design and computer processing. However, Schoenbaum,[2] Greg, and others have argued that authorship studies should be based on early printed editions or manuscripts. In addition, there are few modern editions of any plays by Fletcher. Of the fourteen plays that Hoy determined to be the unaided work of Fletcher, four existed in machine readable form. Two of these were authoritative: the 1647 F1 text of *Bonduca*, and the Ralph Crane manuscript version of *The Humorous Lieutenant* (which is entitled *Demetrius and Enanthe* on the manuscript). Two more existing texts had been prepared from a copy of the second Beaumont and Fletcher folio of 1679, although the text for these plays was derived from F1. These texts were used as the test set for Fletcher. Four other texts were entered into the computer, using Bowers's old-spelling editions.

The use of early authoritative editions does introduce a variety of problems, including some that influence which undisputed plays could be included in the control set. A number of principles were used to select plays not to be included in the study. First, any play with serious questions of authenticity was omitted. Second, I only selected plays that have one authoritative source text, since otherwise I would have to bring together readings from several texts to form a composite version (in other words, become an editor). This principle was violated in minor ways in a number of plays (for example, the witch scenes in *Macbeth* and the passages of French in *Henry V* were ignored; the deposition scene from F1 of *Richard II* was added to the quarto text; and so on). The changes I made in the electronic copies of these copy texts required no editorial judgment other than a sound knowledge of the relationship of the various early versions of the plays. Similar principles were applied in selecting plays by Fletcher.

In choosing to use stylometry to approach a problem, the researcher faces two fundamental choices: what features to count or measure in the texts, and what statistical techniques are most appropriate to evaluate the significance of this data. There are many choices for each of these issues, and differences of opinion among advocates of stylometry have led to controversies within the field. Tallentire argues that the choice of what to measure can be made in two very different ways.[3] The first approach is more natural for a traditional literary scholar: an analyst uses statistics to provide an objective component of judgment regarding features that have been first recognized through careful reading of a text. The second approach is often used by a statistician or scientist working in stylometry: the analyst measures many features (perhaps chosen arbitrarily) in control texts and uses statistics to find those features that produce statistically significant differences. For example, in applying the first approach to the current problem, we might use statistics to evaluate the presence of forms like ye and 'em which scholars have long noted are favored by Fletcher. A study based on the second approach might examine a large number of features (such as the set of all pronouns, sentence length, the type-token ratio of vocabulary richness, and so on) to identify which features show the most promise for distinguishing the two authors.

In using the second approach, the analyst trusts the final results not because of a belief in the importance of the literary features studied but because of a rigorous validation procedure which has been carried out on control samples. The scientist may accept the results even if there is no apparent logical explanation that could explain why the chosen features should indicate authorship, date of composition, and so on. In the past, the community of humanities scholars has mistrusted this approach, but for questions of authorship it is important to find textual features that reflect a writer's conscious stylistic decisions as little as possible. Traits apparent to a careful reader would of course be open to imitation. Thus many studies of authorship, chronology, or textual integrity have focused on features such as the occurrence or position of function words, vocabulary measures, sentence length, or word length. The primary results of this study are based on the rate of occurrence of common function words. Such words were also successfully used by Mosteller and Wallace in their well-known study of Hamilton's and Madison's *The Federalist* papers.[4]

This study also uses a statistical approach that differs from many techniques of stylometry that have been used. Some researchers have measured language features in a number of control texts and then computed statistics (for example, the average together with the standard deviation) for a given author. Then the same feature is measured in a disputed play (or scene, and so on). This value is compared statistically to the value that characterizes all of the control texts as a group. Two problems arise from this approach. First, we must have some way of combining the results of a number of such comparisons. The process of combining mathematical results may not be straightforward if the features being studied are not statistically independent. Second, if there is a wide variation in the value being measured, then this variation may not be reflected when one describes, for example, thirty plays of Shakespeare by one numeric value. When a researcher uses this type of approach to compare the overall proportion for a language feature in a large Shakespeare control set to the proportion in a scene from *Henry VIII*, the researcher is asking in effect: How different is the observed value in the disputed scene from the best estimate of what it should be?

A better question might be: What is the likelihood of observing a sample of text with these values, given the pattern of occurrence observed in a number of similar samples by a given author? This second question seems to be closer to what we really want to ask. But it implies that we should measure textual features in samples similar in size and nature to what is disputed, and that the statistical method chosen should clearly address variation within these many samples. That is, if one wants to assign a disputed scene, one should compare it to members of a large set of scenes of known authorship, not just to a summary statistic like an average value. Thus, the researcher should use a quantitative method that compares like to like. The next paragraphs describe a multivariate statistical method that is based on this strategy.

The statistical method used to analyze word rates in this study, *discriminant analysis*, avoids the problems noted above. (Hand's text[5] provides the best description of discriminant analysis as it is used in this study.) First, it is truly multivariate, in that it allows us to combine measurements for a number of features (or variables) and to produce one answer, taking statistical dependence into account. Second, it uses similar samples (the control set) of known classification (i.e., authorship) to create a *classifier* that decides to which group or class a given sample is closest. In other words, after choosing a set of features to measure and analyze, these features are measured in a large number of samples from both the control set and the disputed set of works. Each of these samples is now described by a set or *vector* of values, and the question becomes this: for each disputed sample, is its vector more like those in the set of Shakespeare samples or more like those in the set of Fletcher samples? For this problem, the samples of known classification are the scenes from the plays in the control set (i.e., undisputed works by Shakespeare and Fletcher). For each scene from *H8* and *TNK*, the statistical method determines if that scene's vector is more like the set of all the vectors from Shakespeare's control set scenes or more like those from Fletcher's. In this context the term *classifier* is used to reference a particular combination of statistical method and specific set of variables. The variables might be any type of textual feature measured in a scene, but in this study they are the rate of occurrence of function words. If the set of words to be analyzed is varied, then a different classifier results (although these classifiers might all be based on the same discriminant analysis technique).

The statistics of discriminant analysis are complex, but a simple example using word-rate data from Shakespeare and Fletcher may clarify the general approach. In this example, the twenty plays in the control set written by Shakespeare and the six plays written by Fletcher are divided into acts. In each act, the rate of occurrence of the word *in* is measured along with the rate of the word *of*. (Shakespeare uses these two prepositions more often than Fletcher.) We now have two values associated with each act in these plays; each sample is represented by a two-dimensional vector. We can show this with a two-dimensional plot, shown in Figure 1, in which each sample is positioned according to its value for the rate of *in* (the horizontal axis) and *of* (the vertical axis). Acts by Shakespeare are plotted as solid circles, while Fletcher acts are shown as small diamonds. (In the actual study, measurements are made by scene; this example uses acts to keep the plot simple.)

Examination of the graph shows that there is wide variation within each author for these two word rates; clearly neither author is very consistent in how often he uses these words. If the writers did use these words at a consistent rate, then the plots for each would form small, tight clusters. But despite the large amount of variation, these two common words do a remarkable job separating the set of Shakespeare acts from the set of Fletcher acts. If we consider the curve shown in the figure as the boundary dividing the two authors, then we can see that two of the thirty Fletcher acts and eight of the one hundred one Shakespeare acts fall on the wrong side of the curve and would thus be assigned to the incorrect class (author). We can view this as a *misclassification rate* of $^{10}/_{131} = 7.6$ percent. If we added samples from *H8* and *TNK* to the graph, then we could assign authorship based on which side of the curve these samples' points fell.

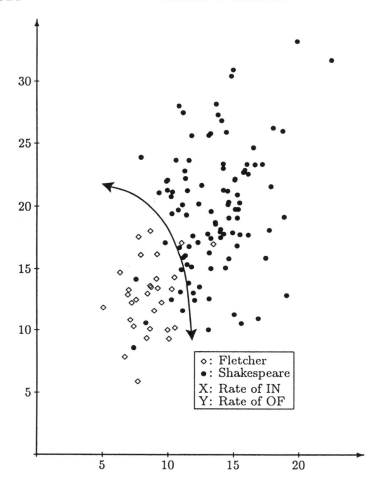

Figure 1. Plot of the rate of occurrence of *in* against *of* measured in acts.

This example illustrates exactly how discriminant analysis works. The method uses the samples of known classification (plotted in the figure) to calculate the curve shown in the figure. This curve serves as a decision boundary for samples of unknown classification. Imagine if three words were used; then the graph would become a three-dimensional plot in which the authors' samples would be clouds of points floating in a three-dimensional space. (If the three variables do a good job in distinguishing authorship, these clouds would not overlap much.) In general, discriminant analysis treats each sample as a point in an n-dimensional space.

If one then chooses any point in this space (say, any position in the plot in Figure 1), then the method can calculate the probability that a sample with those values belongs to one class (author) or another. The ratio of these probabilities becomes the likelihood that the sample belongs to a given class (i.e., that the scene was written by a given author). A sample falling exactly on the curve shown on the plot would have a fifty-fifty chance of belonging to either playwright, according to the probabilities calculated by the statistical method. The farther you move away from the boundary separating the authors, the higher likelihood that a sample is safely assigned to one author. The statistical method allows us to use what is known as a *reject option* to define a region adjacent to the boundary. Samples falling in this region are considered too close to call and are not assigned to either class. (In the results described later, a reject option was used so that samples were not classified unless the likelihood was four-to-one for one author or another.)

The skeptical reader may have several questions at this point. First, why should this statistical method be accurate in assigning a small sample from a possibly collaborative play to Shakespeare or Fletcher? There is no reason to think so unless one has a method for evaluating how successful this approach can be. This evaluation should be carried out before applying the classifiers to the disputed plays. For the example above we began such an assessment when we noted that the method failed for ten of the 131 acts in the control samples that were used to create the graph and make the calculations. Recall also that a set of plays were kept apart from the control samples; this test set is made up of two more Fletcher plays and four more Shakespeare texts. Acts from these plays could be assigned to one author or the other by the method, and the misclassification rate evaluated. These test set plays are not used in any other way to help establish a classifier, so they provide a completely independent test. This approach is used to quantify the accuracy of the classifier (i.e., the method together with the chosen variables) used in the final analysis. Our confidence in the likelihoods produced by the method are based solely on how well the method does in classifying all the samples in both the control and test sets (which are all of known authorship).

Another question might be: How does one decide which variables to use with the method? It is important to note that the statistical method discriminant analysis is really just a technique for assessing information collected from the plays, and thus it will not work well if the data measured in the samples does not really differ enough between the authors. The goal of this study was to try to find the best language features for discriminating between these two authors. Initially several simple statistical techniques were used to identify a large set of possible features that might suffice. Afterwards the discriminant analysis method itself was used with various smaller subsets of these features to find a small set of variables that are best for classification by author. Choices are based on which subsets produce the smallest misclassification rates on the control samples and/or the test samples. This process is known as *feature selection*. There are a number of statistical methods for carrying out feature selection (all beyond the scope of this paper). Each involves trying various combinations of variables in an effort to improve the accuracy of the classifier when applied to the samples of known classification.

No matter what statistical method is used for a stylometric study, we must collect measurements from the texts themselves. Identifying and counting function words might seem to be a straightforward task, but homonyms, spelling variants and contracted forms in old-spelling dramatic texts present problems when using a computer. Many common function words have several variant spellings (e.g., *been* can be spelled *beene, bene, bin*, and so on). Other forms can represent a number of lexical forms; for example, besides the indefinite article, the single-letter word *a* can mean *he, of, on, ah*, and so on. Some forms of compound contractions involving function words are frequent (e.g., *let's, o'th', 'tis*, and the many contracted forms of *is* like *it's, Caesar's, he's*).

These problems were solved by developing a system to produce a revised version of the computer file containing each play in which all forms of common words can be recognized automatically. This system has three components. First, a set of special codes is added to texts' computer files to identify and distinguish homonyms and variants. For example, *a#1* represents occurrences of *he, a#3* represents *on*, and so on. Occurrences of *beene, bene*, and so on will later be automatically replaced by the standard form, but occurrences of *bin* meaning a container are marked *bin#1* to avoid mistaking this as a form of the verb. Second, *replacement and expansion lists* give a "normalized" form for all of these forms involving common function words. For example, these lists include an entry showing that *a#1* should be replaced by *he* in the new version of the computer text. These lists also give the expanded forms of many compound contractions, indicating for example that *'tis* should be replaced by *it is*. Lists of compound contractions and their full forms were compiled from experience and with help from Partridge's book *Orthography in Shakespeare and Elizabethan Drama.*[6] However, a simple replacement strategy is not powerful enough to handle apostrophe-*s* and -*t* forms. Special codes (similar to those shown above for homonyms, and so on) were inserted into the text files to distinguish apostrophe-*s* contractions involving *is*, *us*, *his*, and so on from possessive forms, and contractions of *it* from forms like *banish't*.

The third component of this system is a program named RE-PLACE that uses this system of codes and these replacement/expansion lists to create a "normalized and expanded" version of the computer file containing the text of a play. These versions contain no compound contractions, and all forms of common function words can be easily identified using a computer program. Once such versions were prepared for each play by both authors, we could determine the extent of each author's use of compound contractions. In almost every case, Fletcher uses more of these forms than Shakespeare, although the latter uses more contractions as his career progresses. Because of this secular change and the possibility of alterations introduced by scribes, compositors, or revisors, the expanded versions of the plays were used in the remainder of the study. Thus any subsequent mention of samples or scenes of, say, 1,000 words in this paper reflects the count after the expansion of compound contractions. This process revealed some interesting results based on differences in Shakespeare and Fletcher's rate of use of compound contractions. In particular, Fletcher's rate of use of compound contractions involving *is* is a great deal higher than Shakespeare's. While this finding might be useful in the context of this authorship study, such contractions are features that might easily have been modified by a scribe or compositor. Therefore this feature is not used in any of the statistical analyses described in this paper. Nevertheless, I cannot resist noting that *H8* 4.2, usually attributed to Fletcher, has an extremely low rate for contractions of *is* that is unparalleled in the scenes of the eight undisputed Fletcher plays examined in this study.

Before beginning the discriminant analysis, I searched for a set of words that seemed to have the most potential as authorship markers: words that are used more often by one author than by the other. Starting with several hundred common words, several procedures were initially used to narrow these down to a smaller set of good markers. These procedures included the use of the well-known distinctiveness ratio (DR) and statistical *t*-test. Some words that exhibited relatively large degrees of variation in Shakespeare's works according to genre or date of composition were then eliminated. Finally, as noted above, the discriminant analysis technique itself was used as part of the feature selection technique to further reduce the number of words to be used for the final analysis.

The distinctiveness ratio is calculated for a given word by dividing the overall rate of occurrence for one author by the other author's rate. The DR values did identify some words that turned out to be good markers (such as *dare, too,* and *which*). It also found the forms that Shakespeare and Fletcher have been known to use differently (such as *ye, hath, has, them, 'em*). However, a large DR only occurs for words that one author uses very infrequently, and this method does not identify more frequent words that both authors use but at different rates. For example, the rate for *the* is very different in the two writers; Shakespeare's rate is 32.6 per 1,000 word occurrences, while Fletcher's is 23.7. The DR is 1.38, not a large value. Another criticism of DRs is that they do not take within-author variance into account at all. The *t*-test is a calculation normally used by statisticians to determine if the mean values calculated from two separate sets of samples are statistically equivalent; it does take within-sample variance into account. My results show that this test is probably more useful than the distinctiveness ratio test for identifying good markers.

Perhaps these markers occur at different rates for reasons other than authorship. A statistical procedure called *analysis of variance* was used to test for variation in these word rates that might correspond to date of composition or genre. This was only done for acts of the twenty Shakespeare control-set plays. Many of the words showed significant variation, including some of the best markers identified in the previous steps. After some discussion with a statistician, I decided to eliminate any of the markers for which the average rate for one of the subgroups (i.e., comedies or early plays) did not differ significantly (based on the *t*-test) from the overall Fletcher rate. Thus this kind of variation among Shakespeare's works did not eliminate a marker from consideration if the extreme values were still different enough from the Fletcher rate.

Some of the variations within Shakespeare's works might raise a linguist's curiosity. Shakespeare's comedies are characterized by high rates for pronouns and *a*, together with low rates for *the*. Tragedies have low rates for *a*. The histories have very low rates for personal pronouns (as noted by Brainerd[7]) and high rates for *in, of* and *and*. *In* occurs infrequently in the romances, while *so* is much more frequent in this genre than the other three. The late plays have a high rate for *the*.

There were a number of words that are used at different rates by the two dramatists but did not occur frequently enough to be used as individual variables. However, one way of possibly using them would be to take all of the Shakespeare markers and count them together, then do the same for the Fletcher markers. This produces two new variables, which I call "infrequent marker pooled sets." There are some statistical reasons why this approach is not completely sound. But I decided to see how this might work, hoping that using these two variables together with the other individual word markers might minimize any problems due to statistical dependence. These two new variables turned out to be the best individual discriminators. But because of their somewhat questionable nature, the final discriminant analysis was repeated twice: once using the infrequent marker pooled sets and once without.

The process of evaluating marker words led to the discovery of a trait which, although it cannot be used in the discriminant analysis method, might provide additional evidence. When looking for spelling variants when preparing the replacement and expansion lists described earlier, I noticed that Shakespeare uses more words beginning with *there-* or *where-* (e.g., *therefore, therein, wheresoever*) than Fletcher. In fact, only eight such "*there/where-* compounds" (as I call them) occur in all eight Fletcher plays I studied, whereas Shakespeare uses twenty-seven in the twenty control-set plays. When Fletcher does use such forms, he uses them much less frequently; the combined rate is 1.53 per 1,000 word occurrences for Shakespeare but only 0.13 for Fletcher. This yields a distinctiveness ratio of 11.8, which is as high a value as that of the well-known marker *hath*.

These *there/where-* compounds do not occur very often, and some occurrences in Fletcher and the disputed plays occur in stock phrases (such as "and thereby hangs a tale") or in a song (that may have been borrowed). Because of their very low frequency they were not included in the formal statistical analysis. However, two scenes in *H8* and *TNK* that are usually attributed to Fletcher contain what I feel are significant occurrences of these words. *H8* 1.3 contains two (*wherewithall* and *thereunto*); this would be an extremely high rate for Fletcher. *TNK* 4.3 contains one occurrence of *thereto*; this scene was attributed to Shakespeare by some early scholars. This is the first of the mad scenes of the jailor's daughter, with its echoes of *Lear* and some other Shakespeare plays. To anticipate the results

	Fletcher		Shakespeare	
	Mean	Std. Dev.	Mean	Std. Dev.
all	7.41	3.15	4.39	1.98
are	6.46	2.53	4.06	2.16
dare	1.23	1.01	0.24	0.49
did	0.86	0.92	2.10	1.78
in	8.55	2.99	13.39	4.06
must	3.41	2.16	1.75	1.51
no	6.18	2.39	4.73	2.02
now	5.34	2.70	3.09	1.70
of	12.74	3.92	19.83	6.72
sure	1.58	1.39	0.36	0.52
the	22.82	6.38	32.31	9.32
these	2.82	2.43	1.49	1.34
too	4.52	2.49	1.72	1.37
which	1.24	1.12	2.87	2.00

of the final discriminant analysis, the use of function words in these two scenes is much more like Shakespeare than Fletcher.

After identifying good markers using the DR and *t*-test and then eliminating those that varied too much according to genre or date of composition, sixteen markers remained (fourteen individual words and two infrequent marker pooled sets). These seemed to have the best chance of discriminating between Shakespeare and Fletcher. Above are some simple statistics for the fourteen individual words used in the final analysis. The mean (or average) and the standard deviation (a measure of variability among the samples) are listed, each calculated using control-set scenes containing at least 1,000 words.

The discriminant analysis method is known to work better with a smaller number of variables, so the feature selection techniques (described above) were used to select the subset of variables that produced the best results in classifying the control set itself. I used two different methods to do this, which produced two slightly different sets of words. I then repeated the process, including the infrequent marker pooled set variables; one of the resulting subsets of variables misclassified more samples of known authorship than the other three, so I dropped it. Thus I had three sets of word-rate variables to use in the final analysis, each containing seven or eight words from the fourteen words listed above plus the two pooled sets of infrequent markers.

To determine how short a sample of text could be accurately classified using this method and these variables, I applied the clas-

	Correct	**Incorrect**	**Rejected**
Control set: 371 scenes	358	0	23
Test set: 88 scenes	75	2	11
Overall: 459 scenes	435 (94.8%)	2 (0.44%)	34 (4.8%)

sification method to scenes of different length from both the control and test sets (of known authorship) and looked at the misclassification rates. I first tried all scenes of 1,000 or more words, then 750 or more words, and finally 300 words. Not surprisingly, the method's performance decreases as smaller samples are included. A short scene has fewer occurrences of the markers and therefore less information that can be used by the statistical procedure. The five-hundred-word limit appeared to be a good choice; the accuracy was acceptable in my opinion, and most of the scenes in *H8* and *TNK* are at least this length.

As noted above, I chose to use a reject option that allows samples to remain unassigned if the evidence is not strong. I used a rather strict threshold in comparison to most other statistical applications of discriminant analysis: any likelihood ratio less than four-to-one was "rejected." In addition, because I ended up with three sets of word-rate variables (and thus three distinct classifiers), I needed a decision rule to resolve conflicting or ambiguous results from these three different sets. After examining the performance results on the control and test sets, I classified scenes even where the probability for one of the three classifiers was less than the reject threshold as long as all three results were consistently in favor of one author.

Finally the point has been reached when we can evaluate how well discriminant analysis performs analyzing the scenes of known authorship in the control and test sets. If the word-rate information and the statistical method are not successful when classifying scenes for which we know the answer, there is no point applying the procedure to the disputed plays. The table above shows the number of scenes correctly assigned, incorrectly assigned, and the number that could not be assigned due to the reject option on scenes of five hundred words or more. These results demonstrate very acceptable performance on relatively small samples of known authorship. Almost 95 percent of the five-hundred-word scenes were assigned correctly, and an outright error was made for less than one-half of one percent of the scenes.

Two other important tests were performed before analyzing *H8* and *TNK*. First, I took the six plays of the test set and extracted samples that were composed of the speeches of the individual characters (those who speak at least five hundred words). When the three classifiers were applied to these sixty-two samples, the misclassification rate only increased slightly. Although this is only a limited test, it suggests that characterization does not affect the use of these variables with this procedure to any great degree (at least for the purpose of distinguishing Fletcher from Shakespeare).

Second, to see how the classification procedure handled scenes of joint composition, I took text of known authorship (from the test set) and created twenty samples of about eight hundred fifty words that were roughly half Fletcher and half Shakespeare. These results were not so encouraging. Half of the scenes were assigned to one author or the other (using the same rules which produced the error rates described in the preceding paragraph). Twenty-five percent were left unclassified, and the other 25 percent produced ambiguous results: at least two of the classifiers produced high probabilities one way or the other, but these disagreed regarding which author wrote the scene. This interesting result only occurred for 3.4 percent of the test-set scenes analyzed earlier that were written wholly by one author. It appears that scenes of joint composition may be assigned to one author or the other by the method developed in this study. On the other hand, strong but conflicting results for a scene may well indicate joint composition.

Finally, the statistical method was applied to function word data collected from the possibly collaborative plays. The final procedure was applied to the scenes in H8 and TNK that contained at least five hundred words. As indicated in the introduction of this paper, the results of this function word analysis indicate that both plays are collaborations. Several scenes thought by many to represent Fletcher's work resemble Shakespeare more closely in their use of function words. Figures 2 and 3 show these results together with the length of each scene and the attribution by other authorities. The statistical results given for each scene of five hundred words or more include the probability and authorship attribution calculated using each of the three sets of markers chosen with feature selection. The last column indicates the verdict as determined by the decision rule described earlier. The strength of the result (based on the relative degree of the calculated probabilities) is indicated by preceding the verdict with "like" or "very like." Scenes that could not be clearly assigned by the decision rule are indicated by a question mark.

A detailed analysis of each scene is beyond the scope of this paper, but here are some of the more interesting results. Of the

Figure 2. Discriminant analysis results for *The Two Noble Kinsmen*.

	Words	Attr.*	Set T1		Set T2		Set FR1		Verdict
			Probabilities for Authorship						
I.i	1821	Sh	Sh	1.00	Sh	0.97	Sh	0.99	very like Sh
I.ii	954	Sh	Sh	1.00	Sh	1.00	Sh	1.00	very like Sh
I.iii	804	Sh	Sh	1.00	Sh	0.99	Sh	1.00	very like Sh
I.iv	413	Sh	—	—	—	—	—	—	-too short-
I.v	108	Sh?	—	—	—	—	—	—	-too short-
I.i	497	?	Sh	1.00	Sh	1.00	Sh	1.00	very like Sh
II.ii	2402	Fl	Fl	0.91	Fl	0.75	Fl	0.85	like Fl
II.iii	744	Fl	Sh	0.64	Sh	0.84	Sh	0.92	like Sh
II.iv	288	Fl	—	—	—	—	—	—	-too short-
II.v	573	Fl	Fl	1.00	Fl	1.00	Fl	1.00	very like Fl
II.vi	355	Fl	—	—	—	—	—	—	-too short-
III.i	1051	Sh	Sh	1.00	Sh	0.97	Sh	1.00	very like Sh
III.ii	343	Sh?	—	—	—	—	—	—	-too short-
III.iii	502	Fl	Fl	0.99	Fl	0.99	Fl	0.98	like Fl
III.iv	250	Fl	—	—	—	—	—	—	-too short-
III.v	1241	Fl	Sh	0.60	Sh	0.96	Fl	0.52	?
III.vi	2717	Fl	Fl	0.95	Fl	0.98	Fl	0.59	like Fl
IV.i	1353	Fl	Sh	0.85	Sh	0.68	Fl	0.70	?
IV.ii	1349	Fl?	Sh	0.62	Fl	0.96	Fl	0.79	?
IV.iii	877	Fl?	Sh	1.00	Sh	1.00	Sh	1.00	very like Sh
V.i	1392	Sh‡	Sh	1.00	Sh	1.00	Sh	0.99	very like Sh
V.ii	1039	Fl	Sh	0.53	Fl	0.53	Fl	0.81	?
V.iii	1211	Sh	Sh	1.00	Sh	0.97	Sh	0.93	like Sh
V.iv	1158	Sh	Sh	1.00	Sh	0.99	Sh	0.95	very like Sh
Pro.	169	?	—	—	—	—	—	—	-too short-
Epi.	273	?	—	—	—	—	—	—	-too short-

*Attribution of each scene according to Proudfoot[8] and Hoy.[9]
‡Except for the first 33 lines (276 words).

scenes that are classified as Shakespeare's, perhaps TNK 2.3 is the least exciting. No one else has ever wanted to claim this for him. Perhaps Shakespeare really did write it, or perhaps it is one of the errors we expect (with low probability) from the method. Or perhaps someone else wrote it. Discriminant analysis only tells us which of known candidates is most likely, so it is not very useful for situations where one does not know all the possible classes.

The other interesting result in *TNK* is 4.3. This analysis concludes that the evidence for Shakespeare's authorship of this scene is strong. The function word results show that this scene is as much

Figure 3. Discriminant analysis results for *Henry VIII*.

	Words	Attrib. by*		Probabilities for Authorship						Verdict
		Sped.	Hoy	Set T1		Set T2		Set FR1		
I.i	1868	Sh	Sh	Sh	1.00	Sh	1.00	Sh	1.00	very like Sh
I.ii	1742	Sh	Sh	Sh	1.00	Sh	1.00	Sh	1.00	very like Sh
I.iii	587	Fl	Fl	Sh	0.99	Sh	0.73	Sh	0.80	like Sh
I.iv	941	Fl	Fl	Fl	0.79	Fl	0.90	Fl	0.99	like Fl
II.i	1439	Fl	both	Fl	0.93	Sh	0.74	Fl	0.56	?
II.ii	1220	Fl	both	Fl	0.95	Sh	0.80	Sh	0.72	?
II.iii	898	Sh	Sh	Sh	0.90	Fl	0.73	Fl	0.70	?
II.iv	1924	Sh	Sh	Sh	1.00	Sh	1.00	Sh	1.00	very like Sh
III.i	1525	Fl	Fl	Fl	0.69	Fl	0.73	Sh	0.70	?
III.iia	1663	Sh	Sh	Sh	1.00	Sh	1.00	Sh	1.00	very like Sh
III.iib	2185	Fl	both	Fl	1.00	Sh	0.98	Sh	0.89	?
IV.i	999	Fl	both	Sh	1.00	Sh	1.00	Sh	0.99	very like Sh
IV.ii	1431	Fl	both	Sh	0.89	Sh	0.87	Sh	0.77	like Sh
V.i	1507	Sh	Sh	Sh	0.99	Sh	0.69	Sh	0.93	like Sh
V.ii	296	Fl	Fl	—	—	—	—	—	—	-too short-
V.iii	1550	Fl	Fl	Sh	0.51	Fl	0.78	Sh	0.95	?
V.iv	807	Fl	Fl	Sh	1.00	Sh	1.00	Sh	0.99	very like Sh
V.v	653	Fl	Fl	Fl	1.00	Fl	0.61	Fl	1.00	like Fl
Pro.	132	Fl	?	—	—	—	—	—	—	-too short-
Epi.	268	Fl	?	—	—	—	—	—	—	-too short-

*Attribution of each scene according to Hoy.[10]

like Shakespeare's other scenes as the generally accepted portions of the first and last acts. The linguistic results described by Hoy[11] do not really support Fletcher's claim here. This scene has one occurrence of *has* compared to two occurrences of *hath*, and no occurrences of *ye* but ten occurrences of *you*. Only nine of 106 of the Fletcher scenes in the control set contain two or more occurrences of *hath*, and there are no scenes with ten or more occurrences of *you* with no occurrences of *ye*. Also, this scene contains one of the *there/where-* compounds, *thereto*.

In *H8*, the results of the discriminant analysis are perhaps less clear than in *TNK*. Almost all of the scenes that are generally accepted as Shakespeare's (1.1–2, 2.4, 3.2a, and 5.1) have function word rates that are very unlike scenes by Fletcher. In the last thirty years, some scholars (e.g., Foakes[12] and Hoy[13] have suggested that Fletcher touched up Shakespeare's work in 2.1–2, 3.2b, and 4.1–2. My results may support this theory of revision, since 2.2 and 3.2b have the "strong but disagreeing" results that characterized 25 percent of the "joint composition" scenes put together to test the method. The results for act 4 are more interesting: in both scenes the use of function words is very unlike Fletcher. Also, as noted earlier, the rate of contraction of *is* in 4.2 is lower than for any other scene by Fletcher examined in this study. Thus my results suggest that Fletcher had little or nothing to do with this act. The authorship of these scenes has been controversial; my results indicate that Katherine's final speeches cannot be credited to Shakespeare's collaborator, as some have argued. If this raises difficulties in the interpretation of the play's structure, then these problems cannot be explained away as Fletcher's misunderstanding of Shakespeare's intentions.

Two scenes in *H8* that are usually assigned to Fletcher alone are much more like Shakespeare in terms of function word occurrences. The first is 5.4, the prose scene involving the porter and his man. Here the word rates are unusual for either author, but the scene is far more unlike Fletcher than Shakespeare. Although Fletcher hardly ever wrote prose, the scene has been assigned to him by other scholars because it contains thirteen occurrences of *'em* to none of *them*, and eight occurrences of *ye* to fifteen of *you*. These rates for *ye* and *'em* in one scene are unparalleled in Shakespeare's known work. Assuming the validity of the function word results, a very interesting question arises regarding the copy text: why does a scene by Shakespeare contain linguistic forms that he does not normally use? Revision by Fletcher is one possible explanation.

The second of these results in *H8* is 1.3, which Mincoff calls "the most unmistakably Fletcherian scene in the whole play."[14] The function word evidence here is not as strong as in other scenes assigned to Shakespeare, but it does indicate that the general pattern of use is more like him than Fletcher. Also, the scene contains two occurrences of *there/where*- compounds (*wherewithall* and *thereunto*). These two occurrences in a short scene are unlike any other Fletcher scene in either the control or test sets, and cannot be traced to the sources behind this scene. On the other hand, this scene contains some of the more convincing examples of Fletcher's stylistic traits, including proportions of *'em* and *ye* that are not paralleled in any scenes by Shakespeare in the control set. Again, revision appears to be a possible explanation for the presence of these two types of contradictory evidence.

Inspection of Figure 3 shows that in *H8* the three classifiers left many of the scenes usually assigned to Fletcher unclassified and did not assign many scenes to Fletcher with high probability. It appears that the method may not recognize Fletcher samples with the same certainty as Shakespeare. This may be due to the larger number of Shakespeare samples used to create the classifiers (twenty plays compared to six), or because the most frequent of the markers used are all Shakespeare "plus" words. I do not believe this casts doubts on the assignments of scenes to Shakespeare; the classification results on scenes of known authorship presented earlier are the best indicator of the procedure's accuracy and limitations.

Now that the results of applying this method to the two plays have been presented, a number of advantages of this study of function words should be noted. One of the strengths of my study is the amount of text examined. The classifiers are based on samples comprised of more than 400,000 words of Shakespeare and almost 90,000 words of Fletcher. (For comparison, Mosteller and Wallace[15] used 94,000 words of Hamilton and 114,000 words of Madison in their main study.) Naturally, there are more questions about the integrity of these plays than for the texts in some authorship problems, but the plays I selected were (for the most part) free from any serious textual problems.

The marker words examined are relatively frequent. Of the sixteen variables initially chosen, twelve were used in at least one of the three classifier's sets of markers. These twelve represent about 10 percent of the total word occurrences in both authors. Further work needs to be done in the area of recognizing the effects of context. I relied on the discriminant analysis feature selection process to eliminate any word with serious (or frequent) context dependencies. However, I can give examples where rates for words like *the* and *of* are seriously affected by the subject matter. (In my complete description of this study,[16] the analysis of the results for the disputed plays was accompanied by a close examination of the word occurrences that led to the results.)

Before concluding, it is useful to reexamine the basic approach of this study. The first stages of the analysis of function words were an attempt to answer these questions: Is there a difference in the rate of occurrence of function words in these plays that corresponds to a difference in authorship? If so, how close is this correspondence, and how often does it lead to apparently incorrect decisions about undisputed samples? After finding useful answers to these questions, the next step was the application of the tests to the scenes in the two disputed works.

But how should one interpret the results? When the discriminant analysis method is applied to the word rates from a disputed scene, the "verdict" should perhaps be formulated along these lines:

> The rates for these words in this scene are more similar to the rates found in undisputed scenes written by Author A than those scenes written by Author B.

The only grounds one has for making the jump to the statement:

> Author A wrote this scene

are the results for samples of known authorship that showed that such a conclusion was correct for 96.5 percent of the 365 scenes in the control set and for 85.2 percent of the scenes in the test set (94.8 percent overall). The probabilities produced by the discriminant analysis procedures also provide some indications of the certainty of the decision (and a means of recognizing scenes that the method should leave unassigned). This is important, for as Hoy notes, "With linguistic evidence it is all, finally, a matter of more or less"[17]). In the scene-by-scene analysis of *TNK* and *H8*, one must recognize that the evidence for some scenes was much stronger than for others.

This study has shown that common function words can be studied as internal evidence of authorship, and one should consider how this evidence compares to other forms of internal evidence. This becomes especially important when the results of an analysis of function words do not agree with results based on more traditional forms of evidence. One reason that function words might be a reliable form of internal evidence is that, because of their frequency and lack of prominence, they are presumably less likely to be altered by scribes, printers, editors, or revisers. For the procedures used in this study, this will only be true if alterations in the counts (due to corruption or revision) do not affect the words rates enough to drastically change the probabilities of authorship calculated using discriminant analysis. It should be noted that one or two insertions or deletions of an infrequent marker such as *dare* can produce a large change in the word rate, especially in short scenes. Classification results that appear to be strongly affected by a rate for one infrequent marker are thus less trustworthy than a result due to one or more frequent markers such as *all, the, of,* and *in.* (Again, in the complete description of the study, I examine how the results for some scenes would be affected if small changes were to be made to the counts for one or two words in that scene.)

My result for *Henry VIII* 5.4 probably represents the most serious disagreement between the analysis of function words and other examinations of linguistic evidence. The marker word rates in this scene are much more like those in Shakespeare's control set samples than in Fletcher's but one cannot ignore those occurrences of *ye* and *'em.* If one accepts that my result indicates Shakespearean authorship, one must then explain these very Fletcher-like proportions for the pronoun forms. Either Shakespeare was capable of breaking from his normal practice, or these forms were introduced into the copy by a scribe or by Fletcher as a reviser. Both of these explanations require a serious departure from the assumptions made by most textual scholars.

The nature of the copy text used in printing the play in the 1623 folio is central to reconciling these conflicting results. Most would agree that *Henry VIII* presents a more complex problem than does *The Two Noble Kinsmen.* Hoy has maintained (and my results support his conclusions) that Fletcher revised some scenes in this play that Shakespeare wrote. Their hands do not appear to be so closely intermingled in *TNK.* Neither the goals nor the methods of this study are intended to address new hypotheses regarding the play's copy text. However, the fact that two different forms of linguistic evidence could lead to opposite conclusions if considered on their own suggests that scholars should reevaluate the relation between the copy text of *Henry VIII* and the various internal evidence that it contains.

Such a reexamination would be unnecessary if the conclusions derived from a statistical analysis of function words could be easily dismissed. However, the function word data and the statistical method have been shown to be effective through a rigorous analysis of twenty-four plays by Shakespeare and eight by Fletcher. When applied to scenes of at least five hundred words in these plays, the method correctly assigned almost 95 percent of these to the correct author. Applying this method to *TNK* and *H8* confirms that both plays are collaborations. While the results agree with the generally accepted division between the two playwrights, a number of scenes considered by some to be Fletcher's work have a function word vocabulary much more like Shakespeare's. During the study other useful linguistic evidence was identified: the rate of contraction of *is,* and the use of *there/where-* compounds. In several instances, this evidence supports the function word results.

Notes

1. Thomas B. Horton, *The Effectiveness of the Stylometry of Function Words in Discriminating between Shakespeare and Fletcher.* Ph.D. diss., University of Edinburgh, 1987.

2. S. Schoenbaum, *Internal Evidence and Elizabethan Dramatic Authorship: An Essay in Literary History and Method* (London: Edward Arnold, 1966).

3. David Tallentire, "Confirming Intuitions about Style, Using Concordances," in *The Computer in Literary and Linguistic Studies,* ed. Alan Jones and R. F. Churchhouse, 309–28 (Cardiff: University of Wales Press, 1976).

4. Frederick Mosteller and David L. Wallace, *Applied Bayesian and Classical Inference: The Case of the Federalist Papers* (New York: Springer-Verlag, 1984; 2d ed. of *Inference and Disputed Authorship: The Federalist* (Reading, Mass.: Addison-Wesley, 1964).

5. D. J. Hand, *Discrimination and Classification* (Chichester: John Wiley & Sons, 1981).

6. A. C. Patridge. *Orthography in Shakespeare and Elizabethan Drama: A Study of Colloquial Contractions, Elision, Prosody and Punctuation* (London: Edward Arnold, 1964).

7. Barron Brainerd, "Pronouns and Genre in Shakespeare's Drama," in *Computers and the Humanities* 13 (1979): 3–16.

8. John Fletcher and William Shakespeare, *The Two Noble Kinsman,* in *Regents Renaissance Drama Series,* ed. G. R. Proudfoot (London: Edward Arnold, 1970).

9. Cyrus Hoy, "The Shares of Fletcher and his Collaborators in the Beaumont and Fletcher Canon (VII)," in *Studies in Bibliography* 15 (1962): 71–90.

10. Ibid., 70.

11. Ibid., 89.

12. William Shakespeare, *King Henry VII,* in *The Arden Shakespeare,* 3d ed., ed. R. A. Foakes (London: Methuen, 1957).

13. Hoy, "Shares," 79–81.

14. Marco Mincoff, "*Henry VIII* and Fletcher," *Shakespeare Quarterly* 12 (1961): 239-60.

15. Mosteller and Wallace, *Applied Bayesian.*

16. Horton, *Effectiveness,* 298–307; 316–29.

REVIEWS

The Three-Text Hamlet: Parallel Texts of the First and Second Quartos and First Folio. Edited by Paul Bertram and Bernice W. Kliman. New York: AMS Press, 1991.

Reviewer: Paul Werstine

Paul Bertram and Bernice Kliman have given us a big and valuable book with more *Hamlet* in it than can be found anywhere else. To open this book is to be confronted by four columns of modern typography. (1) On the far left is a diplomatic reprint of the First Quarto (Q1, 1603), long called a "bad quarto" because its text often is gibberish. (2) Next to it is a text of the Second Quarto (Q2, 1604–05), a much longer and far more intelligible version that is the basis of most modern editions. (3) Next is a text of the Folio (F, 1623), a somewhat shorter version than the Second Quarto, but one which contains passages not in the Second Quarto, passages familiar to most readers because editors add them to modern texts based on the Second Quarto. (4) Finally, the fourth column is entitled "Q1 Transpositions." This helpful add-on to the parallel texts is a response to the peculiar structure of Q1, in which some passages, most notably the "To be or not to be" soliloquy and the so-called "Nunnery" scene, appear in quite different places than in Q2 and F. In the "Q1 Transpositions" column, Bertram and Kliman print the Q1 passages a second time, opposite their counterparts in Q2 and F. For this book's wonderful accuracy in reproducing all these texts, for sheer ease of use, and for (relative) inexpensiveness, Shakespeareans are sure to be most grateful to the editors.

With practical utility as a primary consideration in the presentation of the texts, Bertram and Kliman seem to have taken us beyond a stage in the reception of early printed texts that has marked the last decade or so in Shakespearean studies. I am thinking of those who will cite Shakespeare only in photoquotes of the early printed texts; or who protest that Shakespeare should be read *only* in (often expensive) facsimiles of the early printings; or who announce solemnly that they have discovered in looking at these early printings that every version printed is the work of Shakespeare, and, they *know* Shakespeare never intended that any of these versions be combined either on stage or in print. There are those, too, who direct Shakespeare so that every punctuation mark inserted by a compositor in an early text is scrupulously marked in performance. Because Bertram and Kliman make no bones about their editorial mediation in their reproduction of the (always already mediated) early *Hamlet* texts, their work holds out no attraction for readers to treat it as a fetish. Rather, in its serviceable layout and typography, the book offers us a chance to study these early versions of *Hamlet* that so steadfastly resist theories of their origins, but that continue to intrigue readers with their differences and likenesses.

The Oldcastle Controversy: Sir John Oldcastle, Part I and The Famous Victories of Henry V. Edited by Peter Corbin and Douglas Sedge. Manchester: Manchester University Press, 1991.

Reviewer: Roslyn L. Knutson

A few scholars have been able to eke controversy out of the Oldcastle issue, but Peter Corbin and Douglas Sedge are not among them. Gary Taylor stirs interest by the decision to restore the name of Oldcastle to the character of Sir John in *1 Henry IV.* His arguments for the change, paired with arguments against it by David Bevington, define the debate.[1] Richard Dutton stirs interest by arguing that Edmund Tilney allowed the Oldcastle name for Sir John to pass uncensored, "knowing full well how it would be received," because he was aligned with the Hunsdon faction at Court.[2] R. J. Fehrenbach offers Dutton evidence of Tilney's being at odds with the Lord Cobham who became Lord Chamberlain in August 1596.[3] At the lunatic fringe, articles in the *Edward de Vere Newsletter* argue that the Earl at Oxford wrote *Sir John Oldcastle,* and Mark Dominik asserts that

Shakespeare had a hand in the text.[4] I myself attempt to stir interest by suggesting that the Chamberlain's men placated the Cobham faction not only by altering Oldcastle to Falstaff but also by acquiring a play that celebrated their ancestor as a religious hero; further, I claim that this new *Sir John Oldcastle* was the offering performed in March 1600 for *audiencier* Verreyken.[5] I would go further and claim that it was the play staged by the King's men in 1631 and 1639.

Despite their title, Corbin and Sedge treat the Oldcastle issue as if it were long since settled. Their format is like a Norton Critical Edition without the scholarly essays: an introduction, the texts of *I Sir John Oldcastle* and *The Famous Victories of Henry V*; and four appendices. In the first section of the introduction, "Oldcastle: the Man and the Legend," they provide a biography, *DNB*-like but shorter, in which they claim that Oldcastle was the subject of "contrasting hagiographic traditions" in the sixteenth century. In appendices, they document one of the traditions, that of Lollard martyr, with excerpts from John Bale's *A brefe chronycle concernynge the examinacyon and death of . . . Syr J. Oldecastell, the Lorde Cobham* (1544), John Foxe's *Acts and Monuments* (1583), and John Weever's *The Mirror of Martyrs* (1601). In a fourth appendix, they provide excerpts from Holinshed's *Chronicles* (1587), which is by their description a "balanced" and "objective weighing of the evidence" (8).

But no excerpts provide the sixteenth-century arguments that Oldcastle was a traitor and a heretic. Such material does exist. Corbin and Sedge cite a treatise by the Catholic polemicist Robert Parsons and Archbishop Arundel's account of Oldcastle's trial is cited in the *DNB*. The editors might have provided excerpts from histories by Robert Fabyan, Edward Hall, Polydore Vergil, Thomas Walsingham, and others who, according to Gary Taylor, were despised by martyrologists such as Foxe.[6] For the voices of Oldcastle's accusers, there is only an excerpt from Foxe in which he argues against the interpretation of events by Nicholas Harpsfield, alias Alanus Copus. For the Harpsfield polemic itself, Corbin and Sedge direct readers in a footnote to "See . . . *Dialogi Sex* (1566). But isn't the point of a volume like this one to supply sources that are not readily available? I can read Holinshed and Foxe at the UALR library, but I cannot read Parsons and his partisans without a trip to the Folger.

In two sections of theater history ("The Oldcastle Controversy" and "Oldcastle in the Seventeenth Century"), Corbin and Sedge repeat the traditional interpretation of the commercial and political context of *Sir John Oldcastle*. It is clear that they have not reconsidered any of the issues. For example, they drone that the "Oldcastle project . . . was obviously an answer to Shakespeare's *1 & 2 Henry IV*" and as such "appears to have cashed in on a topical controversy" (9). No one argues the connection with Shakespeare's plays, but the timing is worth at least a question. In what sense was the Oldcastle issue "topical" in October 1599? Textual scholars seem to agree that the name change in *1H4* from Oldcastle to Falstaff occurred during the composition of *2H4* and *Wiv.*, that is, early in 1597. As for "cashing in on a topical issue," the touchstone is the coincidence of *Poetaster* and *Satiromastix*, which were written and played within weeks of each other. In comparison, the debut of the two-part *Sir John Oldcastle* was at best a belated response to stage runs of Shakespeare's plays.

And what of the politics behind the *Oldcastle* plays? The Lord Cobham who was Lord Chamberlain in 1596–97 and who putatively first took offense at the treatment of the family name died in March of 1597. The pressure to dramatize the martyrdom of Oldcastle must therefore have come from his son and/or other surviving relatives. By citing the doctoral thesis of David McKeen (1964), Corbin and Sedge hint that there is more to the Cobhams' interest in 1596–99 but they do not pursue the issue (why do they cite the thesis and not the book published from it in 1986?). There is more of the Cobham narrative in "William Shakespeare, Richard James, and the House of Cobham" by Gary Taylor,[7] but Corbin and Sedge do not appear to have consulted this article. Rather, their source on court power structures is R. B. Sharpe's thesis of pro- and anti-Essex factions that seemed reductive even in 1935. Thus they provide very little fresh and no new information on the historical political context.

Further, they make nothing of the bland treatment of Oldcastle himself in part one of *Sir John Oldcastle*. I would want more hagiography for my expenditure of influence if I were an offended Cobham. The orthodox claim, and Corbin and Sedge make it too, is that the second part "no doubt . . . placed considerable dramatic weight on the nature of Oldcastle's martyrdom" (20). But no one including Corbin and Sedge considers some curiosities of this assertion. Why, for example, was this part not published with part one, with which it was registered in August 1600? I do not assume that part one was the more popular and therefore more publishable because I do not believe that unpublished plays were necessarily more unpopular than published ones. Yet I am intrigued by the vaunted commercial appeal of these plays. Granting that the dramatists were motivated initially by the Cobhams, I wonder if something else might have been responsible for the success of the plays in performance. An obvious possibility is the ending of part two, in which Oldcastle might have been "hanged in a chain by the middle, and after consumed with fire, the gallows and all" (Holinshed).[8] A rival to the flaying of Sisamnes and the skewering of Edward II, such a scene of onstage violence is more likely to have generated an audience at the Rose in the winter of 1599–1600 than public empathy with the Cobhams' injured pride. It is certainly more likely to have generated an audience for the play in 1602. Corbin and Sedge assume that Thomas Dekker was paid for additions to both plays in 1602 (they say 40s; he got 50s.). If so, I will wager that it was not the lackluster figure of Oldcastle in the first part but his horrific martyrdom in the second that justified the revival.

As for new editions of the texts of *Oldcastle* and *The Famous Victories,* I do not see the need. For accessibility, the latter is included in Bullough's *Narrative and Dramatic Sources of Shakespeare* (4); the former is available in facsimile (Tudor Facsimile Texts and Malone Society Reprints) and modern editions (Brooke, Rittenhouse). In the classroom, I need a cheap paperback. For scholarly work, I will use the quarto of each play in *The Microbook Library of English Literature.* I have compared one scene from *Oldcastle* in the Revels Companion edition with Rittenhouse's edition, and I think Corbin and Sedge are more indebted to Rittenhouse than they acknowledge. Furthermore, given their own editorial matter and presumed audience, they provide unnecessary notes. The most obvious is the one on "valiant martyr" (Prologue, 1.9), in which readers are directed to the introduction after being instructed that "Oldcastle was regarded as a martyr for the Protestant faith and, as such, was celebrated in Foxe's *Book of Martyrs.*" Of the texts in the appendices, Weever's *The Mirror of Martyrs* is the only source without a modern edition (why it was not included in Honigmann's *John Weever* for the Revels Companion Library in 1987?).

"The whole business seems trivial at this remove," says Richard Dutton of the Cobham family's complaints, and the editors of *The Oldcastle Controversy* give us no reason to think the business is not dead as well. What may be controversial—if only in faculty lounges—is how such a book got published. As theater history it is old-fashioned to the point of perversity. As stage history, it ignores the theatrical worth of the *Oldcastle* plays and *Famous Victories;* indeed, Corbin and Sedge barely conceal the tired old agenda of interest in the plays only because of their relation to Shakespeare's. The historicists have made the issue of the stage as an instrument of power politics newly controversial, but Corbin and Sedge seem unaware of that line of argument. Likewise they seem unaware of reception studies, such as the argument that both plays reach out to a diverse audience through a mix of hegemonic and subversive elements.[9] The Revels Companion Library series purports to "provide a fuller context for the plays of the period by offering new collections of documentary evidence on Elizabethan theatrical conditions and on the performance of plays during that period and later" and "to offer modern critical interpretation" (vii). This volume does not fulfill these aims.

Notes

1. Taylor, "The Fortunes of Oldcastle," *Shakespeare Survey* 38 (1985): 85–100; Bevington, *Henry IV, Part 1* (Oxford: Oxford University Press, 1987), 108–10.

2. *Mastering the Revels* (Iowa City: University of Iowa Press, 1991), 102–6, esp. 104.

3. "When Lord Cobham and Edmund Tilney 'were att odds,'" *Shakespeare Studies* 18 (1986): 87–101.

4. Numbers 12 (February), 14 (April), 15 (May), 16 (June), and 17 (July) of the newsletter in 1990 contain articles on de Vere's authorship of *Sir John Oldcastle;* Dominik's book is *A Shakespearean Anomaly: Shakespeare's Hand in* Sir John Oldcastle (Beaverton, Ore.: Alioth Press, 1991).

5. *The Repertory of Shakespeare's Company, 1594–1613* (Fayetteville: University of Arkansas Press, 1991), 95–97.

6. Taylor, "Fortunes," 95.

7. *Review of English Studies,* n.s. 38 (1987): 334–54.

8. Taylor points out that Shakespeare in a grim joke "envisages Oldcastle as 'a rosted Manningtre Oxe'" ("Fortunes," 95).

9. Larry Champion, *"The Noise of Threatening Drum"* (Newark: University of Delaware Press, 1991).

The Making of the National Poet: Shakespeare, Adaptation and Authorship, 1660–1769. By Michael Dobson. Oxford: Clarendon Press, 1992.

Shakespeare Verbatim: The Reproduction of Authenticity and the 1790 Apparatus. By Margreta de Grazia. Oxford: Clarendon Press, 1991.

Reviewer: Maurice Charney

Both of these books deal with Shakespeare's reputation in the eighteenth century, or, rather, with the postmodern topic of the construction of Shakespeare in the Enlightenment. Dobson discusses theatrical history up to the Stratford Shakespeare Jubilee of Garrick in 1769, whereas de Grazia concentrates on Edmond Malone's edition of Shakespeare in ten volumes in 1790. De Grazia, however, relies on the history of Shakespeare editing in the eighteenth century and both books use similar Foucauldian assumptions. Dobson refers freely to de Grazia's book, which preceded his by one year.

The Making of the National Poet is an engaging theatrical history of Shakespeare on the stage from the Restoration through three-fourths of the eighteenth century. Its strength lies in its linking Shakespeare with contemporary political ideas. Thus the image of Shakespeare and the kinds of Shakespearean adaptations being presented in the theater keep being accommodated to popular taste, which in itself expresses dominant mores and desiderata.

Dobson distinguishes four different periods during which the conception of Shakespeare changed significantly. From 1660–78, Shakespeare was revised to conform with the norms of Fletcherian romance. We tend to forget that well into the eighteenth century Jonson and Fletcher were much more popular dramatists than Shakespeare, who was eminently the exemplar of Nature (rather than Art) and therefore needed to be changed considerably to suit a more refined age. Romantic tragicomedy in the mode of Fletcher was seen to be a royalist literary genre par excellence, and the free revisions of Shakespeare sought to undo the existence of the Puritan revolution and the Interregnum. In other words, Shakespeare was recreated as a late Jacobean and Caroline dramatist. In this vein, Shadwell boasts that his *The History of Timon of Athens, the Man-Hater* (1678) took Shakespeare's raw material and "made it into a Play" (33, n.44). Shakespeare's plays were also adapted to show off the qualities of notorious Restoration actresses.

In a second phase from 1678 to 1688, Shakespeare was used to express political opinions about the Exclusion Crisis (which sought to exclude James, the Catholic brother of Charles II, from the throne). Edward Ravenscroft's *Titus Andronicus* (1678) was presented as a satire on Titus Oates and the Whigs, and Dryden's version of *Troilus and Cressida* (1679) was understood to be a royalist polemic. In the sentimental "she-tragedy" that was then developing, Thomas Otway was imagined "as a slightly inferior version of Shakespeare" (93).

The most important phase in the making of the national poet occurs in the years 1688–1735. This was the period during which Shakespeare was "respectabilized," purged of low elements in order to be canonized as a decorous Enlightenment author. Shakespeare-as-author emerges, often as a ghostly presenter of his own plays, and the bard and bardolatry are solidly established. This situation creates a paradox to which Dobson devotes considerable attention: namely, the important connection of adaptation and canonization. The two seemingly contradictory impulses are really complementary aspects of the same process:

> to present Shakespeare's plays in forms that, free of all transgressive blemishes, display "such Thoughts as we could justly attribute to Shakespeare" and to confirm and promulgate a suitably elevated "Idea of the Man." (130)

Shakespeare, the Poet of Nature, is "corrected retrospectively" (124). The movement is away from the theater to print culture, with Shakespeare as a text to be read rather than performed. The crowning of Shakespeare as a classic author is clearly a move against his connection with popular culture.

The period 1735–69 consolidates Shakespeare's exalted status as the national poet, symbolized by the statue of Shakespeare by Peter Scheemakers erected in Westminister Abbey in 1741. Dobson offers an extended, original account of the Shakespeare Ladies' Club, who were instrumental in the erection of this statue. Ladies of quality and ladies of feeling (like Richardson's Pamela) have a natural affinity with the refined sensibility of Shakespeare, who promotes decency and inspires virtue. David Garrick is the epitome of Enlightenment values. Although he was the definitive Hamlet of his time and officially idolized Shakespeare, in his own adaptation of *Hamlet* he declares: "I had sworn I would not leave the Stage until I had rescued that noble play from all the rubbish of the 5th act" (172).

Dobson's account is vivacious and well informed, and I think he effectively demonstrates how much Shakespeare is a product of Restoration and Enlightenment thinking. Margreta de Grazia's book, *Shakespeare Verbatim*, goes over some of the same ground as Dobson, but it concentrates on the editing of Shakespeare in the eighteenth century and especially on the new perspective on Shakespeare in Edmond Malone's edition of 1790 and related writings. In other words, de Grazia's scope is the Enlightenment and its aftermath. Her book makes more important use of literary theory than Dobson's, and it develops a much more original, postmodernist thesis about the new construction of Shakespeare by Malone.

"Authenticity" is the key word for all of Malone's projects, and it's a pity that de Grazia calls her book *Shakespeare Verbatim*, since "verbatim" is not an exact synonym of "authentic." De Grazia ranges widely on the topic of editing Shakespeare and its underlying assumptions. Her approach is not chronological, which creates a useful analytic account of the topics that interest her. Chapters 2 to 5, for example, are called "Authenticating Shakespeare's Text, Life, and Likeness," "Situating Shakespeare in an Historical Period," "Individuating Shakespeare's Experience: Biography, Chronology, and the Sonnets," and "Shakespeare's Entitlement: Literary Property and Discursive Enclosure," respectively.

The most surprising chapter is the third, where we learn that Malone advised the American painter, John Singleton Copley, on the canvas, *Charles I Demanding in the House of Commons the Five Impeached Members*. Malone supplied Copley with written and pictorial sources for the painting, and when it was first exhibited at the Royal Academy in 1795 the painting was accompanied by a brochure documenting the sources of its major portraits. Copley was an artist-antiquarian who did research on his subject in order to represent it with exacting fidelity to minute historical details. This was precisely Malone's attitude to Shakespeare, which separates him radically from earlier eighteenth-century editors, such as Rowe, Pope, Capell, and Johnson.

Editing for Malone depended at every stage on documents. The editor's threefold object was "to support and establish what Shakespeare wrote, to illustrate his phraseology by comparison with his contemporaries, and to explain his fugitive allusions to customs long since disused and forgotten" (98). Malone's edition in 1790 (expanded with the help of James Boswell, the younger, in the 1821 variorum) preserves the documents that Malone unearthed. It presents an invaluable "Historical Account of the English Stage," first published in 1780. Malone's voluminous exploration (500 pages) of forged documents in 1795, *An Inquiry into the Authenticity of Certain Miscellaneous Papers and Legal Instruments,* uses the same kind of documentary evidence to expose Ireland's forgeries. Malone's footnotes to Shakespeare's text are dedicated to exploring the language and the customs of Shakespeare's time; in other words, they attempt some sort of historical recreation of the Elizabethan period. Malone attempts to undo the eighteenth-century refinement of Shakespeare's vulgarity, who, after all, wrote in a barbarous age. His objective was to fix Shakespeare's works in their final, authentic form.

De Grazia begins with a chapter on the 1623 Folio and the Modern Standard Edition in order to show how much the assumptions of the present-day editing of Shakespeare derive from Malone. His editorial practice individuated Shakespeare in the sense that great attention was devoted to finding out what Shakespeare as author intended in a certain passage, what he thought, or, by historical research, knowing so much about Shakespeare and his times that one could enter into his mind and say what he probably meant. In this sense, Shakespeare's own works could be used intertextually to explicate each other. Malone was the first editor to publish the 1609 Quarto of Shakespeare's Sonnets in an edition of his works (rather than the defective 1640 collection). He made important use of the Sonnets for biographical purposes, which leads de Grazia to remark shrewdly: "Like the factual particulars that prompted them, these inner feelings or experiences further sequestered Shakespeare from the reader, ensconcing him in an introspective space of his own" (152). Shakespeare is now "the engaged poet who observed himself" (159). Malone's extensive "Life of Shakespeare" (525 pages with a 175-page appendix) follows in the same spirit, as well as his important and original chronology, "An Attempt to Ascertain the Order in which The Plays of Shakspeare Were Written." Malone's attempt to identify topical references in the plays acted to record "Shakespeare's thoughts and feelings as stimulated by contemporary events" (143).

I am just touching on some of the rich detail in de Grazia's book, which makes an overwhelming case for how different Malone's assumptions were from earlier eighteenth-century editors. The last chapter, "Shakespeare's Entitlement," situates Malone in Enlightenment publishing history, especially the perpetual copyright that the Tonson's established for Shakespeare's works. Malone was, in fact, the first major eighteenth-century edition of Shakespeare to which the name of Tonson was not associated. Malone's was definitely not "House Shakespeare."

Aside from its formidable scholarship, there is a pleasing eccentricity in *Shakespeare Verbatim*. De Grazia has a certain nostalgic appreciation of the legendary, transgressive Shakespeare that Malone banished from his pages. Malone's Shakespeare, supported by abundant selected documents, is very much an Enlightenment gentleman, of whom the Shakespeare Ladies' Club would approve. No poaching, no tending to horses outside the Elizabethan theaters, no grand speeches every time he (or his father, the whittawer) killed a calf. There is a fleeting sense in this book of The Shakespeare We Have Lost, as if Malone, alas, abolishes all the fictions and fantasies of Shakespeare we delight to linger on. Paradoxically, de Grazia produces a work of scholarship that Malone himself would have been proud of. It would be very difficult for her to argue herself— Foucault and Barthes notwithstanding—out of that predicament.

Shakespeare and the Politics of Protestant England. By Donna B. Hamilton. Lexington: The University Press of Kentucky, 1992.

Reviewer: Margaret Loftus Ranald

With this complex, impressively researched, accessively written, and detailed study Donna Hamilton stakes out new territory "in situating some of Shakespeare's plays within the context of church-state politics" (ix), reaching beyond a mere reconstruction of power relations in terms of Shakespeare's representation of the monarch, and demonstrating the playwright's familiarity with religio-political issues, giving voice to the marginalized through the rhetorical aegis of a "discursive field [of church-state controversy] that has all but disappeared from the view of modern audiences" (192). Therefore she scrutinizes political rather than doctrinal controversies among nonconformists and conservatives within the established church, together with the problematics of Roman Catholics hoping for relief under James.

In the past such material has been applied in "rediscovering" Shakespeare's own personal religious beliefs, an approach Hamilton cautiously and prudently avoids as irrelevant to her purpose (xiii). Instead, she portrays Shakespeare as an active and reactive member of English society with ties to a specific group of patrons at a given time and place. Her aim is to rehistoricize him by recreating the circumstances and conflicts of church-state relations as understood by Shakespeare and his patrons in an attempt to throw some new light on the playwright and his thinking, not the full story, to be sure, but adding further details to our "partial narrative" (ii) of the playwright and his circle.

Certainly this deliberately logocentric book does not imply that Shakespeare adopted all the political opinions of his patrons, but rather that he positions himself along their lines in matters of church-state controversies and demonstrates a great interest in Protestantism. Six exemplary plays are chosen for their portrayal of the way in which the individual English person was affected by governmental policies, emphasizing "the right to privacy" and acknowledging the existence of creative, but not disloyal dissent (192).

Adducing a wealth of documentation, Hamilton concludes that *King John, The Comedy of Errors, Measure for Measure, Twelfth Night, Cymbeline*, and *Henry VIII* are reactively politico-religious, frequently critical of official, and sometimes even patronal policies. She also discusses the political insecurities felt by courtiers during the transfer from Tudor to Stuart dynasties. That religious disputes manifested themselves in Shakespearean drama has, of course, been noted peripherally in other studies of *King John, Henry VIII*, and to a lesser extent, *Twelfth Night*, but that *The Comedy of Errors* and *Cymbeline* may also be quite so deeply grounded in the polemical literature of current church-state conflicts is indeed new.

A useful introductory chapter, "The Elme and the Vine," studies the Shakespearean politico-religious milieu in its identification of major problems resulting from the break with Rome, emphasizing monarchical power and ecclesiastical organization, notably where the episcopal hierarchy was concerned. In fact, with the establishment of the ecclesiastical High Commission, demanding submission to the Thirty-nine Articles, enforced by censorship of dissentient documents, and more personally, by the oath *ex officio mero* (which in effect required self-incrimination) the English Church substituted one form of repression for another.

Thus trial, self-incrimination, imprisonment, and censorship of printed matter remained in effect throughout the closing years of Elizabeth's reign, with conformist propaganda maintaining politico-religious orthodoxy. By 1589 the playing of divinity onstage was prohibited and further control was imposed by the 1599 outlawing of formal satire. Ideologically conservative texts by Foxe, John Jewel and their ilk were also being reprinted, along with crypto-nonconformist texts like Thomas Wilson's *Arte of Rhetorique* and George Puttenham's *Arte of English Poesie*, an occurrence which may help situate the rhetorical comedy of Shakespeare's own earlier plays.

Among Shakespeare's patronage group Hamilton identifies a certain fluidity of thought "opposing absolutist tendencies" and supporting "the liberties of the subject" (xii), possibly in the insecure light of an inevitable change of monarch. She sees Southampton as the key, with connections reaching back to the Sidney-Leicester nexus, and forward into the Essex and Pembroke alliance, all oppositionist and nonconformist groups. Pembroke proved a shrewd survivor, avoiding the taint of rebellion and later serving with Southampton on the commission for union. Given that Shakespeare's Pembroke connection continued, even posthumously in the dedication of the First Folio, it is reasonable to assume that the playwright expressed, though not necessarily espoused, his patron's politico-religious views concerning "privacy and property, and authority and obedience" which he dramatized for the theater (29). Shakespeare's situation certainly became more complicated under James VI and I when that monarch indicated support of the Essex faction by releasing Southampton, and then adopted the Lord Chamberlain's Men as his own.

In this chapter Hamilton cites James's unsuccessful attempt in his Hampton Court meeting of 14–16 January 1604 to achieve peace between conformists and the Puritans who had supported his succession.This foundered on James's absolutist position that refusal to subscribe to the odious *ex officio* oath constituted an attack on his authority. Thus in February 1604 a new prayer book was issued, the *Constitutions and Canons Ecclesiastical* were promulgated, and in January 1605, nonconformists began to be deprived of their livings. Further collision between authority and the rights of individual subjects, this time of Catholics, occurred after the Gunpowder Plot of 1605. Again, after the assassination of Henri IV of France (1610) a royal proclamation further restricted the activities of Catholics, banishing their clergy and requiring that everyone over the age of eighteen take the oath of allegiance, with loss of property the penalty for refusing twice.

The six chosen plays demonstrate the effect of these governmental policies on the individual: notably "the right to privacy" and acknowledgement of the existence of creative, loyal dissent (King John), while The Comedy of Errors adds the locking out of a centrist character who insists upon freedom of speech. Twelfth Night treats a closed society in which competition for place is "strictly controlled" and the self-righteous Malvolio is marginalized. Measure for Measure returns to the right to privacy and "individual autonomy" and their institutional suppression, while Cymbeline and Henry VIII leave the "audience with an image of the needs and virtues of those who are being negatively affected by policies of intolerance and exclusion" (193). In these last two plays Belarius represents exemplary justification for toleration, while Katherine, epitomizing conscience and patience, dies in a state of grace, signified by a theophany.

In "King John: The Church, the Courts, and the Law," Hamilton identifies an attack on conformity, beginning with questions of property and its inheritance. Even more important is the nonconformist attitude toward legal privileging of private conversation, in opposition to the ex officio oath. Hence the opening scene is read as a treatment of "differing attitudes . . . concerning interrrogation, self-accusation, and privacy" (38). Similarly, the law of marriage is invoked to uphold the bastard's inheritance of his putative father's land.

Most important here are Shakespeare's alterations to his source play, The Troublesome Raigne, to transform the debate between jure humano and jure divino into a struggle between papal authority and invocation of divine authority. Seemingly minor changes are interpreted as subtly subversive of the official Elizabethan stance on resistance. Thus, in its questioning (and patriotic) subjects King John champions individual freedom of conscience— epitomized by the Bastard's decision to relinquish his property rights to assume the prerogatives of his royal bar sinister.

Hamilton's approach is, I suggest, most successful in "The Comedy of Errors: The Parody of Errors and Heresies," particularly in

its application to church-state controversies. Further, the circumstances of one of its major performances at Gray's Inn indicate an
audience sensitive to its "ecclesiastical contexts" (59). In fact the
very word "errors" in the title signifies more than merely mistaken
identity, but competing doctrinal stances.

"Domestic, marital, and filial relationships are at issue" (61)
throughout, with St. Paul's specific equation of marriage and the
human equivalent of Christ's divine relationship to the church a
transparent metaphor for hierarchy. Thus the debates between
Adriana and Luciana concerning the place and powers of husbands
and wives, with the apparent infidelity of her Antipholus, are interpreted as evoking the relationship of nonconformists to the organi-
zational mode of the Established Church. More tenuous is the
suggestion that the tolerance and understanding advocated by Luciana may also be aimed at enlightening the Queen herself, who
would (or so it was believed) eventually come to accept the Puritan
position. But did she know about this play? Performance records
would help here. However, Hamilton is enlightening in resituating
the Ephesian setting by suggesting that its complex missionary in-
ternecine ecclesiastical turmoil is in "biblical resonance" (66) with
the episcopal and presbyterian struggles over church government
in late-sixteenth-century England.

Parody and irony carry over into the literal treatment of madness
and possession with their rhetorical equivalents in the prose of
church officials who so designated their nonconformist and Marti-
nist enemies. Adriana, on the literal level, believes that her husband
is indeed diabolically possessed and suggests exorcism, while on
a second level she can be interpreted as the conformist church
attacking her opposition. The solution is found by the Abbess, who
offers reconciliation—or, as Hamilton puts it "a broad, all-inclusive
concept of the true universal, Catholic church" (80).

Finally she turns to the gold chain and the shipwreck. In this
reading the gold chain stands for salvation, a suggestion ratified by
references to numerous Puritan, conformist, and Catholic commen-
taries. The shipwreck is then interpreted as the cause of familial
(religious) separation, but at the end all are integrated in the *kom-
moi* of classical comedy, here also interpreted as a eucharistic rec-
onciliatory meal. This reading is highly ingenious, and given a
Gray's Inn performance, it possesses a singular plausibility, though
for the popular audience these arcane references must have passed
unnoticed. For them the traditional knockabout farce of Plautine
comedy would presumably have sufficed.

In her chapter "*Twelfth Night*: The Errors of Exorcism," Hamilton asserts the equation of the play's linguistic idiom with the "lexicon of church politics" (86), suggesting that Olivia's reclusiveness echoes that of the Virgin Queen herself. In Malvolio's "exorcism" she also sees an echo of the case of John Darrell, a Puritan exorcist "imprisoned from 1598 until his presumed death in 1602" (87). This, of course leads her to reflect on Shakespeare's treatment of the Puritan in *Twelfth Night* and the oppression of those in real life who challenged conformity. Thus, if Malvolio is a sanctimonious caricature drawn from anti-Puritan propaganda, it follows that Sir Toby and his tricks "demystify official policy and practice in regard to nonconformists" (94). They, too, are caricatures—so that the play satirizes Puritans and conformists while also demonstrating and criticizing oppressive tactics, most particularly in the matter of exorcism, here shown "as the playacting that the authorities undertake to persecute the Puritan" (99), with Malvolio's vengeful departure a parody of Christ's forgiveness.

Throughout the play, she perceives Shakespeare offering "a stabilizing orthodox context for his evaluation of church officials within the church" (109), showing that scapegoating and exclusion are inimical to true Christianity. However, the conclusion is unresolved because the marriage of Viola and Orsino has not yet occurred. It awaits her putting on a new garment, that of her true self, the godly garment of Christ's church. The strangely melancholic conclusion may also have politico-religious significance if one considers Olivia as analogous to the reclusive Queen, moving toward death, with unresolved aspects of her reign left for Time to untangle.

Chapter 5, "*Measure for Measure*: The Transition to Stuart Rule," is, as its title promises, more concerned with background material than interpretation. Substitution is an important aspect here. In displacing the ruler, the "precise" Angelo raises the issue of James's ability to act as head of the English church. The "system could go awry" (114) if either the episcopacy were to dominate the monarch, or the ruler were to use oppressive law against his subjects—as the literal-minded Angelo does. In this reading, the final act shows the ruler once again taking control and dispensing justice in moderate form—signifying a hope that James would adopt a centrist position with emphasis on the rights of the subject.

Thus Hamilton argues that *Measure for Measure* restates the same views that Shakespeare articulated in *King John*, concerning the right to privacy, and also the centrist view that called for inclusion within society of those who held unpopular views. Certainly James did achieve a Protestant consensus in his reign—largely because all were united against a common enemy, the Church of Rome, while the jurisdictional conflict was fought in the courts.

In "*Cymbeline*: The Oath of Allegiance and the English Catholic," Hamilton interprets the Imogen plot as the conflict between true and false churches with Shakespeare turning his attention "to a defence of the status quo," emphasizing the act of allegiance, and adopting "the official protestant position" (129). Thus she interprets the rock and air of act 5 as Imogen, the indestructible, indivisible true church. The Queen Mother then equates with the Whore of Babylon, attempting to subvert Cymbeline the monarch, with Cloten as the deceitful, disguised Roman church, whose decapitation signifies his total defeat. But the awakened Imogen mistakes him for her beloved, momentarily representing the church in error—an important nod in the direction of those Protestants who allowed themselves to criticize the true church.

In this context Belarius is the Catholic who retains his allegiance to the king and realm, a figure for whom Shakespeare has sympathy, despite his lapse of loyalty. The real Roman Antichrist, of course, is easily defeated, for he is Iachimo "a slight thing of Italy" (5.4.64), who cannot himself subvert Imogen as true church, but whose accusations are sometimes believed.

Hamilton then raises the central issue of tribute and national autonomy, which she relates to the central Protestant issue of the relationship between spiritual and temporal power, or between obligations to Caesar and to God. In other words, did kingly power come directly from God (as Catholics believed), or derive from the centrist position that the king's power derived from God, but that the people had designated the identity of the sovereign who exercised it—in a kind of social contract? Patriotically, Shakespeare seems to support this centrist position in *Cymbeline* by calling on all subjects to support the king in face of foreign attack. Thus the Jovian theophany vouchsafed to Posthumous is full of Jacobean iconography. The true church is restored in Posthumous's reconciliation to Imogen, and true succession continued through the image of the cedars of Lebanon, while the Roman eagle looks ahead to England's future imperialism.

In her final chapter, *Henry VIII* and its relationship to "The Protestant-Catholic Court in 1613," she suggests that Shakespeare and Fletcher apply Henry's struggle against an "impure religion" (164) to contemporary "secular court and privy council politics," particularly to the Howard faction and its Catholic members, analogizing them with the values of Wolsey and his followers in the play. She believes that Shakespeare criticizes Jacobean court politics by means of an attack on this group which could in fact be accused of disloyalty. Thus Shakespeare makes unusual selection of details in his treatment of Henry VIII, particularly in his emphasis on court cabals. The rhetoric of "conscience and private conference, two idioms associated with evangelical Protestantism, clerical Puritanism and reform" (182) are seen as crucial to understanding the central ironies of the play.

Donna Hamilton has performed a valuable service in resurrecting and analyzing these contextual historical conflicts, particularly in such lucid prose. Nonetheless I find myself asking how it all played. Was a popular audience capable of comprehending such complex religious arguments or equations, or was the play's entertainment value sufficient? Also, her argument makes Shakespeare much more the coterie dramatist than new historicists have been willing to concede, since the topics he dramatizes were of more importance to the aristocratic and powerful than the exploited and powerless.

Judicious, well documented, and with a welcome absence of jargon, this ingenious, information-packed study supplies further pieces of the Elizabethan-Jacobean jigsaw puzzle. The book itself is well produced, with very few typographical errors and an excellent bibliography, though a couple of times the index failed me. Although the subtlety and complexity of Hamilton's arguments can become restrictive and reductive, and one can disagree with her interpretations, this book certainly opens up new vistas for future exploration of contextualized Shakespeare—even if he becomes more court propagandist than crossover playwright. Certainly, readers will enjoy the inventive and challenging reinterpretations while finding the massive documentation most useful.

Forms of Nationhood: The Elizabethan Writing of England. By Richard Helgerson. Chicago: The University of Chicago Press, 1992.

Reviewer: Arthur F. Kinney

Richard Helgerson's first book, a study of late Tudor fiction writers called *The Elizabethan Prodigals* (1976), was something relatively

new—a forceful generational study which argued that the common-
alities of a generation of writers overrode technique and individual
agency. Consequently, through a checking and balancing of various
writers, they together opened a window to an entire culture.
Bounded by the generation of the 1580s and 1590s that produced
Lyly, Greene, Sidney, and Nashe, this book was also firmly rooted
in Helgerson's overriding paradigm of the prodigal son who, feeling
his oats in adolescence, lived long enough to reconsider his behavior and, like as not, repent, lending to Tudor fiction both genuine
experience and a tone of moral rectitude.

Helgerson's second book grew naturally out of the first: *Self-
Crowned Laureates: Spenser, Jonson, Milton and the Literary System* (1983) is also essentially about generational pressures and the
fluctuation of paradigm, although in this instance the paradigm
(or "literary system") is at once richer and subtler, at times even
subterranean, in its use of a postmodernist interest in semiotics
(the ways signs function in a culture, in representing a culture, and
in representing the self in that culture) and, often working out binary oppositions which are meant to suggest, but never to secure,
the definitions which the paradigm needs amidst its temporal and
authorial fluctuations. What is at the heart of *Self-Crowned Laureates*, even when it is called self-presentation or self-fashioning, is
really a shared set of performances, shared largely because of a
shared community of discourse forged in the establishment of a
literary sensibility by self-appointed agents attempting to create
both a literary culture and their leadership within it.

In the first book, the argument develops through a binary opposition of a kind of allegory and detailed realism shared by all the
fiction writers alongside a firmer definition awarded each individual writer by playing him against the others. The essential method
holds, too, for *Self-Crowned Laureates*, although the advancing of
three generations essentially allows both sides of the binary split—
the individual poet and the cultural milieu—to multiply. Thus each
of the poets, when played off against the other two, is defined by
both similarity and difference. Always there is a dual pressure in
the arguments of both books, the poles of which (while never this
pure or explicit) are repetition (where all the writers are basically
similar almost to the point of being identical) and different and
individual (almost to the point of being unique). Helgerson is—has
always been—one of the most rational and logical of Renaissance
scholars, and his deep yearning for deep structure, something all
of us more or less share, makes his work richly researched and

cogently, even densely, written, work which provides its own rewards on every page.

Now enter *Forms of Nationhood: The Elizabethan Writing of England*. Whereas purpose and agency had been central in the previous studies, statehood and nationalism, or cultural discourses, are
now center stage. This is purposeful and timely, since one of the
frequent debates now both in literary and historical studies, ever
since the rise of New Historicism, historical revisionism, and Marxism, is that between the relative force of Tudor and Stuart absolut-
ism and imperialism and the rise of parliamentary and dissenting
movements to counteract such tendencies. (This is encapsulated
with special neatness in Helgerson's notice that the capital C which
embraces the portrait of the seated and reigning Elizabeth I at the
start of John Foxe's *Acts and Monuments* begins [in 1563] the word
Constantine, the prototype of imperialism, and is changed [in 1576]
to *Christ*, the prototype of the solitary Puritan.) Beyond this—in
the introduction, at least, called "The Kingdom of Our Own Language"—we are in familiar Helgerson territory. Thus he begins,

> Spenser's *Faerie Queene*.
> Coke's *Institutes of the Laws of England*.
> Camden's *Britannia*.
> Speed's *Theater of the Empire of Great Britain*.
> Drayton's *Poly-Olbion*.
> Hakluyt's *Principal Navigations of the English Nation*.
> Shakespeare's English history plays.
> Hooker's *Laws of Ecclesiastical Polity.*

> These texts belong to different fields. But they also belong together. All
> were written by men born within a few years of one another, from 1551
> to 1564. All take England—its land, its people, its institutions, and its
> history—as their subject. All are massive in size and scope. And, with
> the exception of Speed's *Theater* and Drayton's *Poly-Olbion*, all have
> had a major influence on some large area of English life (1).

What interests Helgerson at the outset is the generational identity
and the shared interests of that generation: "In chivalric romance,
historical narrative, and topographical description, these poets
sought to articulate a national community whose existence and
eminence would then justify their desire to become its literary
spokesmen" (2). What makes them important at first for Helgerson,
as unlikely partners as some of these writers might at first seem
(Spenser and Coke? Hakluyt and Hooker?) is precisely what it is
they share because they are of the same generation, born into

roughly the same culture at roughly the same time. Thus they were, he finds, essentially all doing the same work in their different genres, the work of pushing the statehood of monarchy toward the nationhood of a community of varying believers. "In seeking to establish their own authority and the authority of the different groups they represented, the younger Elizabethans were often guilty of an involuntary (and sometimes not so involuntary) lèse-majesté. They pushed claims that subverted the absolute claim of the crown. In their books—and more particularly in the discursive forms assumed by those books—we thus find traces of the difficult and, in England at least, never quite complete passage from dynasty to nation" (10). While "as poets, lawyers, chorographers, propagandists for overseas expansion, playwrights, and churchmen, they also belonged to different discursive communities and, as a result, wrote England differently," nevertheless "The boundaries between such communities were erected and reinforced as a funciton of the Elizabethan writing of England. In observing them, we attend to the pluralist communal base of the early modern nation-state, its resistance to the hegemony of either the crown or any other interest" (5). Despite apparent differences, despite varying genres and even communities of discourse on occasion, there remains the paradigm there after all. Within all, in fact; and beyond all.

Cultural materialists of whatever origin will have no difficulty, then, with this attempt to see a whole culture by seeing whole pieces of it; and it is always Helgerson's way to proceed by binary opposition rather than analysis, or, perhaps more accurately, to analyze by comparison and contrast in which an examined text is always itself—he calls himself a historical formalist at one point— and at the same time always and necessarily representative of texts as a body of texts, and as semiotic retrievals. So, he writes, in an extraordinary twist on the humanist thinking of the old historicists, of the act of imitatio, or the practice of rhetorical invention in the antique sense of that term: "every form I discuss depended for its meaning and its effect on its difference from some openly or latently competing form. Rime opposed quantitative verse; common-law reports opposed Roman-law institutes; chorographical description opposed chronicle history; voyage, like chivalric romance (though to a quite different end), opposed epic; Shakespeare's kind of English history play opposed Henslowe's; and apologetic discourse opposed apocalyptic" (7). In this sense, the line that he says inspired the book—Spenser's remark in a letter of 1580 to Gabriel Harvey that "Why a God's name may not we, as else the Greeks, have the kingdom of our own language?" (1) is itself both humanist and binary if we set it back into its own context from which this initial appearance wrenches it: what Spenser actually wrote (as Helgerson reveals on p. 25) is this: "For why a God's name may not we, as else the Greeks, have the kingdoms of our own language and measure our accents by the sound, reserving the quantity to the verse?" Helgerson's own response at this point mocks surprise: "So *that* is what Spenser was talking about: the comically misguided effort to base English prosody on the rules of ancient quantitative meters." But it is, of course, anything but comic. It is one generation discovering itself in opposition to the generations that have gone before it, one culture writing its own cultural formation out of displacement of earlier models. This is the model, then, of the Elizabethan prodigals writ through the genres; it is the humanist urge to imitate by divergence, to create (the laureateship, perhaps) by deliberately uncreating and then recreating (in both senses, in a way). But what I want to suggest is that while Helgerson seems to continue much of the debate of recent reexaminations and redeployments of humanist thought and practice, especially in the late Tudor period, and much of what he has said in his two earlier books, it is his sense that the end result is to rewrite a whole culture in political terms—politics as polity, as Hooker realizes in the double entendre of his title *Laws of Ecclesiastical Polity.* But bifurcation helps him to this, too. "At one pole in the reciprocal process by which England was written is the nation," Helgerson concludes, "—or rather, if we are to recognize the most obvious tension within that pole, the kingdom/nation. At another pole, also fissured, is the text/form. The kingdom/nation authorizes—indeed, authors—the text/form. And the reverse is also true. The text/form authorizes and authors the kingdom/nation" (12). If at first this seems a clever chiasmus, it really is not; here the equations are borne out in a great number of ways, some of them predictable, some not, some sensible, some dazzlingly brilliant, in the pages that follow. For in the body of his argument, Helgerson manages a *discors concors* of his own: in seeking the postmodernist deconstruction of meaning through the mobile semiotics of his chosen exemplars, he nevertheless (in a much more old-fashioned way) emulates them as well. He unwinds his texts with the best of Spenser, visualizes the spaces of thought with the best of Drayton, dramatizes his examples with the best in Henslowe's stable, and reasons with a binary logic that rivals Hooker or Foxe.

Helgerson's first case study is that of epic. "Certain rules of verse, certain poetic genres, certain discursive orderings of the law taken either from Greco-Roman antiquity or the middle ages provided the recognized models of civility and barbarity against which English writings were inevitably measured," he proposes (23). Civility descends from antiquity, from classical civilizations that argued quantitative meter, and from the early Christian society that argued for a life morally centered and derived from one holy magistrate. Gothic barbarity with its looseness of form and self-indulgence opposed this, even as it gives purpose and value to individual expression, to (in another sense) qualitative meter. It is a matter of tradition and its discontents. Thus the aesthetic argument that Spenser and Harvey entertain on the advisability of quantitative meter has deeper, more pervasive roots and powerful if more deeply rooted significance. Thus Helgerson attempts to define *The Faerie Queene*, an epic without a single hero, an epic in fact without the appearance of the title character, against Tasso's *Gerusalemme Liberata*. This is Spenser's antique model, his exemplar, not Ariosto, where the borrowing is only more localized. Tasso's epic is the work *against* which Spenser writes. Tasso's hero is the sovereign Goffredo whose Christianity gains him power and prestige—invincibility, in fact—against such pagans as Rinaldo and, in the later redaction of 1593, *Gerusalemme Conquistata*, the knights themselves drop out. "He cut Armida, Rinaldo, Erminia, and the Ariostan episodes associated with them; he chastened his language, eliminated marvels, increased the number of battles, stayed closer to history, and succeeded in alienating his readers almost as completely as the classicizing Gian Giorgio Trissino had done with his significantly titled *Italia Liberata dai Goti*" (47). Thus Tasso's epic firmly upholds monarchy, absolute rule, prescriptive behavior. Not so *The Faerie Queene*, which privileges several individual knights, each struggling toward a kind of conquest and rest but, in the course of Spenser's poem, never achieving final victory. Their multiple perspectives on magnanimity and their chief if partial virtues—temperance, justice, courtesy—are personal and in a sense fragmented. "The private side dominates, and the political is kept waiting for some unreachable narrative prolongation. But that exclusionary deferral is itself an inescapably political act" (49). Indeed, the striking absence of the Faerie Queen who is "kept out of sight on the poem's furthest periphery" allows "those figures of royal power that do enter the poem—all dangerously recognizable likenesses of Queen Elizabeth—[to] inspire more apprehension than allegiance" (55). It is not Spenser but Milton who comes closest to Tasso in his sense of the single source of hegemonic power, but he is, of course, of another generation and of another cultural moment.

What is true of Spenser's *Faerie Queene* is also true of Coke's *Reports* and *Institutes*. The title of the latter work suggests the Roman Justinian and the rational ordering of Roman law which the writer Tribonian (and others) attempted to record as a royal set of laws for a singular royal authority. This is, in fact, what Bacon intended to do for James, and in precisely the spirit of imitating Justinian's *Institutes* to establish absolute monarchy. But what Coke sets against this is his codification of English law by the detailed recording of common-law precedents in all their unruly, disconnected fragments. Absolute royal prerogative is replaced by a reconstruction of law based on past notations and reports. "Equality, certainty, antiquity, efficiency, and accessibility were the very qualities others attributed to the written law of Rome, qualities they found sadly lacking in England's unwritten law," Helgerson writes. "Coke denied all that. Though he admitted that the Romans may 'justly . . . boast of their civil laws,' he argued that even they recognized the superiority of English law. Had they not thought it superior, they would have changed it during the centuries when they occupied ancient Britain. But this they didn't do, for the law now practiced in England is the same that Brutus brought from Troy a millennium before the Roman invasion" (81). Its very messiness was its strength and the source of its efficacy. In registering its reports it resists codification. Even Coke's commentary on Littleton in its own way deconstructs by surrounding the earlier text with later cases and commentary. "From this perspective, the law seems rather a diachronic practice than a synchronic system. Always faithful to itself, it can nevertheless not be fully apprehended in any one schematic representation" (97). If for James the king came before the laws and wrote them, for Coke, laws were never made by kings—nor interpreted or applied by them either. The philosophy of law in Coke's work, then, is ideological.

In many ways, the chapter on maps and mapmaking is the most fascinating. We speak loosely of Saxton's maps which, formulated in the later sixteenth century, Helgerson still finds the original from which all others depend; yet Saxton merely executed them as servant to Master Thomas Seckford and it was his arms that illustrated them at first and then royal arms that were added to authorize them. But even that changes in time: first Seckford's arms drop off and then, in time, the royal arms, too, are displaced by a cartouche or an inset map, or some other insignia. "Maps thus opened a conceptual gap between the land and its ruler, a gap that would eventually span battlefields" (114). This was, momentarily, stayed and overtaken by the frontispiece of Drayton's *Poly-Olbion* in which England (or/as Elizabeth I?) is shown as a monarch with scepter and cornucopia and dressed in a robe which is itself the map of England. Later maps, showing counties, stress not the overriding monarchy but local particularizations. Richard Carew's *Survey of Cornwall* (1602) gives information on individual landowners and their families—there is something like this provinciality and self-assertiveness in the Cornwall of Shakespeare's *King Lear*—while the *Dorset* of John Coker provides 295 coats of arms. Perhaps the most famous product of this increasing sense of localization is the law of gavelkind that we now know was peculiar to the inheritance laws of Kent and was also doubtless behind *Lear*. "Sovereignty," mapmakers agreed, "was properly invested in the present kingdom and its monarch. But the memory of a not wholly departed local autonomy remained a powerful sign of individual identity" (136). Indeed, for Drayton the local *becomes* the sovereign: "*Poly-Olbion* contains not one but many claims to sovereignty. The Dert, the Parret, the Severn, the Lug, the Thames, the Trent, the Humber, and the Teis, Dean Forest, Malvern Hill, the Vale of Evsham, and the Isle of Man are all called king or queen" (141). Drayton's traveling Muse in this chorography, in fact, is not only inspirational but perambulatory, decentering the world that is the center of Drayton's attention. This "displacement of the monarch works in favor of both the individual authorial self and the enabling community to which he belongs. . . . Together the poet and the Muse go on progress, but the function of their progress is to provide the occasion and the inspiration for the land's self-expression" (145).

But this was the period when inland geography also, and more frequently, gave way to overseas voyages faithfully recorded and collected by Richard Hakluyt. If Helgerson can define Spenser best by putting him alonside Tasso, as Coke is placed alongside Justinian and Drayton alongside Saxton, then Hakluyt's various pamphlets, reports, and letters, fragmenting and composing the *Voyages*, is defined alongside the single epic *Lusiads* of Camões. The *Lusiads* is a poetic rendition of the historical voyage of Vasco da Gama, but the epic has no single hero, according to Helgerson; it, too, is the epic of a nation for here Portugal is identified with its "barões"— "not its 'men' or even its 'heroes,' though the word is often translated in both ways, but its 'noblemen,' its 'barons.' In choosing this term and making it plural, Camões enforces both the aristocratic and the nationalist ideology already strongly associated with the classical epic. But that very emphasis betrays a tension, an uncertainty imperfectly masked by assertiveness" (155). While de Gama's voyage, we now recall, is one around the Cape of Good Hope and across the Indian Ocean in search of the wealth of the Orient, in Camões' hands, as Helgerson reads his epic, "Da Gama and his companions voyage in search not of wealth but rather of honor, conquest, and the opportunity to spread the Christian faith" (157). Thus "Profit—proveito—is as strongly negative a term in Camões's lexicon as glory and fame are positive. Desire for profit grows in the 'base heart' (8.59) of the heathen ruler; the noble-hearted Portuguese seek only fame. Or at least in the ideal time of The Lusiads, a time less historical than mythic, they sought only fame" (158). By contrast history, not myth, characterizes the works Hakluyt publishes. And from the first, the motives are not wealth and proseltizing but the necessary establishment of markets in the service of the English nation. "Exploration, military action, colonization: all must be made to serve the overriding objective of economic well-being" (166). "Conversion, if it is to happen at all, will follow and serve commerce rather than the other way around" (167). "In no body of writings published in England in the sixteenth century—and, so far as I know, in none published elsewhere in Europe—were merchants and their doings presented more fully or more favorably or with less ideological constraint than in Hakluyt's three volumes" (170). But the work was deliberately, designedly ideological. For Hakluyt insisted that these merchants were, like the Gilberts and Raleghs on whom he centered, gentlemen. He created a new class within the culture and gave it great respect and repeated tribute. Thus "his book superimposed the ideological and economic asymmetries of his culture to represent and to enforce a coupling of classes in an enterprise he defined as national" (178–79).

Helgerson's Shakespeare is monarchical, hegemonic, royalist. Even though he uses common players to entertain commoners in the public playhouses of Shoreditch and Southwark, they are nevertheless dressed like nobility: note the opening scene of The First Part of the Contention Betwixt the Two famous Houses of York and Lancaster (2 Henry VI)—arguably his first play: "No one below the rank of earl appears on stage in the opening scene of The Contention. No one above the rank of joiner appeared on stage in the opening scene of The Contention. Both these statements are true"

(204), since one talks about roles, the other about actors. Helgerson cites the well-known attacks on mobs and commons throughout Shakespeare's history plays and notes the association of Jack Cade the rebel with the rebellious, unruly Puritans. And "Puritans were among the theater's most vociferous enemies. To associate them with rebels, an association made easy by the Anabaptist reputation as levelers and communists, was to label their antitheatricalism as seditious" (213). Peasants are associated with fools and clowns; "Prince Hal studies his lowlife companions, so as to reject them" (222). Quite the opposite is true for the plays for which Henslowe paid, as if he were deliberately responding to Shakespeare. "The history plays Henslowe paid for give their attention to the victims of such power. . . . These plays," according to Helgerson, "repeatedly focus on a character who is intensely loyal to the reigning monarch, who has a special relation to the common people, and who suffers as a victim of power. Sir John Oldcastle is such a figure, and so are Jane and Matthew Shore in Heywood's *Edward IV.* In *Sir Thomas Wyatt,* Lady Jane Grey, Guilford Dudley, and Wyatt himself, whose English patriotism finally proves more hardy than even his loyalty to Queen Mary" (234); are all cases in point. "Instead of reproducing Shakespeare's infatuation with kingly power, an infatuation that is often shadowed but never overcome by moral disapproval, these plays eschew ambition and concern themselves with lower-ranked characters who try to maintain their integrity, characters who work to mitigate the effects of power on the common people. Like Jane Shore, Woodstock and Oldcastle are mediators between the king and the commons, and, again like her, they suffer for their virtuous interference. Sympathy with that suffering, an emotion that has gotten these plays the reputation of being sentimental, rather than the heady excitement of mystified kingship, is what they offer" (235). If "The central problematic of Shakespeare's history plays concerns the consolidation of monarchic rule," (238) following the chronicles, Henslowe's playwrights concentrate on the strategies by which power is attained and punishingly employed. Always questioning hegemony, "Caught between their loyalty to the crown and their adherence to a set of values that the crown regularly violated, the protagonists of the Henslowe history plays repeatedly find themselves forced into making choices where either alternative is equally ruinous" (239). Shakespeare shows royal triumph; Henslowe's playwrights show its heavy cost. All the history plays thus do "cultural work" (244) that is ideological,

Shakespeare writing the state and Henslowe's playwrights the nation.

Helgerson's final pairing places the apocalyptic of Foxe alongside the apologetic of Hooker. "*Acts and Monuments* is fundamentally narrative in its structure. Hundreds of individual stories of persecution are subsumed within a larger story of church history based on the Book of Revelation. The *Laws of Ecclesiastical Polity* has a fundamentally argumentative structure. Following an introductory discussion of 'laws and their several kinds in general,' each of its remaining seven books responds to a specific charge that had been directed against the church of England by advocates of further reform" (253). The narrative of Foxe's book is based on the mighty struggle between Christ and Antichrist, God and Satan, the true church and the church of this world. "But apocalyptic also has a predetermined plot, a plot cryptically imaged in the revelations of Daniel and St. John and historically embodied in the Egyptian and Babylonian captivities, the crucifixion and resurrection of Christ, and the sufferings and spread of the apostolic church. . . . These stories . . . reassure the suffering elect that the deaths of their fellow Protestants have not been in vain, maintain the apocalyptic hope on which such self-sacrifice depends, keep believers believing" (256). The "invisible church" of true believers is what inspires and directs; in a time of persecution there is no visible church which is godly. Rather, the church is dispersed, made up of scattered believers each generating his or her own faith. But in Foxe's account, "Constantine and Wycliffe, Englishmen both, mark two of the greatest periods in God's church, the binding and loosing of Satan. Clearly, their Englishness had something to do with their election" (263). Such thought, surely by the 1590s, was associated with dissenters rather than part of Elizabeth I's church settlement, and Helgerson finds it no coincidence that Hooker's *Laws* was published in the same year, so defending the Anglican settlement that Henry Barrow and John Greenwood were executed for sedition (1593). This was also the year that parliament passed the first regulations since Mary I directed specifically against Protestant nonconformity; indeed, the bill was brought before Parliament by Edward Sandys, son of the archibishop of York and Hooker's chief patron and sponsor. Hooker argues for the visible church—visible in church buildings, church liturgy, the *Book of Common Prayer* (used in sevices) rather than the Bible (used for individual meditation). The reasoning of Hooker's treatise builds on a world of hierarchy and order, the ecclesiastical polity stemming from and analogous to that of monarchy itself. But at the same time Hooker argues a singular history and polity he contextualizes both, admitting distinctions and differences even as he tries to argue for a stable and central core to church belief and church history. Inversely, then, Foxe argues for individual consciences which, rising, will eventually converge; Hooker argues for a single apostolic church which, seen historically, takes varying forms. These views have their later proponents in Bunyan's *Relation*, *Grace Abounding*, and *Pilgrim's Progress* and in Walton's *Complete Angler* (on Anglicans); both are consolidated in the remarkable title page of Hobbes's *Leviathan* (1651) where the imperial king overlooks both Anglican and Puritan signs and symbols.

Indeed, this title page could serve as the title page of *Forms of Nationhood* for it refuses to resolve its polarities, refuses even concord to its discordances; rather, it keeps everything in play. What allows Helgerson's play to work in the end, here as elsewhere, I think, is his stubborn refusal to move from his binary oppositions—simple and complex by turn—to the synthesis of a Hegelian diagram. "State/nation, court/country, king/people, sovereign/subjects—if these pairs cannot be neatly mapped onto one another, neither can they be sharply distinguished. . . . Historically, it may be, as recent students of nationalism have argued, that 'nations more often follow states than precede them,' but, once given shape by the state, the nation makes claims of its own, serves as a semi-autonomous source of identity and authority" (296). The difficulty he finds (from implicit start to explicit finish) is that the centralized state is exclusionist in class and gender—remains, in this period, male and patriarchal. It resembles James I. But earlier, that was more of an open question. Spenser chose to make the Faerie Queen a woman, and even if she does not appear in her poem, she enables the adventurous, risk-taking, successful knights who do appear. They, of course, are the Raleghs and Essexes who will grow up to grow away from the throne and even to rebel against it. But the rebellion increases under Stuart rule. This may explain not only why the outcry for nationhood grew into civil war under the Stuarts even as it explains the increasing nostalgia for the age of Elizabeth. Binarisms help us see that, as this resonant and interconnected series of discourses do, in a quite marvelous paradigm that even when talking about exclusionism, manages to include far more than it leaves out. "A unique set of conditions . . . gave men of middling status and humanist education, men born at or shortly following the midcentury, the task of laying the discursive foundations both for the nation-state and for a whole array of more specialized communities that based their identity on their relation to the nation and the state" (299). "But most literate and mobile Englishmen belonged to several discursive communities, were traversed by a plurality of nationalist discourses. Their identity was constructed *within* particular forms and communities, but also *across* them. John Selden was at once a member of Camden's Society of Antiquaries, the annotator of Drayton's *Poly-Olbion*, and Coke's parliamentary collaborator in his struggles with King Charles on behalf of the common law. Fulke Greville contributed to the quantitative movement, patronized Daniel, Camden, and Speed, and wrote his own politic history of Elizabeth's reign, his *Life of Sir Philip Sidney*. And Edwin Sandys not only paid for the printing of Hooker's *Laws* but was also among the most active promoters of overseas expansion" (300).

Discord and concord both. A sense of the state and a sense of the nation in turn. Helgerson's paradign recedes in its control of the argument and, in the end, awards us enlightenment. This dense and comprehensive picture of the making of the nation, of a considerable, unavoidable, and still-present Renaissance not only contextualizes Shakespeare but helps us to understand more clearly and yet more complicatedly the complex culture that helped to construct him as he in his turn went about to construct and reconstruct his culture.

Casting Shakespeare's Plays: London Actors and their Roles, 1590–1642. By T. J. King. Cambridge: Cambridge University Press, 1992.

Reviewer: William Ingram

T. J. King's title is in some ways a misnomer; though his subtitle comes a bit closer, neither accurately describes King's own principal interests in this book, which involve studying the relationship of major to minor roles in a variety of playtexts including all of Shakespeare's; taking note of player-assignments to those roles in all cases where evidence of such assignment survives; assessing the evidence for doubling of roles and applying it to the cases he studies; and (last but by no means least) providing a statistical breakdown, scene by scene, of all the roles in all the plays in his study. There's no room in this agenda for a consideration of "casting," if by casting one means the process whereby players are assigned to parts;[1] nor does a concern for "actors and their roles" (as announced in the subtitle) extend to organizing the data by player, or furnishing an appendix in which one might find, under any given player's name, a professional summary of all the roles he is known or conjectured to have played. Instead the book is organized resolutely in terms of its primary documents, mainly playtexts: players are merely the markers in such a structure, and to work out a career history for any player one has to use the index and chase down page numbers.[2]

That having been said, it remains to look at what King's book actually does do. To begin with, it is full of usefully extrapolated data. An introductory chapter surveys the scanty early scholarship on who-played-what and on the doubling of parts. There isn't a lot to cite by way of earlier work once T. W. Baldwin, G. E. Bentley, A. C. Sprague, and W. A. Ringler are noticed; King's work usefully adjudicates among these earlier theorists, though it scants more recent work such as that by Scott McMillin. A second chapter is devoted to the analysis of eight playhouse documents—four playhouse plots (2 *Seven Deadly Sins*, *Frederick & Basilea*, *Battle of Alcazar*, 1 *Tamar Cam*) and four manuscript prompt books (*Second Maiden's Tragedy*, *Sir John van Olden Barnavelt*, *The Honest Man's Fortune*, *Believe as you List*). A third chapter treats the fifteen plays, some printed and some in manuscript, in which the names of players in principal roles are furnished. A fourth and final chapter considers the possible distribution of roles in each of the thirty-eight plays of Shakespeare. These analytical studies occupy the first 95 pages of the book. They are followed by eighty-one typescript tables, occupying another 161 pages, in which almost all of these dramatic documents, and King's conclusions or conjectures about them, are summarized in tabular form.

Because of this format, King's book is reminiscent of an earlier Cambridge book, Neil Carson's *Companion to Henslowe's Diary* (1988), which also included a number of typescript tables, though proportionately fewer than here. The appearance of typewriter font is always jarring in an otherwise typeset book; no doubt it represents a kind of cost-cutting by the Cambridge Press, though in the case of King's book it has resulted in some carelessness as well. Of the 150-odd pages of tables lying between pages 96 and 254, about a third are formatted vertically and have had typeset page numbers and running heads keylined onto them. The remaining hundred or so pages contain tables formatted broadside, and have been left unnumbered, though they might have been keylined as easily as the others. Because many entries in the index refer the user to the numbers of these unnumbered pages, the omission is genuinely inconvenient.

The book has three appendices. The first consists of transcripts of five playhouse plots (the four mentioned above plus *Dead Man's Fortune*), all reprinted from Greg's *Dramatic Documents from the Elizabethan Playhouses*; the second contains descriptions of seven manuscript playbooks that identify not principal players but players in minor roles (*Sir Thomas More, John of Bordeaux, Woodstock, Two Noble Ladies, the Captives, Edmund Ironside, the Wasp*); and the third is a transcript of Sir Henry Herbert's 1624 order protecting musicians and attendants from arrest. There are three separate indices for persons, plays, and subjects. The book contains twenty-seven plates, sixteen of them reproductions of the player lists in various printed books, and the remainder showing various kinds of manuscript materials containing names of players. The plates are on the whole fairly good reproductions of what are in some cases poorly legible originals.

King's case, in brief, runs like this. In any playing company, the distinction between principal players and hired men was more than just economic. Plays were so constructed that the roles taken by principal players accounted, on average, for 90 to 95 percent of the spoken dialogue in any play. Hired men could usually learn the remaining small parts in a few hours, so early rehearsals could easily proceed without them. Additionally, some principal players were more principal than others. The principal players in Shakespeare's company (whose number varied, and who were not necessarily identical with the sharers) always or almost always took the biggest parts in the plays. Further, the major principal players did not double their parts, even if the logistics of their roles might have allowed them to. Still further, not every principal player performed in every play; bit parts were frequently taken by hired men even when an unassigned principal player was free to take them.

King has found no evidence to support the notion that adult players played female roles, or that boy members of adult companies played adult male roles. If he is right in his interpretation of this negative evidence, cherished notions about Juliet's Nurse or Mistress Quickly may have to be dislodged, and the proposition (by now a cliché) that both Cordelia and the Fool were played by the same performer is made to appear even more fanciful. Robert Armin, who is a likely candidate for having played the Fool though evidence is lacking, was about the same age as Shakespeare, and doubling him as Cordelia would have been silly in any event.

The lesser principal players did double, but precisely how they doubled is difficult to ascertain. The minor players almost always doubled. King distinguishes the documentable claim *that* this was done from the trickier matter of showing exactly *how* it was done; "My tables of parts," he says, "suggest *only one set of possibilities for doubling for each play, not hard-and-fast rules*" (his italics). This is sensibly conservative, but it's also a missed opportunity; one would like to know what the viable and reasonable alternatives were for doubling in any given play, for a consideration of such competing possibilities enables the best kind of informed conjecture.

The strength of King's argument is that so many of the documents he discusses furnish evidence leading to the same set of conclusions about the distribution and doubling of roles. His subtitle tells us that the book's argument covers half a century of theatrical activity; the documents he calls upon are unevenly distributed in this time-frame, however, and the consistency of practice that he adduces across those fifty years may therefore make some readers uneasy. Nonetheless, it's good to have all this material assembled in one place, and to have the statistical analyses that go with it. The downside of this strength is that the book seems filled with repetitive phrases and claims. That the *Battle of Alcazar* "is the only Elizabethan play to survive in both a plot and an early printed text" is stated on page 15, again on page 27, again on page 31. A paragraph in the lower part of page 6 is substantially repeated at the bottom of page 19, another in the middle of page 15 is substantially repeated on page 31, and so on. The phrase "Bourne (or Bird)" is carefully repeated four times in a space of eleven lines. There are typos as well: Bassianus in *Titus Andronicus* appears regularly as Bassanius; Casca in *Julius Caesar* appears as Caska; Calcepius in *Battle of Alcazar* appears as Calcepis; Thomas Towne the player appears as Thomes; and there are more.

But these are quibbles. A more substantive question was raised by Peter Holland when he reviewed King's book as part of an omnibus review in the *TLS* of 7 May 1993. While praising the book's depiction of "a sane and ordered world of busy professionals," Holland found its "arid statistics" uncongenial, terming the book "about as user-unfriendly as books in theatre studies ever get." Holland's objections seem to be to the very nature of King's work; he expresses astonishment that "three-quarters of" the book (an inflated estimate) consists of statistical tables. We may too easily dismiss this as the worst kind of humanist reaction to non-narrative information. But Holland's visceral recoil does point to a legitimate query: to what kinds of proper uses can one put the sort of information the book provides?

Some suggestions come immediately to mind. Theatre historians wishing to understand better the organization and function of playing companies, or the structural differences between a company on tour and the same company in London, or those of a company at the beginning and the end of its corporate life; textual scholars interested in the logistical constraints imposed on playscript construction by Elizabethan theatrical practices; drama critics exploring the effect of doubling upon the complex set of responses generally called "watching a play"; social historians pursuing questions about the use of boy players in adult companies: any of these will want the information in this book. King himself quietly proposes a further, more therapeutic use: "In recent years, several studies have offered imaginative conjectures about possibilities for doubling in Shakespeare's plays, but none of these studies has taken into account the evidence about casting readily available in the extant Elizabethan playhouse documents." King seems to have in mind here not the informed conjecture which his own data would undergird, but the wilder surmises of some present-day interpreters whom he does not name. If King's book can function as a corrective in this fashion, it will serve a useful purpose on that head alone; but it is the fate of such books that they rarely reach the places they are most needed. Peter Holland's dismissive reaction may be paradigmatic.

Notes

1. It may well be anachronistic even to speak of "casting" Shakespeare's plays. We don't really know what word or phrase Shakespeare and his fellows used for the process of allotting parts to players. The earliest notice in *OED* (s.v. 48) of the word "cast" in its theatrical sense dates from the early eighteenth century; Elizabethan *casting* is almost always followed by *aside, away, off, out,* or *up*. Anthony Munday (*Second and Third Blast*, STC 21677, 1580, 111) speaks of "the laying out of parts," and that may well have been the current locution.

2. King's brief doesn't extend to companies of boys, but is limited to adult players in London and their apprentices. Nor is King always careful about those players. He states in a footnote (270) that Lear's Fool "was first played by Robert Armin," though his own text offers no support for this traditional belief. In another place King asserts that Anthony Jeffes is "no relation" to Humphrey Jeffes, a sweeping claim. While the scant evidence suggests that the two men had different fathers, this does not rule out a kinship; and, to complicate matters, Mark Eccles ("Brief Lives: Tudor and Stuart Authors", SP [Texts and Studies] 1982, 133) mentions a document in which Anthony speaks of Humphrey as his brother.

Shakespeare and His Contemporaries: Eastern and Central European Studies. Edited by Jerzy Limon and Jay L. Halio. Newark: University of Delaware Press, 1993.

Reviewer: Marga Munkelt

As the preface tells us, this collection introduces *International Studies in Shakespeare*, a series of "occasional volumes" bringing "to a wider audience the work of non-Anglo-American scholars and critics whose work might otherwise be unknown" (7). The present volume concentrates on works from Eastern and Central Europe, represented by Bulgaria, Czechoslovakia, Hungary, and Poland, and although none of the contributions "has required translation," their original place of publication would have made access difficult.

A wide range of topics and approaches is covered in the thirteen essays, as is a time-span—from 1946 to 1993. The articles are of vastly differing lengths—the longest has some sixty pages, the shortest six. Apart from the focus on Shakespeare and his time, they have no obviously connecting theme. The attempt at representativeness is mainly geographical, and whatever intellectual correspondence there is, is due to the authors' backgrounds rather than to an agreement arranged for the purpose of this volume.

Nevertheless, a group of six essays can be roughly classified as period and/or genre studies: Marco Mincoff's "Baroque Literature in England," Josef Polišenský's "England and Bohemia in Shakespeare's Day," Zdeněk Stříbrný's "The Genesis of Double Time in Pre-Shakespearean and Shakespearean Drama," Henryk Zbierski's "Shakespearean Tragedy: Some Aspects of Its Development and Decline," Małgorzata Grzegorzewska's "*Theatrum Orbis Terrarum* on the Court Stage: Some Remarks on the Cartographic Design of Jacobean and Caroline Masque," and Arthur Blaim's "More's *Utopia*: Persuasion, Polyphony, Genre Pattern."

Mincoff approaches the question of whether one can "speak of baroque literature at all" (11) and whether it is appropriate to extend the definitions and the terminology from painting, sculpture, and architecture to literature. The difficulties in determining a style *and* a period by the same term are self-understood (the English Renaissance, for example, overlaps with the Italian baroque; similarly, Dutch artists of the baroque period lack the typical forms of the time); however, Mincoff ultimately answers his own question in the affirmative. Although the essay was written as early as 1946, the validity of its argumentation is not seriously impaired. Polišenský's essay, originally published in 1965, points out that for most of Shakespeare's contemporaries as for Shakespeare himself "knowledge of Bohemia and of Central Europe . . . was second-hand" (191)—mostly from translations of Italian tales and handbooks on style. His archive material reveals direct relations that "have broadened the knowledge one country had of the other" (193) in journeys between the two countries. The three main types of English visitors (the most famous one was Sir Philip Sidney in 1577) to Prague were Catholics and Jesuits; professional politicians and diplomats; merchants and adventurers. The well-known puzzle of Shakespeare's locating Bohemia on a seacoast finds a possible explanation as well. Trips from Bohemia to England were undertaken mainly by young aristocrats (among them most likely the Moravian nobleman who was the first Czech to see a Shakespeare play performed in 1600); students; miners and glass workers. Polišenský's essay is very rich and contains almost too much in the way of interesting information. Zdeněk Stříbrný wrote his piece in 1969 and has published three sequels since then. His definition of double time is based on earlier works by John Dover Wilson, N. J. Halpin, and Peter A. Daniel. In determining double time as a generic phenomenon, Stříbrný finds that it is a characteristic of the native tradition of English drama with its "elastic" time (111) as opposed to the unities of classical drama. He shows that double time is often the result of two plots that run at different speeds—as in *The Merchant of Venice*—but also typically associated with a "strong compression of history and condensation of dramatic time" (117)—as in Marlowe's *Edward II*. The main part of the essay is a detailed analysis of *Richard III*. *Othello*, a play traditionally used as an example of double time, is only briefly touched on in a footnote. Henryk Zbierski's question of which of Shakespeare's great tragedies are "generally accepted as Shakespeare's best" and why (146) is pursued in an article originally published in 1979. Zbierski holds that Shakespeare "as a dramatist developed as long as he was able gradually to distance himself from the limitations of his contemporaries, and declined when he started to lose his ability and power and finally in his last plays conformed to the dominant trends" (147). He compares and evaluates seventeenth-century tragedies as opposed to sixteenth-century ones and comes to the conclusion that *Romeo and Juliet* and *Titus Andronicus* are "still far away from the perfectly Shakespearean creations of the seventeenth century." Even *Julius Caesar*, "fine play as it is," lacks "concentration on the tragic hero and focus on inward psychological drama" (150). Zbierski singles out *King Lear*, *Macbeth*, and *Coriolanus* as "real" tragedies in which "we have definitely not only hero-concentration but hero-orientation in the causative sense" (152). Everything afterwards is, according to Zbierski, "decline," and after the universality of *King Lear* the deepest fall took place when Shakespeare "fell into the trap of the new genre, tragicomedy" (158).

Both Arthur Blaim and Małgorzata Grzegorzewska use musical language to describe and define the thematic, linguistic, and generic connections in works presenting political or ideological viewpoints. Grzegorzewska's "invitation to *Theatrum Orbis Terrarum*" (240), written for this collection, is very much up to date and obviously part of a larger work in progress. The author applies "verbal-pictorial art forms of the Renaissance and baroque periods . . . to the interpretation of other works of art and literature" (219) and finds close similarities between the cartographer and the masquewright at work. She sees a connection between emblematic vocabulary and the "newly created idiom of colonial discourse" (223). Grzegorzewska illustrates her "cross-interpretation" with examples from Ben Jonson's masques as well as with John Donne's poetry, Du Bartas' *Divine Weeks and Meditations*, and paintings of Jan Vermeer and organizes them in a "new polyphonic text" (240). This interesting article makes one curious for more. The idea of polyphony within one work of art is pursued by Arthur Blaim. He finds that the two themes indicated in More's title are picked up in the "two books that employ two different modes of discourse, Book I (dialogue), in which the prerequisites of the ideal common-wealth are discussed, and Book II (monologue), with the descrip-tion of the newly discovered island" (71). Blaim stresses that the varying points of view found in *Utopia* are dependent on the incon-sistent positions of the two principal narrators that do not allow "a homophonic reading of the text" (80). He holds that contemporary accounts of voyages and discoveries have an analogous relationship with *Utopia* "based on a common cultural tradition" (101). To a certain extent this essay suffers from its separation from the book in which it was originally published in 1984 *(Early English Utopian Fiction: A Study of a Literary Genre)*. Despite the thorough digest of criticism, references to "recent" works need to be handled with caution since they apply to studies written in the 1960s and 1970s.

Five contributors to the book discuss selected aspects in individ-ual plays. István Géher's essay is entitled "Morality and Madness: A Hungarian Reading of *Measure for Measure*"; Martin Procházka writes about "Subjectivity and Dramatic Discourse in *The Tem-pest*." Not untypical in Shakespearean criticism, the majority of essays are on *Hamlet,* all of them published for the first time in this volume: Piotr Sadowski's piece is called "The 'Dog's Day' in *Hamlet:* A Forgotten Aspect of the Revenge Theme"; Marta Gibin-ska discusses "'The Play's the Thing': The Play Scene in *Hamlet*"; and Emma P. Szabó's title is "Shakespeare's *Hamlet* and Paster-nak's Poem."

István Géher's discussion of *Measure for Measure* is reprinted from a chapter in his *Hungarian Shakespeare-Reader* (1990). It is a somewhat disconcerting essay not only in its interpretation of the play itself but also in its cynical tone. The author assesses the dual identities of the dramatis personae as representations of life-styles or moral views and as living characters, and not infrequently he uses one identity to criticize the other. We learn, for example, that as "a personality he [the Duke] is inaccessible, it is only in his impact as a function that he exists" (134). But a little later Géher speculates beyond the play about the same Duke's life and asks, "Could it be that, at one time or another, the venerable Duke Vin-centio happily caroused in the red-lamp districts of Vienna in the company of the dissolute Lucio? . . . True or not, he sounds as though he has never set eyes on Lucio. Perhaps he is suffering from amnesia—or even schizophrenia" (136). The "madness" in the title of the essay is applied to the Duke, whose unintelligible behavior as "the embodiment of Divine Providence" (132) on the one hand

and as a "doctor of the psyche" (141) on the other hand, can best be explained as "deranged" (144). Martin Procházka's not previously published reading of *The Tempest* emanates from 2.1.148–69, the scene where Gonzalo's theory of a utopian state is mocked by Antonio and Sebastian. Following Greenblatt's idea of the play's "doubleness," he emphasizes the "apparent contradiction between the ideal representation of humanity in the style of Renaissance utopian thought and the strategy of the dramatic discourse based on concrete characters, situation, and semantic gestures." Even more so, the island has a doubleness as "place of pure phantasy" and as a "place of power" (208). Prospero illustrates the principle of subjectivity as connected with personality on the one hand and dependent on social change on the other. Although Prospero has indeed authority "both as a character and as a representation of a ruler and his power" (209), his "subjectivity then may not be said to harmonize but to dramatize the conflict between radically different modes of representation in the play" (212).

Piotr Sadowski discusses Hamlet's references in 5.1.291–92 to Hercules and the dog that "will have his day." He finds behind them (accepted by most critics as part of Hamlet's antic disposition) "a well-defined complex of cultural ideas and rituals, particularly characteristic of pre-Christian Scandinavia" (161) where the "transformation of an inoffensive domestic animal into a wild beast [was] a symbol of wild uncontrolled frenzy and savagery" (160) and which in the play applies to Hamlet himself. Marta Gibinska has new thoughts about the play-within-the-play in *Hamlet*. She argues that the dumb show "does not rehearse exactly what is then repeated in the inner play" (176). The dumb show concentrates on Gertrude and the player queen as main "performers" and fulfills what has already been interpreted by Hamlet and the Ghost. Quite differently, the play-within-the-play focuses on Hamlet and Claudius and results in the opposite of Hamlet's prophecies: Hamlet exposes Claudius's guilt, but he exposes also his own knowledge of the crime (187). Emma P. Szabó examines the relationship of the Hamlet myth, Shakespeare's *Hamlet* and Boris Pasternak's interpretation of it in *Doctor Zhivago* and his poem *Hamlet*. The brief essay compares the heroes' choices and concludes that both try to save the values of humankind. "Hamlet's sacrifice takes the form of committing sin in order to set time right. Zhivago's is the sacrifice of surviving as his own person; his way of life is a challenge, a provocation, in itself" (172). In Pasternak's poem (quoted in full at the end of the essay), the two sacrifices seem to be united.

Two articles, László Kéry's and Jan Mukařovský's, present us with pointedly Eastern European views—one of a country, the other of a critic. Both authors portray creative processes in the past that have gained a new dimension of historical significance due to the changed political conditions in the region. Mukařovský gives us a survey of "Shakespeare and Czech Theatrical Criticism" in an essay originally published in 1966. He demonstrates impressively with examples from the careers and works of theater critics, directors, and actors how Shakespeare's plays became central to the growth of a Czech national theater. Kéry's not previously published account of "Georg Lukács on Shakespeare" is an appropriate conclusion of the present collection of criticism. It portrays a critic whose approach to literature was definitely a "historical" one in that he always saw "conflict in drama . . . determined by conflict in the history of society" (260). But Lukács's historical approach is also historical in that his own intellectual history has shaped and modified his assessment of Shakespeare which Kéry sees take place in three phases.

The book as a whole is attractive, and the goals of the series are nothing but praiseworthy. There are, however, also some weaknesses. What comes to mind at first sight is the absence of an essay from Russia—a central European area that would have to be represented. Also, it seems that although one does not expect an equal distribution of countries, there is an overweight of Polish contributions followed closely by Czech authors, all of whom are from Prague or associated in one way or other with the Charles University. But maybe this fact is in itself a statement about the situation of the profession in those countries. It seems likewise strange to have Bulgaria represented by a chapter written almost fifty years ago. Admittedly, Marco Mincoff's stature and reputation then and now make the inclusion of his essay a must, but an additional more recent article or two from Bulgaria would have helped balance the perspectives.

A reader of the book muses why the essays appear in what looks like a random order—apart from the three pieces on *Hamlet* which are printed consecutively. Perhaps an alphabetical arrangement according to contributors or countries would have clarified matters. The excellent idea of having an American editor and one from the area represented by the collection has not been fully utilized. It would probably add to the sense of representativeness if the regional editor made the choice of the contributions a little more transparent. It is, for example, not immediately clear what is typically Bulgarian or Polish or Czech in the present pieces. Even a chapter like Géher's that stresses in the title its "Hungarian" quality does not convey anything vastly unusual (except for the total absence of notes). Apart from the fact that the essays do not always reflect current criticism—and for reasons that we all know and understand—they are not very different from what is published elsewhere. But then, perhaps that is what we want. The most exciting pieces in this volume, however, are those that tell us something that we do not already know—as, for example, the story of Czech theater criticism.

One might suggest a little more consistency and control of both expression and apparatus in the forthcoming collections. The compilation of *one* bibliography in the end (in additon to the endnotes after each individual chapter) should be considered. In any case one consistent style of documentation would be an advantage. The book contains several misprints, errors, and inconsistencies. To give just a few examples: the department of the German member of the editorial board should be "Institut [without umlaut] für Englische Philologie"; Robert Weimann (not "Weinmann") wrote the book on the *Tradition des Volkstheaters* (126, n.3); the Arden Edition is cited as if it were a *Complete Works* type edition (167, n.1) and in another wrong format at 188, n.3, but it should be documented according to the individual play titles *and* individual editors; the title of the German periodical should be *Die Neueren Sprachen* at 105, n.34 and elsewhere. Note 13 at 217 should read "oder" instead of "order," and *Shakespeare Jahrbuch* is misprinted. Confusion in the use of *o, ö, oe* or *a, ä, ae* for the same letter, respectively, is noticeable throughout the notes: at 240, n.1, the author cited should be spelled "Höltgen" (not "Holtgen"); at 217, n.13 we find the German title of *King Lear* as *Koenig* [for *König*] *Lear*; but *ä* and *Ä* are correctly used at 203, n.11, 260–61 and elsewhere. The title of Prochazka's article cited at 217, n.18 should read "Zwietracht" (not "Zweitract"); and Jan Vermeer (228, line 8) is from Delft (not from Delf). The list of contributors could also be made more consistent in information and style.

The variety of the critical viewpoints presented in this collection is very welcome. It would be interesting to compare the volume with an enterprise of its kind after, say, five or ten years of open communication between East and West.

The *Masks of Hamlet*. By Marvin Rosenberg.
Newark: University of Delaware Press, 1992.

Reviewer: Robert F. Willson, Jr.

Marvin Rosenberg's *The Masks of Othello* (1961), *The Masks of King Lear* (1972), and *The Masks of Macbeth* (1978) constitute a major body of work in the field of performance criticism. In all these studies Professor Rosenberg followed one production of each tragedy through rehearsals to first performance. (Richard White's 1990 Berkeley production, with John Vickery as Hamlet, was the paradigm for this study.) He also recites details about other performances, using reviews and verbal accounts from a large group of witnesses. His goal is to give the reader some idea of the wide range of interpretive choices made by directors and actors. He seems especially fascinated by reports from "naive" spectators who have never read or seen these tragedies. His style is that of a reporter, not a scholar; he strings together beads of commentary and rarely pauses to evaluate the emerging strand. Never does he reject a director's or actor's interpretation out of hand, preferring instead to suggest that certain performances are less readily accepted in the stage tradition than others. The aim in these exhaustive studies is comprehensiveness, and the reader is regularly urged—"If more thou dost perceive, let me know more . . ."—to report to headquarters any news of productions that might have been overlooked.

In *The Masks of Hamlet*, Professor Rosenberg appears to have scoured the planet for scraps of information about productions of this tragedy. The book's 925 pages record every conceivable detail about performances on stage, screen, radio, and television. Although he structures this encyclopedic volume as a scene-by-scene analysis of performance choices (relying on Q2 and F for his texts), he makes frequent stops along the way to discuss the main characters' "polyphony" and how that complexity had been realized by actors on the British, American, German, Russian, French, Italian, and many other European and Asian stages. These discussions commence as each character is introduced in the play, the analysis of Hamlet masks coming just after a short canvass of readings of the hero's response to Claudius and Gertrude in 1.2. Rosenberg's review of the history of Hamlet interpretations requires four parts or chapters that total ninety-three pages. The reader is returned to an investigation of the rest of 1.2 (parts 3, 4, and 5) only after being brought up to date on the many Hamlets from performances past. Such an arrangement inevitably induces frustration, since the intent of the study appears to be a close reading of passages and events in each successive scene without regard for the reader's ability to absorb the many comments on performance choices. One yearns for the structure of reference guides like F. E. Halliday's *A Shakespeare Companion* or Kenneth Rothman and Annabelle Henkin Melzer's *Shakespeare on Screen* after only a few hundred pages of *The Masks of Hamlet*.

The reward for persistence is Rosenberg's four-chapter account of the hero's many and various faces. In "Hamlet *(Part 1)*," the reader learns that despite numerous variations the world's stages have produced two archetypal Hamlets: "the sweet and the powerful." The poles are not stable, however. "The sweet Hamlets may turn bitter; the bitter ones sweeten with consolations of philosophy. The victim may turn heroic; the hero become victim. The lovable may turn harsh with experience; the harsh be softened by suffering. . . . The polyphony is restless, ever changing." Kenneth Tynan's intriguing list of descriptive terms to identify the contrasting styles of Gielgud and Olivier satisfies Rosenberg's need to further clarify the terms "sweet" and "powerful." Gielgud's ascetic Hamlet is the poet—spiritual, intellectual, feminine, introverted, "claret." The dynamic Olivier can be called earthy, emotional, animalistic, masculine, extroverted, "burgundy." On the English stage the two classical avatars of these types were John Philip Kemble and Edmund Kean. Their interpretations strongly influenced the work of actors on the European and American stage as well; Sothern, Forrest, and Booth revealed marks of these masters in their performances. Kemble's prince was "a figure of beauty," whose movements were graceful but somehow also suited to his melancholic humor. Hazlitt saw in Kemble "the sweet and graceful, the gentlemanly Hamlet. . . . The beauty of the performance was its introspective air. . . . His youth seemed delivered over to sorrow." Kemble's reading, however, lacked the fire that is necessary in Hamlet's reaction to the Ghost's account of the poisoning and in his verbal attacks on Gertrude and Ophelia.

By contrast, Edmund Kean's 1814 persona was that of a wronged prince, full of energy and impulsiveness. Indeed, Hazlitt thought the enactment "too strong and pointed," unmodulated even in the friendly encounters with Horatio and the players. Kean quickly became the new stage idol nonetheless, as Leigh Hunt confirmed with the observation that "he knew the real thing, which is the height of *passion*, manner following it as a matter of course . . . as the flower issues from the entireness of the plant."

In nineteenth-century Europe, where the restlessness and yearning of Romantic ideals found fertile soil, the sensitive and graceful Hamlet—one who never made audiences feel the dangerous presence of reality—began to give way to more powerful types. Germany's Bogumil Dawison portrayed an irascible, determined Hamlet, one never lacking in will. His gift for exploring intention and conscience led many critics to label him the first modern prince. (Perhaps Dawison's intensity proceeded from his own inner conflict. He sometimes fought with directors off stage and was belligerent with fellow actors. He eventually succumbed to insanity.) Russian Hamlets of this period were aesthetes, in a constant state of mourning, and "Quaking Hamlet" came to be a synonym for "coward" or "incompetent." But revolution struck with the actor Mochalov's performance using a new translation. The critic Belinski believed that Mochalov had in fact changed the text, giving "more power and zeal to Hamlet than a man tangled in internal struggle and staggered under the unbearable burden of his misfortune could afford to express." Unconcerned about textual changes, Kozintsev praised Mochalov by linking him with Kean as one who replaced Hamlet's ideal traits with more "natural" ones. Nineteenth-century French and Italian Hamlets were hot-blooded, tempestuous, sometimes truly "fat and scant of breath." Rossi, the Italian actor, was observed huffing his way through the final duel, leaning on the throne chair during breaks in the action. While these were nonetheless powerful Hamlets, Edwin Booth's prince was androgyne, slight, nervous, small, and lithe. Booth himself declared his belief in the character's femininity; he was fascinated by Vining's suggestion that Hamlet was really a woman.

"Hamlet *(Part 2)*" lists the sweet and powerful Hamlets since 1900. Gielgud, Michael Redgrave, Paul Scofield (according to one reviewer "the greatest and noblest Hamlet of our time"), and Michael Pennington make the lists of "sweets." On the power team are Henry Ainley ("This Prince has leapt from Gascony into Denmark," wrote one reviewer), Donald Wolfitt, Olivier, Ben Kingsley, and Richard Burton. Derek Jacobi's stage and BBC-TV renditions were for Rosenberg exemplary of the character's polyphony—a combination of sweetness and strength—the actor striving to be "spendthrift" in his performance. Mel Gibson's film Hamlet was "vulnerable," but Zeffirelli's heavy-handed direction made the realization of a "whole Hamlet" impossible. Such has been the case with other productions, especially those since 1900, with the emergence of single-minded actors and *auteur* directors.

Questions about the character's age and appearance are central to "Hamlet *(Part 3)*." If Hamlet is young (and the texts offer little help here), he has been portrayed, like Barrett's 1884 persona, as a boy easily influenced by fears and doubts, in search of shelter from a threatening adult world. Barrett played the hero in this manner because he could not imagine a Gertrude of fifty; his interpretation depended heavily on his belief in the queen's "passionate adultery." A mature Hamlet can also be argued for if we acknowledge the wisdom of his speculations about human nature and metaphysics. Here, too, relationships with other characters affect the choice: If Ophelia matches Hamlet's maturity, why is she still unmarried? "The resonances change with the ages, and can seriously shift perspective in the play," intones Rosenberg. In "Hamlet *(Part 4)*" the author uses Ophelia's poignant blazon (3.1.153−64) to catalog the roles that qualify Hamlet to be a Renaissance man. We don't see Hamlet the soldier in action, but we know him as such by implication because the guards turn to him immediately following the Ghost's appearance armed for battle. Rosenberg supposes (without any evidence) that Hamlet served in his father's army before leaving for Wittenberg. Hamlet's scholarship, like his soldiership, is described as impeccable, his education marked by the fervor of Lutheran humanism. The values that were instilled at school also set him sharply at odds with Claudius's Elsinore world: he is shocked by excessive drinking, sexual infidelity, and hypocrisy. Rosenberg outlines the hero's religious, spiritual, professorial, antic, and psychic roles as well in this chapter, speculating whether the plethora of identities signifies a yawning absence at the character's center. As is the case with several strawman-like propositions in *The Masks of Hamlet*, this question, too, is unequivocally answered in the affirmative: "Hamlet's capacity for love and friendship, . . . impatience with pretentiousness, . . . athletic grace, . . . resonance with a world of spirit beyond this one, the reach for nobility"—these are constants in an otherwise protean personality. Multiple masks in this interpretation do not signify multiple personalities, despite the fact that Hamlet's melancholic humor so distracts him that he searches desperately for an identity he can truly recognize as his own.

The tragedy's ending should reveal the "core Hamlet," if he truly exists. Here Rosenberg encounters a host of possible roles for the hero. Indeed, he lists twenty-eight interpretations of the significance of the final scene's massacre in determining Hamlet's "death mask." The prince's inaction alone, according to one perspective, has brought about the apocalyptic debacle; metaphysical forces—for good or ill—cannot be implicated. One possible reading stemming from this interpretation is that Hamlet glimpses his guilt and dies in a state of self-accusation. From another perspective, Gertrude and Ophelia are to blame because they betrayed the trust that Hamlet placed in them. Accordingly the hero dies a confirmed misogynist, another man victimized by the archetypal Terrible Woman. Hamlet could also be regarded as a scapegoat whose death serves as a sacrifice required to cure the state's sickness. In this role he joins the ranks of the other innocent dead, falling prey to the communal disease spawned by Claudius's damnable sin of brother murder. But Rosenberg concludes that, like the other Shakespearean tragic heroes, "Hamlet's final vision [proves] as mysterious, as asymmetric, as the rest of the play." Only the enigmatic "The rest is silence" suggests the acquisition of self-knowledge by the prince. Is he, however, cynically describing the vast abyss of Nothingness, or greeting the solicitude that comes with escape from the heavy weight of this world? Rosenberg and his fellow participants at the October 1990 Berkeley conference can only conjecture about the meaning of the lines, reaffirming in their many interpretations the play's and hero's polyphony.

Scholars familiar with Rosenberg's earlier work will find in *The Masks of Hamlet* the same indefatigable attention to reports about worldwide productions of the tragedy. They also will find an oft-repeated characterization of Hamlet's complexity—and that of other characters—as polyphonic. The term poses a particular problem of meaning, however, because it applies appropriately to music, not drama. A piece of fugal music could indeed be described as polyphonic—many melodies are harmonized into a single work. But *Hamlet* consists of words and actions as well as sounds, and its world has rarely been characterized as a harmonized whole. The volume's heavy freight of notes, reviews, and individual reports, described and responded to in often breathless, staccato-like commentary, fails in the end to convince one that multivalence and polyphony are the same thing. Despite Rosenberg's attempt to demonstrate this concordance—not by means of argument but with a catalog of performance "evidence"—the reader is left with the clear impression that only two archetypal Hamlets—one sweet, one powerful—in fact have emerged in productions throughout the world. The others, to borrow another musical adage, are simply variations on these themes.

Index